THE GLOBALIZERS

THE GLOBALIZERS

The IMF, the World Bank, and Their Borrowers

NGAIRE WOODS

CORNELL UNIVERSITY PRESS
Ithaca and London

CORNELL STUDIES IN MONEY
edited by Eric Helleiner and Jonathan Kirshner

First published 2006 by Cornell University Press
First printing, Cornell Paperbacks, 2007

Printed in the United States of America

Library of Congress Cataloging-in-Publication Data

Woods, Ngaire.
    The globalizers : the IMF, the World Bank, and their borrowers / Ngaire Woods.
        p. cm. — (Cornell studies in money)
    Includes bibliographical references and index.
    ISBN 978-0-8014-4424-1 (cloth : alk. paper)
    ISBN 978-0-8014-7420-0 (pbk. : alk. paper)

    1. International Monetary Fund.   2. World Bank.
3. Debts, External—Political aspects.   4. Loans, Foreign
—Political aspects.   5. International finance—Political aspects.   I. Title.   II. Series.
HG3881.5.I58W66 2006
332.1'52—dc22

                                        2005035784

Cloth printing   10 9 8 7 6 5 4 3
Paperback printing   10 9 8 7 6 5 4 3 2

To Eugene and all my family

CONTENTS

Acknowledgments ix

Introduction 1

1. Whose Institutions? 15

2. The Globalizing Mission 39

3. The Power to Persuade 65

4. The Mission in Mexico 84

5. Mission Creep in Russia 104

6. Mission Unaccomplished in Africa 141

7. Reforming the IMF and World Bank 179

References 215

Index 241

ACKNOWLEDGMENTS

I owe a huge debt of gratitude to many people for helping me think about, research, and write this book. Many people read various early drafts of the manuscript and gave me invaluable suggestions, criticisms, and comments. I am hugely indebted to each of them for their generosity of time and effort. I owe particular thanks to Gerald Helleiner, Robert Keohane, Peter Evans, Eric Helleiner, Roger Haydon, Lou Pauly, and Chuck Myers for reading the entire manuscript at some point in its evolution and giving advice on both its overall argument and on specific chapters. I am also grateful to Emmanuel Adler, David Bevan, Jim Boughton, Ariel Buira, Martha Finnemore, Rosemary Foot, Nigel Gould-Davies, Richard Higgott, Brett House, Andrew Hurrell, Vijay Joshi, Devesh Kapur, Tim Lane, Carol Leonard, Eugene Rogan, Margaret Rogan, Diana Tussie, David Vines, Andrew Walter, Kevin Watkins, Jennifer Welsh, and Alexander Zaslavsky for their comments on specific chapters.

There are many others who have in formal interviews or informal conversations helped me find information and understand parts of the story. I am particularly indebted to Amar Bhattacharya, Tom Bernes, Jack Boorman, Michel Camdessus, Charles Dallara, Boris Fedorov, the late Joseph Gold, Stephan Haggard, Alexander Kafka, Abbas Mirakhor, Robert Picciotto, Jacques Polak, Alex Shakow, Brad Setser, Leo Van Houtven, and James Wolfensohn, each of whom at some point or other shared their time, recollections, or analysis with me. I am hugely grateful to Nicola Meyrick and the analysis team at the BBC for helping me learn to write accessibly and teaching me to pick up the telephone and "get on with it," ringing officials, policymakers, and analysts in faraway lands. As academics we often put off such immediate contact. One direct result of this learning is that I must also thank, for long and extraordinarily enlightening conversations, officials in the IMF, the World Bank, Mexico, Russia, Turkey, Venezuela, Peru, Jordan, Uganda, South Africa, Nigeria, Kenya, the United Kingdom, the United States, Canada, and Italy, many of whom are mentioned in the footnotes of this book but some of whom are not.

I am grateful to a number of institutions for their support of this project. Thanks to Tom Carothers and Jessica Matthews, I spent a glorious couple of months at the Carnegie Endowment for International Peace in Washington D.C., and as a result I also owe especial thanks to Kathleen Higgs and the excellent librarians at the CEIP. The Leverhulme Trust gave me a one-year Fellowship that enabled me to complete parts of the research. Earlier in the project Ricardo Haussman and Nancy Birdsall arranged for me to spend six weeks in the Inter-American Development Bank, which proved a very useful vantage point from which to view Washington's other multilateral institutions. I want to thank Monica Serrano and her colleagues at the Colegio de Mexico for facilitating my research in that great country. In the last stages of production, Karen Laun at Cornell University Press did a great job in finalizing the manuscript, and I must also thank Vivien Hendry, Devi Sridhar, and Sameen Gauhar for their assistance in chasing down elusive references. Finally I must thank my colleagues at University College, Oxford, and in the Department of Politics and International Relations. It is a great privilege to work in such an extraordinary university and to be surrounded by such talented and creative colleagues and students.

THE GLOBALIZERS

INTRODUCTION

The IMF and World Bank are targets of endless criticism. Left-wing groups denounce them as tools of U.S. imperialism. Antiglobalization websites accuse them of enforcing global capitalism. Right-wing think tanks accuse the Fund and Bank of supporting corrupt elites and governments that cripple their economies, maul their environments, and oppress their people. In 2004 it was revealed that even the terrorist group Al Qaeda may have planned an attack on the institutions.

Protesters see the IMF and World Bank as bastions of capitalism and globalization. Some would like to reverse both processes. Others criticize the institutions but see them as vital if governments are going to manage the global economy—an alternative to unfettered capitalism in which firms and private actors compete without restraint and governments stand by and watch. So what are the IMF and the World Bank, what do they do, and how well do they do it?

Since at least the early 1980s, the IMF and the World Bank have encouraged countries to integrate into the world economy. Each institution presents dazzling figures about the overall gains to be made from integration. If the world were further to liberalize trade, the World Bank estimates, within ten years developing and industrial countries would stand to gain additional income of US$1.5 trillion and US$1.3 trillion respectively, with the gains lifting an additional 300 million people out of poverty by 2015 (World Bank 2003). The IMF highlights the potential gains to be made by freeing up flows of money and opening up capital accounts, pointing out that net flows to developing countries tripled, from roughly $50 billion a year in 1987–89 to more than $150 billion in 1995–97 (IMF 2005).

This vision has been translated into a determination to ensure trade liberalization, privatize state-owned enterprises, open up developing countries to foreign investment, and deregulate labor markets in member countries. Yet unleashing these market forces was not the core part of the original mandate of each organization. These public sector institutions were created not to feed global markets but to step in where markets fail and mitigate the harsh effects of global capitalism.

The founders of the IMF and World Bank created them to help balance growth in the world economy. They wrote charters for the institutions directing them to protect employment and standards of living in all countries, and also to facilitate the *balanced* growth of international trade, stimulate employment and real income, and develop the productive resources of all member countries. In each institution these goals were to be achieved through a pooling of resources, credit risk, and information and research capacity. Working together, governments could overcome barriers to cooperation and mutual assistance. Politics and political influence would be kept out of institutions. Boards of proficient technocrats would run them, and highly trained economists would staff them.

What happened to that dream? In 2000 Joseph Stiglitz controversially described the IMF's economists as "third-rank students from first-rate universities" and argued that their use of out-of-date economics had forced East Asian countries and Russia to undertake the wrong economic policies and driven them deeper into crisis (Stiglitz 2000, 2002). On the face of it, his remark suggests that economic theory—good or bad—defines the work of the IMF and the World Bank. Stiglitz and others characterize the institutions as technocratic agencies, generating and applying economic knowledge. On this view a new and better Washington consensus applied by the institutions could rectify their alleged wrongdoing (Stiglitz 2002). I disagree.

The IMF and the World Bank are political institutions created by governments to achieve particular purposes that have changed over time. In every decade, their major shareholders have set clear financial and political limits on what each agency does. Equally powerful in shaping the agendas of the Fund and the Bank are the staff and management, who seek to protect and advance their turf. Like most bureaucracies, these two tend to fall back on existing habits and solutions to deal with unforeseen and unexpected problems, tailoring their solutions or advice to match available resources. What they do is not just a product of how good their economics is or isn't.

This book is about the relationship between political power, economists, and borrowing governments in the work of the IMF and the World Bank. It sets out to untangle how politics, ideology, and economics drive them. It explains why the institutions do what they do, how they learn (or fail to learn) from their successes and failures, and how their behavior has evolved over time. That said, I focus specifically on the lending relationships between the institutions and their members and not the role of either institution in monitoring, regulating, or reporting on relations among industrialized countries (cf. Pauly 1997).

The Globalizers

The greatest success of the IMF and the World Bank has been as globalizers. As this book will show, they have integrated a large number of countries into the world economy by requiring governments to open up to global trade, investment, and capital. They have not done this out of pure economic zeal. Politics and their own rules and habits explain much of why they have presented globalization as a solution to challenges they have faced in the world economy.

By the late 1990s the IMF and World Bank were particularly focused on three different problems in the world economy. The first and most obvious was crisis management. In East Asia and Latin America the institutions were called on to manage and contain financial crises. A second and sometimes overlapping role was transition. In Russia and the former Soviet republics, both the Fund and the Bank were deployed to foster transition from centrally planned to market-oriented economies. The third role shared by the institutions was development in the poorest, often war-torn parts of the world. In Africa and in some of the least developed countries in the world the institutions have been attempting to jump-start development and to alleviate poverty.

In each role, the institutions have been guided by the governments that created and run them and in particular by their most powerful member states. They have also availed themselves of impressive resources—economists, research, data, personnel, and lendable funds—all mainly based at their headquarters in Washington D.C. Yet the efforts of both institutions in all their three major roles have been widely criticized, even within their own walls. In financial crises they have been derided for imposing harsh and ineffective conditions. In Russia and the former Soviet republics they have been accused of fostering crony rather than market capitalism. In respect of Africa, critics converge in accusing both institutions of contributing to an ongoing crisis of indebtedness, stagnation, and poverty.

Evidence of failure has provoked ongoing change in each institution. Some would say they have learned from their experiences. In the IMF in recent years the scope and content of conditionality have been questioned and to some degree rewritten. Operational methods have been expanded. The institution has created an office of independent evaluation to better learn from its experiences. In the World Bank change has been more dramatic. The institution has not only sought constantly to improve its thinking or "development framework," it has also gone through several bouts of internal restructuring and reform. In both institutions the experiences of the 1980s and 1990s have led to a rewriting of what outsiders call the Washington consensus. The result is that the Bank and Fund now advocate a set of policies that emphasize good governance and the need for sound political and legal institutions as a prerequisite for effective economic policy.

What is not clear is how far the institutions will take their learning process. Their rhetoric increasingly emphasizes goals of equitable economic development and poverty alleviation in borrowing countries, yet they face the same resource constraints as before in dealing with these issues. Both institutions have paid lip-service to a new, more participatory and inclusive formulation of policy, emphasizing stronger "country ownership and participation." Taken seriously, this approach would entail a radical change not just in the content of conditionality but in the day-to-day work, headquarters, structure, and staffing of each of these Washington-based institutions. Each institution has decentralized a little—the

World Bank far more than the IMF. However, more profound changes are unlikely to be in the minds of the most powerful member countries that control the institutions.

Riding Three Horses at Once

This book explains why the IMF and World Bank do what they do. Neither institution fails because it is run by economists incapable of dealing with contemporary economic problems. Instead, three distinctive forces shape what the institutions do and determine how effectively they do it.

First, powerful governments influence the agenda and activities of both the IMF and the World Bank. The political preferences of the United States and other industrialized countries provide a strong bottom line or outer structural constraint within which the IMF and World Bank work. In high-profile cases where major economic or geostrategic interests are at stake, such as in Argentina, Korea, or Russia, the U.S. Treasury leaves a clear trail. But this leaves a lot unexplained. Competing and different interests within the United States can lead the institutions in different directions. Furthermore, the United States does not always take a strong interest in the activities of the IMF and World Bank, such as in parts of sub-Saharan Africa.

Beyond the bottom line set by powerful governments, the work of the IMF and the World Bank is influenced by professional economists whose labors are in turn shaped by a particular institutional environment. The work of economists is vital in providing roadmaps for policymakers contemplating change. Technical work is almost always a necessary condition for policy change. But policy is shaped by other forces. Often Fund and Bank prescriptions are based neither on clear evidence nor on pure expert analysis or predictions. Instead they reflect bureaucrats trying to square political pressures and institutional constraints.

Finally, the Fund and Bank rely heavily on relationships with borrowing governments. Without a strong demand from member governments for loans as well as monitoring, the institutions would have no fee-paying clients. When they work with governments, their influence is in part persuasive and in part coercive. They can lend, catalyze other lending, or indeed stop lending. Equally, they can define, impose, and monitor tough conditionality on borrowers. This gives them obvious bargaining power. But the record of failed conditionality reveals that borrowing governments seldom actually do as they are told (Killick 2002). The power to enforce conditionality by withholding money or the like can be easily dissolved by powerful political pressures to continue lending. Equally, the institutions sometimes have their own reasons for not enforcing conditionality, such as to ensure repayment of their loans. This puts an emphasis on a more subtle, persuasive kind of influence.

The IMF and World Bank bring potential solutions to policymakers in crisis-ridden member countries. These solutions are backed up by the status and imprimatur of the institutions and sometimes they tip the domestic political balance.

Put another way, where a policymaker wishes to pursue a particular policy, Fund or Bank conditionality can give him or her an additional bargaining chip with which to persuade or marginalize domestic opponents particularly in the context of a crisis. Reformists in South Korea, for example, after the financial crisis in 1997, were able to rapidly pass institutional reforms in the financial sector that had previously been recommended by a national Financial Reform Commission and rejected by legislators (Haggard 2000, 102). Equally, in Mexico and Russia, as chapters of this book reveal, external pressure has played a critical role in weighting the case of one group of policymakers against another.

The persuasive influence of the IMF and World Bank is at its height when dealing with able and willing interlocutors in borrowing governments. Where government officials are sympathetic to the policies prescribed by the Fund and Bank, and where these officials enjoy power and authority to implement such policies, the Fund and Bank will succeed. Paradoxically, this success becomes more and more difficult as policy-making is opened up to greater numbers of participants, more interest groups, and further debate. Throughout the 1980s the Fund and Bank enjoyed particularly secretive and insulated relations with government officials. This enhanced the institutions' capacity to offer sympathetic policy-makers some leverage. However, by the end of the 1990s, each institution was calling for more open and participatory processes of economic policy-making in borrowing countries. This alters the bargaining power which accrued from the secrecy of negotiations.

Democratizing economic policy-making erodes the influence of the IMF and World Bank but this is not a bad thing—unless you believe that the Fund and Bank promulgate economic policies which are bound to have beneficial effects. In fact, controversy rages as to whether the prescriptions of the IMF or the World Bank improve the economic prospects of countries. Critics argue that they do not, at least in part because the Fund and Bank emphasize the wrong priorities and sequencing of economic measures. By contrast many staff within the organizations point to failure on the part of borrowing governments that lack the resolve to implement prescribed policies.

The evidence about IMF and World Bank impact is mixed. Each institution has undertaken rigorous studies. Up until 1990 the IMF had undertaken nearly a dozen internal analyses as to the effects of its structural adjustment programs. The results highlight possible successes but also instances where specific conditionality was probably wrong or based on underestimations, and overall there is little conclusive evidence of a net positive effect (Khan 1990; Boughton 2001, 614–29). Outside experts and critics have been more damning (Killick 1995, Cornia et al. 1987).

The World Bank's internal reviews are no less convincing. Lending is subject to an annual appraisal that judges the satisfactoriness of Bank programs and structural adjustment loans in terms of development outcomes, the impact on institutional development (improving a country's capacity to use its human and financial resources effectively), and the sustainability of the project over the longer term. The results from the late 1980s up to 1997 suggest that around one third, sometimes more, of Bank-supported projects had unsatisfactory development outcomes, close to two-thirds of projects were judged not to have had a substantial impact on institutional development, and over a half were judged to have unsatisfactory or low sustainability. An internal Bank report in 1992 argued that a very low Bank failure rate could suggest that the Bank "was not taking risks in a high-risk business" (Portfolio Management Taskforce 1992, 3), indicating that the Bank would then be doing little more than unnecessarily lending where private sector lenders would lend. The Bank's own rewriting of conditionality since the early 1990s recognizes concerns about the content, appropriateness, and effects of World Bank conditionality.

There is no incontrovertible evidence that the IMF and World Bank know what is good for their borrowing countries. More important, there is even less evidence that what they know translates into what they require of governments. Overall, powerful states set the boundaries within which the IMF and World Bank work. Within those parameters, professional economists and staff draw up the details. They work with an eye on the political masters of the institutions and equally with a view to promulgating their own and their institution's interests. They express their solutions in the language of professional economists. Once solutions are defined, staff take their mission into the field. There they must coerce or persuade borrowing governments to undertake prescribed measures. Their influence in the short term depends on local conditions and whether politicians have an interest in using Fund or Bank resources or conditionality to bolster a particular position or policy. Longer term the influence of the institutions is affected by the perceived quality and economic impact of their advice. Each institution has evolved a particular knowledge and organizational structure to define and undertake their respective missions.

The Fund versus the Bank

Analyzing the World Bank and International Monetary Fund together is controversial. Staff members in each institution cannot bear for the Bretton Woods twins to be described in the same sentence of a book. Although separated by just a few meters of asphalt, the staff and management on either side of Nineteenth Street in Washington, D.C., never cease to remind outsiders of the tremendous cultural, organizational, and ideological gap between the institutions. Picture the underground tunnel that joins the two buildings, permitting staff to dash from one building to the other without having to negotiate traffic and rain. This walkway is aptly painted with a thin blue line—amusing because it echoes the use of a thin blue line by UN peacekeeping forces that bravely separate warring parties. Often the Fund and the Bank are engaged in a form of conflict with one another—a turf war that results when each institution vies for the lead role in promulgating a particular economic reform.

There *are* some significant differences between the institutions. The most obvious differences are in size and culture. The Fund is mostly housed in one building. With a staff of 2,650 (in 2002), the institution prides itself on being cohesive, consistent, and tightly disciplined. By contrast, the World Bank sprawls across several buildings in Washington and has decentralized some of its operations to the field. With a staff of more than ten thousand, the organization presents itself as open, multidisciplinary, innovative, and more in touch with the grassroots and people who drive development. These differences are widely felt by staff working within the organizations and by their interlocutors in borrowing countries. However, cutting across the differences in size and culture is the fact that the senior staff in both organizations share a very similar training.

At the top of both institutions senior managers are overwhelmingly trained at graduate level in economics or a closely related field in a North American or anglophone university. They work within a similar chain of command. Both agencies are strictly hierarchical, with junior staff reporting to senior managers and so forth up the chain of command. Only very rarely do senior staff across the Fund and Bank differ in their views about an approach to economic policy. Often where disagreements arise, they exist within each institution as well as across the street. When the Fund and Bank quarrel it tends to be more about turf than substance. Their disputes are usually about which institution should take the lead on which issue rather than about which policy should be supported.

A deeper difference between the institutions is that they were created with different roles. Established at the end of the Second World War, each institution was given a distinct mandate. The Fund was charged with ensuring a stable international monetary system that would foster equitable growth within and among its member countries. It was expected to undertake surveillance of all members' exchange rate policies and control a pot of resources from which it could lend directly to members encountering temporary balance of payments problems. By contrast, the World Bank was created to channel investment into projects within countries in need of reconstruction and development. The Bank would raise money in capital markets and lend it to members at market interest rates. It would evaluate the soundness of any project for which a member wanted to borrow, giving technical advice where necessary. Hence a natural division was established between the two institutions from the outset. That division has eroded sharply.

In the first place, the institutions have come to service the same pool of clients. The lion's share of their work is with developing, emerging, and transition economies, and they share the same objective in their work—to foster development in these countries. The IMF has lost most of its earlier role managing the exchange rate system, and the World Bank never became the central force for reconstruction in Western Europe after the war. Life rather quickly brought the two institutions into the same arena. They aggregate and analyze data from the same countries and undertake policy-relevant research into what would improve the economic performance of those countries.

In the second place, both institutions are primarily engaged in conditional lending. From its first operations the IMF required certain policy reforms from countries wishing to borrow from it. In formal terms, conditionality was held up as necessary to safeguard the short-term use of the institution's resources. The

World Bank began its operations making very similar requirements of its borrowers. As early as the 1940s it was stipulating overall policy commitments from borrowers as a precondition for a loan (see chapters 1 and 2). Furthermore, membership and the completion of negotiations with the IMF were preconditions for a World Bank loan. The debt crisis in the 1980s brought the two institutions yet more constantly into overlap as each focused intently on structural adjustment in debtor countries in order to safeguard its own lending and to promote an identical set of conditions defined as necessary for long-term growth.

In theory the institutions take charge of different areas of conditionality. A concordat established between them specifies that the Bank has "primary responsibility for the composition and appropriateness of development programs and project evaluation, including development priorities." The Fund has "primary responsibility for exchange rates and restrictive systems, for adjustment of temporary balance of payments disequilibria and for evaluating and assisting members to work out stabilization programs as a sound basis for economic advance" (Boughton 2001, 997, and excellent discussion in chapter 20). Yet in practice each institution finds it extremely difficult to stay out of the other's area of policy, as is evidenced by the periodic attempts to rewrite the concordat dividing responsibilities between the institutions and continual declarations of intent better to collaborate and cooperate with each another. In essence, both the IMF and the World Bank are engaged in leveraging loans to ensure a jointly defined project of policy reform in borrowing countries on top of which the World Bank undertakes project lending.

The overall structure of governance of each institution is very similar. Their respective Articles of Agreement place a Board of Governors comprising national policymakers at the top of hierarchy with the day-to-day work being undertaken by a Board of Executive Directors who live in Washington, D.C. Their senior managers have similar powers and duties. A constituency system is used for the representation of members, and voting power is allocated among members in virtually identical ways within each organization. The funding and resources of each organization are differently structured, but as is explored in chapter 2, the politics of increasing their funding has brought to bear very similar pressures.

All that said, the Fund and Bank interact very differently with the outside world. The Bank has become an extremely porous organization in which the voices of nongovernmental organizations and civil society reverberate loudly. One analyst describes the modern Bank as a Gulliver tied down by endless threads of socially active groups (Wade 2001). An Inspection Panel created in 1993 permits people affected by a Bank project to bring complaints directly to the Bank and to have the institution's adherence to its own rules and operating procedures scrutinized. This has made the Bank's operating procedures and guidelines more transparent. Equally powerfully, in the 1990s the Bank made public the shortcomings exposed in its own investigation into its loan portfolio effectiveness. The ensuing public debate about the Bank has expanded to engage virtually every aspect of the Bank's work and potential impact, including on the environment, gender relations, people with disabilities, and so forth. Meanwhile the Fund has stayed relatively insulated, choosing its own pace and style for interacting with civil and not-so-civil society—"a tidy disciplinarian wanting to be respected but not loved," to quote its historian (Boughton 2001, 996).

For all their differences of style, in the twenty-first century Fund and Bank officials are engaged in four principal activities: research and its dissemination; policy conditionality and technical advice; emergency financing and crisis management; and longer-term debt relief and development financing. They share the challenge of working with a large number of very diverse countries, and yet at the same time each institution needs to demonstrate that it is treating all members fairly and equally and that its advice is consistent and coherent. The record of each institution in meeting these challenges provokes similar criticisms and responses.

Critics claim that the Bank and Fund have a record of unmitigated disaster. They argue that both institutions leave poverty and failure in their wake. Their incompetence, their subservience to the United States or to Wall Street, and their lack of accountability to other members has led them to throw good money after bad and to support bad causes and bad governments. Certainly evidence of failure may be found even in the Fund and Bank's own studies and evaluations. But "success" for these agencies is difficult to measure. They are public, universal agencies for a reason. Missing from the critics' view is the fact that the Fund and Bank exist in large part to go where angels fear to tread. Their task is to support countries, projects, and policies that may be risky, which take a long time and will not necessarily attract private sector loans. They are not private bankers or investors. They are public institutions with public purposes. If they enjoyed a 100 percent success rate and return on every loan, we would have to ask why public institutions were needed. That said, there is a serious gap between what the IMF and World Bank attempt to achieve and what their record shows they can deliver.

From Political Miracle to Vexed Institutions

The book begins by tracing the creation and evolution of the institutions. The historical record helps us critically evaluate the nature of the organizations. Emerging out of a process of postwar accommodation and cooperation and the searing experiences of the Great Depression and the Second World War, the IMF and World Bank promised a way to manage the world economy in a more rational and cooperative way. Their creation was described by one of their founders as a political miracle. Chapter one highlights several original features of the institutions, which made them relatively independent of their political creators. But the chapter subsequently reveals the way the United States and its changing vision of global order and justice has shaped their evolution.

Chapter 2 takes us further inside the walls of the agencies to examine how the Fund and Bank have each come to define its mission. In the 1980s they seemed to converge in the so-called Washington consensus. But why did this happen? The

chapter pits two competing views against each other. Economic theory as analyzed and perfected by the professional staff in each institution is one answer. But
it is unpersuasive. Economic theories are usually subservient to the needs of the
bureaucracy and the demands of the job, and the material interests of the most
powerful members of each organization. Once we take these political pressures
into account, we begin to see what blinkers and hobbles each agency, such as in
the run-up to financial crises in Mexico at the end of 1994 and in South Korea
in 1997.

The mission of the IMF and World Bank is not just to define economic programs. Each agency seeks to persuade borrowing countries to implement specific
reforms. Chapter 3 explores how they might do this. Each institution deploys a
mixture of technical advice and coercive power in bargaining with borrowing
governments, lending or withholding resources, disbursing or suspending payments, and imposing various forms of conditions. Yet the institutions can successfully deploy this power only where they find and work with sympathetic
interlocutors who are both willing and able to embrace the priorities preferred
by the institutions. Willing policy-makers are produced by circumstances as well
as ideology and training. Able policy-makers (who can deliver what they
promise) are affected by the configuration of political institutions within which
they work. Where economic policy is centralized and relatively insulated from
other political pressures, the potential influence of technocrats and their advisers
in the IMF and World Bank is high, particularly in bureaucracies with high
turnover and adaptive capacity. Where legislatures, party politics, and electoral
cycles have a strong influence, the results will be messier, more subject to veto
players, and less easily influenced by the international financial institutions. This
is best seen by tracing some specific cases.

Chapter 4 examines a case where the institutions seemed successfully to ac-
complish their mission. By the 1990s, Mexico seemed completely to have absorbed the ideas of the Fund and Bank. This chapter examines why. It also draws
out what this case tells us about the conditions under which the Fund and Bank
are more and less successful in selling their ideas. Resources and the power to
leverage other investment into a country give the institutions coercive power. At
the same time, the Fund and Bank had persuasive power based on their knowledge and status and the fact that they shared a mindset with specific local interlocutors. In Mexico both kinds of power came together to produce not just a
change in policies but a subtle reconfiguration of the institutions of policy-making, which in turn deeply affected the implementation of reforms. However, once
democratization began in earnest in Mexico, the power and scope of the technocrats with whom the IMF and World Bank had a special relationship declined
sharply, as did the influence of the international financial institutions.

A very different case is that of Russia. The influence of the IMF and World
Bank in the former Soviet Union in the 1990s was always more limited. Having
leapt into helping to transform the Soviet economy, both the IMF and World
Bank soon found that lending for macroeconomic stabilization and specific projects was futile in the absence of a much broader project of systemic transfor-

mation. The result was mission creep or an expansion of their operations beyond their formal remit. Adjustment conditionality was augmented with deep institutional reform and measures to strengthen and modernize state capacity. The IMF and World Bank were soon engaged in producing standards and benchmarks in areas such as the rule of law, anticorruption, popular participation in policy-making processes, social protection, and poverty alleviation. Staff in both institutions negotiated conditionality in areas in which they had no formal training or expertise. The impact on the Russian economy was seldom what the institutions intended. As chapter 5 details, the absence of prerequisite institutions combined with political, social, and economic forces to produce what the head of the IMF referred to as crony capitalism and a team of World Bank researchers described as state capture and corruption.

The experience of the IMF and the World Bank in Russia fostered an ongoing very public, rancorous debate about the institutions. Yet in many respects their mistakes in Russia were much less significant and damaging than those made in a different and much more vulnerable part of the world. Chapter 6 explores the involvement and adaptation of the institutions in sub-Saharan Africa. Some deep failures in countries in that region have led each institution profoundly to question the approach and priorities in dealing with the least-developed countries in the world economy. Within the Fund and Bank a new approach is now being fostered. However, the revised mission in Africa is challenging—not just to how the institutions do their business but equally to what the institutions are.

The conclusion outlines the case for rethinking the objectives, methods, structure, and governance of the IMF and World Bank. In the twenty-first century both institutions face demands to be more democratic and accountable. Their present structure reflects their historical origins as technical, sovereignty-respecting organizations. They were created to work among states not within them. Today they are more politically intrusive. Their roles take them deep into policy-making within countries, and most especially in the developing world. The mission of the Fund and Bank needs rethinking, as does the way they undertake it. In a world which puts a premium on democratic values of representation and accountability, the challenge explored in the final chapter is how new demands can be balanced within the older structures of power and influence.

A Few Choice Cases

In the contemporary study of international relations there has been surprisingly little attempt to examine power, decision-making, and bargaining within the international financial institutions, although an earlier wave of scholarship opened up precisely these questions (Knorr 1948, Kindleberger 1951, Matecki 1956, Cox and Jacobsen 1973, and for a useful survey, Martin and Simmons 1998). This book brings to bear theories that help to illuminate the way power and influence work within the international institutions and in their relations with countries attempting economic policy reforms.

Students of the institutions have generally assumed that U.S. influence is always dominant and focused on explaining the outcomes of U.S. strategic choices (Thacker 1999, Stone 2002). Others have examined the formal structure of principal-agent relations in which the United States participates within the institutions (Martin 2000, Gould 2004). What these analyses do not focus on is how each institution does what it does and with what consequences for people and politics in the countries it most affects

Power and influence are exercised both formally and informally in each institution. Some institutional constraints that shape the actions of the IMF and World Bank can be analyzed as formal systems of incentives (Vaubel 1986). Others are better construed as norms (Finnemore 1996). Building on previous analyses, this book argues that the work of the Fund and Bank is constrained by scarce resources, by the operational habits and norms, as well as by concrete incentives. The senior management and staff have an interest in ensuring that each institution maintains a key role in the global economy. This requires constantly taking on new roles. However, in the face of a new challenge, their response will be shaped by previously tried solutions and operating rules and procedures. The latter serve to protect each institution from external attack, as well as to ensure minimum standards of quality and coherence in the actions of staff and consultants. These institutional features powerfully channel the work of economists within each agency.

I began this book because I wanted better to understand how small or poor countries could best advance their case in dealings with international institutions which seem apparently to be run by very powerful states. That required dissecting the interplay of power, influence, and ideas in each institution and carefully tracing the politics of their interactions with borrowing countries.

In studying the institutions I have used three kinds of sources. The official documents of the institutions have been used wherever possible. For the contemporary period this has been made easier by the opening up of disclosure and archives policies in each institution. Previously, official documents had to be obtained either through member governments or through unofficial channels. Official documents often reveal very little about the politics of negotiations and the informal channels of influence that often shape decisions within the Fund and Bank and their impact on borrowing countries. For this reason a second vital source has been extensive interviewing and contact with officials in the IMF and the World Bank as well as with their interlocutors from countries including Mexico, Russia, Turkey, Venezuela, Peru, Jordan, Uganda, South Africa, Indonesia, Malaysia, Argentina, South Korea, Japan, the United Kingdom, the United States, Canada, and Italy.

A third source on the workings of the institutions themselves has been the rich secondary literature documenting and analyzing the history of the IMF and the World Bank. The early period of the institutions has been dissected and analyzed by a host of scholars in history, economics, and international relations (see chapter 2). Their institutional histories have been documented from within (and just outside) their own walls. There is a long tradition of excellent official and semi-official histories of the IMF (Horsefield 1969, De Vries 1976, James 1996). These sources are bolstered by more recent contemporary accounts of specific crises (Blustein 2001). The latest official history by James Boughton is a remarkable feat of scholarship and good writing and an indispensable source. Likewise the World Bank is well served by detailed and revealing histories, including the frank and insightful early volume by Edward Mason and Robert Asher (1973) and the more recent compendious and richly detailed study coauthored and edited by Devesh Kapur, John Lewis, and Richard Webb (1997).

In studying the relationship of the IMF and the World Bank with borrowers I have focused on three areas of the world: Mexico, Russia, and sub-Saharan Africa. These areas were chosen because in Mexico the Fund and Bank claim to have played a major role in facilitating reform—they, ostensibly, had successful influence. In Russia the institutions are often cast as having had no impact in spite of their vigorous efforts. In Africa the institutions are widely criticized as having failed to catalyze economic growth and development or even to support the kinds of institutions that might lead to development—they are said to have had a negative influence. These different impacts make these areas significant for heuristic reasons. An exploration of each illustrates how the IMF and World Bank interact with and affect domestic processes of economic policymaking. They point to the conditions under which the international organizations have more or less impact on borrowers. They illuminate the political and institutional implications of reform. In each case a variety of sources is used.

In respect to Mexico the process of policy reform is studied from 1982 through to the present day and a separate case is presented on the December 1994 currency crisis. Several sources are used to reconstruct the process, politics, and mechanisms of influence, limits, and impact of the IMF and the World Bank. First, a rich literature on the politics of adjustment and economic policy reform not just in Mexico but throughout Latin America has been used. This includes studies written both inside and outside of Mexico in Spanish and in English. Second, official documents have been used, including government accounts and reports, and documents exchanged between Mexico and the IMF and the World Bank. Third, extensive interviews were undertaken throughout the period 1992–95 with key members of the Mexican government involved in the reforms as well as with Fund and Bank officials with whom they were negotiating and who were overseeing the process (see chapter 4). Finally, contemporary news sources were consulted in conjunction with interviews to assist in correcting for hindsight and post-facto justifications.

In respect to Russia the role of the IMF and the World Bank from 1990 through until the end of the 1990s is examined. As with Mexico, the sources used include a rich secondary literature on the process of transition in the former Soviet bloc, official documents, interviews with key players, and contemporary news sources. I traveled to Moscow in 1996 to conduct interviews for a documentary about economic reform in Russia. This permitted me to record interviews with a number of key politicians and advisers. In subsequent research I also benefited greatly from collaborations with Nigel Gould-Davies, whose fluency in

Russian and familiarity with Russian sources contributed enormously to our joint work on the IMF and economic reform within Russia, and with Russia analyst Alexander Zaslavsy.

In respect to sub-Saharan Africa I have relied heavily on the extensive secondary literature about individual countries as well as the region as a whole. Two strands of work have been particularly useful. The first is a strand of political science that has focused on the political economy of Africa, exploring the relationship between interest groups, governments, institutions, and policy-making across the different countries of the region. In this literature the Fund and Bank are hardly remarked on but the scholarship serves to provide a useful and rigorous framework for understanding the domestic sources of policy. The Fund and Bank are much more central in the vast and diverse scholarship in development economics addressing the causes and consequences of economic failure in Africa. This ranges from fairly orthodox economic analysis to more radical and eclectic approaches. Finally, I have also used the compendious range of documentation, research, and analysis kept within the IMF and World Bank on their members in sub-Saharan Africa. Overall I must underscore the extent to which I am deeply indebted to librarians, archivists, officials, and policymakers all over the world for their patience and forbearance in assisting me in this research.

Chapter 1

WHOSE INSTITUTIONS?

Within the IMF and World Bank several thousand economists do their best to collect, analyze, and interpret data in a professional way. Their training and qualifications in economics and finance are deemed essential to the task of advising, lending, and giving technical assistance to countries. The managers and staff in each organization take seriously their job of guiding and educating member governments in an impartial way, using their expertise to enhance the scope for every country to benefit from a more integrated world economy. Furthermore, each institution was created with a degree of independence from any form of political control or influence. So why have the IMF and World Bank long been depicted as a "US-serving control instrument over the economic and financial policies of other countries, especially the so-called under-developed countries" (Furtado 1959)?

It is easy to see the U.S. influence in the institutions. They were created within the United States mainly by that country and that is where they are headquartered. In general their policies have reflected U.S. economic and strategic interests, particularly in opening up markets in all parts of the world. Yet it would be wrong to assume that there is one set of U.S. interests shared by all parts of the U.S. government and translated into official policy, which in turn determines what the IMF and World Bank do in member countries. One can almost hear U.S. officials who have worked with the agencies crying "if only." More important, if we stop at the observation that in general the United States dominates the institutions, we write off the possibility that other countries or views might in some way influence the work of the IMF and World Bank.

This chapter examines the actual influence of the United States in creating the IMF and the World Bank and in shaping their subsequent evolution. Doubtless, the United States has had an enormous influence over both institutions. But as this chapter reveals, competing views within the United States are an important factor in understanding that influence. So too, as later chapters will elaborate, competing ideas within other governments and within the institutions themselves affect what they do. In small but significant ways, within the political parameters set down by the United States, the IMF and World Bank are influenced by factors other than U.S. mercantilism.

U.S. Power and the Creation of the IMF and World Bank

Two serious problems faced policymakers in the last stages of the Second World War. First, Europe had been devastated by war and needed to be reconstructed. Second, the "beggar thy neighbor" economic policies of the interwar years had led to disastrous outcomes. Countries tried to devalue their way out of crisis, strangling production in other countries through cheap exports and trade protectionism. The result was catastrophic. The challenge for economic officials meeting at Bretton Woods in 1944 was to gain agreement among states about how to finance postwar reconstruction, stabilize exchange rates, foster trade, and prevent balance of payments crises from unraveling the system. This was expressed at the time by U.S. official Harry Dexter White:

> No matter how long the war lasts nor how it is won, we shall be faced with three inescapable problems: to prevent the disruption of foreign exchanges and the collapse of monetary and credit systems; to assure the restoration of growing trade; and to supply the huge volume of capital that will be needed virtually throughout the world for reconstruction, for relief, and for economic recovery. (IMF Records Office April 1942, cited in Mason and Asher 1973, 15)

Two rather different plans for the postwar economic institutions were tabled at Bretton Woods.[1] On the one hand, the British plan was for an agency to which states would clearly delegate monetary powers. It would be an automatic clearing union to which all countries would contribute and in which no currency had a special place. A new supranational unit of account would be created. Transfers to countries in deficit would be virtually automatic. No policy conditions would be attached. This would apportion burdens of adjustment equally on deficit and surplus countries (Keynes 1971–89, vol. 25; Block 1977; Van Dormael 1978).

By contrast the Americans planned an agency over which the United States would retain considerable control and from which it would derive considerable benefit. The new international institution would use the U.S. dollar and gold as its core unit of account. Transfers would be made among countries on a discretionary basis. Indeed, ultimately the institution would have the power to set down conditions for loans from the institution. Although formal authority would be

---

[1] As James (1996) notes, allied thinking about managing the world economy was greatly spurred by the German finance minister's publication in 1940 of an economic plan: Walther Funk, *The Economic Future of Europe* (Berlin, Tarramare Office, 1940).

delegated to the new institution, discretionary powers would permit the United States to influence exercises of that authority (Gardner 1969).

The two plans shared similar economic reasoning but differed along the lines of the political preferences and needs of their promulgators (Gardner 1980, Hirsch 1969, Boughton 2002). Britain was a debtor wanting to protect itself from the impact of U.S.-imposed trade liberalization and to place some costs on long-term surplus creditor states (James 1996, 39). The U.S. was determined to liberalize trade, thereby opening up the closed markets of European empires, to proscribe manipulated exchange rates, and to lay down conditions for U.S. investment in West European reconstruction (U.S. commentary in Horsefield 1969, 136). As a capital-exporter unlikely to need to borrow from the IMF, the United States was keen to lay down conditions on any country wishing to use the IMF (Dell 1981).

The United States prevailed on a number of issues at Bretton Woods. This was unsurprising. The United States was in a classic hegemonic position. It emerged from the Second World War with greater economic, political, industrial, and military strength than any other country. Its exports dominated world trade. Rudimentary national income accounting, which was just beginning at the time, highlighted the extraordinary fraction of global real income being earned by the United States. Furthermore, the timing of Bretton Woods minimized the input of other states. As one economic historian writes, "The United States required an international agreement and wished to secure it even while hostilities in Europe prevented enemy nations from taking part in negotiations and minimized the involvement of the allies on whose territory the war was fought" (Eichengreen 1989).

On one theory the United States was able to prevail because it alone among Western allies could propose and design new supranational institutions. Other weaker states in the system would "acquiesce because they know that the winners are in a position to proceed without them" (Gruber 2000). The choice faced by weaker states in this theory is a simple one: whether they want to be "in" or "out" of the new club. Their desire to keep the old regime becomes irrelevant since it is no longer available. For this reason even where cooperation is not in their interests, weaker states will bow to the agenda set by a hegemon, whose agenda is in turn shaped by domestic political calculations (Gruber 2000).

In reality, once the Bretton Woods regime was established, at some level it is true that all other states had the choice to opt into a powerful new economic bloc or to be excluded from it. At one point in negotiations, UK representative John Maynard Keynes wrote that the Americans "plainly intend to force their own conceptions through regardless of the rest of us. The result is that the institutions look like becoming American concerns, run by gigantic American staffs, with the rest of us very much on the side-lines" (Keynes 1971–89, vol. 26, 217). However, this statement does not capture Keynes' broader view, nor does it capture the way American policymakers themselves perceived their power.

In the above quotation, Keynes was commenting on news he had just received from U.S. Secretary of Treasury Vinson that the United States wanted to situate the IMF and World Bank in Washington D.C. Keynes was extremely vexed by this decision and later wrote that it "appeared that it was primarily a personal decision of Mr Vinson supported only by the Federal Reserve Board (which would find itself strengthened against the New York Federal Reserve Bank by the Washington location), and not supported on its merits by the rest of the American Delegation" (Keynes 1971–89, vol. 26, 222). More generally, the private and public papers of Keynes highlight the opposite: that Keynes believed there was give and take on the U.S. side in negotiations on the structure and role of the IMF and the World Bank.

United States policymakers did not uniformly perceive their own position as all-powerful. Their papers and records show that they believed they had to negotiate and concede issues (Van Dormael 1978, Gardner 1969, Block 1977). For example, the United States proposed a scarce currency measure that could have forced it to take actions not in its interest when running a surplus (see article VII [3] of the Articles of Agreement of the IMF). In a memorandum written in February 1944 Keynes described this action as "a signal mark of their courage, of their fair-mindedness and of their sense of responsibility to the other nations of the world" (Keynes 1971–89, vol. 26, 402). More broadly the structure and scope of the institutions produced by the Bretton Woods negotiations reflect the U.S. desire to compromise and negotiate. As will be discussed below, in both the IMF and World Bank all member states have some voice, and as technical agencies the institutions possess a significant degree of autonomy from member states, including the United States.

The question posed is why the United States, faced with a number of self-interested options, agreed to the Bretton Woods proposals? The fact that the United States was in the position of a fairly unbridled self-interested hegemon does not help us to sort out what John Ikenberry documents as the "range of postwar orders that were surely compatible with an American interest in an open world economy" (Ikenberry 1992, 290; Kindleberger 1977). Indeed, the United States could easily have produced and promulgated a much more modest postwar pact that involved no international clearing union, no contributions by members, and no issue of new currencies. In other words no supranationalism and no delegation to international agencies. Such a plan was proposed by other countries at the time (James 1996, 43; and Horsefield 1969, 97–102). Yet in the final Bretton Woods agreements, the United States agreed to delegate a limited degree of authority to the IMF and World Bank.

For institutionalist theorists delegation to new institutions should be expected. States construct and shape institutions to advance their own goals (Keohane 1984; Koremenos, Lipson, and Snidal 2001a and 2001b), but these goals are defined in an enlightened way. A hegemon will agree to some constraints because international institutions enlarge its choices and the possibilities for mutual advantage among states (Haggard and Simmons 1987). For this reason cooperation results in delegation to multilateral institutions that can prescribe, proscribe, or authorize behavior even of the hegemon. In negotiations creating such institutions even the most powerful states will cede some ground in order to ensure the participation of other states. These realities will be traceable in the design of the institutions, their voting and decision-making structures, their financial arrangements, and their degree of discretion in the exercise of their functions.

But not all features of institutional design are due to concessions to other states. Liberal theorists focus instead on domestic political constraints faced by states creating institutions (Moravcsik 1998). In this respect, the go-it-alone theory discussed above is a liberal one. It proposes that a powerful state will delegate power to international organizations as a response to domestic political exigencies. In essence, U.S. negotiators would use their go-it-alone power to create institutions the design of which would reflect their need to ensure domestic approval and lock in a particular set of preferences. Certainly there were domestic advantages for the U.S. Treasury and State Department in creating the IMF and World Bank—to some degree in so doing they could wrest control from other agencies over international issues, or as Keynes wrote during the negotiations, they could use the Fund and the Bank to "pass on their impending headaches to be treated by the new institutions" (Keynes 1971–89, vol. 26, 229). However, the liberal explanation is not without problems.

More generally the liberal argument would be that the U.S. Treasury needed to ensure a regime that would bind or persuade *domestic* detractors and successors, present and future, including the U.S. Congress. Here the evidence is not so clear. As historians Mason and Asher document, when the Articles of Agreement for the Fund and Bank came before the U.S. Congress for ratification, the Congress tried to make it clear that any loans "for programs of economic reconstruction and the reconstruction of monetary systems, including long-term stabilization loans" should be made by the Bank and not the Fund (Mason and Asher 1973, 25). Yet this was not what U.S. negotiators pushed for, and the Bretton Woods negotiations produced an IMF that would come to make stabilization loans and a Bank initially empowered to make such loans only as an exception.

The U.S. Congress was yet more concerned to ensure that the executive directors of each institution would not be international civil servants but would be answerable to their own governments (Mason and Asher 1973, 34). Yet this argument had already been made by the founders of the institutions for other reasons (Keynes 1971–89, vol. 26). Furthermore, in both institutions the final result was a Board of Executive Directors who would have dual roles as international civil servants, paid by the Fund or Bank and working for the organizations, as well as being answerable representatives of their own governments.

Neither institutionalists nor liberal theorists explain why such an innovative, multilateral plan emerged at Bretton Woods. Several more modest kinds of international arrangements would have fulfilled the modestly enlightened interests of key states. Yet something more daring emerged from a debate between British and American officials. As Keynes declared in 1944: "The proposals go far beyond what, even a short time ago, anyone could have conceived of as a possible basis of general international agreement" (Keynes 1971–89, vol. 26, 15). The "political miracle" that occurred at Bretton Woods requires more explanation (Gardner 1985). Without new ideas from both the United States and the United Kingdom—ideas, principles, and beliefs about what was possible, legitimate, and might be effective—the creation of supranational economic institutions in 1944 would never have been on the agenda.

Certainly, policymakers drew on existing precedents. The proposed World Bank built on an existing private sector experience of bond markets. The proposed IMF built on a history of cooperation among central bankers to maintain the gold standard prior to its collapse, with banks giving temporary, conditional loans to each other to prevent devaluations. Previously, some cooperation had occurred under the auspices of the Bank for International Settlements (BIS), established in 1930 to foster international monetary and financial cooperation and to act as a bank for central banks. Other cooperation had been led by private sector actors (Bordo and Schwartz 1998, Eichengreen 1996, Schloss 1958). During the interwar period, the League of Nations had coordinated emergency balance of payments loans with funds provided by private bankers, again with conditionality attached (Pauly 1997, Gisselquist 1981, Clarke 1967). However, at Bretton Woods policymakers sought to go further. Keynes himself noted that if all went well the IMF would "furnish a truly international body for consultation and cooperation on monetary and financial problems which would serve the purpose which some had hoped, but had been disappointed, from the BIS" (Keynes 1971–89, vol. 26, 221).

In the event, forty-five countries agreed to create two new supranational institutions. The International Monetary Fund and the International Bank for Reconstruction and Development would "facilitate the expansion and balanced growth of international trade" and "facilitate the investment of capital for productive purposes" (see article I, respectively, of IMF and IBRD Articles of Agreement). The IMF would be guardian of a new system of international monetary cooperation, underpinned by stable exchange rates and a multilateral system of payments. The IBRD would facilitate international investment so as to raise "productivity, the standard of living, and conditions of labour" in all member countries, as well as assisting in a smooth transition from a wartime to a peacetime world economy (WB Art 1).

These institutions were dreamt up by economists on either side of the Atlantic. Representing the United Kingdom was the famous economist already cited above, John Maynard Keynes, who had been at the Paris Peace Conference of 1919 and written eloquently about its failures (Keynes 1920). The bold economic theories of Keynes influenced not only the Bretton Woods conference but several decades of economic policy thereafter. The input of Keynes and the British into the Bretton Woods settlement has been traced carefully by historians of the time (Boughton 2002, Gardner 1969, Van Dormael 1978, Eichengreen 1989, Ikenberry 1992).

The United States was mainly represented by Harry Dexter White who shared Keynes's belief that governments could and should foster growth in times of stagnation, indeed he had watched approvingly as Roosevelt implemented such policies in the New Deal. In the late stages of the Second World War, White began to project this view into a new vision of international economic management (James 1996, 39). Initially the World Bank was central to this vision, a new agency that would create credit to ensure reconstruction and growth in an impoverished world economy. In an excellent historical analysis of White's position and the politics of the Bretton Woods negotiations, James Boughton concludes that White's personal convictions were vital in framing U.S. preferences and support for creating multilateral institutions in the face of isolationist and hegemonic interests expressed in the U.S. Congress (Boughton 2002, 20).

Underpinning the positions promulgated by White and by Keynes were domestic debates about how to structure the postwar world economy (Ikenberry 1992, Block 1977). Different agencies and actors in each country pressed for different kinds of settlements. It was neither clear nor obvious which position would prevail. In the United Kingdom there were shifting divisions on trade and whether or not the imperial preference system should give way to a free trade regime.

In the United States, as historians of the period have carefully documented, the State Department led by Secretary Cordell Hull was fixated on ensuring free trade and free capital movements in a multilateral system (Penrose 1953, Pollard 1985, Gardner 1964). Meanwhile, U.S. economic planners and New Dealers wanted no international diversion from their primary goal of fostering full employment and social welfare within the borders of the United States (Block 1977, Gardner 1980) Furthermore, "lurking behind American wartime debates was a domestically minded and tightfisted Congress" (Ikenberry 1992, 305).

The resolution of different plans and goals in the United States and the United Kingdom was not the simple product of power politics or functional exigencies. The design of the new institutions was equally shaped by the new ideas on the table. But this requires further explanation, for ideas do not triumph and shape negotiations purely by dint of their rationality or technical or moral value (Woods 1995, Keck and Sikkink 1998). Rather, a particular set of ideas prevailed because of their resonance among key participating governments and within the societies over whom they governed.

The focus on a new kind of international monetary arrangement at Bretton Woods neatly sidestepped the intransigent coalitions that had formed to champion various trade arrangements. For free traders, the new arrangements were an indirect way to ensure the expansion of world trade. For internationalists, the institutions were at least a step in the direction of global engagement. As Fred Block puts it, the Bretton Woods institutions offered idealistic internationalists a way to institutionalize U.S. commitment to the world economy. Ironically in so doing these left-wing idealists created institutions that strengthened the hand of their domestic economic policy opponents—the so-called "business internationalists" (Block 1977, 37).

The specific elements of the framework agreed at Bretton Woods embodied variants of all contending groups' beliefs (Ikenberry 1992, 317). In this way it bridged the gap between the U.S. State Department and U.S. Treasury (Block 1977). Ideologically, for Keynesians the new regime transposed Keynesianism to the world economy, paving the way to multilateral government intervention to foster growth, employment, and equity. The innovative postwar settlement also represented a set of ideas and solutions that resonated within societies. War-weary populations not only needed new investment and economic growth, they also needed a new vision of international economic relations and management (Ruggie 1982, Hall 1989). This social need helps to explain the rapid public acceptance of the Bretton Woods plan. Indeed, in his study of four news publications in the United Kingdom and United States, Ikenberry has noted how quickly public opinion swung around to a consensual acceptance of the new institutions (Ikenberry 1992).

In summary, the Bretton Woods settlement reflects more than a compromise between the national interests of a very powerful United States and a less powerful United Kingdom. The negotiations embodied large-scale new ideas about international economic governance, which were perceived as necessary and attractive not just by individual statesmen but by the war-weary public they were serving. American negotiators doubtless had more power to wield than their colleagues from other nations. The remainder of this chapter examines to what extent that power was wielded so as to ensure that the United States retained authority over the institutions through voting rights, funding, and control over mandates.

Independence in the Original Design

The original governance structure of the IMF and the World Bank was unlike other institutions set up in the 1940s. The voting structures in both institutions were deliberately unequal or "weighted." Each member was apportioned a quota. The quota translated a country's economic weight and significance in the world economy into a share of contributions and votes (and in the IMF, access to resources). This made the United States the largest initial contributor and gave it the largest individual share of votes.

The man charged with calculating the first allocation of quotas in 1943 has described how he was told by the U.S. secretary of the treasury to "give the United States a quota of approximately $2.9 billion; the United Kingdom (including its colonies), about half the U.S. quota; the Soviet Union an amount just under that of the United Kingdom; and China somewhat less. White's major concern was that our military allies (President Roosevelt's Big Four) should have the largest quotas, with a ranking on which the President and the Secretary of State had agreed" (Mikesell 1994).

Later in 1944, Keynes reported that the United States had made it clear that whatever the formula used for IMF quotas: (1) the aggregate must not exceed $8 billion (2) the Russians must have 10 percent (3) the Chinese must come fourth in aggregate amount (4) the aggregate voting power of the British Commonwealth must not exceed that of the United States (Keynes 1971–89, vol. 26, 69). These requirements reflect the extent to which U.S. political "bottom lines" would shape the institutions.

That said, the voting structure of the Fund and Bank also involved an equalizing principle. Basic votes were allocated to enshrine a principle of equality among member states. These votes were allocated to all states regardless of size or contribution. The historical record shows that U.S. negotiators believed they had to compromise to meet some of the aspirations of other states and that such compromises were vital if the organizations were to be effective. For example, although Harry Dexter White originally proposed that the United States take 61 percent of quota, he modified this to less than 30 percent and concurred in the allocation of basic votes, expressing his rationale in the following terms:

> To accord voting power strictly proportionate to the value of the subscription would give the one or two powers control over the Fund. To do that would destroy the truly international character of the Fund, and seriously jeopardize its success. Indeed it is very doubtful if many countries would be willing to participate in an international organization with wide powers if one or two countries were able to control its policies. (cited in Gold 1972, 19)

The historical context helps to explain this reasoning. In 1944 a concept of equality among states was coming to prominence (Broms 1959). Indeed it would be enshrined in 1945 in the universal membership and voting of the United Nations General Assembly. In the IMF and World Bank it was recognized in an allocation of "basic votes." As Joseph Gold explains:

> The authors of the plans for the Fund and the negotiators felt that the bold step of weighting the voting power of members in a major international organization according to quotas, which in the main reflected economic and financial factors, should be combined with the political consideration of the traditional equality of states in international law. The basic votes were to serve the function of recognizing the doctrine of the equality of states. (Gold 1972, 18)

In a similar spirit, in 1955, when the quotas of small developing countries looked too small the Fund decided to double their quotas and to set up a minimum quota—dubbed the "small quota policy" (Gold 1972, Lister 1984). These measures ensured that smaller, weaker states had a share of votes that exceeded their economic weight and gave some indication of their status as members of a community of states.

Voting power was not the only element of institutional design that would determine U.S. influence over the institutions. Yet more important was the financial structure created for each organization. Other agencies created at the end of the Second World War were designed dependent on regular subscriptions or levies from member states. Hence in the United States payments to the United Nations and its agencies would have to meet with regular congressional approval. This process has given the United States considerable political influence over these organizations (Righter 1995, Rivlin 1996). However, the original financial structures of the IMF and the World Bank made them relatively immune from pressures exerted in the process of maintaining regular funding.

From the start the IMF was funded by members' subscriptions of capital, which formed the IMF's core assets. As is still the case, each member country holds a portion of its quota in the Fund in "reserve assets," meaning gold or U.S. dollars. Naturally this confers an advantage on the United States as core currency, an advantage gained late in the negotiations at Bretton Woods when by "sleight of hand" an amendment ditched the principle of equality of all currencies in favor of the dollar (James 1996, 50). Furthermore since 1968 the United States and all other creditors have been remunerated for providing this credit (Boughton 2001, chap. 17, 53). The key point here however is that quota holdings established core assets that would automatically be kept at the IMF, meaning that the institution would not need to supplicate members for contributions.

The World Bank (IBRD) was founded with four sources of funds: paid-in capital, retained earnings, repayment of loans, and borrowing on the world capital markets. Members contributed capital stock proportionate to their quotas. A small portion is actually paid-in capital subscription, which comprises a very small proportion of the Bank's funds. The other portion may be called in only to meet the obligations of the Bank in extremis. The result is a set of guarantees provided by member states that permit the Bank to raise money in financial markets by selling AAA-rated bonds and other debt securities to pension funds, insurance companies, corporations, other banks, and individuals around the world.

In essence, the Bank borrows from the markets at the lowest market rates, benefiting from the credit ratings of its rich shareholders. It then lends the funds to developing countries at higher rates, which generates net income and covers the institution's administrative and lending costs. From the outset the Bank has not been limited by a hard budget constraint. It sets its own lending rates and, as a result of the income it generates, compared to other public agencies it has always been able to "employ more staff at higher average salaries, hire more consultants, commission more country studies, hold more seminars, issue more publications, and provide its functionaries better creature comforts" (Kapur et al. 1997, 1165).

Neither the IMF nor the World Bank would have to court and await the approval of governments, parliaments, or the U.S. Congress for its operating budgets. Once created, both agencies were relatively free of influence exercised through their finances by their largest contributors. Indeed the United States was turned down when it proposed in 1947 that the Bank lend exclusively to Western Europe for reconstruction, in exchange for a larger U.S. contribution. The proposal was rejected at least in part for fear that this would turn the institution into an American rather than a multilateral organization (Kapur et al. 1997, 76). Nonetheless, time and expansion would later erode some of the financial autonomy of the IMF and World Bank.

The autonomy of the World Bank and IMF has been affected not just by their voting structures and finances but also by their mandate and the degree of discretion granted to their expert staff. This is very clear from the original and subsequent debates about conditionality in and among the member states of each institution.

Regarding the World Bank, the original debate focused on whether the new Bank would be able to lend for "programs and projects" as the United States proposed or simply for "specific projects" as the British urged (Mason and Asher 1973, 24). Harry Dexter White argued for the United States that the Bank would have wider discretion if it could lend more broadly and insisted on inserting a provision for more general loans under "special circumstances" (Baum and Tolbert 1985, citing White's congressional testimony). The end result was that the institution's loans and guarantees shall "except in special circumstances, be for the purpose of specific projects of reconstruction or development" (article III, section 4 [vii]). In the early years of the Bank the focus on projects proved useful. It helped to reassure lenders in New York. It ensured Bank loans had a finite quality to them. It permitted the Bank to avoid political and sovereignty issues. Perhaps most significantly, it required the Bank to build up technical expertise and a staff who could undertake high-quality project work (Kapur et al. 1997, 8). Still, it bears noting that the Bank's first four loans went to Western European countries to finance imports that in no sense could be considered project oriented (Mason and Asher 1973, 2).

The debate at Bretton Woods about the IMF centered on conditionality. Keynes had originally proposed a scheme in which an international credit union would oversee transactions that were automatic. The new regime would be rule-based and would not require the supervision of a large trained and expert staff. This was true delegation as institutionalists would describe it. By contrast, the United States advocated an institution with wide discretion and what Keynes referred to as "grandmotherly" control over member countries (Dell 1981). In the discretionary regime, the IMF would be able to impose conditions on any borrower so as to increase the probability of swift repayment. Keynes feared that this would give the United States too much control over the use of the Fund's resources.

In the end American negotiators insisted that the new institution have control over the use of its resources. Key agencies within the United States believed that Keynes's idea of automaticity had to be vanquished. Yet the United States was unable to persuade other states to accept an explicit statement about conditionality. The result was ambiguity in the Articles of Agreement of the IMF. However, as historian Harold James found in the archives of the Federal Reserve and the National Advisory Council on International Monetary and Financial Problems, U.S. agencies were convinced that automaticity had been defeated (James 1996, 56). Soon after the Bretton Woods agreements were signed on 10 June 1944 the U.S. Treasury issued "Questions and Answers on the International Monetary Fund." Although this was not an internationally agreed document, it was soon treated as a source of authoritative interpretation (Horsefield 1969). By the 1950s the United States had succeeded in enshrining conditionality in the heart of the IMF's lending, even though the articles were not formally amended until 1969 (De Vries 1976, 1:256–57). Within the World Bank conditionality, albeit of a de facto kind, was also introduced at a very early stage (Baldwin 1965; Kapur et al. 1997, 81).

The outcome in respect of conditionality produced a regime in which a highly trained and expert staff in the IMF would supervise the use of resources by member countries, proposing to the board that conditions be applied to loans so as to ensure that Fund resources were swiftly repaid. In the World Bank, project lending would require technical expertise, and the institution's soft budget constraint meant that it could hire the best and build up status and a reputation for high-quality project work. The Bank's lending structure meant that "extra vetting, extra analysis, and extra technical assistance" could be conducted and the cost simply added into the body of a government's borrowing and covered by markup pricing (Kapur et al. 1997, 1163).

In both the IMF and the World Bank, technocrats would guide the lending discretion imbued in the institutions. Lending proposals in each organization would be prepared by the staff in negotiation with the prospective borrower. From the outset this meant that the Fund needed to develop and transmit knowledge about macroeconomic policy, and the World Bank needed to do the same in respect of project lending. Each institution had an important role as developer and transmitter of expertise. The staff and management of the institutions would play a vital role in this.

The staff in the Bank and Fund, unlike the staff of UN agencies, would not be hired according to country quotas. Rather, the managing director of the IMF and the president of the World Bank would appoint staff in order to secure "the highest standards of efficiency and of technical competence" paying "due regard to the importance of recruiting personnel on as wide a geographical basis as possible" (IMF, art. XII; WB art. 5). This expert staff would be immune from political influence, owing their duty entirely to the institution and to no other authority. Every member government would refrain from all attempts to influence the staff in the discharge of these functions (IMF Article XII, section 4; World Bank Art V, section 5).

The head of each organization would oversee the staff. He or she would be formally appointed by the Executive Board. Informally, however, it was agreed that the World Bank president would be from the United States and the managing director of the IMF would not be. For this reason the top post of the IMF has always been held by a European with the United States getting to select the first deputy managing director (Kapur 2000, Kahler 2001).

Overall the institutions were formally expected to work with countries regardless of political calculations and without taking politics into account. The Articles of Agreement of the Bank explicitly state:

> The Bank and its officers shall not interfere in the political affairs of any member; nor shall they be influenced in their decisions by the political character of the member or members concerned. Only economic considerations shall be relevant to their decisions, and these considerations shall be weighed impartially in order to achieve the purposes stated in Article I.[2]

---

[2] Article IV, section 5. It is worth bearing in mind that to some degree policy conditionality has always been part of the Bank's work (Baldwin 1965).

In the IMF there is no such explicit injunction, although the Articles of Agreement provide that in "surveillance" the Fund must "respect the domestic social and political policies of members" (art. IV, sect. 3).

In summary, the original design of the IMF and the World Bank did not give the United States control over the institutions even though it used its dominant position to shape them. The voting structure enshrined a basic principle of equality and reflected economic and geostrategic power. The financial structure of each institution gave it relative autonomy from its members. The discretion accorded to each institution in respect of lending conditionality certainly gave the United States a measure of influence but it also cast a large role for an expert staff of technocrats to advise the board in each institution as to how to use this discretion and as to what conditions to impose.

The Purse Strings Are Pulled

Since their original creation, both the IMF and the World Bank have become more beholden to their most powerful member states and more susceptible to direct U.S. influence. The system of basic votes that initially provided a modicum of restraint on their weighted voting structures was soon diluted. By the end of the twentieth century basic votes that had once constituted more than 10 percent of total votes had dropped to represent less than 3 percent of the total votes in each institution. Weighted voting took over.

Adding to the power of large vote-holders is their capacity to veto. This arises in respect of decisions requiring a special majority of 70 or 85 percent of votes. Holding 17 percent of votes, the United States alone can block any board decision requiring 85 percent. It is the only member with an individual capacity to do this. Other countries and groups of countries could join together to do the same even though they tend not to in practice. For example, Germany, the United Kingdom, and France hold 15.89 percent of votes and together could effect a veto. However most other countries are grouped within constituencies whose voting power cannot be split. For this reason, developing countries as a group cannot in practice vote together in the Executive Boards of the Fund and Bank because they are spread across over a dozen constituencies some of which are represented by the European country within the group (Rustomjee 2005). Likewise the countries of the European Union cannot vote as a group, although some have proposed that the IMF should be organized so that they could (Mahieu, Ooms, and Rottier 2003).

The significance of a veto power has increased over time as the number of decisions requiring a special majority has increased. Originally very few decisions required a special majority. However, the United States has compensated for a declining overall voting power—from 33 percent to 17 percent—by expanding the requirement for special majorities from an original nine categories of decision to some sixty-four (Gold 1977, Lister 1984).

Even more than voting power, a significant erosion of the original independence of the IMF and the World Bank has taken place as their need for funds has increased and new mandates and facilities have been added.

The World Bank's Expansion and IDA

In the period 1968–81 under the presidency of Robert McNamara the World Bank discovered to what degree it could expand. In the latter four years of the McNamara presidency, lending expanded more than threefold in real terms, the professional staff of the organization rose fourfold, and the administrative budget increased 3.5 times in real terms (Kapur et al. 1997, 16). In part this expansion was funded by new money raised in private markets with successful bond offerings being made in Canada, Switzerland, the United Kingdom, Germany, the Netherlands, Belgium, Italy, and Sweden (Kopper 1997). In part, the expansion was also facilitated by the use of a relatively new arm of the Bank called the International Development Association (IDA).

The International Development Association was opened in 1960 to give loans at highly concessional rates to poorer developing countries. These loans are made from a special fund donated by governments whose agreement is required for periodic replenishments. As a result, the IDA has opened up a new channel through which the Bank can be directly influenced by its wealthier government members, and in particular the United States.

Initially the largest contributor to the IDA was the United States but this has changed over time. The largest contributor to the IDA through 2005 was Japan, which contributed 22.07 percent of IDA's resources, with the United States in second place at 21.74 percent, followed by Germany (11.84 percent), the United Kingdom (8.08 percent) and France (7.23 percent) (IDA 2005). On the basis of these figures, one would expect to find significant donor leverage over the organization. However, none has been so effective as that of the United States. In 1967 the United States agreed to an increase in replenishment for the IDA, providing its increased contribution was tied to procurement to relieve the U.S. balance of payments difficulties—a demand that led to the creation of the IDA deputies who would make decisions on how the Fund was used (IDA 2001, 3). In subsequent replenishments the United States altered the rules on funding and on burden-sharing in the IDA (IDA 2001).

Furthermore, U.S. influence exerted through IDA replenishment negotiations has gone further than the institution. Even though the IDA itself accounts for only about 25 percent of IBRD/IDA total lending, there have been several instances where the United States has used threats to reduce or withhold contributions to the IDA in order to demand changes in policy, not just in the IDA but in the World Bank as a whole. For instance, during the late 1970s the Bank was forced to promise not to lend to Vietnam in order to prevent the defeat of that round of the IDA budget (called IDA 6 in World Bank jargon). In 1993, under pressure from Congress, the United States linked the creation of an Independent Inspection Panel in the World Bank to its contribution to IDA 10. As one writer put it: "With the Congress standing behind or reaching around it, the American administration was disposed to make its catalogue of demands not only insistent but comprehensive on replenishment occasions" (Gwin 1997, 1150). This was played out again in 1999 when both houses of the U.S. Congress passed bills reducing the U.S. contribution to IDA 12, citing not just their own budgetary pressures but the World Bank's decision to continue working on a loan to China even after the United States had voiced disagreement with the project (Wade 2001).

Further strengthening U.S. leverage in IDA replenishment negotiations has been a condition that was applied during negotiations in 1977: that all other members could reduce their own contributions pro rata by any shortfall in U.S. contributions (see IDA 1998, 29). Although this pro-rata provision ensures an evenly shared burden across contributors, nevertheless it also magnifies the impact of any U.S. threat to diminish its contribution: for if the United States does so, all other contributors can follow suit.

Finally, the World Bank group has also become more porous to political pressures through an increase in the use of trust funds. In order to increase their capacity to lend, the Bank has steadily increased its use of cofinancing and trust funds. By the financial year 1999, these arrangements had come to amount to nearly half of World Bank disbursements, reflecting a 17 percent increase in trust fund disbursements.

Both trust funds and other forms of cofinancing give a much more direct control over the use of resources to donors whose Trust Fund Administration Agreement with the Bank governs how the funds are used (See "Operational Policies," World Bank, *The World Bank Operational Manual* at www.worldbank.org). It bears noting, however, that this does not mean that Trust Funds have become a conduit of exclusively U.S. influence. Indeed, the U.S. contribution in 1999 was less than those of the Netherlands and Japan, and it was not initially a contributor to the HIPC Trust Fund—the Bank's largest—which means initially it did not exercise direct influence over that fund. Overall, however, the growth of trust funds and cofinancing arrangements signals an increase in bilateral and selectively multilateral control over Bank lending and a decline in straightforward delegation to the Bank.

The IMF's Expansion

In the IMF political influence by the United States has been greatly enhanced by the process of increasing the institution's resources. At least every five years the quotas determining contributions to the Fund are reviewed (see table 1.1 below, which summarizes the increases). Any increase in quota requires a special majority (85 percent) of votes on the Executive Board and hence the United States has an individual power to veto such decisions. Furthermore, within the United States an increase in resources allocated to the IMF requires congressional approval. For this reason, at each quota review the Fund is subjected to particular scrutiny by U.S. political actors and pressure from them. In the 1990s this trans-

TABLE 1.1
Increases in the IMF quotas

Date	Increase in quotas (%)
February and April 1959 (Special Review)	60.7
1965 (Fourth General Review)	30.7
1970 (Fifth General Review)	35.4
1976 (Sixth General Review)	33.6
1978 (Seventh General Review)	50.9
1983 (Eighth General Review)	47.5
1990 (Ninth General Review)	50.0
Tenth General Review	No increased proposed
1998 (Eleventh General Review)	45.0
2003 (Twelth General Review)	No increase proposed

lated into attempts by Congress to influence Fund conditionality over issues such as worker rights, the role of the private sector, human rights, and military spending with significant successes (Geithner 1998).

In the second half of the 1990s, negotiations took place in preparation for the 45 percent increase in quota agreed by the Fund's Executive Board in September 1997. The U.S. Congress approved the increase only on the condition that an International Financial Institution Advisory Commission be created to recommend future U.S. policy toward the IMF as well as the World Bank and other multilateral economic organizations. In November 1998, the so-called Meltzer Commission was established and reported to Congress in early 2000.

The report of the commission established by the U.S. Congress took a different line from the U.S. Treasury on many issues. Indeed, it launched several attacks on the U.S. Treasury and its policy toward the IMF: accusing Treasury of "circumventing the Congressional budget process" by using the Exchange Stabilization Fund to assist Mexico in 1995; of "commandeering international resources to meet objectives of the U.S. government or its Treasury Department"; and of leading the initiative to create contingency credit lines in the IMF that were "so poorly designed that, to date, no country has applied." In the first two of these criticisms, the Treasury is being accused of laying claim to U.S. policy in exactly the way Keynes suggested in 1946, vesting authority in the IMF so as to wrest control over economic policy away from Congress and other agencies.

In its attacks on the U.S. Treasury, the commission's report highlights differences of view and different bases of power that exist within the U.S. government. It is not obvious that such differences diminish U.S. influence by making its objectives less clear or more diffuse. Indeed, a recalcitrant Congress may even enhance and magnify U.S. influence in two ways. First, it has created a separate and additional channel of communication with the Fund and the Bank: indeed, one of the first acts of the new managing director of the IMF appointed in 2000 was to meet with the head of the Meltzer Commission to discuss the recommendations that had been made in the latter's final report. Second, the fact that everyone is aware that a feisty U.S. Congress needs to be brought on board can give the U.S. Treasury and its officials within the IMF extra leverage and a credible threat to hold over other shareholders and Fund officials.

Although the main source of financing of the IMF is through quotas, the institutions' resources have been increased by other means. In the 1960s the Fund needed access to more resources because of a weakening in the U.S. position (De Vries 1976, 376) and a growing need to offset international capital movements (Gold 1977, 25). If quotas had been increased at the time, both Germany and France would have increased the size of their quotas (Gisselquist 1981). Instead in 1962 the IMF established the General Arrangements to Borrow (GAB). Under the GAB the institution could borrow up to SDR 6 billion from ten industrialized countries (and as of 1964 from Switzerland) to help finance drawings from GAB creditors.[3] In 1977, for example, it was used, along with a bilateral borrowing from Switzerland, to finance standby arrangements for Italy and the United Kingdom (De Vries 1985, 192–93).

In 1983 the GAB was reviewed and extended. The Latin American debt crisis had strained the Fund's resources and under the revised arrangement the institution could borrow up to SDR 17 billion plus an additional SDR 1.5 billion under an associated arrangement with Saudi Arabia. These resources would now be used to lend to nonparticipants in the GAB—as indeed they were in July 1998 when the GAB was activated for the tenth time in its existence to finance an Extended Arrangement for Russia (see chapter 5). At the same time the New Arrangements to Borrow (NAB) were put in place after the Mexican financial crisis in 1994 in order to double the credit available to the IMF under the GAB. The NAB would henceforth be the first recourse for the Fund when it needed additional resources. Credit could be provided by some twenty-five members and institutions participating in the NAB. The new arrangements have been invoked just once to finance a standby arrangement for Brazil in December 1998

Scholars differ in their view of the impact of the GAB. Robert Solomon argues that in the 1962 agreement European negotiators took the opportunity to express their newfound power relative to the United States, insisting on procedures under which they as lenders would have the chance to make decisions (Solomon 1977, 43). However, the GAB also gave the United States a chance to increase the resources of the IMF without increasing the quotas of its allies Germany and France. Moreover, as Eric Helleiner argues, the GAB met the needs of a larger U.S. and UK agenda to create the necessary conditions for freer capital movements. The GAB-resourced IMF would be in a position to offset increasing capital movements as financial actors in London and New York and major multinationals began to compensate for the restraints of national capital controls by increasing their participation in international capital markets (Helleiner 1994, 96).

A clearer sense of the rise of other major creditors in the IMF is to be found in the financing of the institution's activities in the 1970s and early 1980s. Dur-

---

[3] SDR stands for "special drawing right." It is an international reserve asset created by the IMF in 1969 whose value is determined by the market exchange rates of the euro, the yen, UK pounds, and U.S. dollars.

ing this period both Saudi Arabia and Japan greatly enhanced their formal position. Saudi Arabia became the largest lender to the IMF after contributing the lion's share of resources for a special IMF lending program (oil facility) created in 1973–74, a second oil facility, and then a supplementary financing facility created at the end of the 1970s (Boughton 2001, 885, 889). These contributions made Saudi Arabia one of the largest two creditors in the Fund, thereby permitting the country to appoint its own executive director to the IMF rather than remain in a constituency with other countries. Eventually after long negotiations with the institution, the country's quota was also radically increased to reflect its status as the largest lender to the Fund (Boughton 2001, 890). Japan, which also became a major creditor of the IMF also eventually increased its quota after a long and bitter struggle to do so (Ogata 1989, Rapkin and Strand 1996). Although both Japan and Saudi Arabia shifted up the ranks in terms of their quota size and formal voting power, there is very little evidence that either country has used that formal power to push a particular agenda or to limit or constrain other members of the IMF. Japan's leadership on reviewing the Fund Board's policy for appointing the managing director in 2000 surprised many and did not lead to any substantive change in the status quo. More influentially, Japan pushed in the 1990s in the World Bank for a study of the reasons for growth in East Asia, facilitating a controversial debate on the same (Wade 1996). Yet these are exceptions to a general picture of members deferring to the United States.

In summary, although autonomy was built into the original financial structure of the IMF and the World Bank, both have become more porous to U.S. influence as they have expanded. In particular since the 1980s every increase in IMF quotas or replenishment of the Bank's IDA has been accompanied by negotiations with a U.S. Congress using the opportunity to threaten to reduce or withhold the funds, being yet more prepared than even the executive agencies—Treasury and State Department—to set down special preconditions for U.S. contributions. As a result, in the IMF and the World Bank other shareholders and officials within the institutions have grown used to placating not just the powerful departments of State and Treasury, but also a demanding U.S. Congress.

Missing from the story of political encroachment thus far have been the other large shareholders such as Japan and the European countries, particularly Germany, France, and the United Kingdom, each of whom has its own representative on the boards of each institution. Occasionally these members have pushed a particular issue, and these instances show that several other industrialized countries do have a significant voice in each institution, and certainly a larger voice than all other non–U.S. members. Examples include not only Japan's championing of the East Asian Miracle study within the World Bank but also the push by France, Japan, and the UK's push for debt relief for the poorest countries. These examples, however, do not diminish the pattern of overall U.S. dominance.

Particularly puzzling is why European countries, especially since monetary integration, have not pooled their voting power or coordinated their positions more systematically to increase their voice. One reason mitigating against European collective action is the fact that most European countries are spread across different seats and constituencies (Bini Smaghi 2004). Another reason is that they have found themselves on different sides of key debates. For example, when the United Kingdom and France helped lead a new debt relief initiative in 1996–97, Germany sided more with the United States than with its European partners (see chapter 6).

The Pressures of the Cold War and Beyond

Soon after the IMF and World Bank were created, U.S. priorities changed. Institutionalists may well have expected the existence of the new institutions to have constrained or locked-in U.S. preferences (Morrow 1994). In the short run this did not occur. By 1945 Britain was no longer a partner in creating the postwar regime but a supplicant seeking loans from the United States. At the same time the Cold War was beginning (Yergin 1978). The United States shifted its focus to geopolitical rather than economic security. The Anglo-American Loan Agreement of 1946 and the Marshall Plan of 1947 sidelined the IMF and World Bank. The U.S. dollar rather than gold took center place in the international monetary system. The United States argued to "postpone the Fund until more favorable conditions have been developed for its operation" (Williams 1947, 257). The World Bank was sidelined as the agency of reconstruction in Western Europe. The Marshall Plan was used to rapidly build up that region's economies and strengthen political alliances with the United States (Milward 1984).

Where the World Bank was used, its work became inextricably linked to the geopolitical imperatives of the Cold War. In 1948 when Yugoslavia broke from the Soviet bloc, the World Bank stepped in with loans. This fulfilled the advice of George Kennan, the architect of the U.S. containment strategy that the West should offer the country "discreet and unostentatious support" (Kapur et al. 1997, 103). In Nicaragua, the World Bank supported the Somoza regime with a disproportionate number of loans while that country offered the United States a convenient base for prosecuting the Cold War in Central America. This included the training and launching of the 1953 overthrow of Guatemalan president Jacobo Arbenz, who was seen as a Communist sympathizer. It also included the 1961 Bay of Pigs invasion of Cuba (Lake 1989).

In the Middle East, Iran was heavily supported while it offered an important way to contain Soviet-sympathizing Iraq. Indeed in the period 1957–74 Bank lending to Iran amounted to $1.2 billion in thirty-three loans (Kapur et al. 1997, 500). In Indonesia after General Suharto assumed power in March 1966, the Bank immediately began a very close and special relationship with the country. The very substantial levels of corruption, the regime's human rights record, and its failure to meet World Bank conditions regarding the state oil company Pertamina were all overlooked. Rather more important in explaining the Bank's relationship with Indonesia was the backdrop of U.S. strategic concerns about Southeast Asia and communist insurgency (Green 1990). In this case, as in so many others, loans were used to support and win allies in the Cold War against the USSR.

In fact, U.S. administrations were required by law to ensure that any assistance to which they contributed met U.S. geopolitical needs. The U.S. position on the uses of foreign assistance was clearly spelled out in the Mutual Security Act of 1951 (U.S. Statutes at Large, no. 373, tit. 5, sec. 511[b]): "No economic or technical assistance shall be supplied to any other nation unless the President finds that the supplying of such assistance will strengthen the security of the United States." This philosophy (opposed at the time by many NGOs in the United States: see Ruttan 1996, 67) shaped U.S. bilateral programs, including the Economic Support Fund, the Military Assistance Program, the Development Assistance Program, and the Food for Peace Program (or PL 480) (Ruttan 1996). It also shaped U.S. preferences and policies toward the World Bank and the IMF.

The new, more political calculus ran directly counter to the original design of the World Bank, whose Articles of Agreement explicitly state that "the Bank and its officers shall not interfere in the political affairs of any member; nor shall they be influenced in their decisions by the political character of the member or members concerned. Only economic considerations shall be relevant to their decisions, and these considerations shall be weighed impartially in order to achieve the purposes stated in Article I" (art. IV, sect. 5). Yet, as we will see below, economic and technocratic considerations were not and could not be written out of the institution's work.

The IMF was less centrally involved in the Cold War until the late 1970s. Indeed, in 1961 the *Economist* described the managing director of the IMF as "Mr Krushchev's secret weapon" on the grounds that the IMF's stabilization programs under the new Polak model (discussed in greater detail in chapter 2) were so harsh that they risked creating social eruption (James 1996, 142). More seriously, the main clients of the Fund up until the end of the 1960s were industrialized country members: an analysis of countries drawing funds from the IMF 1966–71 reveals that the largest users of Fund resources ($8 billion of $11.7 billion) were eight industrial members (the United Kingdom, United States, France, West Germany, Canada, Belgium, Italy, Denmark) most of whom stayed within their gold tranche and therefore were not subject to conditionality (with the exception of standby arrangements for the United Kingdom and France) (De Vries 1976, vol. 1, 311).

In the later years of the Cold War the IMF's work became much more entwined in the security priorities of the United States. Indeed, one scholar models the loans of the IMF as a direct reflection of U.S. preferences, asking which set of U.S. preferences determined their loans (Thacker 1999). Strom Thacker's simple macroeconomic model tests two hypotheses about IMF lending to developing countries between 1985 and 1994. The first hypothesis is that IMF loans are used to reward friends of the United States; this is labeled the "political proximity" hypothesis. The second hypothesis is that loans are used to reward friendly overtures toward the United States and are withheld in order to punish unfriendly behavior; this is called the "political movement" hypothesis. A third hypothesis is mentioned but a priori rejected. This hypothesis is that specific economic interests drive U.S. policy, as argued by modern political economy or neo-Marxian scholars. Measures of U.S. exports and foreign investment are used to test this view, but Thacker rejects it summarily, although accepting that a subtler model specification and further research would be needed to untangle the cross-cutting nature and impact of these interests (Thacker 1999, 58).

What kinds of results emerge from such a statistical testing of U.S. influence? Thacker's results suggest that during the Cold War his "political movement" hypothesis had the strongest support. In other words, realignment toward the United States improved a country's chances of receiving a loan from the IMF regardless of that country's starting position. Statistically this proved stronger in the tests than the simpler "political proximity" hypothesis, at least until the end of the Cold War (1985–89). This is interesting because it counters our expectation that being an ally of the United States would lead directly to more access to IMF loans.

Since the end of the Cold War, however, Thacker argues that his results support the idea that both proximity to the United States and overtures toward the United States have strongly influenced IMF lending. Thacker interprets this finding as evidence that the United States is using IMF loans in "playing the realignment game as vigorously as ever and is rewarding the allegiance of those who stay close without necessarily moving any closer" (Thacker 1999, 64).

The study is thought-provoking, but two limitations in respect of our purposes must be noted. By assuming that the United States speaks with one voice and controls the IMF, the model does not set out to investigate the multiplicity of voices within the United States and the limits of that country's influence. It ignores the role played by other members of the organization and the staff and management, which varies case to case. As this book will describe, the senior staff and Executive Board are always aware of the preferences of the largest shareholder with interests in a particular loan or country. However, this does not translate directly into the United States either calling all the shots or not, or having loans reflecting U.S. priorities or not. In cases where the United States has no particular interest at stake, other countries play an influential role. Where no large shareholder has particular interests, or indeed they are deadlocked, the staff and management are highly influential.

The other problem with testing U.S. influence is that U.S. preferences are not always clear or obvious. Within the model described above, U.S. interests and preferences are assumed to be revealed by key votes in the UN General Assembly. Thacker admits that these are not an ideal measure of political motivation. Indeed, key votes in the General Assembly are used for a variety of diplomatic effects, which do not necessarily match the preferences pursued (usually by the U.S. Treasury) in the IMF. In Thacker's study General Assembly votes are used to distinguish "political proximity" from "overtures to the United States." For example, IMF loans to Hungary, Yugoslavia, and Romania are all presented as reflecting moves by these countries toward the United States in the 1980s, while the lack of loans to Czechoslovakia and Poland reflects the opposite. This reasoning does not bear up under close scrutiny. Certainly Poland reflected a politically charged decision within the IMF. However, to say that Romania was moving towards the United States in the 1980s is contentious, and in respect of Czechoslovakia the argument is not valid. Czechoslovakia was not a member of the IMF and therefore ineligible for any kind of loan regardless of political circumstances.[4]

Using a larger data set and a wider measure of U.S. preferences, Edwards (2003) makes the following findings, which add to the picture of where and how U.S. influence affects outcomes. First, there is only very limited, weak evidence that states adopting UN voting positions close to that of the United States are under Fund programs longer. Once other measurements of U.S. preferences are included, being a U.S. ally does not increase the duration of a state's stay under an IMF program. To quote Edwards, "There is no indication that US influence gives states in this sample beneficial treatment from the IMF" (Edwards 2003, 20). Nonetheless, other evidence shows that U.S. influences affect the punishment interval of countries that breach their commitments under IMF programs (Stone 2002). Edwards also finds no significant difference between U.S. allies and adversaries in terms of their performance or their propensity to cheat on their programs. Finally, what Edwards does find in terms of political influence is that states with higher voting power in the IMF seem to be permitted to run consistently higher deficits (Edwards 2003).

The findings from correlations between U.S. preferences and IMF lending patterns suggest that U.S. influence is significant in the institution but that it is difficult precisely to track. One important factor behind these studies is the question of how clear U.S. preferences are and what happens when there is no clear unitary set of U.S. geostrategic priorities that might define the work of the IMF and World Bank.

The Limits of Geopolitics

Bureaucrats and politicians within the United States do not always share the same view of what U.S. policy toward a particular country should be. Furthermore, even if they share the same goals, they will not always share or even have a view as to which instruments would best achieve those goals. India and its relations with the United States, the IMF, and the World Bank in the 1960s and 1970s offers an intriguing example.

By the early 1960s India was by far the largest borrower from the World Bank, having borrowed a total of US$2.55 billion by 1971, which was more than the next two largest borrowers (Pakistan and Mexico) combined (Mason and Asher 1973, 195). Similarly in the period 1966–71 India was the largest developing country user of IMF resources, ahead (in order of borrowed amounts) of South Africa, Colombia, Chile, Yugoslavia, Turkey, Indonesia, Philippines, Peru, Ceylon, and Egypt (De Vries 1976, vol. 1, 330–32).

---

[4] I am very grateful to James Boughton for sharing these insights with me. His own history of the Fund offers a rich historical analysis of these examples (Boughton 2001). The cited point is also made by Kapur 2002, 340.

India's geostrategic relationship with the United States during the 1960s and early 1970s was an ambiguous one. In 1964, the U.S. Congress had failed to approve aid for a public sector steel plant at Bokaro and Indian prime minister Nehru turned to the Soviet Union for support instead. The following year, the United States had suspended its aid to both India and Pakistan when the two countries went to war. Further to these tensions, India was consistent and vocal in its opposition to the U.S. engagement in Vietnam. In 1971 the United States suspended aid to India in the wake of the Bangladesh crisis, supported Pakistan, and sailed the U.S. aircraft carrier *Enterprise* into the Bay of Bengal. India's then prime minister Mrs. Gandhi concluded a treaty of mutual defense and support with the Soviet Union leading to a sharp cutoff in U.S. flows of aid to India.

Throughout the tumultuous geostrategic relationship of the 1960s, U.S. aid to India continued. United States policy reflected a number of competing priorities and lobbies within the United States. American officials had become deeply involved in trying to influence agricultural reform in India. These efforts involved the budget bureau in the Executive Office of the president as well as the National Security Council. As John Lewis has detailed, the U.S. aid community placed a high priority on India, devoting considerable resources and personnel to it, including not just the government but powerful private players such as Ford and Rockefeller foundations. Together with other departments and groups, the U.S. Agency for International Development (USAID) constituted a very strong India lobby within Washington, D.C., which favored a generous aid program backed by quiet negotiations. Countering this view in the mid 1960s was President Johnson and a Congress that was becoming increasingly disenchanted with foreign aid. They favored using threats of aid suspension to motivate greater reform efforts on the part of Indian policymakers (Lewis 1997, 94–99)

The multiplicity of voices in the United States created a space for alternative policies in the international financial institutions. This meant that U.S. preferences did not always converge with World Bank actions. For example, at the time of the breakdown in U.S.-India relations in 1971, the World Bank put together an ambitious proposal for further debt relief for India, requiring the approval of all donors who comprised the U.S.-led Aid India Consortium. The result was a clash between the World Bank and the United States, which reduced but did not succeed in preventing a more modest one-year agreement for $100 million debt relief. Probing beyond this outcome, an examination of the figures on India's sources of external assistance over this period reveals that while the United States dropped its assistance from $2.1 billion (1966–69) to $1.5 billion (1969–74), the World Bank (IBRD and IDA assistance taken together) increased its assistance from $593 million (1966–69) to just under $1 billion (1969–74) (Veit 1976). In essence, the World Bank was countervailing U.S. reductions in assistance to India.

The explanation given by scholars who have examined the history of loans to India is that the Bank's lending reflected concerns of the U.S. aid community (Ruttan 1996). Highlighted is the multifaceted nature of U.S. policy. On India there were several competing voices within Washington, D.C., including the White House, the budget bureau of the Executive Office, the National Security Council, USAID, the State Department, and the Department of Agriculture (Lewis

1997). An in-depth study of the U.S. politics of aid to India documents that in the spring of 1966 the departments of State and Agriculture were pushing for more food aid with less conditionality for India (Paarlberg 1985, 144–57). Taking the opposite view was the White House and a very hands-on president determined to keep India on a short leash, particularly in light of India's criticisms of U.S. policy on Vietnam (Varshney 1989, 313). What the U.S. executive seemed not to understand was that the more strongly they pushed the Indian government to submit on economic policy, the more the Indian government had to prove that it was not kowtowing to the United States—principally through ever stronger criticism of the United States in Vietnam (Paarlberg 1985).

The United States is the largest shareholder and the home base of the IMF and World Bank. It enjoys a high degree of influence over both institutions, which it has maintained even as its relative contributions to the institutions have decreased. Yet the U.S. government, riven with competing foreign policy cliques, does not control all that the institutions do.

In the 1940s ideas, beliefs, and values played a critical role in creating the institutions. A bold new vision of international cooperation displaced an alternative, less formal, decentralized form of coordination that could have met U.S. interests. In the design and governance of the institutions a modest equalizing principle was enshrined and a degree of independence was conferred on the institutions, belying the view that the most powerful state at the time would simply create a structure maximizing its own control.

Through time the relative independence of the IMF and the World Bank has been eroded. The Cold War added political imperatives to the preferences of their major shareholders, as did the end of the Cold War and the desire to ensure a particular kind of transition in the former Soviet bloc. Furthermore, as each institution has expanded, it has become more reliant on direct U.S. approval for some portion of its resources. This has given the United States more influence within each institution. However, this does not mean that the United States dictates all policies of the institutions.

U.S. preferences are not always clear cut. Nor are the means to achieve them. As this chapter has illustrated, there can be competing voices and lobbies within the United States about a country and how it should be treated by the multilateral organizations. This opens up a space for the institutions to provide alternative technical ideas and financing plans for a member country, and to broaden the debate about the goals of their policies within that country. Furthermore, as I will explore in the next two chapters, even where the preferences of the most powerful shareholder in the IMF and World Bank are clear, those goals still need to be translated into policies that are in turn implemented and enforced by other governments.

Put simply, U.S. geostrategic motives and pressures have defined the parameters within which the IMF and World Bank work. But translating those preferences into policy requires ideas about ends and means, and instruments and institutions to implement them. Here the IMF and World Bank play a crucial role, not entirely controlled by the Unites States, which we will now explore.

Chapter 2

THE GLOBALIZING MISSION

When the Bank and Fund were created, there was no existing history or economic theory that would assist in defining to whom they should lend or under what conditions. Nor did their charters assist in answering how they might practically achieve the broad objectives set for them. Each institution would have to define its tasks and tools. Although from the start political influence was rife within each institution, national interests could not determine operational decisions. Why? Because as Krasner has so aptly put it, life at the Pareto frontier presents several alternatives (Krasner 1991). Even where a powerful state's objectives are clear, the choice of how to achieve those objectives is often unclear.

The IMF has to interpret the "adequate safeguards" provision—so brutally fought for in the Bretton Woods negotiations. What conditions should be imposed on borrowers to safeguard the institution's resources? In the World Bank, staff members decide which projects best foster development and what constitutes an appropriate program to support with loans. Economists offer competing answers to these questions. So what determines the result? In essence economic theories and politics collide and merge in the work of the IMF and World Bank. New ideas, debates, and theories certainly seep into each agency—especially when political and bureaucratic incentives are aligned. If a powerful shareholder does not back an idea or policy it is highly unlikely that it will be (at least openly) pursued. Equally vital are the incentives staff face to adopt new ideas. In the World Bank, for example, ideas that open up new lending possibilities will best fit with the "disbursement culture" that has long rewarded staff for how much they lend rather than the quality of those loans (Portfolio Management Task Force 1992).

This chapter burrows into the economics behind the IMF and World Bank, exposing how technical ideas are shaped by political and bureaucratic imperatives, starting with the first efforts of the Fund and Bank to implement their mandates.

The IMF Defines Its Tools

Once conditionality was established at the core of the IMF's work, members and staff of the institution had to work out what conditions to set for the use of Fund resources. Countries would approach the Fund for assistance. The IMF staff needed a way to diagnose the problem and prescribe or adjudicate a solution. What theories could be used to determine what borrowing countries should do in order to rectify a balance of payments deficit?

Obviously on some occasions direct political pressures would be brought to bear on the content of conditionality. Powerful members would add or shape conditions, attaching these to assistance such as occurred in the standby arrangement with Korea in 1997 (Feldstein 1998, Blustein 2001, Kirk 2000). However, not all cases attract such political attention and even when they do, the IMF staff still require an approach to understanding balance of payments difficulties that permits them to set down and justify conditionality.

Early on in the life of the IMF a particular model emerged that promised to resolve these questions. The Polak model, named after its author, offered staff a way to diagnose and prescribe conditions for any economy facing a balance of payments crisis (Polak 1957, De Vries 1987, Frenkel and Goldstein 1991). As Polak himself has written, the simplicity of the model was essential to its success (Polak 1997). The original model required few data. It focused attention on a key variable that governments could control—domestic credit creation. Crucially, it linked a country's domestic economic policies to its balance of payments position. This opened the door for IMF conditionality. It meant that to help resolve a balance of payments problem, the IMF would need to address domestic economic policy in its member countries.

The starting point of the Polak model is what was known as the "absorption approach" to the balance of payments, that a country with a balance of payments deficit was absorbing too many resources in consumption and investment, relative to what that country can produce. With a couple of simplifying assumptions, it will follow that a country which increases domestic credit too rapidly will encounter increasing balance of payments deficits reflected in a loss in central bank reserves. The golden rule of the model is that a country's money supply should expand at a rate not faster than the country's growth of real gross national product (Polak 1997). On the basis of this analysis, where a country has a balance of payments deficit the Fund's prescription focuses on reducing government spending, increasing taxes, and reducing domestic credit creation. The model implies a very neat set of policy prescriptions.

The Polak model emerged neither as state of art economics nor as pure practical expediency. It arose out of theoretical work Polak was undertaking in Washington, D.C. (Polak and White 1955) and a practical mission he led to Mexico in 1955. In Mexico, officials had for some time been working to stave off a balance of payments crisis. In his work with the Bank of Mexico, Polak formalized a technique for ensuring external stability and avoiding a new devaluation of the peso. His report on Mexico proposed a way of estimating the amount of money that could "safely" be created over a four-year period, based on estimates of output and of the increase of foreign exchange reserves and loans to the government (Polak 1997; James 1996, 140, cites the original report). The great advantage of Polak's new approach was that it used data on assets and liabilities in the banking system, which were more widely available and reliable than the national accounts data that other previous approaches to analyzing the balance of payments required. In other words, it was eminently practicable.

Subsequently the original Polak model evolved to take into account improving data and a wider range of instruments governments can use to control their economies. In the late 1990s the model began to give way to other approaches to understanding and resolving financial crises. Over four decades, however, the Polak model was the foundation for IMF financial programming and conditionality, and had profound implications for countries seeking to use IMF resources.

IMF conditionality requires countries to rectify balance of payments problems using stringent fiscal and monetary policy measures. The original rationale for this was that other policies would not work. For example, import restrictions could lead to only a short-term improvement in the balance of payments deficit. For this reason the IMF conditionality for a long time set purely monetary targets for borrowing countries, even though the Fund argued that this did not make Fund programs necessarily "monetarist" (IMF 1987).

Even during its early days the Polak model was subject to much criticism for imposing too much austerity with too little attention to the social consequences. Indeed, some of the criticism surfaces in the documents of the IMF and World Bank themselves. Contrasting with the official positive line (Fleming 1963, De Vries 1987), an internal IMF memorandum of 1963 concludes that it was "not too strong to say that the Colombian case tends to support many of the recent criticisms of [Fund] stabilization programs" (James 1996, 143). In 1966 a World Bank report accused the Fund of discouraging savings, undermining confidence in developing countries, and imposing harsh stabilization measures in the wrongheaded belief that balance of payments problems were short- as opposed to long-term (James 1996, 143). By the 1980s these kinds of criticisms became more vociferous as Fund conditionality was applied to debt crisis countries and accused of increasing poverty and curtailing growth in those countries.

Critics have long argued that built into the Polak model and its successor "financial programming" models are conservative biases. For Fund staff working with countries in deficit, a critical variable is output. This has a value that officials themselves must estimate, for the "safe" level of money that a government can create is based on an estimate of the country's growth of real gross national product. In practice, the IMF plays it safe, calculating output on the basis of an estimate of the country's capacity to pay for imports, whether from exports of goods and services, or from inflows of capital. For this reason the result, in the words of two analysts, is that "a conservative judgment is usually made" and "this leads to austere policies in terms of government expenditure" (Fine and Hailu 2000, 5).

A recent review by the IMF's Independent Evaluation Office highlights a slightly different reason for the perception that Fund programs produce auster-ity. "Programs typically assume rapid recovery, and therefore tend to push for greater fiscal adjustment to make room for private investment." However, as it turns out, the assumptions about the pace at which private investment demand will recover are unrealistic (Independent Evaluation Office 2003, 47).

Stepping back from financial programming models in the IMF, it is worth con-sidering the alternative ways the IMF might have defined its task and tools, for there were other theories on which the IMF staff might have based a diagnosis and solution to balance of payments problems (cf. Barnett and Finnemore 2004, chap. 3). In his original plan for the institution, Keynes laid out one possibility, which is reflected in article VII, "Replenishment and Scarce Currencies," of the IMF's Articles of Agreement. Keynes wanted to treat balance of payments sur-pluses and deficits as systemic phenomena requiring international rules and re-sponsibilities on the part of both surplus and deficit countries. Any surplus country would be required to take action to reduce their surplus or to have their currency declared a "scarce currency" by the IMF, which would permit other countries to take restrictive measures in respect of that currency thereby affect-ing the exports and so forth of the surplus country (Keynes 1971–89, vol. 25, 401–2, 474).

Another alternative for the IMF would be to focus on deficit countries but to address more squarely the external causes of deficits. For example, the institu-tion might pay more attention to exogenous shocks that create mayhem in vul-nerable economies such as their inability to increase export earnings, short-term fluctuations in commodity prices, and volatility among key currencies (Killick 1990b). The Fund has only ever taken incidental actions in respect of these is-sues—establishing compensatory loans to deal with the former, and surveillance reports to deal with the latter (more on this in chapter 6), yet they were exten-sively analyzed some two decades ago (Dell and Lawrence 1980, Helleiner 1986a). More recently, others have shown that balance of payments crises are influenced by financial contagion and the volatility of global capital markets and consequent vulnerability of countries almost regardless of their domestic policies and institutions (Williamson 2002). Criticism of the IMF's approach in neglecting international causes resurfaced prominently after the East Asian crisis (Radelet and Sachs 1998, Sachs 1998, Krugman 1999).

Why has the IMF eschewed these alternative approaches to analyzing and re-solving balance of payments problems? Two interrelated reasons stand out, one institutional and the other political. Institutionally, it is much easier for the IMF to deal with the domestic causes of balance of payments deficits. It has the tools and the leverage to exact promises of policy reform from borrowing govern-ments. It has no such capacity in respect of industrialized country trade protec-tionism, macroeconomic policy, or currency arrangements. The Fund could encourage members to use capital controls, and it does have the power to declare a currency scarce and permit other countries to impose limitations on the free-dom of exchange operations in the scarce currency (article VII [3]). In this regard the Fund runs up against the explicit preferences of its most powerful member—

the United States—which over recent years has pushed hard in the opposite direction, urging the membership of the IMF to rewrite its mandate to forbid capital controls and ensure the liberalization of members' capital accounts. Hence by the end of the 1990s even as the IMF's analysis was uncovering the costs of capital account liberalization in countries without highly developed and strong domestic financial system, the institution was nevertheless still positively advocating liberalization (IMF 1999b).

In defining its craft, the IMF is heavily constrained both by its capacity and by the limits put on it by its most powerful members. Within these constraints for a long time the Polak model and successor financial programming models made life relatively easy for the Fund. They provided a way to use available information to diagnose problems and to prescribe solutions that lay within the jurisdiction of the institution. That said, financial programming was severely challenged during the 1980s as the IMF sought an appropriate response to the debt crises that afflicted so many developing countries. Subsequently the IMF's approach would be further stretched in the Fund's efforts to facilitate systemic transformation in the former Eastern bloc countries and in dealing with collapsing and conflict-ridden states in Africa. In each of these later phases the Fund worked closely with the World Bank in defining and promulgating policy conditionality—even though the Bank's starting point, to which we will now turn, had been a different one.

The World Bank and the Pursuit of Economic Growth

From the outset the World Bank's objectives were broader than those of the IMF. Once postwar reconstruction had been dealt with (principally by the Marshall Plan), the Bank's central objective was development—a broad mission for which the Bank would employ a wide range of instruments. From early on development was defined as the promotion of economic growth, although the contents of the Bank's growth model have changed over time.

In the early years the Bank lent primarily for large public sector infrastructure projects, reflecting a particular view of growth and the need for industrialization. The Bank's view of development was based on a widely accepted belief that in developing countries resources needed to be transferred out of the traditional sector and into an advanced sector whose growth would be driven by the investment of profits generated in that sector (Lewis 1954). Owing to the savings-investment gap and the balance-of-payments constraint faced by developing countries, foreign lending and aid were required to facilitate this process (Bruno and Chenery 1962). The government's role in developing economies was central.

The World Bank had an important part to play. Industrialization required an adequate infrastructure of railways, roads, power plants, port installations, and communications facilities. This "public overhead capital" "customarily provided by the public sector" required both planning and investment (Mason and Asher 1973, 458). The Bank could assist by helping to meet foreign exchange requirements for capital infrastructure and providing technical expertise on investment planning and engineering. The result was a loan portfolio dominated by power and transportation projects, which came to account for 78 percent of lending to poorer countries by the end of the 1950s (Kapur et al. 1997, 86). At the same time, the Bank could guide the overall economic policy of its borrowing members so as to ensure "sensible public sector development programs" and "policies designed to promote the mobilization of foreign and domestic capital and its allocation through market forces to its most productive uses" (Mason and Asher 1973, 459).

Subsequently, the World Bank's view of its contribution to economic growth in borrowing countries expanded in two significant ways. First, there was a shift away from the focus on large public infrastructure loans toward a broader range of projects. This enabled the Bank to lend more and reflected the Bank's increasing involvement in India, Pakistan, Sri Lanka, and in Africa. Previously, the Bank had been reluctant to move into areas such as agriculture, industry, commerce, and financial and personal services for these were seen as the realm of private investment. However, by the late 1960s the Bank began to emphasize industry and agriculture. Its experience in India had demonstrated the need to ensure balanced growth across the economy and to reform prices in agriculture. In Africa the Bank became more aware of the importance of human resource development and lending to support education (Mason and Asher 1973, 472).

As well as broadening its range of projects, the Bank's view of development also shifted toward the overall policy framework and institutions within borrowing countries. Early Bank lending in Latin America had already made clear the importance of macroeconomic policy. In 1947 the Bank rejected a loan proposal for Chile on the grounds that the country was suffering from "unbalanced budgets and deficit financing, its need to limit non-essential imports and build up foreign exchange reserves . . . unsatisfactory system of multiple foreign exchange rates . . . unsatisfactory tax and exchange relationships with foreign enterprises" (Kapur et al. 1997, 82). In refusing to lend to Chile the Bank was exercising de jure conditionality over issues on which it would later focus more avidly. In India by the mid 1960s the Bank's focus became agricultural and macroeconomic policy reform to address artificially low interest rates and the overvalued exchange rate (Mason and Asher 1973, Kapur et al. 1997).

The Bank's concerns with exchange rate and macroeconomic policy soon brought it face to face with IMF missions attempting to address the same issues. Resulting tensions between the agencies led to a formal concordat between the Bank and Fund in 1966. The IMF was given primary responsibility for exchange rates and restrictive systems, adjustment of temporary balance of payments disequilibria, and financial stabilization. The World Bank would deal with development programs and the evaluation of projects (James 1996, 144). Yet this issue would recur with a vengeance in the 1980s.

The big change in the World Bank came in the late 1960s when Bank president Robert McNamara attempted to change the Bank's focus on development defined as economic growth measured as the rate of increase in per capita gross national product (GNP). McNamara rapidly expanded the Bank both in terms of lending and research. He advocated a broader conception of development, which paid attention to nutrition, literacy, family planning, employment, and income distribution, to which end he demanded detailed analysis—on this he is worth quoting:

> We do not want simply to say that rising unemployment is a "bad thing," and something must be done about it. We want to know its scale, its causes, its impact and the range of policies and options which are open to governments, international agencies and the private sector to deal with it. (McNamara, cited in Mason and Asher 1973, 476)

Two institutional features hindered the Bank's move into a broader conception of development—and indeed have plagued any such move since the 1970s. First, there was a political problem with expanding the Bank's goals beyond growth in per capital GNP. The Bank's Articles of Agreement prevent it from taking politics into account in making lending decisions, and equally from any political interference in its member countries. These decisions are left squarely within the realm of sovereign governments. If the Bank were to aim explicitly at political, social, and welfare objectives, it would fall foul of this injunction. At most it could aim to enhance the capacity of a government to address these other objectives. That said, even if governments agreed to a wider set of policies, the Bank would have to be able to define what these were.

The second problem for the Bank was a practical problem. The institution did not have the research or expertise to analyze and explain the social and political conditions in borrowing countries. The institution started out with a research department described as "small and underfunded" (Mason and Asher 1973, 467), particularly in comparison with the IMF (Horsefield 1969). This department was hugely expanded under McNamara (Kapur et al. 1997), yet the challenge of making a broader conception of development operational would remain elusive into the twenty-first century. In 2000 the Bank staff still complained that they lacked the knowledge necessary to understand the politics of economic reform and to take it into account in designing conditionality (Branson and Hanna 2000, 6).

Revealingly, the Bank's analysis has always been deeply affected by the way the institution is organized. From its inception the Bank was organized into technical departments, which appraised projects, and area departments, which examined growth rates, import requirements, and so forth. Practically it is easy to understand why the Bank, initially created for project lending, would be structured in this way. Falling between the stools of technical and area departments was a capacity to systematically trace how development policies and processes came together in specific settings—an analysis that would have been invaluable in forging practical cases or models for use in formulating development strategies. As the Bank's historians Edward Mason and Robert Asher put it:

> The Bank's research has never been organized so as to generate a systematic account of development processes or for the principal variants from the norm or model illuminating the relationship among the main variables that would need to

be taken into account in assessing development prospects. (Mason and Asher 1973, 467)

An alternative approach would have been for the Bank to use country comparisons or groupings significant to development to test a range of theories and alternative models of development (Stiglitz 1998 echoes this). Mason and Asher argue that this would have generated more useful models specifically applicable to different kinds of economies. Countries might have been grouped as labor-surplus economies or export-oriented economies or with due regard to characteristic differences in structure of production between small economies and large economies at similar per capital income levels, and among economies of similar size at different per capital income levels. The conclusion about the Bank's research that Mason and Asher regretfully came to in 1973 was that "the only grouping of developing economies that has emerged from Bank experiences is the product of administrative organization rather than of politico-economic analysis" (Mason and Asher 1973, 467).

A later criticism of the Bank was that it exhorted all countries to undertake similar policies without properly analyzing the likely effects of them all so doing. By organizing policy advice region by region, the overarching implications were lost. A key example is commodity exports. As the Bank exhorted developing countries across the world to increase their commodity exports in the 1980s, it failed properly to analyze the impact on world prices of all countries doing the same thing. Writing in 1990, Killick bemoans how little research had been done on this issue, citing just one study of such effects that is confined to African producers (Koester et al. 1987, cited in Killick 1990b). In that study, the evidence showed that an increase in exports of cocoa from all African producers would seriously reduce the world price of cocoa such that producers would lose instead of gaining from additional investments in the crop (Koester et al 1987). For other commodities, one would need to take into account the effects of export increases in other parts of the world being advised by the World Bank. A similar criticism would later be made of the IMF and its failure to properly leverage its capacity to collate, aggregate, and analyze the effects of policy across regions and across the world economy (IMF, External Evaluation 1999a).

In summary, the structure and operational needs of the Bank and the IMF have shaped the ways each institution defines and operationalizes its purposes. Both the IMF and the World Bank draw heavily on economic theory and a staff of expert economists. However, the knowledge they draw on is equally shaped by institutional imperatives and limitations. To some degree each institution must fashion its policies to fit the resources available. This means that their knowledge is influenced by the way they are organized, the kinds of information and data available, and the incentive each faces to adopt a model that can be used for all member states. These variables reduce the discretion of staff and make it easier for the institution to maintain consistency and coherence. It is these features that shaped the knowledge and policies of the IMF and World Bank as they evolved in the 1980s.

The Debt Crisis and the Rise of the Washington Consensus

The 1970s were marked by an explosion of international lending by banks. Using growing Euromarkets, major commercial banks began rolling over short-term deposits into what were effectively long-term loans mostly to developing or emerging market economies (Helleiner 1994, Darity and Horn 1988, James 1996). The activities of the banks were fueled by their desire to profitably recycle OPEC surpluses. The result was a "sudden escalation" in developing country debt, which created what the IMF described in 1976 as a serious vulnerability on the part of borrowers to any shift in access to external credit or export earnings (IMF 1976).

The heady 1970s came to an abrupt halt in 1979 when the U.S. Federal Reserve hiked up interest rates in a shift to control inflation through contractionary monetary policy. Debtors faced exponentially higher interest rates and commercial bank creditors unwilling to extend new credit (Aggarwal 1996). Suddenly dozens of developing countries could not meet repayments to commercial and official creditors (Cline 1984). Adding to their woes, they also faced a new political environment in the North.

During the 1970s governments in the United States, the United Kingdom, and Germany had been willing to open up a dialogue about international economic management and North-South relations (Brandt 1980, Cox 1979). However, by 1980 in each country a strongly market-oriented government of the right had come to power. The new "neoliberal" governments were skeptical about foreign aid and critical of the profligacy and corruption within developing countries. President Reagan had won the U.S. election promising a much tougher foreign policy toward the "evil empire" of the Soviet Union as well as toward all other countries hostile to the United States. In economic policy the Reagan administration, like Prime Minister Thatcher and Chancellor Kohl, focused on monetary policy as a tool to control inflation and on privatization as a way to improve efficiency in the public sector. After a decade of big governments, the new political agenda in these countries was about rolling back the state and unleashing market forces. But the debt crisis forced each of them to accept a form of public intervention.

When the Latin American debt crisis broke in Washington, D.C., in 1982 it was immediately obvious that creditor governments would need to intervene. Several large international commercial banks were heavily overexposed in Latin America (Cline 1984). Creditor governments needed to ensure that their own large, overexposed banks did not go bust and bring down the international financial system (Kaletsky 1983). Several institutions could play some part in averting this threat, including the IMF, the Bank for International Settlements, the World Bank, the U.S. Treasury and Federal Reserve, and their counterparts in other industrialized countries. Adding to the economic pressures, creditors also feared that a politically unstable Central and Latin America would fall prey to geostrategic advances by the Soviet Union (Kissinger Commission 1984).

The IMF soon emerged as the lead agency managing the debt crisis. Unsurprisingly, it turned its existing tools and expertise to the task at hand. The Polak model defined the problem as a short-term liquidity crisis or balance of payments deficit due to excessive domestic credit creation and prescribed contractionary policies, which would stabilize the economy and permit the servicing of debt. Each debtor government was required to clamp down on government spending and increase interest rates. In all cases this led to a severe contraction in the economy and did little to alleviate the crisis. For some this was unsurprising for even outside of the debt crisis, the Fund's approach had been described as "overkill" because the Polak model systematically underestimated the demand-side effects on output (Dell 1982).

The IMF's approach had evolved as a solution to countries facing a short-term liquidity problem. However, in the early 1980s this was not the ailment faced by Latin American governments. High interest rates, poor investment decisions, a global economic downturn, and massive debt burdens meant that their repayment obligations far exceeded their capacity to pay. In essence, the debtors were insolvent. However, the IMF had no tools on hand to deal with that larger problem.

In 1982 neither the IMF nor any other international agency had the powers of an international bankruptcy mechanism to ensure that while safeguarding the system, the costs of dealing with bad debt could be fairly apportioned between lenders and borrowers. Indeed, such a system was not proposed within the IMF until 2002 (Krueger 2002, IMF 2002d). In the 1980s at most the IMF might have exercised power under article VIII (2b), which provides that certain international contracts will not be enforceable in the courts of member countries when they are in conflict with restrictions approved by the IMF. In theory, this could have been used to prevent creditors taking action against a debtor before an orderly debt workout had been negotiated. However, courts in major industrialized countries have interpreted this article in widely different fashions (Gold 1989).

Once deployed, the IMF brought to bear its existing tools and expertise, providing credit (alongside banks and industrialized country governments) to enable the debtors to meet their immediate debt repayment obligations. In return, the debtors were required to undertake "stabilization." Each government had to reduce public sector expenditure and investment, eliminate government subsidies, increase the cost of goods supplied by the government, increase income and sales tax, set positive real interest rates to discourage capital flight and increase savings, rationalize and stabilize the exchange rate, and reduce inflation. This prescription was the first rendition of what would later be called the Washington consensus. It fit well with the new neoliberal ideology being expounded in Northern creditor countries.

The combination of new loans and tough conditionality worked to protect the international financial system using existing international institutions. No major bank collapsed in spite of their high exposure to Latin America. The prescription ensured that debtors met their repayments in a timely and orderly way. Indeed virtually all banks continued to pay dividends throughout the 1980s (Sachs and Huizinga 1987). However, as one banker recognized in testimony to the U.S. House of Representatives at the time, borrowing governments were meeting their interest payments by accepting new loans, hence their overall debt mounted and mounted (Bogdanowicz-Bindert 1985). The result was good for the banks but disastrous for the debtors.

By 1985 debtor countries undertaking stabilization were sliding ever deeper into recession and indebtedness. A new debt strategy and some revision to the "stabilization" solution was urged on the U.S. Congress in hearing after hearing as bankers, academics, and officials warned policymakers of the dangers of default, unrest, a collapse in U.S. export markets and threats to U.S. commodity supplies (U.S. House of Representatives 1985a, 1985b, 1985c).

Why did the debtors not default? One group of Latin American debtors had declared after a conference in Quito in early 1984 that debt service ought to come second to development, proposing to limit debt service in relation to export earnings (CEPAL 1984). A more radical position was formulated a few months later by a larger group of debtors meeting in Cartagena (Banco Nacional de Comercio Exterior 1984). The resulting "Cartagena Consensus" was further refined at subsequent meetings in Mar del Plata (13–14 September 1984) and Santo Domingo (7–8 February 1985). Yet no collective action by debtors emerged (Ffrench-Davies 1987, Kugler 1987). Preventing any collective default was the fact that debtors did not all fall into crisis at the same time, and also that each debtor could relatively easily be induced to accept a special deal with creditors (O'Donnell 1985, 1987; Whitehead 1989).

Some individual countries attempted unilateral action. In 1985 in Peru a new president facing debt interest and repayment obligations that exceeded the country's total anticipated export earnings, declared that the country's debt service would be limited to 10 percent of export earnings. In Zambia after large-scale riots broke out at the end of 1986, a new national "alternative" to IMF-sponsored adjustment was announced, including limiting debt service to 10 percent of net foreign exchange earnings and including IMF loans in the unilateral default. In Brazil at virtually the same time a unilateral moratorium on interest payments on Brazil's outstanding debt was announced. However, in all these cases unilateral action proved short-lived.

A change in the debt strategy did not occur until 6 October 1985 when secretary of the U.S. Treasury James Baker III outlined a new plan for managing the debt crisis at an IMF meeting in Seoul, Korea, soon dubbed the "Baker Plan" (Baker 1985). The new plan had three elements. First and foremost the plan reinforced and further entrenched structural adjustment conditionality: "comprehensive macroeconomic and structural policies to promote growth and balance-of-payments adjustment and to reduce inflation" (Baker 1985, 9).

Second, the Baker Plan involved more lending by both the IMF and the World Bank and other multilateral development banks for structural and sectoral adjustment. The U.S. secretary of the treasury referred to the "ample room to expand the World Bank's fast disbursing structural and sector adjustment lending in support of growth-oriented policies and institutional and sectoral reform," proposing that the Bank could raise its disbursements to principal debtors by 50 percent. Together with increased lending from the Inter-American Development

Bank this would provide an addition $9 billion annually or $27 billion over three years (Baker 1985, 10).

The third element of the Baker Plan was to increase private banks' lending to around $20 billion over three years. This led to much debate in the United States about how banks might be persuaded to stump up more money—in essence throwing good money after bad. Congressmen sought to uncover hidden guarantees or promises being made to the banking sector (see U.S. House of Representatives 1985a and 1985b). Yet the short-term key priority for banks was to ensure that debtor governments met their interest payments on time. If interest payments were postponed or capitalized then a bank would have to reclassify the loan. For that reason, banks focused on ensuring new loans were made to debtors. These included both concerted private sector loans and new loans from the multilateral organizations—indeed commercial bank creditors had begun to insist on World Bank financing as a condition of their reschedulings even before the Baker Plan (Watson et al. 1986, Husain and Diwan 1989, Boughton 2001, 1001).

Repaying the banks was further ensured by more stringent conditionality and new forms of monitoring. Debtors were now required to embark on new deeper "structural adjustment," emphasizing supply-side reforms rather than purely demand-side measures. However, the conditionality paid no attention to supply-side measures that developing countries themselves were urging—viz. the need to enhance investment in "tradeables," that is, exporting and import-competing activities (G-24 1986). The Baker Plan implied that the Fund would lend more, apply deeper structural adjustment conditionality, and offer a new role of "enhanced surveillance" whereby the Fund would monitor countries not already within Fund programs so as to report on their performance to private sector creditors (Boughton 2001, 429).

For the World Bank the new strategy channeled more of the institution's resources and research into structural adjustment and policy-based lending. Already in 1980 the Bank had launched Structural Adjustment Lending (SAL) programs and in 1981 the World Development Report had focused on adjustment. The new demands of debt crisis management pushed the Bank further in this direction and also into a new turf battle with the IMF.

The Baker Plan envisaged that the Bank and Fund would work closely together to produce joint programs and conditionality with individual countries (Baker 1985). The United States strongly advocated such a joint approach (the board minutes are cited by Boughton 2001, 647). However, other countries protested vociferously. They argued that cross-conditionality would further reduce the bargaining power of borrowers (G-24 1986). In the end the United States accepted a much-diluted approach whereby the Fund and Bank would agree on a joint policy framework paper, which would be approved by both Executive Boards prior to each institution negotiating its own conditionality. The institutions also elaborated rules about collaboration and began some minimal participation in each other's missions. The result as later described by Fund historian James Boughton was a set of rules that "helped staffs to keep from tripping over each other's feet when they were both responding to the same fire alarms" (Boughton 2001, 1002).

The rules on collaboration broke down over Argentina in 1988 when the World Bank announced a new loan to that country before the IMF mission had completed its negotiations with the Argentine authorities. Argentina had prepared a new economic plan that the United States wanted to support (Pastor and Wise 2001, Machinea 1990). The IMF managing director and staff wanted to see further tightening in Argentina's fiscal policy. Unusually, the IMF's managing director Michel Camdessus refused to yield to direct pressure from the U.S. secretary of the treasury to approve a loan to Argentina until the fiscal policy issues had been addressed (Boughton 2001, 521).

Meanwhile across Nineteenth Street at the World Bank officials were under equal pressure from the United States to approve a loan (*Economist* 11 March 1989; Aggarwal 1996, 441). The World Bank had long disagreed with the Fund's position on Argentina, arguing that more stringent fiscal policy made it too difficult for the government to implement the very reforms the Bank was trying to finance. On 25 September, the president of the World Bank announced his support for a package of four loans to Argentina totaling $1.25 billion. The conditionality attached to the package included a "Letter of Development Policy," which stipulated macroeconomic policies that were at the heart of the IMF's negotiations with the country. The move was a direct affront to the conventions and accords that governed relations between the IMF and the World Bank.

The Bank's loan to Argentina produced a bitter feud between the organizations as the respective heads failed to agree on a form of words that would capture a new agreement about collaboration (Boughton 2001, 1003). The world's press went to town (*Financial Times* 26 September 1988, *Wall Street Journal* 26 September 1988). In the end, the two institutions agreed on a new concordat governing their collaboration (World Bank *Annual Report* 1989b).

Meanwhile the overall debt strategy desperately needed revising. The situation in debtor countries was not improving. Rioting in Venezuela in March 1989 reflected a couple of years of widespread discontent in Latin America as growth failed to materialize. Legislators in Japan, Europe, and the United States found themselves under pressure to come up with a better solution. Public criticism of them was mounting for having used taxpayer money to bail out banks, ensuring first and foremost that public interventions served to have debtors make their interest payments (Sachs 1986, 1989; Calvo et al. 1989). Legislators in the United States began to debate regulating banks to prevent such bailouts in the future (U.S. House of Representatives 1989).

Crucially, by the late 1980s the bargaining position of the banks had changed (Aggarwal 1996). The most exposed commercial banks had provisioned themselves so that their debt exposure no longer posed a risk to stability in the international financial system (Lissakers 1991). Citibank's much publicized decision to add $3 billion to its reserves in 1987 led the way on this. Furthermore, outstanding debt was increasingly being diffused into secondary markets (Cline 1995).

A new approach using debt relief to reduce interest rates was floated by Japan and by France. This became known as the Miyazawa Plan following its announcement at the G-7 in June 1988 in Toronto. Soon other countries began to support the idea of a change in the strategy (Cline 1995). Yet it took until 10 March 1989 for the United States to change its position and thereby unlock a new official approach (Lissakers 1991).

Intellectually the case for debt relief was being put together in several forums. Although it was taboo to refer to debt relief in public, some work was being done within the IMF (Dooley 1986; Corbo, Goldstein, and Khan 1987) as well as in the World Bank (Husain and Diwan 1989, Claessens 1990, Claessens and Wijnbergen 1990), and in the Inter-American Bank economists had been quietly working for some time on the issue (interview with Chief Economist Ricardo Haussman). In June 1988 in the IMF a debt group was set up secretly to generate new ideas—few other staff members knew of its existence (Boughton 2001, 483). Outside of the institutions several prominent economists were also making the case for debt relief (Williamson 1988, Sachs 1989, Frenkel et al. 1989).

There was also an emerging practice of debt reduction through market operations (Blackwell and Nocera 1989). The Fund implicitly supported debt reduction in Bolivia and Costa Rica in 1987, as it did when Mexico concluded a path-breaking deal with Morgan Guaranty Bank to exchange part of its bank loans for bonds, which would be partially guaranteed by the U.S. Treasury (Boughton 2001, chapter 11; Lissakers 1991, 237). Chile had also begun to structure some debt relief (Aravena 1991).

In the U.S. key economic policymaking figures remained opposed to debt relief (Lissakers 1991). These included Secretary of the Treasury James Baker and Federal Reserve chairman Paul Volcker (until mid 1987). It was not until after the new secretary of the treasury Nicholas Brady took office in early 1989 that the United States shifted its official position. He recalls that the debt strategy had become "ludicrous." Banks were being coerced into "doing more of what was bad" (Interview with Secretary of Treasury Nicholas Brady 1994).

After conferences with the IMF, Brady's deputy David Mulford and the G-7 prepared a new approach, which was unveiled on 10 March 1989. The "Brady Plan" permitted some degree of market-based writing down of debt whereby a few debtors undertook to replace part of their debt with bond swaps, which would reduce their overall liability (Fried and Tresize 1989). The banks, recalls Nicholas Brady "hated it but it was the only game in town" and the administration was prepared to "push and shove and keep on pushing and shoving" (Interview with Brady 1994). The conditionality part of the debt strategy was not altered. More structural adjustment continued to be demanded of debtors. The same prescription was also applied to systemic transformation in the former Soviet bloc and to combating economic failure in sub-Saharan Africa. Stabilization and adjustment seemed to provide both Western donors and policymakers in transitional and developing economies with a simple, clear prescription for economic policy in a world full of baffling new complexities and vulnerabilities.

What Embeds the Washington Consensus in the Bank and Fund?

In 1990 economist John Williamson coined the term "Washington consensus" to describe the policies of stabilization and adjustment that prevailed as a framework for virtually all tasks undertaken by the Fund and Bank as of the early 1980s (Williamson 1990). "Consensus" referred to the seemingly unassailable agreement among experts as to the fundamentals of good economic policy. The "Washington" part of the label highlighted that these experts were on the whole based in Washington, D.C.—in the Fund, the Bank, the U.S. Treasury and Federal Reserve, and some of the think tanks that concern themselves with these issues.

The need for a policy consensus arose because the debt strategy depended on debtors tightening their belts. Creditor countries were unwilling to provide greater financing or to force creditors to take more of a loss. If debt repayments were to be made, then financing and adjustment had to be balanced. The less finance made available to debtors, the more adjustment they would have to undertake. In the 1980s the clear priority of the debt strategy was to save the banks (Sachs and Huizinga 1987, Lissakers 1991). The result was that debtors had to adjust hard. As the debt strategy evolved the financing of it was reshuffled alongside a minimal fine-tuning of the terms of adjustment. This underscores the questions of what determined the content of conditionality and how and why was a consensus maintained within the institutions?

The terms of adjustment or the content of conditionality during the debt crisis was influenced by the economic diagnosis and prescription of the crisis *as interpreted* within the IMF and the World Bank (Helleiner 1981). A number of characteristics of the institutions stand out in shaping this interpretation. The first of these is the provenance and training of the staff in each institution, which only in very recent years has begun to diversify.

In the IMF a 1968 study of senior management revealed that just under 60 percent were from English-speaking industrialized countries (Strange 1974, 269). In 2001 this had not changed radically. Some 42.1 percent of department heads were from industrial English-speaking countries along with 55 percent of senior personnel managers (IMF Diversity Annual Report 2001, 21). The IMF's Diversity Report also highlights the severe underrepresentation among senior management of economists from Africa and the Middle East, noting that although the Fund hired record high numbers of new staff in 2000–2001 it "missed the opportunity to improve diversity" (IMF 2001c, 19).

In the World Bank a 1991 study of the Policy, Research, and External Affairs departments showed that some 80 percent of senior staff were trained in economics and finance at institutions in the United States and in the United Kingdom (Stern and Ferreira 1997). In the IMF at the time it was reported that some 90 percent of staff with Ph.D's received them from the United States or Canada (Clark 1996). In 2002 the Human Resources Department in the IMF reported that the institution employed 1,231 economists of whom 59 percent received their most advanced degree in North American universities (IMF 2002c).

Many economists would argue the facts stated above simply reflect that the best economics departments of the world are to be found in the United States (with the UK and Canada trailing close behind), and that the Fund and Bank hire the best. Equally however, several features of the organizations skew them in this direction. Unlike most multilateral organizations, the IMF and World Bank have no nationality quotas to ensure that all countries are represented both formally in the governing councils of institutions, as well as informally among the technical staff. This was rejected by the United States in the early planning stages of the institutions.[1] Furthermore both institutions work exclusively in English with no requirement to work in other languages. Recent historians of the Bank argue that this has weighted employment in the Bank significantly, not just geographically (favoring South Asia over East Asia and Britain over other European countries), but also overwhelmingly toward graduates of institutions that taught in English (i.e., predominantly in the United States and UK) (Kapur et al. 1997, 1167).

The similar graduate training shared by staff in each organization gives them a shared, albeit narrow, methodology and particular understanding of the world, its problems, and their solutions. This makes it difficult for ideas from outside of the "profession" to be taken seriously or to percolate into the mindset of the institutions. The term *profession,* which is widely used by neoclassical economists, I highlight deliberately. It underscores the extent to which this kind of economics is a discipline, like medicine or law, requiring the command of a specific body of abstract and complex knowledge, which is then brought to bear on a particular case (Brint 1994, McDonald 1995).

As a profession, neoclassical economics has both a technical and a normative, value-laden aspect to it. Just as doctors are taught to value human life above other goals, economists are trained to value efficiency above other goals (Evans and Finnemore 2001, 17). The professional discipline becomes a way of examining problems, of defining their essential features, and considering solutions. It becomes a way of "taming" the most intractable problems by reducing them to the core elements that the professional expertise can digest and prescribe from. This professionalism is vital to the work of the IMF and the World Bank. It is on this that their claim to specialist knowledge and technical expertise is founded.

Put another way, the IMF and the World Bank do not claim to know the local circumstances of their borrowers. They do not send anthropologists into the field to examine the social institutions and values that underpin working practices, markets, and political life in a country. They send professional economists who "cut through" the details of local circumstances, and "tame" the complex-

[1] In early negotiations on creating the organizations, the United States blocked any such requirement, although the management of each institution is required "subject to the paramount importance of securing the highest standards of efficiency and of technical competence" to "pay due regard to the importance of recruiting personnel on as wide a geographical basis as possible" (IBRD Art V, section 5, and IMF Art XII, section 4).

ities of economic problems, extracting indicators and specific policy goals from what might otherwise be a morass. This is the application of professional expertise. It has several positive advantages for the IMF and World Bank. It makes it easier to claim that they are treating all members similarly. It keeps politics out of the equation. And it brings all problems within the professional ambit of staff.

There is also a psychological advantage to having a clear, narrow mindset in the work of the IMF and World Bank. Junior officials are regularly sent to far-away places to analyze rather alien and difficult situations. As mentioned above, a clear blueprint of models and policies provide the Fund and Bank staff with a well-structured starting point from which to define the problem, map out the stakes, prescribe a solution, evaluate the chances of success, and assess the implications of their prescription. Obviously, the simpler and clearer the model the more usefully it fulfills these functions.

The downside of professionalism for the IMF and the World Bank is that there is very little room for local knowledge. Local knowledge is messy, political, intractable, and very difficult to make judgments about. Nevertheless, it is vital to the definition of economic problems and their likely and practicable solutions. This point is made by critics of the World Bank (Ferguson 1990, Gran 1986, Escobar 1995). The point is also increasingly recognized by the institutions themselves, as evidenced in their increasing push for "local ownership" of policies and programs (see chapter 5). Their reasoning is that policy prescriptions simply don't work unless there is local ownership and commitment to implementation. However, this poses an inherent contradiction for both the Fund and the Bank. The advantages accruing from professionalism would be difficult to sacrifice in the name of a wholly new "local" and "messy" way of working. We will discuss this further in chapters 5 and 6.

The staff of the Fund and Bank are professionals bringing a particular framework to bear on problems emerging in different countries the world over. Necessarily this implies a degree of insensitivity to local circumstances which many argue persistently hampers the mission of each institution. The advantage has been that the institutions have retained an enviable coherence and reputation for professional expertise. They have also very often managed skillfully to avoid the pitfalls of overtly political analysis and prescription. Nevertheless, in some cases the professionalism and coherence of the institutions can lead to a certain kind of blindness and overrigidity that leaves them unable to deploy their formidable expertise.

Disagreements among staff within each of the Fund and Bank are ultimately resolved by appeals up the chain of command. If a heated debate emerges within a country mission it will go up the chain possibly right to the head of the Area Department. If that person finds that the Policy Development and Review Department disagrees with him or her, they might even remit the issue further up the hierarchy. In the extreme an issue will finally be settled by the first deputy managing director or the managing director of the IMF.

Hierarchy combines with centralization within the IMF and World Bank to ensure a high degree of conformity. Ultimately all staff account back to headquarters in Washington. This prevents staff "going native" or interpreting their work or methods in ways that diverge from the institution. In recent years this feature has become weaker in the World Bank as it has decentralized and come to rely more heavily on consultants and staff outside of its permanent operational structures (more on this later). By contrast, in the IMF the sense of one-of-us is further bolstered by a reluctance to decentralize, a smaller staff, lower turnover, and imperviousness to information, advice, or criticism coming from outside its own walls (see Kuczynski 1988, 124). This is changing at a very modest speed.

In both the IMF and the World Bank political pressures and bureaucratic features combine to entrench a particular world view. This set of ideas is not a direct reflection of the interests of the most powerful members of the organizations, even though powerful members get to influence it. Prevailing ideas are shaped by economic analysis, institutional constraints, and bureaucratic organization. These latter factors also create somewhat of a straight-jacket around the thinking of each organization, as is illuminated in studying their reactions to a crisis.

When Consensus Is Blinding

In 1994 both the Fund and the Bank failed to foresee that their largest debtor was in dire economic trouble. As Mexico's exchange rate and economy went into free-fall at the end of 1994, both the IMF and the World Bank were accused of having had their heads in the sand. Subsequent evidence suggests that the experts failed fully to recognize the risks faced by Mexico and failed to consider anything other than optimistic scenarios for the economy. The case illuminates several political and institutional features that lock the Fund and Bank into a particular pathway, hobbling their ability to foresee or help to prevent a crisis. Some three years later, backing up the lessons drawn from the Mexican case, South Korea would go into financial crisis and be attended to by an IMF hobbled by some of the same factors.

In Mexico a crisis seemed unlikely to the IMF and the World Bank for a number of reasons. In 1993 Mexico's economic future looked set to flourish. Under the tutelage of the IMF and the World Bank, the Mexican government had built steadily on a set of economic reforms commenced a decade earlier. These reforms now seemed to be cemented in place by the completion of the North American Free Trade Agreement (NAFTA) and by Mexico's accession to the OECD. Likewise, a couple of years later South Korea was undertaking liberalization, urged on by the IMF to liberalize more rapidly, and acceded to the OECD in December 1996. In each country, an IMF article IV consultation conducted just prior to each respective financial crisis revealed little concern on the part of Fund staff that the country faced a risk of financial crisis.

In Mexico a financial crisis began just two months after its October article IV consultation. In December 1994, after a period of economic policy difficulties the Mexican government widened the exchange rate band by 15 percent (Lustig 1995; Sachs, Tornell, and Velasco, 1995). Within weeks Mexico was on the verge of default as investors withdrew. The country's vulnerability to capital inflows and outflows suddenly became a nightmare. From Washington, it looked as though risks were posed to international financial stability as Mexico's problems threatened to create a "Tequila effect" spilling across Latin America, causing capital flight from the whole region (IMF 1995b, Gil-Diaz and Carstens 1995, Calvo and Mendoza 1995).

Extraordinarily, in spite of warning signs earlier in 1994 and even back in 1993, neither the IMF nor the World Bank picked up on urgent warnings about Mexico, nor did either institution issue any kind of urgent warning to the Mexican government. Yet there were several warning signs which either institution might have noticed. Many of these are documented in the institutions' own publications from which most of the information below has been derived (IMF 1995a, 1995b, 1995c; World Bank 1996a). Similarly, in the case of Korea, a review by the IMF's Independent Office of Evaluation has uncovered documents and internal debates to which more attention should have been paid (Independent Evaluation Office 2003a, Annex 2, 95, notes the doubts that began to surface in 1997 about the timing and sequencing of financial liberalization as per Folkerts-Landau and Lingren 1998, a draft of which had been circulating within the IMF in late 1997).

In Mexico in early 1994, the country's current account deficit had been exacerbated by an uprising in Chiapas, which the government found very difficult to deal with and which markets were reacting to adversely. Further, an increase in long-term U.S. interest rates forced down bond prices, and in particular the value of Mexico's Brady bonds. In international markets, there was a significant rise in the risk premium being charged on Mexican debt. Yet in official documents neither the IMF nor the World Bank went beyond their usual states of "concern" about the economy (IMF 1994a).

In April 1994, the markets (and the Fund and Bank) became aware that the Mexican government was substituting *tesobonos* (Mexican peso-denominated government bonds, carrying a dollar guarantee) for CETES (U.S. dollar-denominated instruments). Yet an IMF staff visit undertaken in mid 1994 was not alarmed by the swiftly increasing stock of *tesobonos,* even while financial markets were reacting to the shift. While foreign investment continued to flow into Mexico, a closer investigation into the nature of investment would have revealed that it was creating new vulnerabilities for the Mexican economy. Certainly, once Mexican's monetary data up to April 1994 were released (in August 1994), the shifts should have been apparent to both the Fund and Bank. So, too, later in 1994 the institutions should have more carefully noted the shortening of maturity of new government security issues, the drop in foreign holdings of short-term public debt, and the drop in stock market prices.

In South Korea there was a similar failure on the part of the IMF to find and examine negative signals in the marketplace. In that case between August and September 1997, outside analysts have pointed to two such indicators. The yield spread of Korean Development Bank dollar-denominated bonds had begun to widen, and other signals indicated a diminution of market confidence in the value of the currency (Park and Rhee 1998; Independent Evaluation Office 2003a, Annex 2, 97).

In Mexico, equally worrying, figures released in early September 1994 revealed that Mexico's imports had grown by 25 percent over the second quarter of 1993, and that the country's current account deficit had increased to 8 percent of GDP on an annual basis. In the same month, in a vain hope to reassure the investment community, the government announced a Pact for Welfare, Stability, and Growth (PABEC), which did nothing to correct the deteriorating trade balance or to tighten up the loosening financial policies. At least by this point, the IMF or the World Bank should have sprung into action. Yet a senior World Bank official at the time was expressing a positive view (Edwards 1995), as were IMF staff (see IMF Country Report of January 1994, following 1993 Article IV consultations with Mexico). Why was this the case?

Obviously the IMF and Bank cannot loudly report negatively on one of their member economies. If they did, they would risk catalyzing the very crisis they would hope to avoid. Furthermore, the institutions rely heavily on the cooperation and openness of governments in the countries with whom they work. They have no automatic right of access to confidential and sensitive statistics and policy questions. Once granted access, the institutions must use information carefully and without breaching confidentiality. To do their job they must ensure continuing good relations and continuing access. The risk of adverse analysis is that a government would simply close off access. This would prevent the institutions from performing most of their functions. Yet the result is to hobble their capacity to undertake clear-sighted analysis. In the cases of Mexico and South Korea the IMF was given incomplete data, yet failed to follow up on this.

In hindsight it is clear that in April 1994, World Bank staff should not have accepted the assurances of Mexico's Central Bank that they would not defend the exchange rate band if it became unsustainable, and that they were shifting to a monetary anchor (World Bank 1996). The weakness of both Fund and Bank staff in the ensuing months to push for better information and more evidence of assurances has been explained by the Bank as due not just to "respect for the competence of the Mexican technical team" but also to "some element of deference to such a large and important client country" (World Bank 1996: these elements are also highlighted in the IMF's confidential internal study IMF 1995c). In the case of South Korea, the report of the IMF's evaluation office notes that "there was insufficient data on Korea's short-term obligations (though some relevant data sources were overlooked)" and that staff did not attempt to request the appropriate data more forcefully (Independent Evaluation Office 2003, Annex 2, 97).

Finally, although the IMF often notes that Mexico had no standby program with the IMF at the time and therefore little influence—and indeed the same is true for South Korea—this wrongly understates the IMF's responsibilities when it undertakes article IV surveillance of its members, and its overall responsibility for financial stability.

In the case of Mexico the reputations of the IMF and the World Bank were on the line. Both institutions had given the country their "stamp of approval." The reforms Mexico had undertaken over the late 1980s and early 1990s had been perceived by many within the international financial community, including the World Bank and the IMF, as "spectacular, lasting, and the envy of any reform economy" (Dornbusch and Werner 1994, 266). Mexico's special status as a role model for other developing countries is reflected in *Economic Transformation: The Mexican Way,* by the former Mexican finance minister, Pedro Aspe, who describes the "profound transformation of the economy," which rendered it (i.e., in 1993) "much better prepared to face the uncertainties of a rapidly changing and challenging world and to respond more effectively to the social needs of our population" (Aspe 1993, xiii). The involvement of the IMF and World Bank and their commitment of resources to Mexico was a sign of confidence that the government had implemented (and would continue) liberalizing reforms, and that these would almost inevitably lead to economic success.

Not only would a warning or pessimistic note from the Bank or the Fund risk catalyzing a crisis, but it could also signal a failure of the Fund and Bank's more general project: of persuading countries to liberalize and deregulate their economies. Indeed, very soon after Mexico's crisis, other countries such as Brazil, India, and Korea were arguing the case for slower or different types of reform with a note of triumphalism—pointing to Mexico as evidence of failure of the prescriptions of the Fund and Bank (Hale 1996, 2, 21).

In Korea in 1997 a similar stricture existed. IMF staff papers and board discussions consistently reflected a concern that Korea should be persuaded to liberalize faster and more deeply. This was part of a more general over-enthusiasm for greater capital account liberalization (Rogoff 2002, Independent Evaluation Office 2004). The result was to leave little space for economists within the institution to step back and to examine what vulnerabilities the specific timing and sequencing of liberalization had set in place in Korea.

In both Mexico's crisis of 1994 and Korea's crisis of 1997, the international financial institutions had their reputations and the credibility of their policy advice on the line. The failure on the part of officials within each institution fully to recognize the risks of a crisis was not due to the blindness or stupidity of particular individuals. Both crises reveal much about how the structure, organization, and ideology of each institution affect its work.

In Mexico and in Korea the experts became blinkered. The more they invested in a positive scenario, the less they were able to consider alternative outcomes. In Mexico, officials involved at the time admitted in a highly confidential internal assessment of the handling of the crisis that little effort was made to consider any kind of contingency plan should their positive assumptions fall through (IMF 1995c). In Korea, Fund staff displayed "excessive optimism" regarding Korea's ability to prevent speculative attacks on the *won,* and "underestimated the risk of a breakdown in funding the capital account."

Why did this occur? Both the IMF and World Bank have conducted internal and confidential reports about their internal failings in respect of Mexico, and the IMF's Independent Evaluation Office has conducted a study in respect of Korea, all of which are revealing, as are the oral accounts of participants involved (see World Bank 1996a; IMF 1995c, Independent Evaluation Office 2003a; interviews).

What became clear after Mexico's crisis at the end of 1994 was that there had only been one scenario considered on Washington's 19th Street. To cite the Bank's internal report on the crisis: "Insufficient effort was devoted to developing 'what if' scenarios" (World Bank 1996a). Indeed, after the crisis a very senior World Bank staff member pointed out that "what is to some extent intriguing . . . is not that the Mexican economy faced a major currency crisis, but that so many observers were shocked by this turn of events." In his view the "prophetically similar crisis" suffered by Chile in the 1970s should have alerted officials (Edwards 1996). Yet such a scenario was not being considered and that official himself had earlier adhered to the positive view (Edwards 1995). Social psychologists would interpret the over optimism and screening out of any evidence that ran counter to the group's beliefs and story as a form of "group-think" or "belief-consistent behaviour" (t'Haart 1990, Wegner and Vallacher 1980).Their approach offers a useful framework for analyzing responses to events in Mexico and Korea respectively.

Importantly, as both Mexico and Korea headed toward crisis, several analysts *outside* of the IMF and the World Bank managed to read the signals. In respect of Mexico, throughout 1994 highly respected economists were forecasting a variety of warnings. Among the more famous were Rudiger Dornbusch who advocated an immediate devaluation, and Guillermo Calvo who advocated not devaluation but an immediate arrangement with the U.S. Treasury (Dornbusch and Werner 1994, comments by Calvo, 298–303). Most warnings focused on the appreciation (or "overvaluation") of the peso and what it reflected and implied for the economy. The critics of the government policy highlighted the lack of growth and fragility in monetary and exchange rate policy.

By contrast the IMF and World Bank continued to believe in the success story. While outside economists asked questions about the sustainability of Mexico's reforms, inside the IMF and the World Bank the positive consensus remained. For example, the Fund's January 1994 Country Report on Mexico recognized some of the danger signs: both that the Mexican exchange rate was appreciating and that net inflows to the public sector were increasing. Yet, the interpretation was that "it was felt that such a real (i.e. inflation-adjusted) appreciation would not affect export competitiveness significantly because of the positive effects of the structural reforms." Later in the staff appraisal we find: "During 1993 the peso continued to appreciate in real effective terms as customarily measured and eroded further the margin obtained in the 1980s. However, the strong expansion in manufacturing exports would indicate that the structural reforms in recent years and wage restraint have compensated so far" (IMF 1994b, 7, 12).

Similarly in the World Bank, to quote a later document, "the Bank's program in Mexico was shaped by a strongly positive view of the Mexican strategy and the successful stabilization it had achieved." In hindsight, it was recognized that "given the growing warning signs of potential trouble, the Bank should have been better prepared to respond." More specifically, in the area of macroeconomic policy, Bank staff had an "overly-optimistic view on what had been achieved by earlier reforms in the sector" (World Bank 1996a).

In both the IMF and the World Bank, there was a strongly doctrinal rationale for the positive interpretation. Staff maintained a belief throughout 1993–94 that Mexico's current account deficit was not a cause for undue concern because it was essentially a *private sector phenomenon*. They argued that so long as public sector finances were (or seemed to be) more balanced, the private sector could be relied on to adjust itself. Yet, it is unclear that there is any real evidence of an actual case where the private sector has adjusted to such deficits without a damaging spillover into public finances. Indeed, Fund research into the issue had raised this question (Boughton 2001).

In respect of Korea, IMF staff concluded that Korea was "relatively well equipped" to handle further external pressures without making any early attempt to analyze rigorously Korea's vulnerability to a cutoff of external short-term financing (Independent Evaluation Office 2003, Annex 2, 96). Although researchers had exhaustively catalogued the liberalization measures that had been undertaken in South Korea and in other countries, they did not draw attention to the growth in borrowing by Korean overseas bank affiliates. These were simply catalogued as part of the liberalization of outflows of direct investment (Johnstone et al. 1997). By thinking about capital account solely in terms of transactions between residents and nonresidents, the staff failed to treat borrowing by affiliates as potentially equivalent to borrowing by their parent institutions (Independent Evaluation Office 2003, Annex 2, 95). The result was to underestimate vulnerabilities in the South Korean economy.

Not only were officials in both institutions continuing to interpret events according to one rather narrow, optimistic framework, they had also insulated themselves and did not seek out external sources of information. For example, throughout 1993–94 the IMF staff relied on the debt data being published by the Mexican Central Bank, which had a two to three month lag. What they might have done—indeed what some other financial actors, such as Reuters did—was track the Mexican government's debt by following the results of auctions of governments securities (Hale 1996). In respect of Korea, they relied on an incomplete reporting on the part of the Korean authorities about their reserve position (Independent Evaluation Office 2003, Annex 2, 96), and as mentioned above, failed to investigate market signals. The crucial point here is that alternative sources of information were available, yet the Fund staff chose to rely on what the Mexican and South Korean governments made available to them. In the case of Mexico, they were even prepared to endorse this information by using it as a basis for giving assurances about the Mexican economy to the Bank for International Settlements in mid 1994.

Looking back, what we find is that in respect of Mexico while the IMF and the World Bank issued their usual caveats and concerns in economic reports and forecasts, along with some credit rating agencies and many private investment institutions, they held fast to the view that the appreciation of the Mexican currency was a natural companion to capital inflows and foreign investment and reflected a high rate of absorption in the Mexican economy. This contrasted with private investors' forecasts (Hale 1996). Debt, or a trade deficit, on this view, was not a problem so long as it was in the private sector.

In a raft of Fund and Bank publications, we find the belief in Mexico's reform process buttressing optimistic accounts of Mexico's prospects and covering over warnings or evidence to the contrary. Indeed even after the August 1994 elections, both the Fund and Bank were prepared to continue giving upbeat and optimistic assessments of the Mexican economy. Their reports and statements tended to report sources or signals from the market that were *positive,* yet only very exceptionally to pick up and report any major *negative* signals or outside commentaries. In essence, the experts were screening out any alternative information or warnings and at the same time constantly buttressing their optimistic accounts, which in retrospect, looks ever less warranted by the facts they might have paid more attention to at the time.

The optimism of the IMF and the World Bank rested largely on the belief that Mexico's successful program of stabilization, privatization, and deregulation, topped off with NAFTA and OECD membership, gave it a credibility and strength that would carry it through temporary difficulties. The maintenance of this view, even in the face of evidence to the contrary, was astonishing. The positive consensus seems to have seriously eroded the standards of evidence, which ought to have been applied alongside critical appraisal of the Mexican economy and policy. A similar statement can be made in respect of the IMF's work in South Korea.

Further exacerbating the failure to read the warning signs were the pressures within the institutions not to rock the boat. As in most hierarchical organizations, staff do not try to "second-guess" the upper management or, if relevant, the Executive Board, preferring instead to play the tune their superiors would most like to hear. The effect is a subtle form of self-censorship and a suppression of strongly critical or alternative views, which has been recognized by staff in both the IMF and the World Bank. In the words of a Bank official: "The ethos of the Bank is that no one challenges his supervisor, there is no room for boat rocking" (Sherk 1994, n. 19).

Finally, in respect of Mexico there was all too little sharing of information within and between the IMF and World Bank themselves. To cite the World Bank's analysis of lessons to be learned, "the macro concerns of staff were not well-known to top management . . . and within the country department, many staff and even some managers working on sectoral issues were unaware of the macro concerns of their colleagues. As a result, their policy dialogue continued to be based on the assumption that the stabilization program would stay on track" (World Bank 1996, IMF 1995c). Furthermore, the Executive Board of each institution remained silent. A later enquiry into the IMF's response to the crisis found that members of that Executive Board simply did not robustly push doubts or concerns that they may have had at the time (IMF 1995c).

The events of 1994 highlight several institutional features of the IMF and the World Bank that entrench a policy consensus. Having lent significant resources to the country and strongly endorsed it, the institutions obviously had a big stake in Mexico's success. Their prescription for growth and stability had solidified into one optimistic scenario, which was adopted as an article of faith. An equivalent, optimistic faith seemed to guide the IMF staff's interpretation of South Korea's vulnerabilities in 1997 in the wake of that country's initial ventures into capital account liberalization.

The faith-based blindness or seeming groupthink within the international financial institutions comes about partly because they rely on a template. The Bank and Fund have each forged conditionality that permits it to reconcile limited lending with the objectives of enhancing macroeconomic stability (in the case of the IMF), growth, and development (in the case of the World Bank).

The template is necessary because it guides staff working in countries all over the world, permitting them to act with the full backing of their institution and to put agreements in place with a minimum of time and resources. Put another way, staff have no incentive to venture beyond what the institution, as a whole, will take responsibility for. The result is conformity, which is entrenched by the hierarchical way in which each institution is organized. In both Mexico and in South Korea, the United States and its G-7 partners who command a controlling share of votes on the boards of the Fund and Bank failed to mitigate or contain groupthink in either institution. To the contrary, the explicit preferences of the United States seem to have driven the institutions further into a blind spot from which a crisis could not be seen.

The debt crises of the 1980s thrust the IMF and World Bank into the role of preservers of international financial stability. Major shareholders gave neither institution the political incentive, expertise, or resources to do anything but require debtors to undertake costly rescheduling and harsh stabilization and adjustment. It was in this crucible that the Washington consensus was born. Only once the vulnerability of international commercial banks had attenuated was any rebalancing of the debt strategy considered. But the imprimatur of the Washington consensus lives on not just for political reasons but equally for institutional ones.

Although changes have been undertaken in the IMF and World Bank since the Mexican crisis of 1994 and the South Korean crisis of 1997, core tensions persist and are perhaps inevitable. The staff of the IMF and World Bank must work with a vast array of countries, prescribing targets and sectoral reforms intended to enhance economic growth and performance. At the operational level there is very little room for experimentation or for taking account of local circumstances and knowledge. Individual staff members face a strong incentive to stick to a blueprint belonging to their institution they risk less personally if things go wrong. If all staff speak with one voice and prescribe the same things, then it is the institution as a whole that must bear the brunt of any criticism. At the general level this has its political justifications. The institutions must be seen to treat borrowers "equally" in terms of access to resources and conditionality. They need to ensure quality control and managerial direction over hundreds of professionals working in all corners of the world.

Templates permit the Fund and Bank to "stand above" local knowledge and to claim a universally applicable expertise, based squarely in the discipline of economics. Disciplinary boundaries and methods assist them in forging coherency and unity, as do their own governance structures and hierarchy in particular. However, just as these features make life easier for the institutions, they also hobble them, as is illustrated by the crises in Mexico at the end of 1994 and in South Korea in 1997.

The institutions themselves are the first to admit that their success or failure lies in politics. Ultimately economic growth and equity depend on the strength and efficacy of a country's governance structures and institutions. But these preconditions for success lie beyond what the IMF or World Bank systematically takes into account in prescribing economic policies. Both are aware of the gap. The World Bank has attempted to begin at least to capture policy processes and the practices of policymakers in its series of "Prem Notes." The IMF has made various attempts to explore what a political economy analysis might add (Wimmer 2002). Yet as this chapter has demonstrated there are powerful incentives for each institution to continue to define its mission in narrow, more technocratic and replicable ways—and for staff members to want to work in this way rather than risk doing things differently and being held individually responsible for results. In the next chapter I examine the results from the other side of the equation, exploring what factors in borrowing countries lead the IMF and World Bank to succeed or fail in their respective missions.

Chapter 3

THE POWER TO PERSUADE

The mission of the IMF and World Bank is not just to produce and propose ideas but to persuade borrowing countries to implement them. On the face of it, this may seem easy. The IMF and the World Bank are powerful and coercive instruments of the international community and bastions of a dominant way of thinking about economic policy and the global economy—or so they are perceived across developing, emerging, and transition economies. Wealthy countries dominate the board of each agency and have arrogated to themselves the right to choose the head of each organization. Furthermore, when the institutions lend, their wealthiest members can bolster conditionality by bringing to bear considerable political pressure of their own.

Yet the IMF and World Bank do not always succeed in their mission. As staff within each agency put it, "politics" too often gets in the way. To succeed the IMF and World Bank must find willing and able interlocutors in borrowing governments. In the 1980s the prospects looked hopeful. A wave of market-opening economic reforms in a host of borrowing countries brought to power technocrats and like-minded policymakers from Latin America across to parts of sub-Saharan Africa. On one view this wave was due to a shift in consensus about economic policy, which the IMF and the World Bank helped to disseminate across the developing world. This chapter examines this and how subsequently the institutions have sought to transmit ideas and how their work is affected by the configuration of politics within borrowing countries.

Fostering a Global Consensus

In the 1980s many Latin American countries embraced the market-oriented reforms of the Washington consensus. The explanation for the regionwide transformation was simple, or at least appears to be. Economically literate technocrats came to power and implemented a new kind of economic policy. These technocrats, mostly trained in the United States, embraced the new economic consensus and networked with one another, sharing advice and information. Former participating policymakers who shared "similar educations and beliefs in neoliberal solutions to key economic problems," attended the same conferences, subscribed to the same journals, and exchanged views in the same publications describe always feeling only "a telephone call away from each other" (Interviews: Naím 1995, Aspe 1995, and see also Williamson 1994). Their ascendancy in turn created openings for the IMF and World Bank to give advice and further disseminate the new economic policies. The result was a tide of economic liberalization in the 1980s (Dominguez 1997, Naim 1993, Nelson et al. 1994, Kahler 1992a).

Sociologists of ideas look to economics to explain the rise of the new consensus. Some write of a transformation of the discipline into a highly internationalized discipline, dominated and defined by an emerging class of "global experts" with "highly internationalized training (usually American)" who "claim to possess a universally applicable variety of expertise" (Babb 2001, 12). Subsequently the values and norms of the new economics were diffused by institutions, producing normative changes (Meyer and Rowan 1977) as well as changes in preferences and routines (Hoffman 1989, DiMaggio and Powell 1991). Governments became persuaded through dissemination, performance monitoring, seminars, publications, and the like (Kraatz 1998) and through a range of transmission mechanisms that has been elaborated by scholars of policy convergence, policy diffusion, and policy transfer (Dolowitz and Marsh 2000, Stone 2000). The result was a transformation ostensibly driven by beliefs and disciplinary training.

In Argentina, for example, Harvard-trained finance minister Domingo Cavallo brought about a "homogenization of economic thinking in Argentina," providing "the bridge that brought to Argentina the 1980s international consensus in favor of economic liberalization" (Corrales in Dominguez and McCann 1996, 51). Prior to Cavallo, Argentina had been divided between the advocates of statism (the stronger and more vocal majority) and those of free markets (a weaker and less self-persuaded minority). Yet in 1996, it was said that "today a consensus exists in Argentina, even among the left, that Cavallo's harsher version of economics—free convertibility, free trade, privatized public services, simplified tax systems, fiscal austerity—ought to be indelible features of the new Argentina" (Corrales in Dominguez and McCann 1996, 51).

In Argentina Cavallo's consensus did not persist. Within four years the bridge described by Corrales had collapsed. Argentinians of widely different political views converged in an anti-IMF and antineoliberal view of economic policy in the wake of that country's financial crisis. However, the rise of individuals imbued with a vision of economic reform that converged with that of the IMF and the World Bank had been crucial to the successes of the institutions not just in Argentina but elsewhere. So what role had the international financial institutions played?

Both the IMF and World Bank had facilitated negotiations between debtor countries and their creditors. When governments enter international negotiations they open themselves up to new ideas, creating incentives for their own bureaucracies to prepare and advance ideas on an issue, often requiring their own officials to hire new experts or access new intellectual technologies. During negotiations governments learn not only from one another, but equally from their own adapting bureaucracies. The results often change their preferences (Putnam and Bayne 1987, Putnam 1988, Evans et al. 1993).

If we consider the case of Argentina, we can see how this process might work. Negotiations with foreign creditors and the IMF began in earnest in the early 1980s. Successive finance ministers had to fashion accords with both private and public international creditors. These finance officials soon came to know their counterparts in other countries across Latin America and worked intimately with interlocutors in international agencies. Negotiations were closely focused around the issues of external financing and debt rescheduling. The conditions seemed ripe for the kind of learning and international influence on which scholars of international relations focus.

Policies requiring technical expertise are the most likely to induce the "learning" effects of international cooperation. This is because "the diffusion of new ideas and information can lead to a new pattern of behaviour and prove to be an important determinant of international policy coordination" (Haas 1992). Where governments face uncertainty in international policy, they turn to networks of professionals with recognized expertise and competence in a particular domain. These networks soon form "epistemic communities" whereby professionals brought in to frame policy share normative and causal beliefs as well as notions of validity and a common policy enterprise (Adler and Haas 1992). The "epistemic community" not only informs international agreements, but shapes agreements in ways that entrench the positions of experts at the national level, leading to international cooperation and convergence which would not otherwise occur.

Underpinning the transmission of ideas are facilitating institutional arrangements. For a policy to succeed it will need to be taken up and pushed by an appropriate institution within government (Haas 1990, 1992). Indeed, international development agencies have long been aware of this. In the 1950s, the World Bank encouraged the creation of planning agencies, energy authorities, and the like within national governments that would be insulated from domestic pressures and responsive to bank preferences (Krasner 1999, 147). In the 1960s, the Inter-American Development Bank and the UN Economic Commission for Latin America gave technical support that bolstered the position of planning agencies and central statistics offices (Sikkink 1991, Tussie 1995). In the 1970s ideas about state-centered development "fit" very naturally in planning ministries (Sikkink 1991, Finnemore and Sikkink 1999, 268).

In the 1980s, the World Bank's desire to push trade liberalization did not find a home within trade ministries that derived power and revenue from tariffs and import duties. It was through other agencies with no stake in the protectionist regime that the World Bank pushed liberalization. For example, in Mexico the Central Bank supported trade liberalization, believing that trade liberalization might assist in the control of inflation, not to mention in the control of the trade ministry (Heredia 1987).

The "epistemic" role of the IMF and World Bank is reinforced by the fact that they often step into crisis situations in which governments are uncertain. Armed with technical knowledge, the institutions foster the emergence of "technocrats" who understand and are sympathetic to their reform agenda. The practicalities of debt rescheduling and negotiations with the Bank and Fund constrain negotiations to a small, relatively insulated group. The result is to give specific policymakers and agencies considerable leverage. Hence the IMF and World Bank can bolster the position of policymakers who wish to undertake unpopular policies (Drazen 2001, Vreeland 2000, Ramcharan 2002, and see the older literature Putnam 1988, 457; Spaventa 1983, Remmer 1986, Edwards and Santella 1993, Vaubel 1986, and Dixit 1996). In Argentina, Cavallo's special relationship with the Fund and Bank gave him leverage over other agencies within the Argentine government, making him gatekeeper of the country's access to loans as well as to the ongoing support of the institutions, which was influential in persuading private capital markets to keep investing.

Behind the story of an emerging "epistemic community" lie political processes within countries that are equally if not more important. Economic reform during the 1980s was hugely contested in all countries and no less so in Argentina—as reflected in the vast literature on the politics of structural adjustment during the 1980s (Haggard and Kaufman 1989, Nelson et al. 1994, Remmer 1986). In other countries technocrats sometimes did not succeed in implementing neoliberal policies. Occasionally even in the absence of technocrats, neoliberal policies were put in place. In Argentina, a new democratically elected government took power from the military in 1983 and embraced a new and heterodox set of economic policies, which led it into confrontation with its creditors by the end of 1984 (Bouzas and Keifman 1985). Subsequently, as Robert Kaufman has analyzed, Argentina's policies were shaped by domestic politics and by economists with a different view of the IMF's then-orthodoxy (Kaufman 1990).

Far from snuggling into a new epistemic community, Argentinian policymakers attempted throughout the 1980s to play off the various actors within the community, variously invoking the U.S. Treasury and the World Bank in bids to persuade the IMF to soften its line. This alters the "epistemic community" view of why Argentina and other countries changed their economic policies, and it suggests two important caveats in respect to the relationship between "technical knowledge" and policy-making.

First, beneath every consensus lie many disagreements. In practice, technocrats often disagree about values, priorities, and even economic theories (Kapstein 1992). This is understated in the epistemic communities literature. Furthermore, even where experts or technocrats agree, the consensus among experts will not necessarily drive policy. John Ikenberry's account of the role of experts in the creation of the IMF and World Bank shows that the result was not driven by a preexisting expert consensus. Rather, what became a consensus was forged in response to policymakers' exigencies and questions. Politics drove the technocrats, and not vice versa (Ikenberry 1992). As evidenced in the previous chapter, the mission of the Fund and Bank is not informed by pure theory and empirical evidence. Institutional pressures and political factors also contribute to defining the mission of each institution. When they try to "sell" the result to borrowing countries, it is likely that even borrowers sympathetic to the underlying world view of the Fund and Bank will reject at least some elements of their prescriptions.

More profoundly, technical ideas shape politics only where they resonate with the political needs of the moment and provide opportunities to bridge old political divisions and build new coalitions (as elegantly put by Ikenberry 1992, 293). Ideas prevail not because they are the "best" ideas in a technical or professional sense but because they best meet the social, organizational, and political needs of key actors (Lakatos, and Musgrave 1970; Deane 1978; Blaug 1987). In the 1980s the Washington consensus offered a simple, intuitively appealing set of ideas and a vision of future competitiveness and wealth. In many ways this mindset fulfilled the role of an ideology in attributing blame and letting off steam, creating morale and optimism about the future, engendering solidarity or a particular identity, and permitting advocacy (Geertz 1964). Blame for the debt crisis and its aftermath was attributed to poor policy-making in developing countries. The future would be bright with the short-term pain of adjustment and reform leading to high growth and renewed access to capital markets. Old nationalist identities and solidarity were replaced with a new identity of entrepreneurialism, modernization, and integration into the world economy. Specific economic goals were prioritized and policies advocated. Neoliberal ideas offered not just a clear way to respond to a crisis but a whole new social language and rationale for reform (Woods 1995).

Like all politics, economic policy is the art of the possible. The IMF and World Bank operate in a marketplace not just of ideas but of politics and social forces. They supply ideas and prescriptions based (to some degree) on their technical analysis. They know that actual policies will be shaped by practical exigencies. Borrowing governments, for their part, will formulate policies in response to political, social, and institutional pressures, paying some heed to what Fund and Bank experts diagnose as the problem and propose as workable solutions.

In the 1980s the debt crisis discredited the more statist economic policies that preceded the Washington consensus and reconfigured social forces and priorities within debt-ridden countries. Thrown into crisis, policymakers in developing countries grappled for new solutions. In this context the prescriptions forged by the IMF and World Bank had attractions of their own. They offered governments a new paradigm that fitted policy into existing resources and promised a future of economic growth and recovery. The Washington consensus had the backing of institutions renowned for their technical expertise and resources. That said, it was also backed by significant bargaining power and leverage on the side of the international agencies.

Bargaining Power and Requiring Governments to Reform

The IMF and World Bank enjoy considerable bargaining power in their relations with borrowing governments. Countries mostly approach the institutions when they have little access to alternative sources of finance.[1] Bank and Fund loans are less attractive than private sector loans because they have many strings attached, including both formal conditionality and informal pressures and influences over the design, implementation, and procurement within programs and projects. For this reason governments heading into difficulty are often reluctant to approach the institutions—indeed, recall that in 1997 South Korea was determined not to approach the IMF. Only under strong U.S. pressure did South Korea eventually agreed to meet with the IMF's most senior officials dispatched to Seoul at the eleventh hour (Blustein 2001).

Once a country approaches the Bank or the Fund, it opens up a number of opportunities for the institutions and their most powerful government members to wield influence through penalties, conditionality, and advice. The institutions can refuse to lend to the country, thereby depriving a country of the emergency resources sought. Furthermore, when the institutions turn down a request for assistance, their action carries a second kind of penalty. Their refusal to lend will be interpreted by many other investors as an unwillingness to certify that a country's economic policies and prospects are sound. This can send a strong message to the markets and other potential lenders. Indeed, some countries will seek a positive certification even in the absence of a loan in the hope that this will help to catalyze funds from elsewhere.

When a loan is made to a country it is accompanied by conditionality. In practice, this involves some formal and some less formal requirements. In the World Bank rigorous requirements have always been complemented by looser, less formal agreements to undertake particular actions. Even three decades ago, as World Bank historians Mason and Asher detail, the Bank would complement detailed explicit conditionality with "supplementary letters" setting out the Bank's expectations with respect to borrowing government agencies on matters less formal than those covered in covenants, as well as "oral understandings concerning reciprocal obligations of lender and borrower" (Mason and Asher 1973, 420).

In the IMF conditionality is described across a spectrum from "hard" to "soft." Hard conditionality describes measures a country must meet in order to access any money. Typically this involves "prior actions" and "performance criteria," which are specified in the formal agreement. These can be waived where minor deviations from agreed targets are considered to be of a temporary or reversible nature. Soft conditionality refers to a wide range of other elements that the Fund will take into account in deciding whether or not to "complete" the reviews that are necessary to permit the disbursement of each portion of the loan.

---

[1] Normally this means they do not have adequate foreign reserves (Bird 1996). Economists debate the extent to which countries turn to the IMF because their balance of payments deficit increases (cf Santaella 1996, Goldstein and Montiel 1986 vs Knight and Santaella 1997, Conway 1994, Edwards and Santaella 1993).

Such soft conditionality includes things such as structural benchmarks, indicative triggers, and general undertakings in the country's letter of intent (Independent Evaluation Office 2002).

In formulating conditionality, the institutions' resources and "expertise" can be overwhelming. The technical weight of the analyses of the Fund and Bank staff put critics at a distinct disadvantage. In the words of one study, domestic actors simply cannot compete with the expertise and sophistication (or the "weight" and "depth") of the international financial institutions' technical work: "One interesting feature of the power dispute with the international agencies is the use of technical competence and research as a strategy to negotiate policy with the local administration and the intelligentsia. The imposition of technical criteria and the heavy emphasis on detailed and quantitative research about the problems at hand put local administrators at a great disadvantage" (Castro and Althan 1996, 18). In many cases, local officials wishing to present alternative policy recommendations have great difficulty matching the kind of technical work the Fund and Bank prepare. Proposing an alternative involves a long and arduous process of preparation to meet the Fund and Bank technicians head on.

Once agreed, conditionality is monitored by the IMF and the World Bank who have formal powers to apply sanctions if necessary on countries borrowing from them. If a country falls behind in implementing its agreed program or project, the institutions can suspend or cancel disbursements of loans (disbursements are made contingent on evidence that conditions being met). More serious sanctions can be imposed on a country if it falls behind in its repayments to the institutions. In the IMF this is covered by its arrears policy and in the World Bank by the nonaccrual policy. Further to this, until the late 1980s, the institutions would withhold funding from countries if they fell behind on their wider repayments obligations to the private sector.

The powers of the IMF and World Bank to require governments to reform are significant. They do not lend large proportions of global development financing but the timing of their loans gives them considerable leverage because they lend at times when governments have few alternative sources of finance. In spite of this advantage, it is easy to overstate their power and influence.

The imprimatur of the institutions is always cited by policymakers and commentators as an important signal to private investors, although in fact the evidence of the catalytic effect of IMF agreements is ambiguous at best (Mody and Saravia 2003, Cottarelli and Giannini 2002, Mosley 2000).

Conditionality is nowhere near as effective as either institution would like. They certainly can and do require a range of conditionalities from governments. But available evidence suggests that, for a number of reasons, they are seldom successful in imposing this (Killick 2002).

Where a country has strong support from a powerful shareholder within the IMF and World Bank, this can influence the package of policies the Fund and Bank are able to extract from a borrower. A government-in-need may be less compelled to agree if, as in the case of Russia, major shareholders on the boards of the Bank and Fund are prepared to exert informal pressure to ensure more "understanding" agreements and conditions. In other words, when the economic and security interests of large powers are at stake, the Fund and Bank staff may find themselves on a leash. Similarly, when a country's crisis poses a threat to the international financial system, its government may find that it has more leeway since the institutions are under equal pressure to find a speedy solution—the usual package may be modified.

Access to information about their borrowers is vital for the IMF and World Bank, for on this depends their capacity to structure and offer loans as well as monitor conditionality. Yet each institution has to negotiate how much access they are granted to crucial information, policy debates, and decision-makers. A government wishing to hinder or limit the role of either international institution can simply close off access, albeit in many cases at obvious costs to its relations with the Fund and Bank staff. For example, prior to 1983 the World Bank was constantly frustrated by the Mexican government, who denied it access to crucial sectors of the economy. In the months leading up to Mexico's debt crisis in 1982, the World Bank (who had considerable exposure to Mexico) had virtually no information at all on Mexico's external public debt situation (Interviews: Knox 1995, Husein 1995, Binswagen 1995). Apparently the government claimed that statistics were held up due to computer difficulties. Without access, however, it was difficult for the Bank or the Fund to do its job and sensibly advise on areas of key economic policy.

In a more subtle way the nature of access to information can facilitate the mission of the IMF and World Bank. For a long time both sides could negotiate almost entirely in secret (now all countries are under pressure to permit the IMF and World Bank to disclose the content of agreements). The result was to forge a particularly narrow relationship between the Bank and Fund staff and very senior officials in specific economic agencies (typically finance ministries and central banks), cemented by each side's privileged access to information. The Fund and Bank would gain access through special relations with officials who in turn would benefit from the fact that they were the only policymakers with full information about the negotiations and positions of the Bank and Fund staff. This gave them a special gatekeeping role vis-à-vis the rest of government, empowering the individuals and the agencies with whom the Fund and Bank deal most directly.

The Fund and Bank have significant bargaining leverage in the face of crises, which force governments to supplicate for assistance. But this does not give either institution the power to impose a Washington-prescribed medicine. Rather, their mission has to begin by seeking out sympathetic policymakers or persuading existing leaders that specified reforms should be undertaken.

Finding Sympathetic Interlocutors

Where the Fund and Bank staff share technical expertise, methodology, and an orthodox economist's understanding of problems and solutions with officials in a borrowing country, their capacity to transmit (or reinforce) ideas is heightened.

As analyzed in chapter 2, a particular professional mindset dominates the work of the IMF and the World Bank. Where they encounter officials who share that same mindset as a way of managing political and economic problems, the task of persuasion is a joint effort in which the Fund and Bank staff team up with sympathetic local decision-makers to persuade others.

Two cases that reach back into the 1960s and 1970s highlight the ways in which the international institutions and foreign donors have relied on relations with particular officials with whom they can forge jointly agreed projects or policies. The cases indicate that it is not just a question of finding individual policymakers. Equally critical are the structures of government within which those individuals work and the bureaucratic and political incentives they face. The first case is that of India where the country's considerable national economic policy-making capacity and active sense of sovereignty and independence have for a long time forced the IMF and World Bank very actively to seek out and work with sympathetic interlocutors.

In the early 1960s the U.S. administration worked very closely with the World Bank setting up what became the Aid India Consortium. Further close cooperation resulted in sending two expert missions to India to examine its economic policies: the "three wise men" led by Oliver Frank in 1960 and the Bell Mission of the mid 1960s. The latter resulted in significant pressure on Indian policymakers to reform agriculture, liberalize industrial and trade controls, and devalue the rupee. India had a deteriorating balance of payments driven by two successive monsoon failures and two wars—with China in 1962 and with Pakistan in 1965. The result was an increase in the economy's dependence on foreign aid and loans (Joshi and Little 1994, 49).

The IMF, the World Bank, and the United States collectively used promises of external assistance to induce India to devalue and rationalize its tariffs and export subsidies. There was little domestic support for the devaluation (Joshi and Little 1994, 49). Subsequently, its perceived negative impact was blamed on World Bank pressure (Frankel 1978, Thapar 1991, Lewis 1997). The IMF would much later reflect that the result was "political backlash which gave reform a bad name and resulted in a fifteen year period before reforms could be tried again" (Krueger 2003). In fact reforms were attempted in concert with the IMF some nine years later in India.

Our concern here is with the conditions under which the World Bank team was originally able to persuade the government to reform. Retrospectives of the World Bank's work in India during the 1960s focus closely on the able, sympathetic, and technically competent interlocutors within the Indian government (Lewis 1997; Kapur et al. 1997, 293–98, 463–67). These interlocutors fostered a sense of success and ongoing commitment in the Bank and likewise in the Fund and the U.S. administration. The architect of the agricultural policy reforms so desired by the World Bank in India was C. Subramaniam, food and agriculture minister from 1964 to 1966. His beliefs about Indian agriculture have been traced by Ashutosh Varshney who depicts their culmination in an agrarian model that complemented the World Bank's thinking about these issues (Varshney 1989). Equally important to the uptake of the World Bank's model was the bureaucracy and the way in which Subramaniam's institutional base—the prime minister's Secretariat—rose while the hitherto dominant Planning Commission was tamed (Varshney 1989). Subramaniam was able to attract critical elements of party support and finance for his reforms, and to build up a base of sympathetic colleagues. It was with this group that the World Bank worked so successfully.

Once a relationship with key policymakers had been established, outside agencies could use that relationship discreetly to find ways to smooth over problems. From an official perspective, USAID official John Lewis details the way the United States and World Bank turned to Subramaniam in 1965 in order to break an aid log-jam. Confidential negotiations that included President Johnson resulted in a secret treaty in which the Indian minister agreed to undertake specific policy commitments—over the objections of his colleagues—in return for an unlocking of U.S. aid (Lewis 1997, 113).

Finding the right interlocutors in the Indian case did not mean that the Bank, or any other external agencies, enjoyed plain sailing with India. In dealing with their Indian interlocutors, Bank staff seemed to have oscillated between respect and frustration. Indeed, in their 1973 history of the Bank, Mason and Asher wrote that by the end of the 1960s "what had previously been viewed as technical excellence in India was characterized as doctrinaire arrogance" (Mason and Asher 1973, 683).

In the early 1970s a radical-populism defined India's economic policies as Mrs. Gandhi surrounded herself with radicals in the wake of winning a heady unconditional surrender from Pakistan when that country attacked India by air in December 1971. But the radical-populism was short-lived. Mismanagement of food supplies and the oil price shocks of 1973 and 1974 contributed to political and economic disarray that drove Mrs. Gandhi to alter course.

In 1974 Mrs. Gandhi gathered around her an interministerial task force of senior bureaucrats to devise an anti-inflationary policy. These technocrats introduced tax and monetary measures that brought inflation under control and successfully devalued by stealth, manipulating the currency basket to which the rupee was fixed (Joshi and Little 1994, 54–56). One result of the new policies was to reforge relations with the IMF and World Bank. In 1972–73 India received no credit from the IMF and net multilateral loans of US$473 million. In 1974–75 India accessed US$522 million from the IMF and US$961 million in multilateral loans, which rose to US$1.29 billion in the following year (Joshi and Little 1994, 137).

In India where failure pushed policymakers to seek a new approach in the economy, the World Bank and the IMF gained openings into the policy debate. However, these openings could only be used effectively where sympathetic interlocutors in the Indian government were prepared to work with the international institutions. This meant that the IMF and World Bank had to tailor their advice and aspirations to fit within the domestic Indian economic agenda. They were most influential when policy was made by a small group relatively insulated from the wider political system. A similar set of factors affected relations with Indonesia.

Indonesia offers another case in which the World Bank and the IMF became highly involved during the 1970s. U.S. strategic priorities set the backdrop for their involvement. The extent of the international agencies' work in Indonesia depended on their relations with government officials. As with India, a consortium, initially called the Inter-Governmental Group on Indonesia and later the Consultative Group on Indonesia, was formed to bring together Western donors and lenders to Indonesia. Under that umbrella more specific working partnerships were formed.

Indonesia joined the IMF in 1967 and was required to implement a series of economic reforms orienting the economy toward exports and limiting the country's budget deficit, initiating a period of significant IMF influence over policy (Sutton 1982). Subsequently a very close relationship developed between the staff of the Bank and Fund and their interlocutors in the Indonesian government—a group of young U.S.-trained economists (or "technocrats" as they came to be called) who were brought into government by General Suharto (MacIntyre 1993, Yoon 1991, Soesastro 1989). In 1968 the Bank set up a Resident Mission in Indonesia (the Bank's first ever such arrangement), cementing the close relationship that existed between the Bank and Indonesian counterparts. It then increased its lending rapidly during the 1970s, giving its most senior staff member in Jakarta unprecedented powers to make loans and report directly to the World Bank president (Operations Evaluation Department 1999, Kapur, Lewis and Webb 1997, 467–71). On the Indonesia side, the bureaucrats were important since they wielded a lot of power over economic policy due to the heavily statist, centralized, and clientelistic system that had developed under Suharto (MacIntyre 1989).

The Fund and Bank lost some degree of influence once their technocratic Indonesian interlocutors lost some of their special position and power as the constraints faced by Indonesia changed in the late 1970s. Yet even within the "special relationship" between the government and the World Bank there were drawbacks. As later reported in an official evaluation of the World Bank's relationship with Indonesia: "The special relationship . . . created a situation where the Bank did not succeed in persuading the Government to heed some crucially important, but unwelcome messages to the country, let alone impose unwanted policies, lest the relationship be broken" (Operations Evaluation Department 1999, 16). The same would happen later on in Mexico (see chapter 4).

It is important to recall that the World Bank depends on lending to countries such as Indonesia who can borrow and repay, thus generating both opportunities for the Bank to lend large sums, and net income for the Bank from its lending activities. Added to that, Indonesia's impressive record of economic growth and poverty reduction were seen as adding luster to the Bank's reputation.

Elements of the relations forged with India and Indonesia can be found in the Fund and Bank's work with many other strongly statist countries allied to the West with whom the World Bank and/or the IMF formed close relations during the late 1960s and 1970s: for instance, Turkey, Mexico, Iran (in particular in the late 1970s), and the Philippines. Strong relations were initially developed with a particular group of young technocrats. Economic difficulties enhanced the leverage of both the ideas and the resources proffered by the IMF and World Bank. However, once the technocrats lost influence in government, the Bank and Fund lost a degree of leverage and influence. For this reason we need to examine the political institutions within which technocrats either rise or fall.

The Bureaucracy and Institutions of Government

We have seen that the IMF and World Bank are most likely to succeed where economic decision-making is undertaken by the executive or an insulated elite at the top of the government bureaucracy. This does not imply that authoritarian governments are better placed to pursue economic reform than democracies (the debate about this is reviewed by Sirowy and Inkeles 1990, Przeworski and Limongi 1993, Helliwell 1994). Although early studies suggested that authoritarian governments undertake "tough" economic adjustment more readily than democracies (Haggard and Kaufman 1992), subsequent studies contest this (Hellman 1997, Joyce 2004). In the end, the studies of authoritarian versus democratic regimes do not tell us under what conditions economic reform is most likely to be undertaken (Haggard 1986, Remmer 1984, Geddes 1995, Edwards 2003). But core political structures do affect when and where the IMF and World Bank are likely to be most influential.

In some political systems economic policy is made away from the hurly-burly of politics. This gives greater scope for the IMF and World Bank to engage technocratic interlocutors. There are several ways economic policymakers can be insulated from the rest of a political system, permitting them to pursue economic policy in close cooperation with the IMF and World Bank with relatively little constraint. Obviously at times of economic crisis executive authority is expanded (Haggard 2000). Or put in the words of the first deputy managing director of the IMF, a crisis can suspend "politics as usual" and provide a government with "considerable freedom—more than is usual in politics—to undertake reforms"; furthermore, "new governments may enjoy something of an advantage, especially those in democracies that enter office with a mandate for change" (Krueger 2003). Economic policy-making can also be insulated from broader political processes through delegation to specialized agencies such as independent central banks (Cukierman, Webb, and Neyapti 1992; Eijffinger and de Haan 1996), quasi-judicial structures for the management of trade policy issues (Hall and Nelson 1992), and centralized budgetary processes (Alesina and Perotti 1996; Perotti 1997; succinctly described in Haggard 2000, 42).

Where economic policy is mostly made within part of the bureaucracy, we must delve inside the bureaucracy to discover under what conditions the IMF and World Bank are most likely to find or persuade willing interlocutors. For inside government institutions, the impact of particular ideologies or ideas is affected by patterns of recruitment and administration as well as the capacity of institutions to innovate (Evans 1995, Evans et al. 1985, Hall 1986, Steinmo 1989, Adler 1987). The kinds of experts appointed to senior jobs and the qualifications demanded and recognized can shape the upper echelons of a government. If re-cruitment takes place almost exclusively among individuals with a particular type of training or degree, this can easily bias receptivity toward one set of ideas (Haas 1989, Miller-Adams 1997, Ascher 1983, Finnemore 1996).

Equally important are the bureaucratic structures that permit, or hinder, a turnover of staff. In the United States and Mexico, for example, the political ap-pointment of senior civil servants means that each new president brings to office a new staff and potentially a new mindset. Change is thus more likely and more rapid than in the erstwhile UK-style career civil service where new ideas wait be-hind a long queue of retiring civil servants (Weir 1989 and others in Hall 1989). In the post-Communist world, Steven Fish has shown that "elite turnover" deeply affected the propensity of governments to reform (Fish 1998b).

Bureaucracies powerfully shape the actions of those who work within them. This requires us to pay attention to the norms, values, and processes of any agency tasked with economic policy. March and Olsen remind us that institu-tions are "collections of standard operating procedures and structures that de-fine and defend values, norms, interests, identities, and beliefs" (March and Olsen 1989, 17). James Q. Wilson, in his empirical study of bureaucratic agencies, re-minds us that preexisting attitudes, predispositions, preferences, and peer judg-ments, combined with the imperatives of the situation, all powerfully shape the responses and actions of bureaucrats (Wilson 1989).

Until recently the IMF and World Bank could work relatively easily with bu-reaucracies who enjoyed relative independence from the rest of the political sys-tem within borrowing countries. Each international institution could exercise some influence over domestic policy struggles by using the timing and quantity of small amounts of rapidly disbursable resources together with conditionality to bolster the position of their favored interlocutors. They could enhance the au-thority and resources of individual policymakers, privileging some and disem-powering others. They were aided in this by the secrecy surrounding negotiations with the Fund and Bank and the fact that only a chosen few were party to nego-tiations. As required by their Articles of Agreement, they negotiated exclusively with one small group of officials—those at the head of the Ministry of Finance, Ministry of Planning, Central Bank, or the like. As a result, their interlocutors had privileged information and influence within their own political system.

More recently, the nature of relations between the Fund and Bank and bor-rowing governments has changed. Increasing transparency and publicity has opened the work of the institutions, making the old, more secretive approach dif-ficult to sustain. Furthermore, as the reform agenda has deepened to include far-reaching institutional and social reforms, it has become apparent that a top-down approach does not produce sustained reforms. In the 1980s and early 1990s the "top-down" macroeconomic policies and trade liberalization reforms being urged by the IMF and World Bank did not require "deep" political implementa-tion—a small group of technocrats *could* take these kinds of decisions. However, the deeper "good governance" reforms being urged by the mid 1990s could not be pursued in the same way (Naim 1995, Nelson et al. 1994). Recent thinking in the Fund and the Bank recognizes the fragility of a reform process that relies on key individuals, suggesting that sustained reform requires a deeper commitment or support from the broader political system and society.

In several cases the mission of the IMF and World Bank has been blocked by the actions of parliaments. For example, in Russia in July 1998, the parliament flatly rejected a number of the tax reforms that were key conditions of an IMF loan that had been approved a day before. As will be discussed in chapter 5, the Russian president then turned to instituting the required reforms by decree. In Argentina in December 2001, after defaulting on $155 billion in foreign debt, the government acceded to IMF demands for monetary adjustments, spending cuts, and politically sensitive reforms to the system of revenue-sharing with the provinces. However, the parliament refused to move on a bill converting savings to bonds and flouted IMF orders by passing bills reforming bankruptcy rules and punishing "economic subversion"—removing money from the cash-strapped economy even though this sank Argentina further into threat of default on its loan payments to the World Bank (Valente 2002). In Turkey in 1998, parliament forced the government to break its promise to the IMF to hold down the wage increases of public sector workers.[2] In 1999 and 2000, the Moldovan parliament repeatedly rejected IMF-mandated privatization of wine, brandy, and tobacco enterprises in a political fight that brought down a government. (Eventually, despite Communist opposition, the privatization took place and the IMF relationship was restored.)[3] The Indonesian government declared in January 2003 that it would break free from its commitments to the IMF; parliamentary pressure, including a decree in October 2002 requiring the government not to extend the current IMF program, was a vital part of this decision.[4]

Both the IMF and the World Bank now adopt the view that they must go beyond ensuring that their counterparts are intellectually convinced about new policies, prepared to initiate reform, and use their political will to implement new policies and build a consensus around them (Johnson and Wasty 1993, Frischtak and Atiyas 1996). Each institution has begun to work with and to consider more systematically a wider range of processes within borrowing countries.

Nonetheless, there has always been an awareness within the IMF and World Bank of the way political institutions affect their role. A comparison of Mexico and Brazil is instructive. The Bank built a closer relationship with key government bureaucracies in Mexico than in Brazil, which had a far more complex political structure, a more open society, and a more prescriptive constitution. As the former director of the Latin American and Caribbean Department of the World Bank put it to me in an interview in 1995, when Bank-friendly technocrats came to power in Mexico, they all too quickly passed through (Husein interview 1995).

Within the political process there are several actors who may have a veto over

---

[2] "Politics cloud the economic horizon," *Middle East Economic Digest* (7 August 1998): 7.

[3] "Moldovan Government Resigns," *Deutsche Presse-Agentur*, 9 November 1999. "Moldova 'may face default' after parliament rejects privatization," *BBC Worldwide Monitoring*, 18 April 2000.

[4] Smitha Francis, "Indonesia's battle of will with the IMF," Network Ideas, 25 February 2003, http://www.networkideas.org/themes/trade/feb2003/tp25_Indonesia.htm.

economic policy. At the apex of any political system is the executive—the president or prime minister whose authority and strength depends on how much he or she must rely on the support of a political party, coalition, or legislature. The president, cabinet ministers, parliament, parliamentary committees, bureaucracy, and implementing agencies may all need to agree in order for a measure to be adopted and implemented. In theory, the more actors along the way who can veto or block a policy, the more difficult it will be to reform but the easier it will be to maintain stability and credibility (Tsebelis 1995). In practice, outcomes will depend on the respective roles of the executive, parliaments or legislatures, and political parties.

A large number of political parties within a political system will produce "fragmentation." Forging agreement among a large number of parties is difficult and further compounded when the system is strongly polarized, meaning that strong ideological differences drive actors in the system to differentiate themselves as occurred in Russia and in Turkey in the late 1980s (Haggard 2000).

Equally important is how political parties are organized and what incentives politicians face—such as to fall in behind a leader or to focus on individual, narrower interests. Some political systems encourage politicians to seek publicity and popularity for themselves with little need for party backing or support. This makes top-down economic reform difficult. The evidence demonstrates this in respect to "open list" systems where political parties do not control who gets to run for election (Carey and Shugart 1995) and multiple-member constituencies where there are several representatives from each constituency and so politicians have an incentive to appeal to selective parts rather than the electorate as a whole (Cox 1990, Myerson 1994). The structure of campaign financing can magnify these effects. By contrast, in a single-member constituency in a closed-list system, politicians face a much stronger incentive to tow the party line and the result, according to one study, is a greater provision of public goods and less spending on special interests (Edwards 2003).

In sum, political parties and the way they compete for power will affect the kinds of economic policy a government favors. So too will the electoral cycle. Econometric studies tell us that the higher the uncertainty about whether a government will be reelected, the more likely a government is to spend more and to tax less in order to try to buy support for itself (Roubini 1991, Edwards and Tabellini 1991, Annett 2000). Furthermore, a government facing an election is unlikely to initiate a program with the IMF within six months before the election (Bird and Rowlands 2000, Vreeland 1999, Dreher 2002, 2003), and more likely to enter into an agreement with the IMF after the elections are over (Przeworski and Vreeland 2000).

Political institutions heavily influence the leverage of the international financial institutions over policy. The IMF and World Bank have the most scope for influence where policy-making is highly centralized and insulated from the broader political arena. But this has increasingly failed to translate into an ability to ensure implementation. This is because each institution is trying to foster policies that require broader support and implementation by agencies outside the narrow circle with whom the Fund and Bank negotiate. The result is a difficult trade-off between centralized and insulated policy-making that prioritizes a particular view of economic effectiveness, versus a messier, complex democratic process that is more open and transparent but can result in poor economic policies. Specific cases of this trade-off are further explored in subsequent chapters. Playing into either system are actors outside the political institutions—first and foremost among which are powerful interest groups whose support or rejection of particular measures can often influence policy.

The Role of Interest Groups and the Scope for Policy Capture

The IMF and World Bank have long held the view that they must persuade and garner support not just from governments but also from the private sector and other parts of civil society within countries if their mission is to succeed. Although they must work formally through the government, both the IMF and the World Bank engage and consult with an increasing range of interest groups in borrowing countries. So too they have begun to analyze the impact of policies on such groups through stakeholder analysis, which examines which societal groups will benefit or lose out from reform (World Bank 1996b). But where and how do interest groups shape policy and thereby the influence of the Fund or the Bank?

Governments rely on some degree of support from interest groups to stay in power (Ilchman and Uphoff 1969). These interest groups "enter the political arena in pursuit of their interests, with major effects on political outcomes" (Frieden 1991a, 7). As the incentives for groups and sectors changed—such as in the 1980s in the wake of the debt crisis in Latin America—so too government policies changed to accommodate new powerful interests (Bates 1981, Olson 1982). Put simply, international economic shocks created new opportunities and constraints that altered the agenda of powerful interest groups, empowering some and disempowering others (Frieden 1991b). On this view economic reform will be possible when a crisis or shock reconfigures social interests.

But what role does this suggest that interest groups play—do they set the agenda for politicians or do they exercise a veto over policies forged by politicians? The answer is to be found in political economy research. If interest groups were to set the agenda they would need to be organized in stable coalitions with dynamic sources of ideas that best reflect the interests of members. But this is not borne out by the evidence. Imperfect information means that interest groups simply do not know or are uncertain about the benefits they will enjoy if a particular policy is pursued (Rodrik 1996, Fernandez and Rodrik 1991). Alternatively, interest groups know how they will benefit but are hindered by uncertainty about how the overall benefits are distributed and how their rivals and others will benefit (Drazen and Grilli 1993, Alesina and Drazen 1991).

Imperfect information and uncertainty mean that interest groups tend not to set the agenda. Rather they respond to an agenda set by the government. In Africa, for example, Robert Bates depicts politicians creating and maintaining coalitions of interests in order to ensure their political survival (Bates 1981). So-phisticated cross-class coalitions *result* from government policies. For example, farmers who benefit from seemingly adverse policies by using the market defen-sively coalesce with urban clienteles including both business and workers created by governments' use of nonmarket instruments. In this analysis, interest group coalitions are fluid and reactive.

The failure of interest groups to set the agenda is also born out in a later study by Bates and a team of researchers examining and comparing eight developing countries. They reported that "one of the most surprising findings of our case studies is the degree to which the intervention of interest groups fails to account for the initiation or lack of initiation of policy reform" (Bates and Krueger 1993, 454). A similar finding is made in a study of Indian agricultural policy (Varshney 1989). Indeed, sometimes interest groups are even unwilling to support policies that favor their interests. In Brazil, Chile, Ecuador, Egypt, Ghana, Korea, Turkey, and Zambia, scholars found that "in the context of comprehensive economic pol-icy reform it is difficult for particular groups to calculate where their interest lie. Ideological struggles therefore can outweigh competition among organized in-terests as a determinant of policy change" (Bates and Krueger 1993, 456).

The power of interest groups lies in shaping policies within the preferences set out by governments and bureaucrats. Sometimes they even succeed in capturing the process of detailing and implementing policy. For example, Korea's financial liberalization began in earnest in 1991 when the government began to license merchant banks and to lift administrative controls on commercial credit. The re-sult, as described by Stephan Haggard and Jungkun Seo, is "a case-study in how financial reforms can be captured not only in their implementation but in their basic design" (Haggard 2000, 37). The government was captured by the intense lobbying efforts of corporate conglomerates who used kickbacks to bureaucrats and politicians in order to shape both the design and application of policies.

The private sector is a powerful lobby within government, and sometimes this includes the lobbying of foreign direct investors. It is often assumed that in-creasing foreign direct investment (FDI) will open up an economy and result in lower protectionism (Bhagwati 1987 gives evidence of this). However, more re-cent studies show that the opposite can occur. For example, when foreign direct investors moved into import-competing sectors in Mexico, those sectors became more highly protected than other import-competing sectors with no FDI (Grether and Marcelo 1999). Industrial groups as a whole were very active in lobbying the government (Kraemer 1995). Foreign director investors were yet more effective in lobbying a government increasingly sensitive to their interests (Grether and Marcelo 1999). Overall, as a trade policy review of Mexico reported in 1993, a very high level of well-organized cooperation and linkage between the govern-ment and the private sector pervaded Mexican policy-making through the 1980s and early 1990s (GATT 1993). The real question is what should balance this influence?

In Africa although organized interest groups play virtually no role in setting the economic agenda, this has not prevented subsequent capture by specific interests (Van de Walle 2001). The weakness of government capacity to implement policies and achieve outcomes has resulted in a government apparatus in many countries that has been used to create and extract rent (Mbaka and Paul 1989). Indeed, in some countries politicians are seen as "brokers of wealth transfers between the various interest groups" (Kimenyi and Mbaka 1993). Key to perpetuating such systems is the lack of any checks on governments by societal pressures, parliaments, opposition parties, or a free press (Migdal 1989).

The IMF and World Bank have long recognized private interests as a powerful force in politics. In an interview, a senior Bank official recounted that in Venezuela in the early 1990s the Bank failed adequately to understand rent-seeking and its relationship to particular government institutions. After strongly supporting a reformist government, they soon found that the well-established rent-seekers struck back, collapsing the reforms and revealing deep shortcomings in the Bank's analysis of fundamental policy structures and relationships and the likely impact of change (Husein interview 1995). Subsequently World Bank researchers have begun to flesh out the conditions under which policy becomes "captured" by private sector interests (Hellman 1998, Hellman et al, 2000).

The challenge for the IMF and World Bank is that they are likely to have influence where "rational economic policy" can be formulated away from the hurly burly of politics (Krueger 2003). Yet so too are vested interests, who may capture and distort outcomes for their own benefit. The alternative is economic policy made in a more transparent, openly contested, publicly debated, and democratic way. That process is likely to be messy, complex, and time-consuming, it will often thwart rapid reform, and it will certainly marginalize the role of the IMF and World Bank.

The IMF and World Bank transmit ideas about economic policy to a wide range of countries. Their influence depends not just on the individuals with whom they work but on the configuration of political institutions within borrowing countries. The rise of the Washington consensus in Latin America was facilitated by U.S.-trained technocrats prepared to embrace prescriptions proffered by the IMF and the World Bank. However, this occurred only in the context of an economic crisis that had thrown previous policies into discredit and imposed a new resource constraint on governments. Even then, however, not all governments facing similar circumstances adopted the same policies at the same time—Brazil and Mexico, for example, each responded differently in the 1980s and early 1990s to fiscal constraints.

The IMF and World Bank deploy a mixture of technical advice and coercive power in bargaining with borrowing governments. Each institution can variously lend or withhold resources, disburse or suspend payments, and impose various forms of conditions. Yet the institutions can successfully deploy this power only where they find and work with sympathetic interlocutors.

Sympathetic interlocutors must be both willing and able to embrace the priorities preferred by the institutions. Their willingness is influenced by circumstances and prevailing sets of ideas. For example, the debt crisis not only discredited some existing ideas about economic policy but also demolished the resources necessary to implement them. In that context, new policies were actively sought and taken up by indebted governments. The Washington consensus offered one solution. Its persuasiveness was doubtless bolstered by the resources and expertise thrown behind it by the IMF and World Bank, as well as its roots in prevailing economic theories of the time in which many finance officials had been trained. But even then, the Washington consensus was implemented only under particular political conditions.

The ability of interlocutors to implement reforms is shaped by the configuration of political institutions, or "governance" within countries. Where economic policy is centralized and relatively insulated from other political pressures, the potential influence of the IMF and World Bank is high, particularly in bureaucracies with high turnover and adaptive capacity. Nonetheless, such systems are often characterized by only the narrowest form of accountability. Where economic policy is subject to a broader set of processes, party politics and electoral cycles will have a strong influence. The results will be messier and less easily controlled—albeit more open, and more transparent. In more open systems, the capacity of the government to change policy will depend on the number of "veto players" in the policy process.

Among potential veto players in economic policy, interest groups play a rather specific role. They do not set the agenda. Rather they respond to priorities set by the government. Despite their reactive nature, interest groups can capture the process of policy implementation, thereby altering the outcomes of economic policy. Their capacity to do this is greatest in systems that are not transparent and where formal systems of accountability do not function. These effects are illustrated in the next chapters.

Chapter 4

THE MISSION IN MEXICO

During the 1980s the IMF and the World Bank worked closely with Mexico. The debt crisis forced Mexico to turn to the IMF for financial assistance in 1982, and during ensuing years a close and evolving relationship emerged between policymakers in Mexico and staff, management, and board members in the IMF and the World Bank. Obviously several features make the case of Mexico special, not least its special relationship with the United States and the size of its borrowings from the international financial institutions. That said, the development of the relationship between Mexico and the Fund and Bank illuminates how the international institutions seek to discharge their mission, persuading, advising, and where necessary, coercing borrowing governments.

This chapter explores how the IMF and World Bank built up a working relationship with the government of Mexico from the period 1976 onward. In the first period, 1976–82, the bargaining power of the IMF and the World Bank grew out of the material incentives each institution could offer policymakers to undertake particular policies. In a second period, 1982–88, the international institutions developed relations with sympathetic interlocutors who came to occupy key roles in the government—this enlarged the role of the advice and lending of the Fund and Bank. In the third phase, 1988–94, there was a further deepening of relations and lending from the IMF and World Bank as Mexican interlocutors continued to prove both willing and institutionally capable of undertaking prescribed reforms. Secret negotiations and assistance were a part of this relationship, as revealed in interviews with the key actors. In the final period since 1994, individuals have remained in key economic policy-making positions; however, political changes have altered their institutional position and capacity, and so too the influence of the international financial institutions. Using archives and interviews undertaken with officials in Mexico and in Washington D.C., I will trace the ways domestic institutional changes alter and shape the possibilities of influence of the IMF and World Bank.

The Case of Mexico

Like many other countries, Mexico radically reshaped its economic relations with the world during the 1980s, throwing open borders to trade, finance, and investment. Accompanying this transformation of economic policy was a change in the role of the state, described by former finance minister Jesús Silva Herzog as a profound change, virtually a silent and peaceful revolution (Silva Herzog 1993). Although the IMF and the World Bank had intensive relations with Mexico over this period, most policymakers' accounts of the transformation give little hint of their involvement (Aspe 1993, Ortiz 1994, Rogozinski 1993, Martinez and Farber 1994, Gurria 1993, Blanco 1994, Silva Herzog 1993). A prevailing view favored by economists in both Washington and Mexico is that Mexico simply undertook the most rational, technically sound policies available. The transformation from 1982 to 1994 is portrayed as both planned and inevitable from the start.

Underplayed or ignored in mainstream accounts are the tough debates and vociferous contestation that preceded each step of liberalization in Mexico. In 1984 the idea of replacing the gradual, negotiated trade liberalization with rapid unilateral liberalization was opposed by President de la Madrid and by most of the major agencies of the Mexican government, including the Finance Ministry (Secretaría de Hacienda y Crédito Público), the Ministry of Budget and Planning (Secretaría de Programación y Presupuesto), the Ministry of Foreign Affairs (Secretaría de Relaciones Exteriores), the Trade Ministry (Secretaría de Comercio y Fomento Industrial), the Ministry of Energy, Mines, and Parastatal Industry (SEMIP), and the Ministry of National Patrimony and Industrial Development (SEPAFIN) (Mares 1985). Furthermore, both unions and large business associations such as CANACINTRA and CONACAMIN were also opposed to trade liberalization (Heredia 1987). The government's view on investment was that foreign investment should not replace existing national enterprises, nor remove more resources from Mexico than it earned in exports (De La Madrid 1982).

In spite of widespread domestic political opposition to accelerated liberalization, the Mexican government launched a rapid series of trade liberalization measures in 1985, acceded to GATT in 1986, and eventually signed up to the NAFTA accord and undertook investment and financial liberalization (Story 1982). Having once extolled the benefits of independence and controlled relations with world markets, the Mexican presidency now became an evangelist of the benefits of foreign investment and open access to world markets (Salinas 1989). By the 1990s many hailed the transformation as inevitable. Yet closer investigation reveals pervasive political contestation. A change in economic policy was inevitable but the modalities, pace, and sequencing of change were not.

Several factors demanded change in the Mexican economy prior to the trade liberalization in 1985–86. Economic problems in mid 1985 were compounded by earthquakes on 19–20 September 1985, an IMF announcement that Mexico had failed to meet the conditions set down in its agreement on 21 September 1985, and a crash in oil prices in January 1986 (Szymczak, 1992). The debt crisis had decimated the political power of existing sectors in the Mexican economy and created powerful new interests that supported liberalization (Frieden 1991b).

That said, at the end of 1984 the Mexican government was enjoying a modest sense of economic recovery, having completed two years of economic adjustment, reduced inflation to an annual rate of around 60 percent, and rescheduled the external debt into multiyear arrangements. The successes of 1983–84 were diminished toward the end of 1984 when the government began to loosen up its fiscal policy—some would say in order to achieve a spurt of growth so as to help to secure victory in midterm elections in 1985. Yet, although inflation picked up, the public financial deficit grew, the trade balance deteriorated, and foreign reserves dropped, the pace of economic activity remained strong well until the second half of 1985 (IMF 1985).

Paradoxically, it was during the more positive phase described above that the Mexican government decided to accelerate trade liberalization. For this reason, "crisis" and lack of choice are not accurate determining factors. Furthermore, the evidence shows that within the Mexican cabinet at least three different alternatives were recognized and debated (Lopez Portillo 1995, and interviews with Undersecretary of the Finance Ministry Guillermo Ortiz 1994, Undersecretary of Foreign Trade Luis Bravo Aguilera 1994, Cabinet Minister Jesús Silva Herzog 1994, and Undersecretary of the Ministry of Foreign Affairs Andrés Rozental 1994). Gradualists within the government favored continuing hard debt negotiations with the IMF, the commercial banks, and the U.S. government and maintaining the gradual process of liberalization started in 1983. Radicals favored using a debtors' cartel to negotiate for better terms, limiting debt repayments to an amount set aside from export earnings, and negotiating trade issues separately. The liberalizers who supported the Washington consensus argued that the government should undertake a rapid, unilateral dismantling of trade protections and use structural reform to deal with inflation and debt.

The critical question is why and how did the liberalizers prevail? Furthermore, when the Washington consensus ideas seemingly failed to produce the hoped-for results in the later 1980s, why did they continue to dominate? Did the IMF and World Bank play any significant role?

The Role of the IMF and the World Bank

It is clear that in Mexico the IMF and World Bank could not and did not play a definitive role, imposing the Washington consensus on the Mexican government. There are several factors that mitigate against such a role. When Mexico comes up in the IMF and World Bank, the United States is prepared to "push and shove until it gets what it wants" (interview with IMF Alternate Director from Mexico Roberto Marino 1994). The sensitivity of the United States to political and economic stability across its southern border has given Mexico more opportunity to push for special treatment from the Fund and Bank staff than most other countries enjoy.

Additionally, unlike most developing countries, Mexico has access to large alternative private sources of finance and indeed, because of this, when crisis looms Mexico poses a risk to financial stability in the rest of the world. This means that intervention is rapid and necessary for systemic reasons. For the IMF and World Bank this means they must work amid other political pressures and priorities, which can undermine their own leverage and coercive power over the Mexican government.

Finally, Mexico has a large and sophisticated bureaucracy and government infrastructure. To quote IMF officials I interviewed who had worked with the Mexican government throughout the 1980s, "The thing you must understand is that we can't patronize Mexican officials" (Interview with Claudio Loser and Eliot Kalter 1994). Similarly a World Bank head of mission recalls taking a very good—but not absolutely the best—economist from the Bank on mission to Mexico with him and watching Mexican finance official Jaime Serra Puche simply "rip the guy to bits, bit by bit in the most sophisticated way." His conclusion was that if the Bank wanted to have influence in Mexico, it would have to "offer the best" (Interview with Rainer Steckhan 1995). All these features lessen the capacity of the IMF and World Bank to "impose" prescriptions on Mexico and make the Mexican case both a tough and an interesting one in trying to trace their influence.

The story of Mexico's intensive relationship with the IMF and World Bank, and contemporaneous transformation in foreign economic policy, covers four periods (1976–82, 1982–88, 1988–94, 1994 onward), which offer useful phases within which to describe the relationship. The evidence suggests that negotiations with the IMF and World Bank had a subtle effect, playing into the competition among agencies of government, such as Trade Ministry and Finance Ministry, fighting each other for control of a policy or resources. The IMF and World Bank also played into the battle for power within agencies undertaken by individuals or groups wishing to rise to the top, or see their view prevail within a particular agency.

To summarize the story, in the first phase of engagement, the Fund and Bank used material incentives to try to nudge Mexican officials toward policy change. In the second phase, government officials became more closely linked to their interlocutors in the IMF and World Bank, using the incentives and advice of the Fund and Bank to enhance their own power and position, and that of their respective agencies in relation to other parts of government. In the third phase, there was a very high level of cooperation between Fund and Bank staff and Mexican government officials, which accompanied an institutional consolidation within Mexico of economic policy. Officials sympathetic to the approach of the IMF and World Bank (whose careers generally began in the Finance Ministry or Central Bank) took charge of virtually all important parts of government and squeezed alternative kinds of policy off the agenda. In the final phase, political changes altered not only the position of the economic policymakers within the Mexico government but equally the potential and actual influence of the Fund and Bank.

The Use of Incentives

When the administration of the new president Lopez Portillo came into office in 1976 it was greeted by a debt crisis and negotiations with the IMF for short-term balance-of-payments financing. The crisis brought two competing views of economic policy into sharp contrast. Economic nationalists prioritized development and growth. Technocrats argued that Mexico needed to adjust, stabilize, and liberalize in order to lessen inflation, capital flight, and foreign debt.

Among the technocrats were two of the future presidents of Mexico, the then head of the newly created Budget Ministry, Miguel de la Madrid, and the undersecretary of that same ministry, Carlos Salinas de Gortari. The solutions favored by the technocrats matched those advocated by the IMF, whose program required devaluation, fiscal tightening, and encouraging Mexico to open up to world trade and investment. This group came to the fore in 1976, when Mexico was forced to seek assistance from the IMF and to negotiate its first bilateral trade agreement with the United States in thirty-five years.

At the same time, after several years of denying the World Bank access to Mexican economic data, the government agreed to participate in a World Bank review of Mexico's economic performance and President Lopez Portillo forged a new closer relationship with the World Bank, kicked off by a meeting with World Bank president Robert McNamara on 17 February 1977, which led to a doubling of the World Bank's portfolio in Mexico.

Although the technocrats prevailed, there were alternative voices in the Mexican cabinet. The new policies were criticized by the then minister of budget and programming Carlos Tello, who accused the architects of the new policies in the Finance Ministry of being "IMF functionaries" (Ramirez 1982, 8). The structuralists (or economic nationalists) argued that Mexican development was best served by decreasing dependence on the United States and by protection or any measures against the vagaries of uncontrolled international markets. Also advocating a strong state and intervention was the new Ministry of National Patrimony and Industrial Development (SEPAFIN), which emphasized the need to balance economic growth with equity and welfare considerations, and to prioritize production for domestic consumption (SPP 1987).

For a brief period in the late 1970s, the structuralists won. Loans from international banks permitted Mexico to turn its back on the IMF, turn away from GATT, and embark on a nationalist set of trade and investment policies (Mares 1985, Story 1982). However, the heyday of the economic nationalists was brought to an abrupt halt when Mexico was hit by a series of economic shocks. A damaging drought caused widespread crop failures in 1979–80 and was followed by a more damaging rise in U.S. interest rates in 1979, which hiked up Mexico's foreign debt repayment obligations. Furthermore, in 1981 and again in

1982, the price of oil, Mexico's thriving export, dropped. Mexico's economy soon unraveled.

The crisis brought out two contradictory responses. The technocrats in the government appealed to the international financial community for help. The economic nationalists nationalized the banks (1 September 1982), imposed unwieldy exchange and interest rate policies, and castigated the exploitative international financial community. The result was massive capital flight sparked by rising public sector expenditure, external debt, inflation, and increasing reliance on domestic bank credit. In February 1982 the Central Bank withdrew temporarily from the exchange market, leaving the peso to depreciate sharply. In August 1982 the Mexican finance minister made an emergency appeal to Washington (the U.S. Treasury, the Federal Reserve, and the IMF) for assistance in meeting Mexico's foreign debt repayments, while the president prepared a nationalization of commercial banks announced in September 1982.

The clash between nationalists and technocrats was resolved when the crisis brought the incoming government directly back into the arms of the international financial institutions. Indeed, even as the nationalists within the cabinet of 1982 pursued policies which ought to have completely undermined the confidence of the international financial community, the technocrats negotiated agreements with both the IMF and Mexico's commercial creditors. Although president-elect Miguel de la Madrid had not yet taken office, the IMF negotiated with Jesus Silva Herzog and his team, as did the Bank Advisory Group of thirteen banks that was set up in the wake of the crisis (Gurria 1988, 73–74). These negotiations are often presented as a series of confrontations between Mexico and the IMF and the commercial banks. Yet in some ways the real differences of view lay among the Mexicans involved.

In discreet negotiations behind the scenes young members of de la Madrid's incoming team were urging the IMF to take a tough line. For example, a senior IMF official who was negotiating at the time recalls that Gustavo Petricioli, one of de la Madrid's team, would meet him every morning for breakfast during the Fund's mission in Mexico City in order to urge the Fund to be tougher with the outgoing administration (Conversation with IMF official Ted Beza 1995). Petricioli, however, was not a "convert" to the Washington consensus as his later actions reveal (see below).

The incentives the United States and IMF offered to Mexico in 1982, to persuade its policymakers to stay in line with Washington's vision of debt management, were substantial. The Mexican government requested a new loan from commercial banks of US$5 billion for six years and three years' grace, and the IMF backed up their request by requiring banks to confirm their commitment to new lending as a prerequisite of Fund approval for Mexico to draw some US$3.9 billion from the Extended Fund Facility (Gurria 1988, 78). On 8 December 1982, the finance minister communicated to the IMF that Mexico would abide by an economic program supported by the IMF, and to the banks the restructuring scheme for the Mexican public sector external debt as formally agreed with the Bank Advisory Group.

Along with the incentives the IMF could offer, the Fund also proffered clear answers to Mexico's difficulties. They offered a simple, ready-made solution to a government disenchanted with the ideas behind the old foreign economic policy and without the finances to continue it. Just as the staff of the Fund benefited from the professional discipline and relative simplicity of orthodox economics, so too these same characteristics made the ideas attractive to technocrats needing quickly to come up with solutions to difficult and messy problems. In social theory terms, the theoretical logic, the prescriptive simplicity, and the optimistic prognosis all made this a tempting package that would give a strong hand to the individual and the agencies promulgating it.

The political impact of the adjustment Mexico undertook was immediate. The IMF required Mexico to meet macroeconomic criteria that required stabilization and adjustment. The necessary measures, unlike deeper microeconomic reforms, did not require a wide consensus within Mexico but rather could be undertaken by a very small group of senior officials. As a result the Finance Ministry and the Central Bank began to increase their power relative to other agencies.

Both the Finance Ministry and Central Bank had always been powerful in Mexico (Solìs 1970, Maxfield 1990). Previously their power had been counterbalanced by competing views of economic policy and other powerful political ministries. Gobernación, for example, controlled the security and the patronage apparatus of the state through the appointment of governors, municipal authorities, and the leaderships of corporatist organizations. But the power of Gobernación began to erode as soon as the budget cuts required to meet IMF-favored macroeconomic criteria were introduced. At the same time, the recipients of IMF assistance, the Finance Ministry and Central Bank, began to expand their own networks—as did the Budget Ministry (headed by Miguel de la Madrid from 1979 and then by Salinas from 1982), creating a network of regional offices whose heads had more direct access to the budget (Centeno 1994, chap. 4).

However, in spite of the rise of supporters of the Washington consensus there remained competing views inside the cabinet throughout the late 1970s and early 1980s. The new technocrats in the Finance Ministry and Central Bank were continually forced to rebut alternative policies propounded by radical voices in the cabinet. The Washington consensus prescriptions were continually subject to critical scrutiny. With hindsight, a senior World Bank official described the Bank's relationship with Mexico during this period as characterized by "suspicion and difficulty" (Interview with Rainer Steckhan 1995). However, from the Mexican point of view, cabinet opposition served as an important source of leverage in negotiations with the international financial institutions—the technocrats could always use the threat of more radical alternatives to get better terms (Interview with Cabinet Minister Jesús Silva Herzog 1994).

Sympathetic Interlocutors

The debt crisis in 1982 forced Mexico to seek help from the IMF and the government of the United States. Yet Mexican policymakers had some "reverse leverage," which they put to good use. Negotiators were able to play on U.S. fears of radical alternative policies waiting in the wings. If the Mexican government gave in to political demands for a radical policy this would further jeopardize banking stability (due to the heavy exposure of U.S. banks) and exacerbate U.S. concerns about security. Fears of political instability, immigration, and the communist threat were all spelled out in the Kissinger Commission Report of 1984. In the early 1980s Mexican government officials could point to radical alternatives, such as a moratorium on debt repayments, being advocated within the cabinet.

The Mexican cabinet, however, was in the process of changing. The 1982 elections had sealed the outgoing president's choice of his successor—Miguel de la Madrid—whose new cabinet alarmed radicals. The loser in the race for the presidential nomination attributed the change to the domination of the party by the "technocrats of SPP," or the Budget Ministry (cited in Centeno 1994, 158).

The description of the new cabinet as technocratic was to some degree an accurate one. A study of de la Madrid's 1983 cabinet reveals that some 59.3 percent of positions were taken by officials who had started out their careers in the banking or planning sectors of the bureaucracy; just over 44 percent were trained in economics, many in U.S. universities (Centeno 1994, 139). Young technocrats like de la Madrid and Salinas had already set out their own view of Mexico's foreign economic policy during the Lopez Portillo administration (SPP 1987).

The new members in the incoming cabinet were an important point of contact for both the IMF and the World Bank. Indeed, some would say that technocrats had been appointed so as to send out a signal of confidence to Mexico's creditors and private sector, who were hemorrhaging capital abroad. In his memoirs, the outgoing president recalls that he appointed Miguel de la Madrid because as he saw it, de la Madrid was better equipped to deal with Mexico's "financial" problems than was his rival Javier García Paniagua (Lopez Portillo 1988). From the World Bank's point of view, Miguel de la Madrid (and Jesús Silva Herzog) was already perceived back in 1979 as someone who was "very willing" to collaborate with the World Bank, as were several members of his team (World Bank 1979). Indeed, the director of the Latin American and Caribbean Country Department at the time speaks of having "picked out" Carlos Salinas in the early 1980s as a man the Bank could deal with after meeting him at a Business Conference in Cancun in 1983 (Interview with Rainer Steckhan 1995).

The power and status of the young technocrats was immediately enhanced by their role in dealing with the debt crisis and the IMF. Debt posed the most immediate constraint on Mexico's economic policy. The role of the technocrats was central since the IMF negotiated confidentially with as small and as specialized a group of policymakers as possible. This meant that access to the relevant documents and the deliberations and the outcomes of negotiations was tightly restricted. The debt negotiations concentrated power in the hands of the Finance Ministry and Central Bank and the technocrats therein.

The World Bank's negotiations were channeled through the Finance Ministry. A key World Bank official at the time recalls that as trust between Bank staff and Mexico's emerging technocrats grew, their dialogue with Mexican authorities broadened to include officials from other agencies (Interview with Rainer Steckhan 1995). A subtle shift was occurring within and across agencies. The Ministry of Foreign Affairs, for instance, lost even the marginal role it had once played in foreign economic policy (in 1986 losing even the post of undersecretary for economic relations in the ministry) and was relegated, in the words of one of the president's economic advisers, to "dealing with the Third World." Meanwhile several economic functions of the Foreign Ministry were shifted to the neoliberal-dominated Trade Commission (called Bancomext), which grew so that by 1994 it had twenty-eight offices around the world (Interviews with Undersecretary of the Ministry of Foreign Affairs Andrés Rozental 1994, and Deputy director of Bancomext Umberto Molina 1994).

Yet in the mid-1980s there was still strong concern about international infringement of Mexican sovereignty. A debate about this was engendered when the World Bank proposed in 1983 to deepen its dialogue with Mexico. Having been denied access for many years, the Bank proposed a new, high-quality macroeconomic dialogue, focusing on three areas: fiscal policy, trade, and public enterprises. It argued that such an intensive dialogue could potentially lead to several structural or sectoral adjustment loans.

The World Bank's proposed "intensive dialogue" created a storm within the Mexican cabinet. The only Mexican agency then borrowing from the World Bank was the National Industrial Development Bank (NAFIN), and its head, Gustavo Petricioli, argued strongly that such an arrangement would impinge on Mexico's sovereignty and independence. Petricioli lost this argument. Signaling the growing power of the Ministry of Finance, the minister (and key debt negotiator) Jesús Silva Herzog overruled Petricioli's objections and the government ended up accepting the proposal (Interview with Cabinet Minister Jesús Silva Herzog 1994, Kapur 1994). Hence, the World Bank gained deeper access to information across many sectors of the Mexican economy (with notable exceptions of oil and agriculture), permitting ever more specific analyses and advice to be presented to the government.

As of late 1983 the World Bank's advisory role became a regular, institutionalized feature in Mexico with six-monthly country strategy implementation meetings occurring throughout the 1980s, alternately in Washington, D.C., and in Mexico City. In preparation for each meeting the Bank would prepare a ten-page memorandum aimed at senior officials, giving the Bank's analysis of the country's macroeconomic situation. Initially these consultations involved junior officials from the Finance Ministry, but they quickly became fora for higher-level officials in which the minister of finance would take the lead.

The World Bank's agenda was radical liberalization. Trade liberalization was seen as a crucial lever to more fundamental reforms of public enterprises and fiscal reforms (Interviews with World Bank Vice-President Shahid Husein 1995, and World Bank economists Hans Binswagen 1995 and Sweder Van Wijnbergen 1994). Throughout consultations in the 1980s, the World Bank gradually concentrated more and more on advising Mexico of the links between its fiscal problem and the need for trade liberalization. The Bank's influence on trade reform offers a useful example of influence.

Incentives were the most obvious source of influence. The Bank could offer fast-disbursing loans such as the first Export Development Loan to Mexico in 1983, and the subsequent Trade Policy Loans of 1986 and 1987, which were worth $500 million each, in return for trade policy reform. Significantly, these loans were considered by the World Bank as "rewards" for past and for future performance in trade liberalization: that is to say, not only incentives for policymakers to pursue particular policies, but also articles of faith in these sympathetic interlocutors.

A second type of support the World Bank could offer, as mentioned above, was intellectual. In 1985 when the Mexican cabinet was wrestling over crucial decisions on trade liberalization, the Bank very discreetly, without using its name, sponsored a conference on trade liberalization using the private university ITAM and the Mexican agency Bancomext. The speakers at the conference included Anne Krueger and many other World Bank staff or consultants who presented the benefits of trade liberalization. Several policymakers within Mexico cite this meeting as having had an important impact (Interviews with Economic Adviser to the President Fernando Clavijo 1994, Undersecretary of Finance, Guillermo Ortiz 1994, Undersecretary of Foreign Trade Luis Bravo Aguilera 1994). One particularly persuasive argument was that liberalization could assist in the control of inflation. Here the World Bank lent important intellectual support to technocrats pushing trade liberalization within the Mexican cabinet. The real struggle had become, according to officials on all sides, a fight within the Mexican government, pitting a new team in the Ministry of Budget and Planning along with Bancomext and the Central Bank against the Trade and the Finance ministries who were "dragging their feet" (Interviews with Undersecretary of Finance Guillermo Ortiz 1994, IMF officials Claudio Loser and Eliot Kalter 1994, World Bank economist Sweder Van Wijnbergen 1994).

Trade liberalization created conflict within the Mexican bureaucracy and thereby opened up a conduit for the World Bank view. Unsurprisingly, the Ministry of Trade did not want to relinquish the control and patronage it had gained from administering Mexico's deep range of protectionist instruments. The Central Bank, however, was in a different position. The Central Bank was keen to control inflation without having to limit its own control over interest and exchange rates. The World Bank's view that trade liberalization would reduce inflation strengthened the Central Bank's voice on the issue, even though later World Bank research would cast doubt on the relationship between trade liberalization and inflation (Ize 1990). Here the "knowledge" and research of the World Bank influenced a bureaucratic turf battle, thereby creating a hefty partner with whom the World Bank could pursue trade liberalization (Lustig 1992).

The World Bank and Mexico's Central Bank soon became very close partners in pushing trade liberalization within Mexico. In Mexico's 1985 negotiations with the Bank, according to a senior official involved in the negotiations, the Central Bank went behind the backs of the Trade Ministry, and gave the World Bank a set of figures that seriously undermined the Trade Ministry's claims about liberalization undertaken to that date (Interview with Undersecretary of Foreign Trade Luis Bravo Aguilera 1994). One of the World Bank officials involved elaborated that they had actually worked with the Central Bank to produce the new figures based on production weights rather than the obscure system of reference prices which had been previously used (Interview with Rainer Steckhan 1995).

The Trade Ministry tried to push for a more gradualist approach to trade liberalization. The liberalizers argued that this would create political resistance that would slow and probably block the process altogether. The resulting maneuvers illustrate the way domestic actors can use international financial institutions to carry out interdepartmental struggles.

Although the Central Bank won the battle over trade liberalization in 1985, the stakes were altered by renewed economic crisis in Mexico and a crash in oil prices in January 1986. Furthermore the radical trade liberalization overnight destroyed many small- and medium-sized enterprises, which could not compete without some period of transition. The remaining radicals in the cabinet now strengthened their demands for an alternative strategy and gained some support from others in the cabinet. The radical strategy included calling a meeting of the Latin American debtors' group (which had first been established at Cartagena in 1984) and reactivating a more assertive, less cooperative approach to debt.

The response from Washington was rapid. After the Mexican government called for an emergency meeting of the Latin American debtors' group in Punte del Este January 1986, the United States and the international financial institutions sped up a revision of arrangements with the Mexican government and came up with important concessions. The terms of the World Bank's trade liberalization deal were immediately lightened, as were the conditions in the IMF agreement signed soon after.

Two points emerge as particularly important from the 1986 episode. First, the presence of some radicals in the cabinet meant that Mexico could still use the threat of an alternative, more radical policy in bargaining with the United States, IMF, and World Bank. Second (and paradoxically), it also emerges from the 1986 agreements that the Fund and Bank were becoming more and more confident of the commitment of the technocrats in the cabinet to their style of reform. As senior officials who were involved in lightening Mexico's conditions explained in private: there was no longer any need to push Mexico to sign up to such vigorous written terms, since the new breed of Mexican policymakers were committed to liberalizing as far and as fast as they could anyway (Interviews with World Bank officials David Knox 1995, Shahid Husein 1995, and Rainer Steckhan 1995).

In summary, as the 1980s progressed, the economic policy-making agencies (the Budget Ministry, the Finance Ministry, the Central Bank, and the Office of the Presidency) acquired more extensive control of overall policy within the Mexican political system. These agencies provided the IMF and World Bank with sympathetic interlocutors who were able to use the resources and conditionality of the IMF and the World Bank as leverage within the cabinet. Both the Bank and the Fund lent them support, backing up their policy choices with material incentives and extensive technical expertise and analysis. The quid pro quo from the Mexican government was that it granted the institutions ever greater access to information and policy debates within Mexico.

Propitious Political Institutions

The result of Mexico's 1988 presidential election was hailed from the outset as one that would cement close ties and confidence with the international financial community. Like his predecessor, Carlos Salinas de Gortari had been head of the Budget Ministry after a career in the Finance Ministry. Foreign financial press all stressed that the new president-elect had a degree in economics from Harvard. Indeed, the *Economist* cited him in their 1993 Special Survey of Mexico as quite possibly one of the greatest men of the twentieth century.

Critics deprecated the choice of Salinas as the new presidential candidate. He was described as a man controlled by international financial interests (Porfirio Muñoz Ledo in López Gallo 1989, 30). His nomination was described as "the result of private sector forces associated with the multinationals which desire the development of a privatizing, monetarist, and free-trade PRI" (Pablo González Casanova in Ramos 1987, 302). Both those who celebrated and those who criticized the president-elect were right about his close links to the international financial community.

In October 1988, the United States made a "dramatic confidence building gesture" to the Mexican government and its new president-elect amid allegations of massive electoral fraud. Stepping in to assist Mexico's severe economic and political crisis, the United States granted a US$3.5 billion bridging loan from the Treasury exchange stabilization fund. The U.S. loan was soon rolled over into arrangements with the IMF and the World Bank (under the auspices of the Brady Plan announced in March 1989) totaling some US$4.135 billion of IMF financing over a period of three years and credits from the World Bank of US$1.96 billion for 1989. There was also financial support for debt reduction and new loans of US$2 billion on average per year over 1990–92. Importantly, the Brady Plan permitted the IMF and the World Bank to support debt rescheduling in Mexico even in the absence of Mexico completing a deal with its commercial bank creditors (Jones 1988; Lissakers 1991, 228).

The World Bank and IMF moved quickly to make this possible. Although both had been working discreetly on the technicalities of debt reduction, neither had been able to move forward with debt reduction schemes until the U.S. government gave the nod. Once the "fax arrived saying that we had to help Mexico," the IMF and World Bank went into overdrive to implement debt-reduction in deep consultation with Treasury officials (Interviews with World Bank officials Sweder Van Wijnbergen 1995, Rainer Steckhan 1995, David Knox 1995, and IMF officials Claudio Loser and Eliot Kalter 1994). Deviating from normal practice, the World Bank put together a major series of loans to Mexico in just over three weeks: writing reports in the field, agreeing to the loans by Special Committee without the Bank's chief economist (who disagreed with the new U.S. policy of debt reduction), and skipping some of the review mechanisms and appraisals (Interviews with World Bank officials Sweder Van Wijnbergen 1995, Rainer Steckhan 1995).

What few people know is that even prior to Mexico's 1988 elections, the World Bank had become involved in preparing a series of short briefs on major policy issues for Salinas (the PRI candidate) and the PRI. A senior World Bank official describes having his "very best and brightest staff" prepare a series of a dozen policy papers: each based on an issue and no longer than a single digit number of pages (Interview with Rainer Steckhan 1995). The substance of many of these proposals appeared subsequently in the PRI's manifesto. Furthermore, immediately after the elections before Salinas actually took power, the World Bank organized a workshop for Salinas and his prospective cabinet in the mountains a couple of hours drive outside of Mexico City. Here, in seminar-style discussions, World Bank officials claim in private that they cemented relations of mutual trust and confidence with the new team that subsequently played a major part in expediting loans and agreements with the World Bank. "It became clear," recalls one World Bank official, "that these people wanted the World Bank's involvement in virtually everything. They said things in the same way as the Bank." In the words of another Bank official, describing the evolution of relations with the new team: "It no longer mattered what was written down, more important was that these policymakers could be trusted" (Interviews with Rainer Steckhan 1995, Hans Binswagen 1995, Shahid Husein 1995).

The participants in the seminar soon became key members in the cabinet appointed by Carlos Salinas de Gortari. Marking a departure from the Mexican tradition of appointing heterodox cabinets which ensured that the heads of the various ministries had different views and were supported by different factions within the party, Salinas made appointments to key agencies from an overwhelmingly small group of officials who had come up through the Finance Ministry, the Budget Ministry, or the Central Bank (Centeno 1994, 140; Centeno and Maxfield 1992). The four key economic policymakers in the new cabinet—José Córdoba, head of the office of economic advisers set up within the Presidency; Pedro Aspe, an MIT-trained Budget and Finance Ministry official; Jaime Serra Puche, a Yale-trained Finance Ministry official; and Ernesto Zedillo, a Yale-trained, Central Bank and Budget Ministry official—were all technocrats. Even the new head of the PRI was University of Pennsylvania–trained and Budget Ministry–experienced Luis Donaldo Colosio.

The international financial community, the IMF, and World Bank all had a clear stake in these men from the outset. Furthermore, some within the Bank even thought that if a member of the cabinet did not "play ball," they could now make it clear to the government that they would find it easier to work with someone else. For example, the former vice president for Latin America recalls telling the Mexican authorities that he could not work with Education Minister Manuel Bartlett, and soon linked this communication with the fact that the education minister was replaced within a couple of months with the young technocrat Ernesto Zedillo who would later become president (Interview with Shahid Husein 1995). Most Mexican officials recall that these events had many other more political aspects than the Bank official's recollection suggest. Nevertheless, the relations between the IMF and the World Bank and the Salinas administration became ever more marked by trust evidenced by high levels of access, and by a high degree of acceptance on all sides of each other's figures, prescription, and promises.

Increasing trust, access, and acceptance was, of course, always handled (as was the workshop in the mountains discussed above) with the utmost discretion. For example, immediately prior to the unveiling of the 1989 Mexican budget, it was vital that the IMF not be seen in Mexico City where it might be construed as "dictating" a budget to the Mexican government. In fact, even normal Fund missions at this time were always kept secret in order to avoid press attention and possible speculation. However, in this case, the Fund was careful officially not to send a mission to Mexico until after the budget had been announced. Nevertheless, prior to the announcement of the budget, two IMF officials flew into Mexico City "dressed as tourists" to meet with and advise the Mexican team (Interview with IMF officials Claudio Loser and Eliot Kalter 1994).Perhaps unbeknown to the IMF officials at the time, the World Bank chief economist for Mexico was also making secret trips to Mexico City—in order to "coach" the Mexican team for their visit from the IMF (Interview with Sweder Van Wijnbergen 1995).

The secrecy of Fund negotiations and advice was crucial to subsequent events. In the cabinet negotiations on the budget, Finance Minister Pedro Aspe (along with the head of the Central Bank) invoked the need to comply with IMF terms and conditions to bolster their argument for continuing restrictive anti-inflationary policies. Yet, this was a ploy to outmaneuver cabinet colleagues. Crucially, the restrictiveness and secrecy of both monetary policy and Fund negotiations meant that many in the cabinet were unaware that Mexico no longer needed the IMF resources for which compliance with the criteria of the Extended Arrangement was necessary (Interviews with Mexican officials)).

The closeness of relations between key Mexican policymakers and the international financial institutions were cemented during 1989 by the negotiations on the details of Mexico's Brady Plan debt reductions. IMF officials were flying in and out of Mexico at least every two months. World Bank officials were there almost permanently. And even though many governments wanted banks to negotiate directly with Mexico, nevertheless, the Fund and the Bank assisted Mexico throughout. A senior World Bank economist involved at the time recalls spending large chunks of his own time helping the Mexican team and even traveling privately to Mexico City in order to help them sort out how best to take advantage of debt reduction (Interview with Sweder Van Wijnbergen 1994).

This deepening relationship is perhaps best illustrated by the case of agricultural reform. In 1983 Mexico stonewalled the World Bank on agricultural policy. When the idea of deepening World Bank dialogue was floated in 1983, agriculture was consensually agreed to be one of the strictly taboo areas from which the Bank was excluded. By 1989, however, the Mexican government embraced the World Bank's agenda and permitted it to train young technocrats to be put in charge of the Ministry of Agriculture.

The change in agricultural policy began in 1988 when agricultural reform was raised at the pretransition workshop organized with the World Bank. By 1989 the issue had risen to the top of the agenda of President Salinas and Minister of Finance Pedro Aspe, and a team of young technocrats, headed by Luis Tellez, were moved into the Ministry of Agriculture. None apparently knew anything about agriculture (in the words of one World Bank official: "Not one of them knew the difference between wheat and maize"), but they were picked out as "heavy-hitters" in the bureaucracy, capable of implementing market-oriented reform (Binswagen 1995). The training of these young technocrats was provided by the World Bank, with the utmost discretion, during so-called "reverse missions" to Washington and on one occasion at the Wisconsin Land Tenure Center (Interviews with Hans Binswagen 1995, Sweder Van Wijnbergen 1994, Rainer Steckhan 1995).

Looked at more closely, the progression of agricultural policy illustrates the mechanisms of influence depicted in this chapter. The first aspect of change was the shift in policy priorities. Mexico's volte-face on agriculture was greatly facilitated by loans offered by the World Bank along with research and evidence of the potential gains from reform. The dialogue that commenced in earnest in 1988 resulted in some seven major loans for agricultural reforms between 1987 and 1991. Additionally, two sector adjustment program loans and five nonproject loans were approved by the Bank. These loans were an important step to securing policy change. One World Bank official recalls trying to "maximize" the leverage of the Bank by cooperating with the Inter-American Development Bank so as to come up with as large a package as possible to offer Mexican policymakers in return for reform (Interview with Hans Binswagen 1995). So too, the quality of Bank personnel and research was important. At the core of the team working on Mexico were the World Bank's top agricultural expert Hans Binswagen, and one of their star economists Sweder Van Wijnbergen, whose work on the consequences for agriculture of a North American Free Trade Agreement was particularly influential.

A second mechanism of influence was the shift in policy-making power among government agencies reflected in the fact that the push to reform agriculture came from the Ministry of Finance and the Presidency. As these agencies accumulated power over the 1980s, so too the scope of their policy-making initiatives expanded to incorporate most areas of policy—including agriculture, where they took the lead.

A third mechanism of influence was the restructuring which took place within ministries as key personnel were appointed—as we saw in the case of agriculture—who would carry out the agenda approved by both the international financial institutions and Mexico's Ministry of Finance, Central Bank, and Presidency. In 1992, the Budget and Planning Ministry, which had been created in 1977, was folded back into the Finance Ministry to create one superministry.

A final channel of influence was the close set of collaborative relations that emerged between officials in the international financial institutions and Mexican policymakers. Bank officials talk about Mexican policymakers providing them with more and more figures and greater and greater access, and in return, they themselves became more prepared to be flexible in interpreting compliance and noncompliance. The Bank officials cited in this chapter spoke of a change in the mood and ambiance of negotiations from the early to the later 1980s. They say that by the late 1980s, when it came to asking whether a disbursement should be withheld because the terms had not been completely fulfilled, compliance or noncompliance came to be interpreted very flexibly. Some Mexican finance officials felt that they could trust Bank and Fund officials more than their cabinet colleagues at times (Interview with Pedro Aspe 1995).

Over this period, the international financial institutions also became involved in selling the neoliberal project to a wider community in Mexico. Just as the World Bank had sponsored a conference in 1985 on trade liberalization to convert reluctant cabinet members, in 1989 the IMF sponsored a conference on growth, equity, and external financing, the proceedings of which were later published (Morales and Ruiz 1989). This was an attempt to bring the National University (UNAM) into the liberalization strategy from which its very critical economists had distanced themselves. IMF officials speak of their sense that UNAM had been "alienated" from the reform process and needed to be brought on board (Interview with IMF officials Claudio Loser and Eliot Kalter 1994). Such activities highlight the role the international financial institutions see themselves playing. They perceive themselves as not merely setting targets for governments and ensuring policy compliance, but educating and transforming the parameters of domestic policy debate, in fact, furthering and entrenching powerful ideas.

The early Salinas administration years have been said by the World Bank to be the best in terms of their lending to Mexico because they shared a "common vision about required reforms and Mexico needed external financial assistance."[1] That said, intimacy and trust with Mexico led to a degree of self-censorship on the part of the World Bank—just as it had in Indonesia after successful growth in Bank loans there had underscored how good that country was for the World Bank's lending portfolio (see chapter 3). In Mexico in 1992–93, two financial economists in the World Bank were warning of an alarming deterioration in asset quality among some banks in Mexico. However, they failed to induce their senior managers to raise these issues at the highest level of government in Mexico. The Bank rates this as "by far the most serious omission in the Bank's agenda in Mexico" across the period 1989–2000 (Operations Evaluation Department 2001, 11). This failure underscores the inherent problems for the Bank when it seeks successful borrowers and develops very close and positive relations that could be jeopardized by negative feedback.

By 1994, Mexico's transformation had become an "exemplary case" of reform. The Fund and World Bank heralded it as "spectacular, lasting, and the envy of any reform economy" (as quoted in Dornbusch and Werner 1994, 266). Mexico became a member of the North American Free Trade Agreement, opening up new possibilities of inward investment as well as new vulnerabilities to shocks in international markets. Even as new challenges emerged, both the World Bank and the IMF remained confident that the right group of policymakers were in control in Mexico, and that any storm could be ridden out (IMF 1994b, Edwards 1995). Mexico had opened up its economy; any "turning back" through controls on capital or trade flows would be heavily punished by the markets. This vulnera-

---

[1] World Bank/OED 2001, Memorandum to the Executive Directors and the President, 1.

bility had been increased by the lifting of restrictions on the purchase of government bonds, which had been required in 1993 as an entry requirement to the OECD.

In 1994, when it came to the question of who would succeed Salinas, the four main contenders for the job were all from the president's own power base, or *camarilla,* and all were technocrats. They were Ernesto Zedillo (Yale), Pedro Aspe (MIT), Luis Donaldo Colosio (University of Pennsylvania), and Manuel Camacho (who had attended UNAM with Salinas and worked with him at the Budget Ministry from 1980). With the exception of Camacho, all were pretty much in agreement with each other—and with IMF and World Bank officials—as to the nature and solution to Mexico's economic problems. All were part of a new concentration of power over economic policy within the Finance Ministry, the Central Bank, and a small number of technocrats in other institutions. Their position and views had been crucial to Mexico's foreign economic policy transformation and the influence of the IMF and World Bank. But politics would soon change this constellation.

The Impact of Political Change

Later in 1994, a series of shocks hit Mexico. These included an uprising against the government in Chiapas and the assassination of Donaldo Colosio (the man nominated as the PRI's presidential candidate). In December 1994, the Mexican government widened the exchange rate band by 15 percent and within weeks Mexico was on the verge of default as investors withdrew (cf Lustig 1995; Sachs, Tornell, and Velasco 1995; IMF 1995a).

It turned out that the IMF and World Bank were wrong to believe that Mexico's structural reforms would insure it against what the Bank would later describe as "the catastrophic 1994–95 financial crisis" which "thrust millions of Mexicans into poverty" (World Bank 2004b). The new administration headed by Ernesto Zedillo faced a huge challenge, making a number of mistakes early on (Bartley 1997 and cf Gil-Diaz and Carstens 1997). However, their continuing close relationship with the IMF and World Bank was cemented through the large "rescue package" of fast-disbursing loans from both the Fund and the Bank, and in 1995 the IMF stationed a resident representative in Mexico City.

The most significant challenge faced by the new administration was political. While the neoliberals had greatly strengthened their place within the existing institutions of the federal government—achieving control of all-powerful ministries, and benefiting from the hegemony of the PRI—they came to face a much broader political challenge that would greatly weaken the power of both the central government and the PRI.

Mexico's new administration were ushered into office in early 1995 against a background of "a botched succession and political assassinations . . . sandwiched between a guerrilla rebellion and financial collapse," which sealed their fate right then and there according to one scholar (Wallis 2001, 306). The devaluation in

1994 and ensuing crisis precipitated a massive outburst of popular opposition fueled by revelations of extensive corruption, drug trafficking, and murder. At the very least this precipitated electoral reform, putting previous forms of election-rigging out of reach (Shadlen 1999). In April 1995 the PRI suffered its first serious loss in Jalisco where its candidate was defeated in the important governorship election. Subsequently the PRI lost out in a whole series of local and regional elections (Morris 1995a and 1995b, Dominguez and McCann 1996).

Further electoral reform in 1996 had far-reaching impacts. The first ever direct election for the mayor of Mexico City was won by opposition candidate Cuauhtémoc Cárdenas of the PRD. Subsequently the PRI lost control of the Mexico City Legislative Assembly, the two key states Querétaro and Nuevo León, and its constitutional majority in the Senate. Yet more devastatingly, the PRI lost its overall majority in the Congress.

Political change dramatically altered the ability of Mexico's technocrats to control economic policy. The rise of opposition in Congress deprived the executive—the PRI president—of its capacity to legislate with the virtually automatic consent of Congress (Levy and Bruhn 2001, Philip 2002). Important legislation was now scrutinized, debated, and subject to negotiations (Shadlen 1999). As the PRI lost control over local politics, pressure increased for decentralization, which would erode the power of the Federal bureaucracy. The Finance Ministry opposed this move (Philip 2003).

The series of political changes culminated in 2000, with the election of the first non-PRI president since the 1917 Revolution, Vicente Fox of the Partido Acción Nacional (PAN). The Fox administration at first attempted to continue the previous direction of economic policies but soon found itself blocked by a Congress keen to exercise its newly found power. Plans to kick-start oil, gas, and electricity production through foreign investment were all blocked—as was even a presidential trip to Canada and the United States in April 2002 (Peters 2002).

What happened to Mexico's programs with the IMF and World Bank? The IMF reported in 2003 that Mexico's structural reform agenda was limited by a lack of support in Congress where the president's party is in a minority. They also reported with disappointment that Mexico's public debt has edged up and that reforms to electricity generation, labor market regulations, and tax reform have all been blocked (IMF 2003a, 4–5). In the IMF's view, the inability of the executive to implement policy in these areas will damage Mexico's medium-term competitiveness (IMF 2003a, 5).

What stands out is that Mexico is diverging from IMF prescriptions in areas where the executive does not have control. On the narrower set of issues where the executive still has control, the IMF's aspirations continue to be met: inflation has been lowered, the structure of debt has been strengthened, the financial system is being modernized, Mexico participated in an FSAP, and has issued bonds with collective action clauses (IMF 2003a, 5). IMF lending and advice was closely involved in the Financial Strengthening Program 2000–2001, which involved some US$16.9 billion of loans to the Mexican government in July 1999. The IMF portion was a US$4.2 billion standby arrangement (now repaid), with a further

US$5.2 billion being borrowed from the World Bank, US$3.5 billion from the Inter-American Development Bank, and US$4.0 billion in credit lines from the EXIMBANK of the United States (Ministry of Finance Mexico 1999, IMF 2003a).

The small group of technocrats still in command of the central controls over Mexico's economy are still "willing" to pursue a reform agenda in close collaboration with the IMF. But while they are willing they are only able to do this in certain spheres. In the words of an IMF staff report: "The authorities have broadly shared the Fund's views on the priorities in these areas, but political constraints have hindered passage of key reform legislation, as it has been difficult to channel the longer-term economic benefits of these policies into broad popular support" (IMF 2003a, 5).

The World Bank has found similar obstacles in its relations with the politically reformed Mexican government. In a report by the Operations Evaluation Department, staff members repeatedly note the extent to which political factors and increased opposition in Mexico have affected the Bank's operations (OED 2001). Disagreements with the government or the political sensitivity of the government led to withdrawals from lending in sectoral reforms in power, finance, agriculture, and environment, and nonengagement on water supply and sanitation, state modernization, decentralization, and poverty reduction (OED 2001, 19). The pattern of approved loans from the World Bank naturally gives a very rough approximation of the relationship between a country and the Bank given the time it takes to prepare and have a loan approved. That said, from a highpoint of US$2.39 billion in loans approved in 1994, by 1997 Mexico's loans approved had dropped to US$530 million. They picked up thereafter.

The contemporary relationship between the Bank and Mexico is laid out in the Country Assistance Strategy paper completed on 15 April 2004. The Bank will continue to lend Mexico between US$0.8 and US$1.7 billion a year. Its approach, as outlined in the report, aims to be more adaptive and more based on learning and knowledge-sharing in researching unanswered questions in areas such as poverty, water, competitiveness, quality of education, and decentralization (note that these are areas previously defined as particularly politically sensitive). The Bank also intends to be more sector specific, even though this adds more risk that supported projects or policies may be dropped (World Bank 2004d, 3).

The experience of the late 1990s underlines the extent to which the special relationship forged between the IMF and World Bank was based not only on Mexico's need for external finance and the willingness of like-minded Mexican officials to pursue reforms with the advice of the international institutions. Crucial was a political system that insulated economic policymakers from others and not only permitted access to the IMF and World Bank, but gave key policymakers tremendous power over wide areas of policy.

The case of Mexico highlights the combination of bargaining power and persuasion that the IMF and World Bank employ to transmit ideas to a member country. Economic crises and the need for finance drove Mexico into the arms of the IMF and World Bank. Money and leverage enabled the Bank and Fund to help nudge Mexico toward policy change in the early 1980s. Subsequently, as a small number of more sympathetic interlocutors began to filter into the Mexican bureaucracy, the relationship with the Fund and Bank became a deeper one. Mexican officials began to reap the rewards of a close relationship with the Fund and Bank, which assisted them individually in their own advancement and institutionally in aggrandizing the role of particular government agencies. Over time, a very close working relationship of trust, mutual confidence, and assistance flourished between the staff of the Fund and Bank and those officials with whom they shared a similar mindset.

Does this suggest that the Fund and Bank "brought about" Mexico's transformation? Absolutely not. Rather, it reveals some crucial conditions under which the Fund and Bank can influence policy. Several features made Mexico ripe for the IMF and World Bank "mission" of transmitting ideas. In particular, during the 1980s and early 1990s Mexico was essentially a single-party political regime with an enormously powerful presidency and executive. The centralized power of the administration and capacity to orchestrate change from the top greatly facilitated the rise of technocrats and the insulation of these policymakers from other parts of government. Furthermore, as Graham argues, Mexico's federal structure and its process for selecting presidents ensured a succession of candidates who have risen from within the party and the government bureaucracy (Graham 1990). This helped further to entrench a particular view of economic policy. Where these political conditions do not pertain, sympathetic interlocutors may be willing but not able to work with the IMF and World Bank to frame and implement reform. This is highlighted in the next chapter's study of reform in Russia where the influence of the IMF and World Bank was much more sharply limited.

Chapter 5

MISSION CREEP IN RUSSIA

At the end of the 1990s it was widely argued that the "mission" of the IMF and the World Bank had to change. A series of financial crises culminating in collapses in Russia and East Asia, coupled with ongoing poverty and economic decline across most of Africa in the late 1990s, led to harsh criticism of both institutions. Until the mid 1990s both the IMF and the World Bank had steamed forward prescribing the "Washington consensus" combination of macroeconomic stabilization and structural adjustment for most ailing economies turning to them for assistance. Underpinning this advice had been a presumption that "freeing markets" in countries would simultaneously unleash positive forces for deeper institutional reforms. It was assumed that political reform would follow hot on the heels of economic reform as new firms and market actors demanded better legal and political systems. By the end of the 1990s this presumption seemed wrong. Nowhere did this seem clearer than in Russia.

Both the IMF and the World Bank became engaged in Russia from 1990 onward. Although neither institution had experience in transforming centrally planned economies into market-based systems, each had some experience and expertise in advising heavily managed, developing economies on structural adjustment, privatization, and reform. They were seen as capable of bringing a formidable range of technical capacities and knowledge to bear, as well as the leverage of significant financial resources, on Russia and the transition economies.

The subsequent work of the IMF and the World Bank in Russia has generated a wide debate as to their impact (Operations Evaluation Department 2002, EBRD 1997, Aslund 1997, IMF 1998a, 66–78, Stiglitz 1999). Over the 1990s, the Russian economy collapsed, as evidenced by at least a 50 percent drop in gross national product, which shrank from more than US$600 billion in 1990 to around US$250 billion by the end of the 1990s (World Bank 1998a, 390, and Operations Evaluation Department 2002, 3). In 1998 the IMF was reporting a deep decline in output (IMF 1998a and 1998i), and the U.S. Congress heard that

TABLE 5.1
GDP, GNP, and real wages in Russia, 1990–2001

Indicator	Fiscal year											
	1990	1991	1992	1993	1994	1995	1996	1997	1998	1999	2000	2001
GDP growth (annual %)	−3.0	−5.0	−14.5	−8.7	−12.6	−4.1	−3.4	0.9	−4.9	5.4	9.0	5.0
GNP per capita growth (annual %)	−3.6	−5.5	−15.3	−8.4	−12.5	−4.4	−3.5	0.7	−6.4	3.3	11.2	7.5
GNP, Atlas method (US$ billion)		569	469	412	343	333	348	383	331	256	246	253
Inflation, consumer prices (annual avg. %)	5.6	92.6	1345.1	895.3	303.2	188.7	47.5	14.8	27.7	85.7	20.6	21.5
REER index (1997 = 100)	161.2	121.5	16.5	34.0	56.6	68.0	91.7	100.0	72.0	46.0	58.9	70.4
Real wage rate (annual growth)					−8.0	−28.0	6.0	4.7	−13.4	−22.0	20.9	
Corporate profit, current prices (% of GDP)			3.0	2.4	1.3	1.6	0.6	0.7	0.7	1.5	1.5	
Gross domestic fixed invest. (% of GDP)	29	23	24	20	22	21	21	19	18	16	18	18
Exports (annual % growth)		−30.0	−28.7	2.1	3.3	10.3	8.7	4.6	−2.3	−1.7	2.7	2.8
Current account balance (% of GDP)			0.1	0.7	0.2	1.7	2.5	0.4	0.3	10.5	16.1	11.2

Source: Official statistics and World Bank *Unified Survey, 2002*.

along with a 40 percent drop in output since 1992, male life expectancy had dropped from 65.5 to 57 (Weisbrot 1998). Real incomes, even after a decade of decline, shrank by a further 22 percent in 1999, and by the middle of that year 55 percent of the population, especially children and the elderly, was living in absolute deprivation (Operations Evaluation Department 2002, 2–3). Table 5.1 outlines these changes.

Some Russians believe that the transition to the market was all part of a devilish plot to weaken Russia, hatched in the West and undertaken on the West's behalf by the IMF and the World Bank. In a less conspiratorial vein, others argue that the Fund and Bank did too little (Sachs 1994 and 1995), or that they messed up Russia by pressuring successive governments too rapidly to adopt radical measures ill-suited to local conditions (Bogomolov cited in Bohlen 1998, Arbatov 1992). These accounts all attribute large amounts of influence to each of the international institutions. At the opposite end of the spectrum, it has been argued that Russia's problems were primarily of its own making, and that foreign assistance had little influence on domestic outcomes. Russian policymakers simply made bad policy choices (Yevstigneyev 1996, Rutland 1996, Gomulka 1995). On this account, the work of the IMF and the World Bank was much less significant.

This chapter analyzes the role of the IMF and the World Bank in Russia, examining their mistakes and the constraints and opportunities they faced. The institutions neither crafted nor implemented Russia's policies. At most they had the potential to use their limited bargaining and persuasive power to tilt political forces within the Russian government. Neither institution could ensure that agreed policies were implemented or enforced in Russia. Both the IMF and the World Bank had some leverage at the point of loan approval when fast-disbursing loans could be dangled in front of a government in need of immediate financial assistance. Each also had a potential persuasive power based on their economic expertise, ideas, and prestige, providing they found and could support sympathetic interlocutors.

The new set of ideas the IMF and World Bank brought to their mission in Russia was particularly important in the context of the end of the Cold War. The pre-1990 Soviet economy had begun slowly collapsing and the centrally planned model and associated expertise were not only discredited but proffered no new or optimistic scenarios for the future. By contrast, the IMF, the World Bank, and a host of Western economic advisers held out a vision of reform and optimism. At the time, some called their prescription "shock therapy," evoking an image of electrotherapy or short-term painful shocks that jolt a system out of a depressed state and into a new more positive one. In fact "shock" reforms were never implemented, although the process of transition certainly proved to be a painful one.

The reforms prescribed for Russia were based on the prescriptions of the Washington consensus, which had been perceived in Washington to have been successfully applied in Poland (Johnson and Kowalska 1994). Yet after a decade of advising the Russian government, both the IMF and the World Bank revised the scope and substance of the model. Their experience in Russia reinforced lessons both institutions were learning elsewhere. The new element of the Washington consensus was "good governance." Throughout the 1980s officials from the IMF, the World Bank, and other agencies had recognized the need for institutional transformation and strengthening in Russia. However, in practice, it was much easier to focus on macroeconomic stabilization and microeconomic reform. By the end of the 1990s it was widely accepted that economic growth and development could not be achieved unless a country enjoyed sound institutions of regulation and law enforcement, in brief an effective state. These issues came to dominate the rhetoric of both institutions and to frame a new, wider consensus embodying "good governance" and the need for "institutional development and strengthening."

In this chapter I use the work of the Fund and Bank in Russia in the 1990s to illustrate the way in which the IMF and World Bank tried to influence policy-making in what is now known as the Russian Federation. For the sake of simplicity the term *Russia* is used throughout the chapter, even in reference to the country when it was still part of the USSR. The research for the chapter was undertaken using official documents, newspaper reports, academic writings, and interviews undertaken in Moscow during the presidential elections of 1996, and subsequent interviews and conversations in Washington and London.[1]

The result reveals the extent to which the Fund and Bank rely not just on material incentives but on sympathetic interlocutors who are not just willing but also able to decide and implement economic policy. Where interlocutors are willing but not able, the Fund and Bank have little influence. Technically they can attempt to enforce conditionality by withholding disbursements or canceling loans; however, even this power is eroded where geostrategic interests intervene. In Russia a mixture of Western goals and U.S. priorities eroded the leverage of the Fund and the Bank. In the face of these external pressures neither institution could fully utilize its normal bargaining power, and this had implications in turn for the institutions' capacity to persuade.

The Mission in Russia

From the outset it was never the case that the IMF and the World Bank were fulfilling a purely technical job in Russia. When the Cold War ended the United States and the West faced serious geostrategic challenges. Who would control the nuclear arsenal of the Soviet Union? Could there be a stable political regime in Russia? How could the West ensure this? Gone was the old apparatus of control within the USSR and gone were the institutions and the balance of power that had provided external stability.

In the absence of other levers, the West turned to the IMF and the World Bank (much smaller amounts of assistance were channeled through USAID, the European Bank for Reconstruction and Development [EBRD], and other bilateral agencies). These were international institutions which could deploy economic incentives to facilitate a successful transition to a market economy. Liberalization and deregulation, it was believed, would create new firms, consumers, and market actors who would then demand wider, deeper democratic reforms. In short, both democracy and open-market capitalism were desired for Russia, and it was hoped that economic reform would complement political reform and thereby the West's broader interest in ensuring Russia was a benign and stable partner.

The U.S. desire for the IMF and World Bank to lead was based on several factors. It was clear to the United States government that vital security interests were at stake. Yet purely bilateral assistance from the United States would be costly and require politically difficult agreement from Congress. The IMF and World

[1] Including General Alexander Lebed (presidential candidate), Gregor Yavlinsky (politician and presidential candidate), Galina Starovoitova (politician and presidential candidate), Boris Semaga (communist member of parliament), Sergei Glazyev (trade minister under Gaidar), Victor Borisyuk (president's analytical department), Andrei Illiaronov (economic adviser to Gaidar, Chernomyrdin, and Yeltsin), Sergei Karaganov (adviser to the president on foreign policy), Vladimir Goussinsky (general director of the Most Group), Yuri Levada (head of the Russian Center for Public Opinion and Market Research). I am also hugely grateful to Boris Fedorov (minister of finance) and Carol Leonard (former U.S. adviser to the Russian government on regional financial sector reform) for their comments on this chapter.

Bank, by contrast, provided a much less controversial and less expensive route, yet one which U.S. Treasury officials could carefully guide (Wedel 1998). As discussed in chapter 2, the United States contributes some 18.5 percent to the IMF capital and guarantees a small percentage of the World Bank's callable capital. Yet U.S. influence, particularly in respect of countries it defines as strategically important to it—as this case study shows—far exceeds this voting share. Furthermore, the United States recognized early on that the IMF and World Bank would be less likely to evoke concerns in Russia about infringement of sovereignty than any direct U.S. assistance would.[2]

The U.S. position was shared by several other major shareholders in the IMF and the World Bank, many of whom had made munificent promises to Russia on which they had been unable to deliver due to a combination of recession, electoral cycles, and weak leadership (Sachs 1994). The main objection to using the IMF and World Bank for stabilizing Russia came from developing countries. Their concern was that scarce multilateral development resources would be diverted away from developing countries (or made more expensive for them) in the pursuit of strategic and economic goals in the former Soviet bloc countries. For this reason in 1991 the coalition of developing countries in the IMF and the World Bank argued that the necessary transfer of resources to the formerly centrally planned economies "should not be at the cost of assistance to developing countries" (G-24 1991, para 27). Likewise in April 1992 they "emphasized once again that the transfer of resources and assistance to these countries should be additional, and not at the expense of, financial and other assistance to other developing countries, which are still trying to cope with pervasive poverty conditions, heavy debt burdens, and barriers to their exports" (G-24 1992, para 12).

In retrospect, developing countries' concerns were well-founded. In spite of pledges of bilateral and G-7 assistance, official financial flows overwhelmingly ended up coming from the IMF and the World Bank. In 2001, Russia's was using 20.24 percent of the IMF's General Resources Account (IMF 2001b, 190), and even after a significant reduction in Bank lending, in 2000 Russia was still taking 3.3 percent of IBRD lending (WB 2000, 147).

The IMF and World Bank each had its own interest in becoming involved in Russia and the transition economies. The IMF was actively searching for a new role and its managing director and most (but not all)[3] senior staff were eager to take the lead in policy toward Russia and the transition economies. It bears recalling that by 1990 the Fund had lost a key part of its original purpose. Its responsibility to manage a fixed but adjustable exchange rate regime had come to

---

[2] Of course, the IMF does provoke nationalist reactions and criticism that it infringes on its members' sovereignty. Nevertheless, it has a defense against such criticisms, in the words of Managing Director Michel Camdessus (to the Russian press): "We don't impose conditions on governments. Russia is a great country, but if you were a small country, my attitude would be the same. If a program were to be imposed from outside, its chances to be fulfilled, to be implemented, would be minimal. For a program to have its chances, it has to be seen as really the program of the country, elaborated by the country. But it also has to be credible to the international community" (Camdessus 1993, 51).

[3] Fund economist Jacques Polak in an interview with me in 1994 reiterated his constant and unwavering concern about the IMF's involvement in Russia.

an end in the early 1970s. Its other major role, to provide assistance to states facing temporary balance of payments crunches, had brought the institution center stage as the international lender of last resort in the first phase of managing Latin America's debt crisis in the early 1980s. However, by the mid 1980s, the debt crisis had been redefined, leaving the IMF with a less central role (James 1996).

The IMF's managing director Michel Camdessus was quick to seize the new opportunity afforded by Russia's need, even in the face of the obvious risks. In his words: "Our role at the IMF is not to wait for all such risks to be eliminated before taking action, but even in chaotic circumstances of history to sit down with the authorities of a member country and see how we can help" (Camdessus 1995). The World Bank was under intense political pressure and faced similar incentives to follow suit. The grand nature of the task was spelled out in the title of a later Bank report, "Assisting Russia's Transition: An Unprecedented Challenge" (Operations Evaluation Department 2002). Yet the historical imperatives had their costs. Although the institutions saw their role in "transition" as a historic opportunity, in retrospect the record shows that in Russia they had very weak bargaining power and very little persuasive power. The technical expertise they had to offer was impressive in some sectors but very limited in what came to be the defining prerequisite of successful transitional lending—good governance and institution building.

A Promising Beginning

Even before Russia became a member of the IMF and the World Bank in 1992, both institutions had been asked by the G-7 to prescribe reforms for the Soviet economy and conditions that the West should set in offering support to Russia (World Bank 1990, OECD et al. 1991). In August 1991 an opportunity to put their prescriptions into practice opened up. Boris Yeltsin emerged—famously astride a tank—from the dramatic events in which a coup attempt by communist hardliners in the Russian Parliament was quashed. By the end of the summer of 1991, Yeltsin's new government announced itself willing to deal directly with the IMF and the World Bank:

> We are prepared, in cooperation with foreign specialists, to immediately disclose the strategic data necessary for admission into international organizations and to accept the basic principles set forth in the charter of the International Monetary Fund. We will make an official appeal to the International Monetary Fund, the World Bank and the European Bank for Reconstruction and Development, inviting them to work out a detailed plan for cooperation and participation in the economic reforms. (*Current Digest of the Soviet Press* 1991, 5)

Immediately a plan for an ambitious new program of privatization, liberalization, and stabilization designed to rapidly create a full market economy was laid out to the Fifth Russian Congress of People's Deputies on 28 October 1991.

Four days later the Congress granted Yeltsin broad powers to rule by decree for a year. The new prime minister promptly appointed a government of young reformers led by Yegor Gaidar as deputy prime minister with responsibility for economic policy.

At this stage, the IMF had two powerful bargaining chips in its relationship with the Soviet Union. First, Russia wanted full membership of the Fund (from which membership of the World Bank would follow). In October 1991 Russia had been given "associate membership" of the IMF but this gave it rights only to technical assistance and advice, not to financial assistance.[4] It took several months for the IMF to accept Russia's application for membership. That said, once approved in April 1992, the Fund was able to present Russia's successful bid and its larger-than-expected quota as a trump card to reformers who by the spring of 1992 were very much in need of external support.

A second bargaining chip in the hands of the IMF was that the government needed a G-7 package of debt relief, which was being promised by a Bush administration keen to attenuate criticism of inaction on Russia in the run-up to the U.S. presidential elections of 1992. This package was conditioned on the government following IMF advice and permitted the IMF to negotiate a detailed Memorandum of Economic Policy with the new government. The agreement, concluded in February 1992, included commitments to unify the exchange rate by mid April, eliminate export quotas and licenses except on energy-related and strategic goods by July, reduce inflation to 1–3 percent per month, and eliminate the budget deficit by the end of the year.

The World Bank had less coercive leverage than the IMF at this stage. Before Russia became a member of the organization, the Bank used a special $30 million trust fund established by its Executive Board to provide technical assistance grants to the former Soviet republics. In Russia this involved setting up a Resident Mission in the autumn of 1991, advising the Russian Privatization Center, and completing a series of studies indicating how the institution might assist Russia. That said, the time it took to set up these advisory services meant that they did not influence Russia's first reform program (Operations Evaluation Department 2002, 6).

The potential influence of both institutions was greatly enhanced by the reformist composition of the new government in Russia, which focused on economic rather than political reform (McFaul 2001, 118). The new team of "young reformers" led by Yegor Gaidar, desperate to deal with a country "on the verge of economic chaos," accepted advice from several prominent pro-market economists (Gaidar 1997, 13). In particular, they faced hyperinflation, a large and growing budget deficit, lack of currency reserves, monetary chaos

---

[4] The "IMF Institute" was expanded to provide courses for officials concerned with transition to the market, and staff in the Monetary and Exchange Affairs Department, Legal Department, Fiscal Affairs Department, and the Statistics Department were made available to provide technical assistance. By December 1991, it was estimated that between 120 and 130 (or one in six) IMF economists were working on countries in transition, and the IMF announced it was creating a new department to deal with the former USSR (Prowse 1991, 2).

(sixteen different central banks in different republics), an inability to service foreign debt, and growing shortages of basic staples. Old Soviet models offered little solution. There was little disagreement at this stage between Russian economists, the IMF, the World Bank, and prominent Western economists advising Russia.

Russia's first set of economic reforms began on 2 January 1992. Prices for around 80 percent of consumer goods and 90 percent of producer goods were decontrolled. Internal trade was freed. The ruble was floated. Inflation fell rapidly from a monthly rate of 245 percent in January to 12 percent in May. The budget was cut and a small budget surplus was recorded in the first quarter of 1992 (*Russian Economic Trends* 1992, 10). The reformers argued that a combination of maximum possible speed of market reforms and drastic tightness of fiscal and monetary policy was vital if reform was to succeed (Interview with Illiaronov 1996; Gaidar 1997, 14). A mass voucher privatization program was whisked into place in June 1992 with strong advice and backing from the international community, including USAID funding to the tune of $58 million.[5] Writing later, three key advisers to the government privatization claimed that by 1 June 1994, two-thirds of Russian industry was privately owned, the stock market was booming, and 40 million Russian citizens owned shares in privatized firms and mutual funds (Boycko, Shleifer, and Vishny 1995).

Political reforms were taking place at a much slower rate. Neither Yeltsin nor his government—nor Western donors—pushed for a modernization of government institutions that would have increased the likelihood of a sustained set of economic reforms. As Michael McFaul has detailed, the Russian Supreme Soviet and the Congress of People's Deputies were left intact. Yeltsin failed to create his own political party and refrained from convoking a new postcommunist founding election. Instead Yeltsin and his government "used their political mandate to initiate economic transformation." The result was a set of political institutions in which ambiguity, stalemate, and conflict very quickly arose (McFaul 2002, 118). Similarly, Russian economic rather than political reform preoccupied the West. It has been calculated than more than half the bilateral assistance channeled through USAID (the lead agency on U.S. efforts to support democratization in Russia) was directed toward U.S. private sector consulting firms working on market reform (Mendelson 2001, 78). That said, support of any kind was very meager at this point.

The first phase of Russian economic reform took place before any significant foreign financial assistance other than a G-7 debt relief package was disbursed. At most the IMF and World Bank contributed technical assistance and a seal of approval to the ideologically sympathetic reformers in the government. Many in the United States and elsewhere in the West were proposing larger-scale assistance, including one proposal for a "Grand Bargain" of up to $100 billion over

---

[5] The World Bank's privatization loan approved in 1992 did not become effective until the end of 1993, by which time the program was virtually completed with more than half of Russian industry transferred into the ownership of more than 40 million Russian citizens (General Accounting Office 2000).

four years alongside an orthodox IMF program (Sachs 1992, Sachs 1991 cf Reddaway 1994). However, very little assistance was forthcoming (Sachs 1994, appendix and table A.1; and Sachs 1992). Yegor Gaidar would later comment that "although there was mutual understanding of the need to help Russian reforms, real mechanisms to carry it out were not elaborated. Instead, there appeared the simplest, deliberately inadequate solution of shifting the burden of responsibility to the IMF" (Gaidar 1997, 14).

In the United States a standoff was taking place between a Republican president seeking reelection and a Democratic-controlled Congress. The European Union was looking inward as Germany dealt with reunification and the rest prepared for monetary union and further expansion. Nonetheless, German technical assistance was greater than that of any other state. The Group of Seven countries professed at each of their summits that they wanted collectively to do something but did very little. In the end transition was left to the IMF and World Bank, and in the period prior to Russia's first loans they seemed to have some success in persuading Russian policymakers to embark on a series of measures to control inflation and begin to restructure the economy. The first actual IMF and World Bank loans were not approved until 5 and 6 August 1992 respectively. By that time, both the political and economic conditions in Russia had changed as had the leverage and persuasive power of the IMF and World Bank.

The Lending Begins

Already by the spring of 1992 pressure was building against economic reform, and Yeltsin's conviction and support of his own government was beginning to waver (Stone 2002, 118). As Yegor Gaidar called for IMF funding in his defense of unpopular budget proposals (Bush 1992), the chairman of the Supreme Soviet, Ruslan Khasbulatov, dismissed the potential of IMF help and called for "adjustments" to economic policy (*Current Digest of the Post-Soviet Press* 1992, 12).

Inside Russia, new forces were emerging. In particular, powerful industrialists began to petition the government to protect their interests from economic reform. In June 1992, a government reshuffle brought Viktor Chernomyrdin and Georgii Kizha—representatives of the industrial lobbies—into government. The following month Viktor Gerashchenko, the former head of the old Soviet Central Bank, was appointed chairman of the Central Bank of Russia (CBR). He quickly proved a much easier and more responsive source of credit for the industrialists than his predecessor had been. The consequence of these developments was a larger budget deficit financed by credits issued by the Central Bank, and a significant increase in government off-budget credits, which threw Russia into an inflationary spiral, derailing stabilization, and impoverishing Russians on pensions and fixed incomes (Hough, Davidheiser, and Lehman 1996).

A further set of interests had been inadvertently created by the sequencing of policies in the first phase of reform. In essence, massive rents were directed into the hands of a small group of managers of state companies producing oil and metals. The reforms had permitted the creation of private trading firms that exported oil and metals at the world market price. However, this was before commodity prices within Russia had been liberalized. In the spring of 1992 the state price of oil was still only 1 percent of the world market price, and even in 1993, the average Russian oil price was only 8.3 percent of the world market price. As a result, in the peak year of 1992, some 30 percent of GDP was channeled into the hands (or more accurately put, the foreign bank accounts) of a small number of private beneficiaries, including state enterprise managers, government officials, politicians, and commodity traders (Aslund 2000). This laid the political-economic framework for a rent-seeking economy in which industrial lobbies and powerful rent-seekers would constantly hinder further reform.

Ironically, it was at this point that the IMF and World Bank began lending to the government. Following Russia's formal admission to the IMF on 1 June 1992, on 5 August 1992 Russia concluded a first tranche agreement with the IMF, which released US$1 billion on condition that Russia undertook steps to reduce inflation. These included reducing the budget deficit, limiting money creation by the central bank, and supporting a flexible exchange-rate policy within the framework of the ruble zone. The next day the World Bank approved a US$600 million Rehabilitation Loan, which was linked to the IMF agreement.

The IMF and World Bank now had significant monetary incentives to offer Russia. In theory, their influence and bargaining power should have increased. They could afford to demand tough conditionality because if Russia did not agree the institutions could withhold loans. The conditionality laid out in agreements and their enforcement of that conditionality, we might expect, would increase at this time. Paradoxically it did not.

Russia demanded special treatment, at the outset arguing that Fund conditionality be waived and that Russia be granted a two-year moratorium on debt service (Stone 2002, 119; Erlanger, 1992; Uchitelle, 1992; *New York Times* 1992). At first the IMF would not concede. As Russia failed to meet agreed conditions on curbing inflation and reducing the budget deficit, the IMF froze payments of the Stand-by Agreement. This had the knock-on effect of freezing other aid to Russia that had been linked to the IMF program. Negotiations broke down between the Fund staff and the Russian authorities and the IMF postponed Russia's arrangement just ten days before a G-7 Summit was to take place. However, political pressures soon intensified as the Bush administration began to lean on the IMF in the hope of ensuring a positive announcement at the G-7 Summit. IMF managing director Michel Camdessus flew to Moscow and personally ensured a watering down of the conditionality.

Likewise the World Bank was under strong political pressure to lend on lenient terms. In the loan formally approved on 6 August 1992, the Bank poured money into balance-of-payments support with a $600 million Rehabilitation Loan tied to the IMF's first credit tranche arrangement and soon extended to finance imports in an attempt to limit the decline in output occurring in the wake of the devaluation of the ruble. As the Bank would later confess, the loan was approved with "virtually no conditionalities" (Operations Evaluation Department 2002, 7). Under pressure to lend from their largest shareholder, neither the IMF nor the Bank, it seemed, had significant bargaining power.

Unwittingly, the IMF and the World Bank were also eroding the foundations of a relationship with reformers such as that which had so enhanced their influence in Mexico. In their 1992 loans the Fund and Bank took their first steps into a political battle being played out between the president and parliament. The conflict was not a simple one of reformers versus nonreformers. Industrialists had been siding with Parliament in order to press for more credits. President Yeltsin had now brought key industrialists into government and acquiesced to the appointment of a Central Banker who would do their bidding. In so doing, the president had bolstered his own position of power at the cost of sacrificing key elements of economic reform and the position of interlocutors sympathetic to the IMF and World Bank. Reformer Yegor Gaidar was replaced in December 1992 by Victor Chernomyrdin. The new prime minister rapidly secured himself monopoly rights for Gazprom—the natural gas company he had created—granting it extensive tax exemptions at the end of 1993, which amounted to a value of 1–2 percent of GDP (Aslund, 2000).

Conditionality Compromised

The pattern set in 1992 would continue throughout the Yeltsin presidency. The president would alternately play to Russia's most powerful vested interests on the one hand, and to more or less reformist governments, international financial institutions, and bilateral allies such as the United States on the other. In each case Yeltsin sought to maximize his own power and authority.

For the IMF and the World Bank the pattern was an extremely difficult one to manage. Each of their three sources of influence was diminished. Their bargaining power was undercut when each time they tried to insist on stringent conditionality, Yeltsin would successfully appeal to the United States to ensure that they lightened loan terms. The persuasive power and the status of the institutions' technical advice was demolished by increasingly powerful vested interests using arguments of nationalism and patriotism to underscore the costs of reform and to insinuate that the institutions had negative ulterior motives. And finally, the capacity of the institutions to forge a close and trusting relationship with interlocutors in Russia was eroded by the president's shifting loyalties and the new vested interests coming into government. Ongoing economic crisis, however, pushed even the new government back toward reform.

Inflation was soaring. By the end of 1992 inflation in Russia had risen to an annual rate of 1354.1 percent as exports and output dropped dramatically (Operations Evaluation Department 2002, 3), for although inflation had been brought down to 9 percent in the month of August, from October onward it leapt at a monthly rate of 23 percent, 26 percent (November), 25 percent (December), 25.8 percent (January), 24.7 percent (February), 20.1 percent (March) (IMF 1997b and 1997d).

The ruble was losing value, although the IMF data do not support the view that the ruble collapsed after Gaidar lost office as some analysts have averred (Stone 2002, 124, makes this point, see also Odling-Smee and Pastor 2002). In real terms the exchange rate went from a base rate of 100 in July 1992 to 89.5 in December 1992 and actually rose to 95 in January 1993 and again to 101.4 in February 1993 (Balino et al 1997, 21). Very serious problems existed with the ruble area arrangements that had been made with other republics, making it nearly impossible to control the money supply. By spring 1993 the pressure to limit these arrangements was unstoppable.

In this context both the World Bank and the IMF announced concern about the direction of Russian economic policy. World Bank president Lewis Preston criticized Russian policymakers for failing to use loans already allocated to them and condemned the Russian Central Bank for its failure to get a grip on inflation. The World Bank, he argued, would be unable to lend to Russia until the country acted to stabilize its economy (Bush and Lyle, 1993). Meanwhile the IMF resident representative in Moscow announced that the IMF was not ready to approve the proposed $6 billion stabilization fund, underscoring that Russia had failed to meet its IMF target of a budget deficit not exceeding 5–6 percent of GDP in 1992 or in its projected budget for 1993, and that it was unclear that the stabilization fund would be properly used (Bush 1993). The IMF's representative also noted that·a new aid program could not be approved while there was uncertainty over who was in charge of the country. This referred directly to a brewing political crisis.

As the economy descended into a new crisis, Yeltsin's political position was directly challenged. In the Congress of People's Deputies his former political ally, Ruslan Khasbulatov, led a campaign to impeach him. In the wider battle for control between the Congress and the president, deputies in the Congress drafted constitutional amendments that would hugely limit if not extinguish the president's powers (McFaul 2002, 119). Yeltsin's response was to bolster his own position by playing the reformist economic hand. He appointed reformer Boris Fedorov as finance minister and announced a referendum to endorse his presidency and the course of economic reform. He won the referendum, which took place on 25 April 1993.

Up to this point the IMF and World Bank were pointed in their criticisms of the Russian government, which had failed to meet specified targets. Until Russia did so, they argued, the government would not be able to access more loans from the institutions. The Fund demonstrated that it was prepared to enforce its conditionality and withhold lending. The Bank made similar noises. However, their tough positions were swept away by high politics.

Virtually at the same time as the institutions voiced their criticisms, President Clinton was publicly urging the IMF to increase its lending to Russia to $13.5 billion a year and to impose less rigorous conditionality (Whitlock 1993). In a strenuous fit of lobbying, the U.S. administration swiftly put together a package of some $28 billion with a large contribution from the IMF and the World Bank and a rescheduling of Paris Club debt (Stone 2002, 124). This included a lightening of the enforcement of existing conditions and new easier loans.

The new IMF contribution was a generous credit from the brand new Systemic Transformation Facility (STF). The facility was specially created to help with transition, lending to members "experiencing severe disruptions in their trade and payments arrangements due to a shift from significant reliance on trading at non-market prices to multilateral market-based trading." Unlike other facilities the STF carried no standard conditionality, merely requiring that the recipients not "intensify exchange or trade restrictions" (IMF 1993, 60). The STF agreed for Russia in June 1993 was for $3 billion, half of which was agreed immediately with a remaining $1.5 billion to follow after talks on providing more support through a standby arrangement. Once again, as the capacity of the IMF to lend to Russia increased, paradoxically its capacity to influence Russia decreased.

And so too with the World Bank—under intense political pressure to lend more and faster to Russia, even though this was extremely difficult. The Bank's objective was supposed to be to improve social services and restructure various sectors of the economy. However, efforts to disburse sector and project-oriented loans were frustrated by bureaucratic resistance and inertia, and the inability of Russian agencies to implement loans. In 1992 the Bank approved a $70 million loan for employment services and social protection and $90 million for privatization implementation. In June 1993 a further US$610 million Oil Rehabilitation Loan for reform within the oil and gas sector was also approved. Yet by the end of 1994 only 23 percent of approved loans to Russia had been disbursed and about 90 percent of this was the initial Rehabilitation Loan (General Accounting Office 2000, 140).

Bank officials say that they were severely hampered not just by their own lack of expertise on transition issues, but by the fact that they did not have access to high-level officials—nor were they able to develop a stable evolving relationship with Russian counterparts (General Accounting Office 2000, 139). Later the Bank's Operations Evaluation Department would confess: "In the first half of the 1990s, under pressure from shareholders, the Bank approved many technical assistance and investment projects that were overly ambitious, far from ready for implementation, and in sectors with a weak commitment to reform (e.g. oil, agriculture, banking, and highways). . . . Significant project design weaknesses were tolerated at entry in the belief that they could be corrected later" (Operations Evaluation Department 2002, 28). The clash between the Bank's efforts to stick to its own rules and procedures and the preferences of its most powerful shareholders was underscored when the Bank's management held up board submission of a second Rehabilitation Loan until mid 1995 (Operations Evaluation Department 2002, 7).

Although the bargaining power of the Fund and Bank was severely limited by overarching political pressures, there was one place where the Fund exercised persuasive power as it did in the Mexico case. Where it could tilt the balance among domestic actors struggling for power, the Fund's advice or conditions could occasionally be used by reformers to gain an upper hand over others institutions of government. For example, in negotiating the 1993 agreements with Russia, the IMF worked with finance minister Boris Fedorov to strengthen his hand in reining in the Central Bank. Before Russia could access the STF described above, Fedorov urged and the IMF required more restrictive rules governing the way the Central Bank allocated credit. These were subsequently put in place, as described in a later IMF review (Balino 1997; Fedorov 2004).

Was this simply a rewriting of the story by Fund officials and Fedorov himself? Central Bank officials interviewed by Randall Stone argued that the new 1993 restrictions were no big concession since the Bank was already reducing its lending to banks (Stone 2002, 126). In fact, a later report would demonstrate that the Bank had found more covert ways to channel credits to the government and commercial banks (PriceWaterhouseCoopers 1999). However, other sources concur that Fedorov's role in restraining the Central Bank was a crucial one (U.S. State Department 1994), and on Fedorov's own account IMF support was critical to succeeding in this (Fedorov 2004).

Lending into a Political Drama

The situation for the Bank and Fund became yet more difficult as the political situation in Russia turned further against reform and disintegrated. In July 1993, the Supreme Soviet passed a number of measures, including a budget with a projected deficit of 25 percent of GDP. Economists feared that the budget deficit would fuel hyperinflation. Yeltsin feared that he would lose control of an unruly legislature. In turn he appointed reformer Yegor Gaidar to the post of first deputy prime minister on 18 September 1993 just before the *New York Times* reported that the IMF was considering suspending its lending program to Russia because of slow progress on reform (Greenhouse 1993b).

On 21 September, Yeltsin dissolved the legislature by decree, precipitating a bloody showdown with parliamentarians. Their rebellion was supported by tens of thousands of protesters in the streets. But Yeltsin prevailed and subsequently his government, led by Gaidar, passed a series of measures that converged with IMF conditionality. These included bringing the Central Bank under executive control, reducing the deficit, breaking up the ruble zone, and abolishing most export quotas and licenses, which had been lucrative sources of rent. Doubtless here Gaidar was bolstered by the IMF's willingness to suspend the second tranche payment of the STF loan that had been due in November.

Crucially, however, the deficit was reduced by failing to pay wages and pension benefits. This created an immediate backlash bolstering the position of ultra-nationalists and communists who polled 22.8 percent and 12.4 percent respectively in the December 1993 elections. In those same elections Yeltsin succeeded in passing a referendum that granted him enormous powers and greatly diminished the Duma's role. However, this did not boost the position of reformers. Indeed on 16 January 1994 Gaidar resigned, as did Boris Fedorov four days later.

Although by early 1994 the Russian government's capacity and commitment to reform had markedly eroded, outside of Russia political pressures for the international financial institutions to increase lending were intensified. In Washington, officials feared that communists might further strengthen their position and destabilize Russia. This led U.S. vice president Al Gore to call for a loosening of IMF conditionality and senior official Strobe Talbott to call for "less shock and more therapy." Their comments were immediately criticized by Vladimir Mau—a close aide to Yegor Gaidar—as being unhelpful to the reformers within Russia whose main problems lay not with the IMF's position but with Western countries restricting Russian exports (Lloyd 1993, 2).

The IMF and the World Bank were yet again in a bind. They took the unusual step of issuing a joint note justifying conditionality and urging Western countries not to abandon efforts to require Russia to reform (Graham 1994, 2). Within the institutions, senior staff strongly believed that Russia needed to be held to the targets and policy prescriptions on which loans had been based (Odling-Smee and Pastor 2002, and see interviews reported by Stone 2002, 130). However, as the managing director of the IMF would later recount, the political imperatives pushed management to override this view (Camdessus 1996). Both institutions duly agreed to new loans for Russia with the IMF significantly relaxing its conditionality (Greenhouse 1993a, A1; Stone 2002, 129).

Once again Western alarm about political crises in Russia swept away the substance of agreements between the government and the Fund and Bank. The IMF approved a second installment of $1.5 billion from the STF on condition that the government reduce monthly inflation to 7 percent and increase gross international reserves to approximately $10 billion, both by the end of 1994. The World Bank approved six new loans to Russia totaling $1.52 billion for work on highways, financial institutions, land reform, agricultural reform, enterprise support, and oil rehabilitation.

Economic policy in Russia was fluctuating at the time. Pressured by the need to stem capital flight and shore up confidence in the ruble, the government pegged the exchange rate to the dollar and prohibited the Central Bank from extending credit to the government. The immediate result seemed disastrous as the pegged ruble collapsed and fell by 40 percent on "Black Tuesday," 11 October 1994. However, Yeltsin responded by promoting reformer Anatoly Chubais to the position of first deputy premier, permitting him to launch a second stage of economic reforms. The timing was not propitious.

By the end of 1994, as Russian troops began their war in Chechnya, it was clear that the IMF's macroeconomic targets had not been met. Inflation was twice as high as that targeted, and by January was up to 18 percent. The reserves target was missed by a significant margin. Fiscal policy was moving way off track as the government increased spending and failed to improve its tax revenue. Little progress was made implementing the World Bank's loans, indeed by the end of 1994 disbursements on only two of them had begun.

The institutions were in an extremely difficult position. In Washington they were being criticized for imposing conditionality on Russia and at the same time for not ensuring reform was being undertaken. The Senate undertook hearings on the IMF and Russia during which critics argued that conditionality had adversely affected Russia's economic stability and transition to democracy (Riegle

1994). Jeffrey Sachs, for example, who had earlier advocated a "Grand Bargain" embodying orthodox IMF prescriptions for Russia, criticized the Fund's demands for drastic budget cuts, arguing that IMF credits should be used not just to build up reserves, but to assist in the noninflationary financing of the deficit (Sachs 1994). The implications for the Fund and Bank were far-reaching. They make loans on condition that their terms are met. Their leverage is based on their capacity to enforce terms and conditions, withholding further financing where necessary. In Russia it was clear that loan conditions were not being met. Yet still the institutions were being told to lend. Their political masters had, in essence, redefined their mission as a political one, thereby dramatically reducing their bargaining power.

The problem with the new political mission was that it was not a clear one. It was not to bring about political reforms. At most it was to support "reformers" as a route to ensuring economic reform. Yet neither the Fund nor the Bank succeeded in developing a relationship with reformers that might later facilitate more reform through a persuasive influence—as they had done in Mexico. Although their advice conveniently bolstered particular actions at discrete moments—such as the measures to control the Central Bank mentioned above and later in the privatization of 1995—for the most part both institutions were marginalized as political maneuvering continued within Russia through 1995.

Seizing Privatization

By 1995 Russia's policymakers were looking for a way to finance their deficit without creating more inflation. The government's options were very limited, indeed the IMF and World Bank had been criticized for pushing deficit reduction too hard while doing nothing "to find acceptable and non-inflationary ways to finance part of [the deficit]" (Sachs 1994). In 1995 President Yeltsin was also looking for a way to get support from the business elite for his bid in the spring 1996 presidential elections. One solution seemed to offer something to each of these problems—a second phase of privatization.

Beginning in late 1995, the government auctioned off state assets in a loans-for-shares privatization. The bidding process used was neither open nor adequately publicized. Most winning bids fell far short of what was expected and were made by the very same banks managing the auctions. The result was to transfer control of Russia's most valuable assets such as its oil and metals companies to a handful of financial-industrial groups. Helpfully for Yeltsin, these oligarchs returned the favor by offering him a unified block of support in his presidential campaign.

Neither the IMF nor the World Bank had great influence in Russia at this time, but nor did either institution oppose the 1995 loans-for-shares privatization. Each institution was involved in negotiations on their largest loans to date with Russia. Yet each claims that they had no responsibility over the course of the 1995 privatization.

The IMF argues that privatization, being a World Bank issue, was not primarily within its jurisdiction. For this reason, although Fund officials raised concerns about the process, they also argue that they could not link their concerns to any legitimate sanction or enforcement action. The IMF's justification is weakened by two facts. First, privatization has very often been explicitly on the agenda of IMF negotiations with Russia. Indeed, the IMF's April 1995 loan to Russia included a call for further privatization, and the Extended Fund Facility (EFF) approved in 1997 required the Russian government first to announce transparent privatization measures. Second, although Fund officials might have raised concerns, they continued to recommend to the board that disbursements and loans to Russia be completed.

At the time of privatization the IMF's board was disbursing by far its largest ever loan to Russia (a $6.8 billion Standby Arrangement approved in April 1995) with a new exceptionally demanding set of monitoring mechanisms that included monthly as opposed to quarterly reports by a working group comprising IMF staff and Russian agencies, which were reviewed by the IMF's Executive Board. Furthermore, the IMF would approve a further $10.1 billion EFF in early 1996. There was ample opportunity for staff to press their concerns at the very least with the Executive Board of the Fund.

The World Bank's silence on the loans-for-shares issue is equally if not more striking. The institution had played a strong advisory role on privatization from the start. The U.S. General Accounting Office reported in 2000 that a World Bank official in Moscow *did* express serious concerns about the loans-for-shares program but senior Bank officials did not follow this up with any high-level protests (General Accounting Office 2000, 94). Yet the Bank was in the process of approving a large $600 million second Rehabilitation Loan for Russia in mid 1995 (approved on 6 June 1995), a further loan for standards development in November 1995, and yet further loans for bridge rehabilitation, community social infrastructure, and energy efficiency in early 1996.

One explanation for the World Bank's silence on the loans-for-shares issue might lie in the fact that by the end of 1995 the Bank had disbursed less than 10 percent of loans for investment projects that had been approved to Russia. "Improving the Russia portfolio" had become a major priority for the institution (General Accounting Office 2000, 141) and other considerations took second place to the imperative to lend more and faster.

The silence of the Fund and Bank on privatization also reflected other constraints and pressures on the institutions in 1995–96. The high political stakes for the West in maintaining and bolstering the Yeltsin regime increased over this period. By the end of 1995 the Communist Party emerged strongly in the Duma elections and Yeltsin's popularity plummeted. The chances of Communist Party candidate Zyuganov in the spring 1996 presidential election began to look more promising. The IMF and World Bank were under pressure to provide assistance to ensure that the communists stayed in opposition. But this political pressure does not wholly explain the lack of rigor on the part of Fund and Bank experts in analyzing and foreseeing the results of the privatization process.

Each institution also faced incentives to tout its own successes in lending to

Russia as well as to justify them in terms of their official lending criteria. Hence, officially the rationale for more loans even in the face of the loans-for-shares scandal was economic. Both the Fund and the Bank drew selectively on positive indicators of Russian economic performance. Paradoxically each touted the success of Russia's massive privatization in justifying their lending. Early on the IMF's managing director announced that Russia was a "clear leader" in the area of privatization (Camdessus 1994), and the World Bank advertised Russia as "the largest privatization program in history" (World Bank 1997b).

Both the IMF and the World Bank cited the extent of Russia's macroeconomic stabilization in 1995. A ruble corridor had been established in the summer, preserving the value of the currency within a target band set by the Central Bank. Tight monetary policy cut inflation to only 5 percent a month by the end of the year. And the government succeeded in covering the deficit with internal and external borrowing. The Fund could also point to government pledges to cut back on the provision of subsidized credits and trading subsidies and privileges that had been so enormously costly to the Russian economy: one informed estimate valued gross rents in 1992 at 80 percent of GDP (Aslund 1996).

By the end of 1995, the IMF declared that Russia had met all of its macroeconomic targets and that it was largely satisfied with Russia's progress. In fact the IMF was wrong. A 1999 audit demonstrated that Russia misreported and had failed to meet at least two targets in 1995 (PriceWaterhouseCoopers audit 1999). Subsequently the United States General Accounting Office reported on ways to prevent this (General Accounting Office 1999 and 2000).

A careful study of the documents and statements of the IMF and World Bank on Russia reveals the extent of their powerful presumption, indeed ideological belief, in favor of rapid privatization. This had been a fundamental tenet of the Washington consensus since the mid 1980s. Indeed, as mentioned above, by the mid 1990s both institutions were using rapid privatization as a key indicator of its successes in Russia. The assumption in respect of privatization was that new owners of enterprises would push for institutional reforms, such as an increase in their security of property rights over time. In this way privatization was a core part of the technical consensus on how to achieve institutional as well as economic reform.

Yet in Russia the second round of privatization had the opposite effect. The loans-for-shares program led to a once-for-all loss of potential state revenue that a competitive procedure might have netted. Furthermore when the government exercised its option not to repay loans in 1996, it left controlling stakes in the newly privatized companies firmly in the hands of newly established financial institutions. This conferred enormous political power on the oligarchs or financial-industrial groups. Soon they would successfully demand tax exemptions and nonpayment of those taxes for which they were liable. Gazprom, for example, continued to hold billions of rubles in a tax-free "stabilization fund" for investment (World Bank 1998b). Far from demanding the provision of public goods and institutions from the state, the new owners of privatized enterprises directed massive private benefits to themselves. As highlighted in a pathbreaking World

Bank study, far from becoming a competitive market economy, this marked one further step toward Russia becoming a "capture economy" (Hellman et al. 2000).

In Search of Sympathetic Interlocutors

After 1995, the oligarchs entrenched their position in government and across the economy. Partly in response, the IMF and World Bank expanded their prescription for reform. They argued that successful economic reform would require a broader transformation—and deeper conditionality—than originally conceived. Stronger, more transparent, and less corrupt institutions of governance had to be developed alongside structural adjustment and economic reform. The Washington consensus had to be expanded to include "good governance."

In pursuit of the new broader consensus, both institutions became more generous in their assistance to Russia and more rigorous and regular in their monitoring of conditionality. Paradoxically, as their agenda, lending resources, and monitoring expanded, their bargaining and persuasive power seemed further to diminish. The oligarchs were not sympathetic interlocutors to the institutions' new agenda, and only on one occasion did the Fund or Bank seem able leverage tactical support to ensure a specific reform was undertaken.

The presidential elections of June 1996 swept aside the economic agenda in the early part of that year. Anatoly Chubais was rapidly redeployed to run Yeltsin's election campaign—a task greatly assisted by the 1995 privatization, which had delivered not just a constituency but a large source of campaign funding to the president's campaign. He was replaced on 25 January 1996 by Vladimir Kadannikov, an industrialist who had been lobbying hard for subsidies to industry (Rudland 1996).

The president framed his campaign in two contradictory promises. To the outside world he argued that his government would restrain spending, reduce the deficit, and stay the course on economic reform (Parrish 1996). Yet this would be an impossible task if he were to live up to his simultaneous promises to the Russian people to pay wage and pensions arrears and to improve the living standard of the poor (As announced in his New Year's Eve Address to the Nation: Morvant 1996). Subsequently President Yeltsin expanded these promises to include rescheduling $6.7 billion in taxes owed by enterprises and to allocate $2.2 billion to the coal industry in the face of a nationwide miners' strike (Stone 2002, 139).

As the election campaigns raced ahead, Western powers became increasingly alarmed at the prospect of a Communist victory by Communist Party candidate Zyuganov. Predictably, both the Fund and Bank came under pressure to lend more to Russia prior to the election, to bolster Yeltsin's chances. The IMF waived its agreed targets on budget revenue and budget deficit and even turned a blind eye to the dubious accounting methods used by the Central Bank to cover up its failure to meet international reserves requirement (these methods were later detailed in PricewaterhouseCoopers 1999).

Against a background of noncompliance, the IMF offered Russia a new EFF of around $10.1 billion, which would be disbursed monthly over the period 26 March 1996–25 March 1999, and unlocked a comprehensive restructuring of Russia's $38.7 billion debt with the official creditors of the Paris Club in April. The conditions for the loan included further reduction of the fiscal deficit (to 4 percent of GDP in 1996 and 2 percent in 1998) and reduced inflation (to 1 percent a month by the end of the year), structural reforms in privatization and agriculture, and the elimination of all export duties. There was also a new range of conditions such as banking reform, proper auditing of the largest enterprises, and improvements in tax collection that reflected the new technical consensus on good governance.

By 1996, the World Bank shifted its focus away from investment lending at the regional level and into large, quick-disbursing adjustment loans made to the federal government. Between 1997 and 1999 the Bank approved five large loans for structural adjustment and adjustment in social protection and the coal sector, amounting to $4.5 billion and accounting for 84 percent of loans. These loans channeled money straight to the core ministries of the Russian government such as the ministries of Finance and the Economy. One effect was to improve the Bank's access to these officials. Access they got and World Bank staff have said that these loans to the central government facilitated a closer relationship with these agencies (General Accounting Office 2000, 147). However, there is no evidence that the Bank enhanced its leverage over these officials.

Once again in 1996, the West's political aims overrode Fund and Bank conscientiousness in enforcing conditionality. The IMF staff monitoring Russia's progress on a monthly basis had to modify targets to prevent any squeeze on Yeltsin. The Fund was not unaware of Yeltsin's campaign-building but conditionality-breaching largesse. Indeed, just before the IMF Executive Board met in June to decide on the release of that month's credit tranche, it was informed by the government of a transfer of CBR profits to the budget. The board approved the release of the credit nonetheless (Boiko 1996). The first tranche was not withheld until July—after the elections had taken place. As the newspaper *Sevodnya* put it: "Both the Fund experts who conducted the monthly review in Moscow and officials at IMF headquarters in Washington were well aware that too much was at stake at that particular time to raise an international commotion over 'net domestic assets'" (Bekkr 1996).

In the 1996 presidential elections Yeltsin emerged victorious, and so did the oligarchs. Two of the latter were immediately appointed in the new government. Boris Berezovsky controlled two of Russia's oil companies, Sibneft and Lukoil, as well as the television channel ORT and the *Izvestia* newspaper. He was appointed deputy secretary of the Security Council. Vladimir Potanin, who was appointed deputy prime minister, controlled Russia's largest private bank, Oneximbank, which he had set up to finance foreign trade using his knowledge and position as the key communist official concerned in regulating foreign trade under the Soviet regime. He had profited greatly from the privatizations, which took

TABLE 5.2
Russia's shrinking federal tax revenue, 1992–1997 (percentage of GDP)

	1992	1993	1994	1995	1996	1997
Federal tax revenue*	17.8%	11.5%	13%	11.7%	10.7%	10.1%
Federal government expenditure**	26%	20.2%	23.2%	17.6%	22.1%	18.9%

*As calculated by Treisman 1999 from World Bank operational data, taking into account changes in classification of revenues. Treisman notes the importance of regional tax revenue, which is not taken into account in these figures.
**As compiled from IMF, *World Economic Outlook* (May 1998): 100 & (October 1998): 70.

place while he was deputy prime minister, buying stakes in the Russian telephone system Svyazinvest, the oil company Sidanko, and the valuable mining concession Norilsk Nickel, each for a fraction of their real value.

Linked to the rise of the oligarchs, tax collection fell precipitously during the campaign and did not subsequently recover (see table 5.2). Both the IMF and the World Bank became increasingly concerned about the problem of taxation and on occasion the IMF withheld tranches because of inadequate government efforts to improve collection. Yet neither the IMF nor the World Bank had adequate bargaining or persuasive power to touch this problem. The preponderance of tax revenue withheld was owed by a very small number of oligarch-owned companies who had not only become highly influential within the powerful executive but had gained control over most of the print and broadcast media outlets. The World Bank would later estimate that had Gazprom (formerly headed by Victor Chernomyrdin) been required to pay all of its tax obligations in 1995, these would have gone some way toward shrinking Russia's budget deficit by contributing somewhere between 2 and 3 percent of GDP (World Bank 1998b, Box 7.1). However, any move by the government, and by extension any pressure exerted on the government by the IMF, to challenge these interests would inevitably elicit both direct resistance from the oligarchs and efforts to mobilize opinion in their favor—as the subsequent reform-minded government of Kiriyenko would find out in 1998.

As described by politician and reformer Yegor Gaidar, the problem of tax collection was not a normal problem of tax administration. "It was more a political struggle over what constituted the essence of the emerging economic system, whether . . . the relationship between the state and the enterprises was to be regulated by law or whether it would be business as usual, based on political influence and personal contacts" (Gaidar 1999).

The political core of the tax problem became increasingly obvious to the IMF and the World Bank over this time. A few months later, in April 1997, while praising Russia's achievements at cutting inflation, stabilizing the exchange rate, and reducing the government deficit, Michel Camdessus noted that there were still core problems to be addressed, one of which was "the exceedingly close relationship between the government and a number of large enterprises, which allows many to benefit from explicit or implicit tax exemptions, to exploit flaws in the tax system to avoid paying taxes—and even to engage in tax evasion" (IMF 1997c). In 1998 the managing director would speak out yet more stridently against "crony capitalism" (IMF 1998e).

Overcoming Russia's crisis, the Fund and Bank staff came to argue, required deep legal institutional reforms (IMF 1997d; World Bank 2001a). The Fund highlighted the need to create an institutional and regulatory environment that fosters investment and promotes new private sector activity. To this end, the institution recommended reforming the tax system, reducing red tape and bureaucratic corruption, strengthening the judicial system, and improving capital market infrastructure (IMF 1997d). This fit within a more general view of the Bank and Fund that modernizing the state was necessary. To achieve this both institutions advocated accountability, transparency, the rule of law, and an effective judiciary, at the same time as rooting out corruption and building up the state capacity (IMF 1997a, World Bank 1998b).

By the end of 1996 there were powerful obstacles to the IMF or the World Bank wielding influence over Russian economic policy in the areas that the institutions had defined as critical—taxation and good governance. Although Yeltsin had appointed two important reformers to high positions—Anatoly Chubais was made chief of staff and Alexander Livshits was made finance minister and deputy premier—these appointments did not counter the power of the oligarchs and their determination to hinder reform in these areas. More important, as Russia began to develop access to alternative sources of finance from private capital markets, the IMF and World Bank were being supplanted in their role as financiers.

Abolishing Capital Controls—A Moment of Influence?

In 1997 the ever-adaptable President Yeltsin temporarily switched his support and appointed a government of young reformers who seemed keen to take on the oligarchs. Anatoly Chubais and Boris Nemtsov were named as first deputy prime ministers in March 1997. With the encouragement and support of the IMF, Nemtsov, a popular and reforming provincial governor, set about challenging the oligarchs' interests on a range of issues: the elimination of insider privatization, the reform of natural monopolies, and the punishment of tax debtors. The government also took steps to reduce inflation as well as to take on the oligarchs. For example, a special committee was set up under Deputy Prime Minister Chubais in late 1996 to browbeat major companies into paying tax arrears. The workings of this committee soon became a staple of the daily political press (Treisman 1999, 157). That effort was short-lived.

The government's Temporary Extraordinary Commission on Strengthening Tax and Budget Discipline was empowered to seize and sell off the assets of tax debtors. However, such actions, and Fund and Bank support for them, provoked a furious response from the oligarchs, who themselves had become yet more wealthy and powerful from 1995 to 1997 through their investments in the extraordinarily high-yielding GKOs (GKOs being short-term couponless bonds issued by the federal government)(Stone 2002, 150). One of the oligarchs most threatened, the head of the LogoVaz-Sibneft group and close ally of the Yeltsin family, Boris Berezovsky, printed excerpts of letters from the IMF and World Bank to Prime Minister Viktor Chernomyrdin under the headline "Why Does Russia Need a Government of Its Own?" (*Nezavisimaya Gazeta,* 1997, 8). Less than two weeks later the powerful mayor of Moscow, Yuri Luzhkov, weighed in on the same theme of national dependence on the IMF, describing it as a "national disgrace" (RFE/RL 1997a). A growing number of powerful voices were now arguing that the Fund was a threat to Russia's sovereignty—not to mention to their own special privileges.

In spite of the clamor of oligarchs, overall the impact of economic policy in 1997 received plaudits from the IMF. It was "a year of achievement" according to the IMF's first deputy managing director, noting that for the first time since 1992, the economy actually grew. He rightly qualified this latter observation with the words "albeit barely" (Fischer 1998b). In fact, Russia's real gross domestic product increased by 0.3 percent, having declined every year since 1992 (see Table 5.1 above). Russia's budget deficit remained worryingly high at nearly 7 percent of GDP, but the domestic and foreign attractiveness of government bonds encouraged officials to predict that Russia would need no further IMF funds after the full disbursement of the current loan (RFE/RL 1997b). In early January 1998 the IMF completed a delayed review of Russia's Extended Fund Facility and agreed to disburse a further $700 million tranche of that loan.

During this period the IMF used a new window of influence in Russia to push policymakers to liberalize the country's capital account. Russia had earlier agreed to be bound by the provision in the IMF's articles (article VIII) committing members to abolish restrictions on current payments. Initially, however, it had been accepted that Russia could retain some capital controls during a transition period. In early 1997 the IMF and bilateral and multilateral donors began to pressure Russia to dismantle those residual capital controls (this was a standard condition in IMF programs by mid 1990s). The problem for Russia was that while it had a pegged ruble, capital controls were a crucial way of sustaining the value of the currency. So how did the IMF come to exert influence in this area? And why did the IMF not use its influence instead to push for the fiscal and tax reforms? After all, it had marked these out as the highest priority for Russia (Fischer 1998b).

According to one Russian policymaker, capital account liberalization in 1997 was a straightforward quid pro quo. The IMF would be lax in enforcing targets on fiscal policy and restructuring, and in return Russia would liberalize its capital account. It was after all easier for the government to dismantle capital controls than it was to take tough decisions on tax and spending (Aleksashenko cited by Stone 2002, 147). In the battle among policymakers this was the easiest and most likely area in which reform could be leveraged. This was particularly the case in a year when the Russian government could access resources from private capital markets, therefore obviating the need for too stringent a relationship with multilateral lenders. Capital account liberalization could appease the IMF and United States at the same time as ease the government's financing difficulties.

From the IMF's point of view, capital account liberalization not only had the full support of the United States but also of other multilateral organizations, including the Organization for Economic Cooperation and Development (OECD) and EBRD. There was no ambiguity about what external actors wanted and no counterbalancing political influence attempting to dilute that position. Unlike other episodes of conditionality, on this issue there were no political voices in donor countries calling for Russia to be permitted to retain what its Central Bank saw as necessary protective measures. This was the case, even though the IMF itself knew of the fragilities of Russia's banking and financial system, which would facilitate a full-blown financial crisis in 1998 (Fischer 1998b). Capital account liberalization was an issue that the IMF could push—with some success to show afterward, particularly to its major shareholders.

Russia's Central Bank was cautious about easing restrictions, particularly on foreign investor participation in the government securities market. Such a move could attract "hot money," which would fly out of the country in the face of any shock, and there was also real concern about the impact on the domestic banking system. In spite of this concern, in August 1996 liberalization began with the first partial relaxation of restrictions on foreign investment in the GKO/OFZ market. Foreign investors could purchase GKOs through specially controlled bank accounts in specified Russian banks with a requirement that they tie up their investment for a minimum of three months. By November 1996 they had purchased $3.5 billion worth of GKOs in this way, and by mid 1997 some $8 billion, accounting for about 30 percent of the market (Granville 1999). Subsequently the restrictions on foreign investors were relaxed, and by January 1998, as required by the IMF, all restrictions were lifted.

By early 1998 Russia's capital controls had been abolished and access to foreign banks opened up. The Central Bank's capacity to limit the volatility of GKOs and OFZs (ruble-denominated coupon bonds) had been swept away. By May 1998 about one-third of all of these domestic treasury securities were held by nonresident investors (IMF 1998i, 18), most of which were hedge funds (Hale 1998). Since 1995 the yield on GKOs had risen to 110 percent, since the government was paying interest rates of 150 percent on its treasury bills while inflation was around 40 percent. Indeed, as a result Russian banks were putting their funds into GKOs rather than making loans to businesses. There were two serious implications for Russia. First, as capital rushed into the government's coffers there was no hard budget constraint on policymakers—efforts to rein in the deficit or increase tax revenue were bound to be wasted. Second, the rush of foreign capital would test—to the point of breaking—the country's fragile banking and financial system.

In October 1997 contagion from the East Asian financial turmoil forced Russia to defend the ruble by raising interest rates. This in turn increased the already heavy burden of interest repayments on loans and so began a slow spiral into a debt trap. The bond market became overbought and the yields on bonds fell to around 35 percent, shifting speculation to the stock market (Margolin 2000). The fragility of Russia's overall situation was soon exposed—although astonishingly the Fund was upbeat in pronouncing that the country had "successfully fought off contagion effects from East Asia and maintained the currency band" and that "the most important battles in securing macroeconomic stabilization and creating a market economy have been won" (Fischer 1998b).

Meanwhile in October 1997 nonresidents who had rushed into the treasury bill market in droves began withdrawing from the GKO market, leaving the Finance Ministry in search of buyers to refinance its bonds. By late October the Central Bank was forced to intervene to support the bond market, depleting its reserves by about a third in a matter of days even though interest rates were increasing (IMF 1998c, Figure 2.8 at p. 34). Further private foreign inflows were desperately sought. Indeed, by July 1998, accumulated foreign portfolio holdings were nearly 15 percent of Russia's GDP, with the loans from the Fund and Bank amounting to another 4.5 percent of GDP. Russia had become heavily dependent on foreign capital flows.

In March 1998 an ailing and somewhat incapacitated Yeltsin stepped into the political fray, dismissing Chernomyrdin and replacing him with a junior minister Sergei Kiriyenko. This was politically costly. The Duma thrice rejected the appointment of Kiriyenko, and in the end Yeltsin threatened to dissolve the Duma unless legislators agreed with the appointment. Although the new administration brought a zeal and determination to reform in general, and the job of tax reform in particular, unmatched since the early months of 1992, it had no political muscle with which to take on the Duma with its entrenched position against them, nor Gazprom and other oligarchical interests arrayed against it. The results of the tax collection campaign were pretty inconclusive, as reports in the Gazprom owned newspaper *Tribuna* revealed (RFE/RL 1998c). The continuing revenue shortfalls, exacerbated by falling oil prices due to the East Asian crisis and combined with the high debt service burden, which absorbed 36 percent of revenues by July, finally led to crisis in the summer of 1998.

The Crisis of 1998

By May 1998 the GKO market had turned down sharply. One immediate catalyst was the government's failure to attract any bidders for a crucial privatization deal, a 75 percent stake in state oil company NK Rosneft (Dow Jones, 28 May 1998). Unable to attract investment in ruble-denominated securities, the authorities made two large new issues of dollar-denominated Eurobonds in June at successively higher interest rates. The government was fast building up a serious repayment problem. Redemptions and coupon payments would amount to some $1 billion *per week* by May 1999 (IMF 1998i, 18). On 19 June 1998 the Russian government was forced to appeal for foreign assistance as its reserves fell sharply. Capital flight had been triggered by turmoil in financial markets. Fear was rife that Russia could not maintain its high interest payments on foreign debt and defend the ruble. The IMF had earlier withheld disbursement of a monthly tranche of Russia's loan (Freeland 1998).

In late June the IMF approved the previously withheld disbursement amid the beginning of intensive negotiations for a new loan package for Russia. As the crisis developed, so too did intensive diplomatic activity between Washington and Moscow. United States Treasury officials were said to be talking to their Russian counterparts, two, three, or four times a day (Dow Jones 28 May 1998). On 10 July President Yeltsin spoke by telephone to the U.S., UK, French, and German heads of state and the following day to the Japanese prime minister (RFE/RL 1998a).

In July 1998, after difficult negotiations, the IMF announced a total package of some $17.1 billion of new loans for Russia, which included contributions from the World Bank and Japan. It was initially proposed that the World Bank contribute $6 billion to the Russia bailout, a figure that included existing loan disbursements and a third structural adjustment loan for Russia of $1.5 billion, which was approved by the Bank's board on 6 August 1998. In fact the World Bank's contribution ended up being far smaller, with only $1.5 billion committed and only some $400 million eventually disbursed (General Accounting Office 2000, 142: the remainder of the structural adjustment loan was canceled on August 8, 2000).

The IMF was committed to provide $11.2 billion of new funds for currency support. This was an unprecedented use of resources for the organization, which was already stretched due to the huge rescue packages it had extended in South Korea and Indonesia in 1997. Indeed, when the press reminded Stanley Fischer that he had previously said that $10 billion was too much for a single country to draw, the first deputy managing director replied: "Ten billion was too much for us, and we have had to draw on the GAB" (IMF 1998f). He was referring to arrangements not used since 1978 whereby the Fund can borrow from eleven industrialized countries (or their Central Banks). Through this means the Fund raised an $8.2 billion augmentation of Russia's Extended Fund Facility for Russia. The remainder of the new loan was a $2.9 billion credit under the IMF's Compensatory and Contingency Financing Facility, which exists to provide temporary compensation for a shortfall in export earnings. The final package was approved by the Executive Board on 20 July in a nonunanimous vote that reflected difficult politics across the membership of the institution (IMF 1998g).

On both sides of the new multilateral loan package there were significant political difficulties. In the United States, congressional Republicans used the occasion to oppose the Democratic presidency. On 11 June 1998, the U.S. House of Representatives' Republican leadership demanded more information from President Bill Clinton in order to consider the administration's $18 billion funding request for the IMF, arguing that "recent reports of misappropriation of IMF funds in Russia, including the statements of a Russian official, also demonstrate the need for more careful examination of IMF programs" (Kupchinsky 2002). In his reply of 28 July 1998, U.S. treasury secretary Robert Rubin underscored the risk that withdrawing IMF aid to Russia would lead to a market collapse and damaging turmoil in other emerging markets, and that the United States ought "to use the leverage of IMF financing to help the Russian government finally take the myriad steps needed to put its finances on a sustainable path" (Dow Jones, 29 July 1998). The treasury secretary was closely backed by the IMF's deputy managing director whose assessment was that Russia's basics were all in the right direction (Blustein 1998, A16). In the end the administration successfully forced the $18 billion through Congress in the face of significant opposition and debate hostile to the IMF and multilateral lending institutions (Locke 2000).

In other creditor countries, the 1998 loan, coming so soon after the East Asian financial crisis, also provoked opposition within legislatures. In the UK Parliament, the Treasury Select Committee pressed the government to submit an annual report to parliament on IMF issues, the first of which was published in 1999. In France, the National Assembly passed a new law in December 1998 requiring an extensive annual report from the government on the activity of the IMF and France's role therein, and an account of the positions taken by the French executive directors.[6] A similar requirement was passed in Ireland in 1999 (Eggers, Florini, and Woods 2005).

On the Russian side of the equation the legislature also posed obstacles for the new multilateral loans. In the Russian Duma, which had earlier refused to pass IMF-required measures, Speaker Gennadii Seleznev warned that the new loan package could dilute Russian sovereignty and risked passing control of Russia's economic and budget policies to foreigners (RFE/RL 1998b). Eventually measures were approved but as negotiations continued the Russian stock market plunged. The day before Rubin's letter to the Speaker of the House and the IMF's upbeat assessment, the market suffered a 9 percent drop. "It's looking ugly," said one Western economist on 27 July. Said another Western investment strategist: "We're sitting and watching this in shock and horror" (LaFraniere 1998, A1.)

Amid a snowballing financial crisis, the multilateral institutions were determined to act and the Kiriyenko government in Russia made serious efforts to improve its tax collection and reduce the budget deficit. On 6 August 1998 the World Bank approved a $1.5 billion loan to Russia just as the IMF's first deputy managing director traveled to Moscow to review program implementation—a trip described as part of his "war against complacency by Russian officials" (Lyle 1998). On that same day, Russia's Federal Tax Service ordered the seizure of the assets of the oil companies SIDANCO, ONAKO, and Eastern Oil for nonpayment of taxes. Vladimir Popov, head of the department charged with collecting payments from companies in arrears, told reporters that the assets would include buildings, apartments, and cars belonging to the companies' management and subsidiaries. According to Popov, SIDANCO owed 737.8 million rubles ($118 million) and ONAKO 214.5 million rubles. Earlier, Minister of Fuel and Energy Sergei Generalov had announced that SIDANCO and ONAKO would be unable to access export pipelines in August, owing to tax arrears (Corwin 1998). Yet the efforts of the IMF and the government made little impact.

[6] Tavernier 2001, 205.

Overall the massive multilateral loan package did not stave off the crisis. As part of the July 1998 program the IMF helped Russia to convert some of the debt into seven- and twenty-year dollar-denominated Eurobonds, but this affected too little of the overall debt to restore confidence (IMF 1998i, 18). In the last weeks of July 1998, as Treasury bill rates rose and equity prices fell, massive capital outflow put irresistible pressure on the ruble. Only three days after President Yeltsin announced that such a measure would not be taken, Prime Minister Kiriyenko announced on 17 August a 34 percent devaluation of the currency that soon became a de facto float. The prime minister also announced a ninety-day moratorium on some commercial foreign debt and a forced restructuring of short-term government bonds or ruble debt. It soon became clear that the entire $4.8 billion first tranche of support from the IMF had been used up in a failed attempt to support the ruble that served only to assist capital flight. As investors fled, Russia faced not just a *debt crisis* but simultaneously a *currency crisis* as confidence in the ruble evaporated, and a *banking crisis* as fears of bank failures led to a run on the banks.

On 23 August President Yeltsin dismissed the Kiriyenko government and brought Chernomyrdin, the preferred candidate of the oligarchs, back as prime minister designate. The ruble was now in free-fall and on 26 and 27 August the Central Bank suspending trading. Meanwhile, IMF managing director Michel Camdessus flew to Crimea to enter into urgent talks with Chernomyrdin and make clear the dire consequences of populist measures like the printing of money or the reimposition of prices and foreign exchange controls. Camdessus argued instead that Russia must maintain monetary discipline and reestablish exchange rate stability in order to receive any further assistance from the international community (IMF 1998f). As it turned out, Camdessus was talking to the wrong man.

In a move that heralded a resurgence of the Duma and a temporary decline of the power of the oligarchs during the crisis, the parliament refused to endorse Chernomyrdin as prime minister. Yeltsin was forced instead to propose the foreign minister Yevgeny Primakov, who was popular with the Parliament. Primakov then formed a government of Soviet-era survivors like himself, including Yuri Maslyukov, the former head of the state planning agency Gosplan who became first deputy prime minister in charge of economic policy, and Viktor Gerashchenko who had resigned as Central Bank chairman in October 1994 after the last ruble crash. Gerashchenko returned to his old position in place of Sergei Dubinin, who went to work for former prime minister Chernomyrdin at Gazprom, which was still highly successfully avoiding tax payments (Stone 2002, World Bank 1998c).

The new government was far more critical of the Fund than previous Russian governments and its rhetoric was more aggressive. Yuri Maslyukov said of the crisis that "we did not just fall into this pit by ourselves—it was also thanks to our 'skilful' partners in the International Monetary Fund. . . . There is only one way out—we must be understood, and we need help. We demand that help" (Reuters 1998). Russia's threat to default on loans unless international funding was restored was described as "a form of blackmail" by IMF officials (Sanger

1998). The government's proposals for tackling the economic crisis were swiftly criticized by the IMF and the United States. All that said, however, the new government soon proved itself committed to a fairly orthodox tight monetary and fiscal policy and concluded a new agreement with the IMF in July 1999.

Rebuilding the State: What Role for the IMF and World Bank?

After 1998 a further dramatic change occurred within Russia. When President Boris Yeltsin withdrew from politics at the end of 1999, he appointed a fairly unknown successor Vladimir Putin. After Putin won the presidential election in 2000 it was widely thought that his background within the intelligence service and government would put him in a better position than others to "take on" the oligarchs and strengthen the capacity of the Russian state. Certainly Putin's early rhetoric suggested this. An ambitious program for structural reform was outlined by Putin to the Federal Council (upper house) on 3 April 2001 and to the Duma (lower house) on 24 April 2001. In his address to the Duma, the new president spoke of Russia's "rentnaya" (rentier) economy and the need to tackle corruption, poor corporate governance, and the "illegalities" in the past privatizations of Russia's natural resources.

Further enhancing optimism about the government, commentators pointed to Putin's strong working relationship with both houses of Russia's legislature and the way he consolidated the power of the presidency and the federal government. He created seven new "superregions" to facilitate central control over Russia's territory and appointed personnel from the military and intelligence agencies to head six of these superregions (Hanson 2000).

To some degree the oligarchs' underlying control and influence was diminished. For example, Putin went after Boris Berezovsky of Logo Vaz-Sibneft, whose export businesses benefited from the 1998 crisis and currency devaluation that fattened export profits. Using his television channel ORT ruthlessly to discredit Mr. Putin's opponents, Berezovsky had lavishly supported Putin in the 2000 presidential election. Berezovsky was subsequently stripped of most of his media assets, including ORT and opted to exile himself rather than face questioning by Russia's prosecutor general in November 2000. Subsequently his flirtations with Russian party politics were conducted from abroad. After 1998 Vladimir Gusinksy of the Media-Most group saw his Most Bank forcibly merged with rivals Menatep and Oneximbank and he was finally pushed aside in a takeover in 2001 (Fomin 2001).

Other oligarchs retained significant power. Vladimir Potanin of Oneximbank-Interros saw his massive fortune dented but retained his controlling interests in the gas, oil, real estate, and newspapers industries. Alexander Smolensky of the failed bank SBS-Agro seemed seamlessly to relaunch his banking empire (*Pravda* 2003). Under President Putin the oligarchs soon learned to deal in a new way with the Kremlin and presidency. Under Yeltsin, they had significant influence over presidential and gubernatorial elections, government personnel decisions, and government economic policy. Such a deep level of influence in the political machinery of Russia is no longer obvious.[7]

Nevertheless, a handful of oligarchs retain an extraordinary level of ownership and control over large parts of the Russian economy. This makes them a crucial force to be reckoned with, especially in a political system that is lacking in coherent, unified, adaptable alternative sources of power, personnel, and authority. There is weakness and resistance to reform in Russia's state bureaucracy, as well as in coalitions of political parties and the gubernatorial class. Couple these weaknesses with the concentration of economic power in the hands of the oligarchs, and the result makes the ongoing task of reforming the Russian state a hugely ambitious one.

Taxation is extremely difficult in an economy that by 1998 was increasingly based on barter (Gaddy and Ickes 1998). By 1998, over half of all interenterprise payments were being made in barter, and enterprises were increasingly using their tax debts to extract government orders or "offsets" (Commander, Dolinskaya, and Mumssen 2000). This fact led one commentator to conclude that when Putin spoke of strengthening the state, his vision of the state was more one of a "corporate entity" specializing in "the protection of life and property, and coercion services selectively to the business community under guise of 'law enforcement'" (Vassiliev 2000). That said, however, one of Putin's first moves was to push a comprehensive tax-reform package through the Duma, simplifying the tax codes and closing off many loopholes.

Where have these developments left the IMF and the World Bank? Russia's last loan from the IMF was a Standby Arrangement, which expired in December 2000. However, up until March 2002 the IMF was still closely monitoring macroeconomic targets in Russia under its Post-Program Monitoring arrangements (IMF 2002b, 34). Russia still owed the IMF more than SDR5.55 billion, which is about 10.67 percent of the institution's total outstanding resources (IMF 2002g, 168). The institution's potential influence has all but disappeared as Russia's oil and gas revenues have obviated its need for IMF support either in the form of loans or in the form of approval for Paris Club rescheduling. Instead Russia has been repaying its Paris Club debtors and the IMF (Munter 2003).

IMF staff have continued to report positively on dramatic improvements in macroeconomic outcomes in Russia since the August 1998 crisis, citing the strong stimulus to growth provided by the large real depreciation in the currency, and assisted by the sharp increase in international energy prices. Other analysts have commented more critically that the rise in energy prices has led to a new flow of superprofits to Russia's oil-exporting oligarchs. Less positively, the Fund has reported disappointing results in structural reforms, especially in the banking sector and infrastructure monopolies, where plans to restructure the banking, power, and gas sectors have all been repeatedly delayed.

The World Bank's largest ever loan to Russia was the structural adjustment

---

[7] I am grateful to Alexander Zaslavsky (Eurasia Group) for his insights on the position of the oligarchs under Putin.

loan for $1.5 billion approved by the Bank on 6 August 1998 (World Bank 1998d), which was subsequently reduced and restructured into four tranches of US$100 million, US$100 million, US$400 million, and US$600 million. This extended both the period and scope of the loan beyond the original agreement. In subsequent years the World Bank has disbursed a number of smallish long-term loans—mostly of between US$80–150 million and of seventeen-year maturity—including loans for TB and AIDS control, tax administration and fiscal reform, education, and infrastructure (a constantly updated list is available at www.worldbank.org).

Both the IMF and the World Bank have openly recognized that in Russia the political landscape and the lack of development of appropriate institutions have seriously hindered a successful reform process. In the words of the managing director of the IMF:

> It is hard to overemphasize the structural and institutional obstacles to reform that have existed in Russia. . . . Complex political realities have constrained policy options, vested interests have been able to side-track reform measures, and the government has often simply lacked adequate administrative capacity to see difficult reforms through. (IMF 2000a)

Of course this statement reflects similar problems the Fund has faced elsewhere. The World Bank president draws from the Russian experience the lesson that the Bank needs to "structure programs for the possibility of long-term involvement (for institution-building) in Russia" and to "concentrate assistance efforts on areas in which Russians are open to making reform." The Fund seems largely to agree with such a prescription. Yet these lessons overlook some of the factors that drove policies in Russia and at the same time introduce significant new contradictions and tensions into the work of both the IMF and the World Bank.

What Did the IMF and World Bank Get Wrong?

The experience of the IMF and the World Bank in Russia sheds important light on their nature as international institutions. Many expect international financial institutions to act as relatively autonomous agents undertaking technical tasks on behalf of government members who delegate such tasks to them. Yet in Russia, there was no clear-cut delegation. Although the mission in Russia was framed in technical terms befitting the goals and instruments of the institutions, overt political aims underpinned these goals. Although assistance was given according to strictly negotiated conditionalities, these were sidelined when major shareholding governments decided that political exigencies overrode technical qualifications. This occurred in 1993–94 and in 1996 when the West had to be seen as supporting Yeltsin's government against destabilizing Communist and nationalist opposition. The result was to reduce the bargaining power of the IMF and World Bank, diminishing their capacity to enforce the terms they negotiated with the Russian government. Russia highlights the structural constraint within which the institutions work.

When it came to Russia, a perception of "systemic threat" overrode individual country qualifications or the lack thereof. The threat, of course, was not economic. The Russian economy per se does not represent a major part of the world economy. In 1998, for example, the total value of Russia's imports was similar to that of Belgium or Switzerland (IMF 1999a 4–5). Russia's trump card was geostrategic. As a nuclear-armed colossus bordering Europe with a capacity to generate conflict and turmoil spreading right across the continent, Russia commanded attention and special treatment from the West.

Nonetheless, both the IMF and the World Bank had a persuasive power in their negotiations with the Russian government because of their position as centers of knowledge and research about economic policy. Neither the Fund nor the Bank had specific tools or expertise in transforming centrally planned systems into free market economies. Nevertheless, they had a ready set of ideas and prescriptions to offer Russia at a time of uncertainty and crisis. Their technical expertise and data could assist sympathetic and willing Russian officials in formulating policies for the Russian economy.

In their role as persuaders, the institutions faced two kinds of constraints. First, their influence relied on sympathetic interlocutors within the Russian government who were willing and able to push the particular policy preferred by the institutions. Where a policymaker had an interest in pushing a Fund- or Bank-preferred policy, the institutions could coordinate support in favor of the policy, adding incentives and disincentives to the choice, thereby leveraging the negotiating power of those in favor of their preferred policy—as occurred in capital account liberalization in 1997. Where no such internal politics could be played, the institutions had little influence.

The second constraint faced by the institutions was more ideological. Their own experience, preexisting tools, and core beliefs set constraints on how they defined both the problems and the solutions for the transition economies. Their initial prescription for Russia was a standard Washington consensus mixture of structural adjustment, privatization, liberalization, and deregulation. Neither the Fund nor the Bank fully considered the possibility of the catastrophic decline that subsequently occurred in the Russian economy.

More specific critiques of the Fund and Bank point to the institutions' support of policies which were, in retrospect, clearly wrong. For example, the IMF initially urged Russia to retain the ruble zone rather than creating national currencies for the Soviet successor states. This resulted in inflationary pressures, rendering financial stabilization virtually impossible (Goldman 1994, 108–12; Sachs and Lipton 1993; Hansson 1993). The ruble zone benefited a small number of groups such as commodity traders who could exploit the differences in price regulation among various former Soviet republics (Aslund 1999). The cost to Russia was immense. According to the IMF, in 1992 alone it cost Russia 9.3 percent of GDP in financing and 13.2 percent GDP in implicit trade subsidies (IMF 1994a). It was not until 1993 that the Fund took a clear stand against the ruble zone. Of interest to us here is why experts got things wrong. Is there evidence of the problems elaborated in chapter 3, of mindset and ideological blindness in the advice and approach taken by the Fund and the Bank? In at least a couple of major policies, it would seem that there was.

On privatization both the World Bank and the IMF seemed blind to the risks and negative scenarios emerging on the ground. In spite of considerable evidence about the risks of privatization it took a long time for the core Washington consensus presumption in favor of any form of privatization to change. Already by the summer of 1993, in the first round of Russian privatization "insiders had acquired majority shares in two-thirds of Russia's privatized and privatizing firms" and were demonstrating that privatization did not necessarily lead to restructuring and independence from state aid (McFaul 1995, 210). The loans-for-shares privatization of the mid-1990s had yet more dire consequences as discussed in the previous section. It was not until the end of the 1990s that economists within the Fund and Bank began to examine the importance of sound institutional frameworks for successful privatization, and the costs of privatization in the absence of such institutions.

The gaps in the approach to privatization taken by the IMF and the World Bank are highlighted by the World Bank's more recent work demonstrating how privatization can create or strengthen oligarchs who "capture" the state. These oligarchs or captor firms do not put pressure on governments to strengthen institutions. Rather, they purchase advantages directly from the state, such as individualized protection of their property rights. In what are now labeled "capture economies," privatization erodes the capacity of the state to provide necessary public goods and institutions. Instead the state becomes a provider of enormous private benefits, which accrue to the owners of newly privatized firms. Nowhere has this process been clearer than in Russia, which ranks as one of the most highly captured of twenty-two former Soviet and transition economies (Hellman et al. 2000).

On exchange rates and capital account liberalization, the IMF's advice and prescriptions for Russia were ill-advised. Indeed, a later research paper by IMF senior economists would detail the issues and vulnerabilities arising from capital account liberalization (Prasad et al. 2003). In negotiations for the 1995 Standby Agreement, the IMF persuaded Russia to put in place a crawling band exchange rate (IMF 1996, 13). Russia was then urged to open its capital account in negotiations for the 1996 EFF loan, thereby permitting foreign portfolio investment in government bonds and shares (IMF 1997b). Both measures reflected Fund orthodoxy, which was maintained until 1997. The IMF prescribed the crawling band exchange rate to countries as an anchor against inflation. Nonetheless, capital account liberalization, high on the agenda of the United States, had become an article of faith within the organization. Indeed until 1997, moves were afoot led by the United States to amend the Fund's Articles of Agreement to permit it greater jurisdiction in this area. Yet both parts of this orthodoxy proved risky and particularly in combination in the context of globalizing capital markets.

The East Asian crisis definitively exposed the dangers of a fixed exchange rate and capital account opening in economies where a country's banking and financial institutions were ill-prepared to cope with a flood of short-term capital. Surprising, however, is that it took this long for the Fund's experts to revise the orthodoxy. Recall that the IMF had advised with equal enthusiasm both these measures in Mexico in the early 1990s. At the very least, this had greatly exacerbated Mexico's crisis of 1994–95 (see chapter 3). In Russia, in 1998 the results proved equally disastrous.

From the Russian point of view, capital account opening permitted the Russian government to depend increasingly on short-term foreign flows of capital in order to finance its budget. As the Treasury bill yield in Russia increased, more and more capital flowed in. One critic writes, "The Fund reacted to the high yield on treasury bills, by persuading the Russian government to open its treasury bill market to foreign investors rather than pushing for a smaller budget deficit" (Aslund 2000, 20). This criticism seems to ignore the fact that the Fund staff had been urging tax reform and a reduction of the budget deficit throughout negotiations with Russia in 1996 and 1997. However the dangers of these short-term flows were underestimated—just as they had been in Mexico in 1994, even though some Fund staff were already analyzing the problems, fragilities, and vulnerabilities associated with this level of external borrowing (Kapur and Van der Mensbrugghe 1997). The orthodoxy that such flows did not pose a serious sovereign risk seemed to have remained in place, leading to what Fund staff themselves accept was poor advice on these issues in the case of Russia in 1996–97 (Fischer 2001).

Why did the IMF seem to offer poor advice? The Fund was caught between powerful members on one side and scarce resources on the other. The United States pushed the IMF to lend at particular junctures such as in 1993 and 1996 to support Yeltsin—regardless of his economic policies—and to avoid turmoil in the markets when the financial crisis occurred in 1998. In these cases decisions to lend to Russia were being taken outside of the IMF and this left the institution with little negotiating or enforcement power in respect of conditionality. However, in other cases the IMF had more influence.

In respect of the 1993 and 1995 privatizations and the 1997 decision to liberalize Russia's capital account, the IMF was more involved. Each of these decisions was driven by the Russian government's need to find a way to fund the government deficit. The IMF's advice on this matter was heavily constrained by its own lack of resources and alternatives. Other than exhorting tax reform and deficit reduction, the institution had neither the resources nor a ready set of ideas to propose or provide an alternative way for the Russian government to finance its deficit. It was unable to mobilize more resources. It was ideologically entrenched in the belt-tightening solution. Equally importantly, the institution was constrained by the interests and capabilities of Russian interlocutors. Whether or not policies were being proposed or pursued in a rational sequence, the incentive for the IMF was to seize any opportunity to implement policies which the institution and its major shareholders preferred. In so doing the institution could at least point to some success in implementing reform and change within Russia and thereby justify its ongoing lending.

Overall in Russia the IMF worked within a structural constraint imposed by its most powerful shareholders. Its actions were also shaped by institutional constraints imposed by its scarce resources and its entrenched contractionary approach to economic reform in a crisis. Finally, it was politically constrained by its dependence on Russian interlocutors to take up and implement specific reforms. Working within these three sets of constraints, perhaps the most serious weakness in the IMF's approach lay in its sanguinity toward Russia's political, legal, and economic institutions and the presumption that they would materialize and strengthen as an organic part of market reform. The World Bank was equally guilty of this.

In its sectoral work in Russia, the World Bank has been accused of "pouring money into central government authorities of notoriously corrupt industries such as coal or agriculture" (Aslund 2000, 26). In total the World Bank has approved $1.525 billion of loans for coal sector adjustment in Russia since 1996 with the aim of making the coal sector more efficient and ensuring social protection for laid off and disabled miners. Critics allege that the Bank's assistance to the coal sector has in part "disappeared down a black hole" and that in 1997, "instead of controlling how the money was spent, the bank handed over cash in exchange for Kremlin promises to reform the industry" (Russian Reform Monitor 316, 1997). The Bank's own staff admit to the constraints they have faced in lending in this area. These include "the lack of stable top management in government" and "the lack of fundamental reform in the banking sector, the lack of clarity in private sector development and the lack of clear government policy as regards oil, gas and coal are constraints" (World Bank 2001a, 7).

Obviously the World Bank is neither equipped nor permitted by its constitution to enter into wholesale political transformation in borrowing countries (nor is the IMF). That said, we still need to ask why the Bank made substantial loans when it knew (or should have known) that institutional weaknesses in Russia would render many of the loans ineffective. The Bank itself admits that in Russia its "efforts have not borne fruit to date on a scale commensurate with the increase in Bank exposure" (World Bank 1999a). Indeed, the Bank's lending to Russia has at times had "the poorest performance in the World Bank's portfolio, for countries with significant borrowing" (General Accounting Office 2000, 70).

One explanation for the lending in spite of inadequate reform was pressure from its most powerful shareholders. As noted above, in 1994–96 the institution came under intense pressure from Washington to increase its lending; in effect this was the structural constraint within which the Bank's work proceeded. But there were institutional driving forces as well. The World Bank exists to make loans. Its large staff earn their salaries by preparing loans that meet the approval of the board. IBRD loans are then repaid with interest, which pays for the working expenses of the Bank. In other words, there are powerful internal incentives within the organization which encourage staff to maximize lending.

The Bank's failures in Russia have led to a constant rethinking of the Bank's mission and its prescriptions. In its coal sector loans to Russia, for example, the Bank has embarked on a more explicitly institutional approach to identifying necessary organizational mechanisms, processes, and institutions through which to work (World Bank 2001a). In effect, the Bank is attempting to overcome the political constraint both it and the IMF work within. Finding stakeholders who are both willing and able to use loans and implement projects or conditionality is one aspect of that constraint, but of course, such policymakers will not always exist and the experience of both institutions is that they do not necessarily materialize in the face of external incentives and pressures.

Both the IMF and the World Bank set out on their mission in Russia with the aim of promoting transition by implementing the core elements of the Washington consensus. What became apparent in Russia through the 1990s was that the core missions of the Bank and Fund could not be achieved in the absence of a deeper development of institutions, rules, norms, and state capacity across Russia. In this sense mission creep has occurred in both organizations. The IMF and the World Bank soon realized that policy prescriptions had to take much greater account of institutions and the political, legal, and social environment in which economic policy was being attempted.

By the late 1990s, a much revised Washington consensus had been drawn up casting the original mission of the Fund and Bank as "first generation reforms" and adding to them a new set of "second generation reforms." These labels "first" and "second" generation give a sense of logical chronology to the mission and evolution of Fund and Bank conditionality. This is misleading. Perhaps one of the lasting lessons of their work in Russia in the 1990s was that some "second generation" reforms need to come before the "first generation" reforms. If privatization is to result in the necessary restructuring and growth, the process needs to take place in a well-regulated, transparent way and subsequent owners need to be regulated and taxed in an appropriate way. Sectoral adjustment loans will only have an impact if they are disbursed through institutions that are effective and accountable.

As mission creep has expanded the activities of the IMF and the World Bank, so too it has increased the challenges posed to them in implementing projects and conditionalities. So-called "second generation" reforms take much longer to achieve than traditional goals and certainly longer than the average short-term IMF loan or even the somewhat longer average World Bank loan. They are also more difficult to monitor. Both institutions are evolving new measures to try to capture institutional reforms. Finally, it is not clear that the staff of the Fund and Bank have the expertise and experience to ascertain and advise governments on the development of sound institutions of governance. Probing more deeply, it is not obvious that there are universal aspects to this expertise that the Fund and Bank could usefully collect and aggregate.

Will rethinking reform have an effect? The Fund and Bank have worked within three constraints in Russia. These constraints have been described above as structural, institutional, and political. When experts within the institutions refine their vision of how to achieve transition and development, it is not necessarily the case that their learning will result in different advice or priorities. The institutions rely on a combination of negotiating power derived from their creditor members and the material incentives they can offer, as well as persuasive power deriving from the expertise of their staff. In any one case the influence of the IMF or World Bank may be subject to overriding political imperatives, resource constraints, and other institutional exigencies, and politics within borrowing countries. However, experts within the institutions have a power to define what is possible and to present and probe the implications of any given set of policies. In so doing they cannot only influence choices made within the abovementioned constraints, but also inform those who impose the constraints.

Chapter 6

MISSION UNACCOMPLISHED IN AFRICA

Sub-Saharan Africa came to rely heavily on the IMF and the World Bank during the 1980s. The 1970s oil price rises, the raising of U.S. interest rates and subsequent contraction in the global economy in 1979, the appreciation of the U.S. dollar, and the ongoing volatility of commodity prices rocked the continent. Deep domestic policy weaknesses and poorly aimed interventions by Cold War rivals, former colonial powers, and aid donors further enfeebled African countries who tried to deal with these problems.

In the face of a continentwide crisis, the IMF and the World Bank became frontline purveyors of advice and conditional resources for Africa. The stakes were high for both institutions, as expressed by World Bank president Barber Conable in April 1986:

> The role and reputation of the Bank Group is at stake in Africa. . . . We have said publicly . . . that we are giving Africa the highest priority. . . . We have been telling Africa how to reform, sometimes in terms of great detail. . . . If these programmes fail, for whatever reasons, our policies will be seen widely to have failed, the ideas themselves will be set back for a long time in Africa and elsewhere. (Kapur et al. 1997, 730)

Africa was recognized as a serious test for both the IMF and the World Bank.

Africa was potentially a showcase for the technical expertise of the institutions because unlike Mexico and Russia, the country-level work of each international institution was not overridden by threats to international financial stability or the need to stabilize a nuclear arsenal. Nowhere was good quality economic advice more needed. Many African governments had limited capacity to analyze global economic trends and shocks, yet their economies are hugely influenced by such forces. The IMF and World Bank also had a very strong bargaining position in sub-Saharan Africa. Borrowing governments faced a disastrous external position and most had few other sources of finance. The Fund and Bank were not only lenders in their own right but gatekeepers to all other aid since individual donor governments followed behind their accreditation, loans, and programs.

In 2002 both the Fund and Bank published evaluations as to why their loans, advice, and conditionality seem to have failed on the continent (World Bank 2002c, Independent Evaluation Office 2002). Scattered through their reports we find evidence of the core factors discussed in this book so far. The advice they offered to governments was not always right. Politics within borrowing countries, and a lack of sympathetic interlocutors and propitious political institutions, made their jobs difficult. And the preferences of their major shareholder sometimes eroded their bargaining power or interfered in other ways. This chapter teases out these factors and explains what drove the mission of the IMF and World Bank in sub-Saharan Africa.

Defining the Mission

In the early 1980s the IMF and World Bank plunged into a widespread debate about what kind of economic reform would work in Africa. Up until the late 1970s most developing countries had favored a statist approach to development, using economic planning, import-substitution-industrialization, price controls, credit rationing, state-owned enterprises, and government control of agricultural marketing (Van de Walle 2001, Lofchie 1994, Killick 1989, Waterbury 1999). In Africa the approach was reiterated in the Lagos Plan of Action set out by the Organization for African Unity in 1980. The concern of African leaders advancing the plan was to shift the continent away from its dependence on the export of basic raw materials, which "had made African economies highly susceptible to external developments" (Economic Commission for Africa 1980, Preamble). To this end, the plan focused on increasing Africa's self-reliance, promoting industrialization, and building up regional and subregional cooperation and integration.

The Lagos approach to development faced two severe challenges in the 1980s. First, it required resources and by the early 1980s most African countries were in economic crisis. Hit by the increase in oil prices in 1973–74 as well as a slump in commodity prices, many had increased their borrowing in the 1970s so that by 1980 they faced a world economic downturn with a huge debt burden on their backs. There was a huge gap between the resources required for a renewed push toward industrialization and what was available. External donors were unlikely to come forward, in part because industrialized countries faced problems of inflation and a downturn in their own economies. Also skepticism had grown among governments in several industrialized countries about the statist approach to development. This was the second challenge faced by the Lagos approach.

The ideological climate in donor countries changed dramatically in the early 1980s. In the United States, the United Kingdom, and Germany, President Reagan, Prime Minister Thatcher, and Chancellor Kohl espoused a new antistate, antigovernment, free-market rhetoric. Their hostility to government spending, industrial policy, and the welfare state soon spread into their view of aid. Suddenly the focus was on the failures of development policy in the 1970s (Bauer 1984, Tucker 1977). In the worst cases in Africa the state-owned, state-driven economic model had created and sustained a kleptocratic state. Across the continent as a whole, economic development seemed at the time to have failed. In the twenty years from 1960 to 1980 the average annual rate of growth for Africa was about 4.8 percent, dropping to 2.9 percent for the least developed countries (Economic Commission for Africa 1980). At the time these figures were treated as disastrous, although in retrospect they look like a golden age of development on the continent. For example, over the period 1990–2001 Africa suffered a negative 0.2 percent average annual percentage decline in gross national income (World Bank 2003, chap. 1).

Against the background of scarce aid resources and skepticism about state-centered development, the IMF and the World Bank defined conditionality for Africa in the 1980s. Two important choices underpinned the approach they took. First, they treated the primary cause of the 1980s crisis in sub-Saharan African countries as internal rather than external to each country. Eschewing African leaders' concerns about external shocks and constraints and how these might be mitigated (a central theme of the Lagos Plan), the institutions focused their attention on actions indebted governments needed to take. They chose to turn away radically from the state-centered industrialization model, which had prevailed until the end of the 1970s, and to focus on reducing the state in the hope that this would enhance the role of the private sector.

The IMF's analysis began first and foremost as a requirement that governments undertake stabilization policies reducing the budget deficit and stemming inflation. This was evident in the conditions attached to loans during the 1970s. The Fund's largest loan at the time was to Zambia, which took out its first standby arrangement with the IMF in 1973 when its border with Rhodesia was closed by that country's white-controlled minority government of Ian Smith, who was trying to suppress the majority struggle for control in that country. Among many other effects, the border closure severely disrupted Zambia's commercial transportation system, decimating the country's trade (Boughton 2001, 787). In 1976 and 1978 Zambia took out two further IMF loans, this time as its economy, heavily dependent on copper exports, was rocked by shifts in the world copper price. In each program the Fund required the Zambian government to take measures to reduce inflation and trim the deficit. In these terms Zambia succeeded and indeed this spurred further IMF offers of assistance (IMF External Evaluation 1998, 95; Callaghy 1990, 290; Boughton 2001, 291). However, a 50 percent reduction in the deficit in 1976–79 was essentially achieved by cutting recurrent and capital expenditure, and this policy soon caused a political backlash that wiped out the gains of reform (Callaghy 1990, 290).

What the IMF soon recognized was that stabilization measures worked only as a short-term measure. In and of itself stabilization did not enhance a country's capacity to repay the Fund. Indeed, even as Zambia met its core program conditions, its debts mounted alarmingly, and by the early 1980s Zambia could no longer repay the IMF in a timely fashion (Boughton 2001, 787). For the IMF this spelled out the need for deeper measures of "structural adjustment," while critics argue that the case of Zambia in the 1970s underlined the extenuating impact of external factors—political, strategic, and economic.

The World Bank's approach was very similar to that of the IMF. In 1981 in a report named after its coordinator Elliot Berg, the Bank set out a tough critique of African governments for failing to provide incentives for agricultural growth, discouraging the private sector, poor public sector management and investment, and poor exchange rate and trade policies. The Berg report underlined the need for the countries of the region to "adjust" (World Bank 1981). Many have treated this as a statement of the "technical consensus" of the time. That consensus, however, was highly contested outside of Washington, D.C.

The World Bank's diagnosis of Africa's economic position in 1981 created a storm of controversy. As historians of the Bank later recorded, "Never before had the Bank been as publicly critical of such a large group of borrowers" (Kapur et al. 1997, 719). At the April 1982 meeting of the Economic Commission for Africa the report was declared to be "in fundamental contradiction with the political, economic and social aspirations of Africa" (Economic Commission for Africa 1982). Of course, one would expect this response from those most heavily criticized in the report. However, African countries were not alone in arguing that the multilateral institutions were taking insufficient account of factors beyond their control such as terms of trade, international economic conditions, and climatic and regional security problems. Nor were they the only ones to reject the consensus expressed in the Berg report. Strong critiques were also expressed at the 1982 meetings of the OECD Development Assistance Committee, by Arab/OPEC countries, the European Economic Community, the United Nations Development Program, and by the United Nations Children's Fund (UNICEF).

It was not strictly true to say that the IMF and World Bank were ignoring external factors or exogenous shocks. The Berg report recognized compounding factors beyond governments' economic policy such as the rise in oil prices, slow growth in industrialized countries, adverse climatic conditions, civil and military strife, and donor policies that supported and even encouraged inappropriate domestic strategies and institutions (Kapur et al. 1997, citing internal World Bank memoranda, 716–17). However, these factors were not emphasized in the prescriptions of the report. The importance of exogenous shocks was recognized in the IMF in 1963 when a Compensatory Financing Facility was established for countries affected by commodity price shifts. But such a facility could only ever provide short-term alleviation of the problem. Furthermore, limited funding and limited shareholder support rendered it very difficult to build on that approach in the 1980s.

The alternative to the tough stabilization approach taken by the IMF and World Bank was a more explicitly gradualist approach to reform as advocated by many development economists at the time and through the 1980s. The Economic Commission for Africa produced an African Alternative Framework as a conceptual starting point, although this did not include specific program designs (Economic Commission for Africa 1989). A more specific alternative was drawn up by an independent team of advisers to Uganda, sponsored by the Canadian International Development Research Centre, who advocated a program of economic stabilization and reform while retaining several key elements of the existing system of centralized planning and control (Uganda Economic Study Team 1987). At the core of gradualist alternatives was an attention to attenuating the vulnerability of African economies to world markets, exogenous economic shocks, and their reliance on exporting primary commodities—in the case of Uganda 90 percent of its export earnings came from global coffee markets (Loxley 1986).

In Tanzania in 1980–81, Robert McNamara arranged, with the agreement of the government of Tanzania, a three-person "wise-men's group" to attempt to find an accommodation between the IMF and Tanzania. After about a year's work by expatriate and local staff an alternative adjustment program was developed. It placed much greater emphasis on supply-side expansion rather than demand-side restraint, took much greater care with the income distributional implications of the required macroeconomic adjustments, and more gradual implementation. That said, in the end, both the IMF and Tanzania turned it down (McDonald and Sahle 2002).

Commodity exports lay at the core of the problem for many low-income developing economies. Their reliance on exporting commodities laid a vicious economic trap for three reasons. First, access to markets for commodities was (and still is) tightly controlled by industrialized countries who instead of opening their markets, operate tight discretionary policies. Second, the price and demand for primary commodities is in a long-term decline, which means that even if the volatility in world prices for commodities is alleviated, an alternative long-term strategy is still required. Finally, the possibilities for poor countries to pursue a longer-term strategy of moving away from raw commodities into semiprocessed and processed goods are blocked by industrialized countries who apply higher and higher barriers to these goods, effectively kicking away the development ladder from any countries trying to move up it: a 1988 United Nations Conference on Trade and Development (UNCTAD) study showed industrialized countries were applying twice the level of nontariff barriers to manufactured goods from developing countries compared to what they were applying to manufactured trade with each other (UNCTAD 1988, Chakravarthi 1989).

An alternative approach to Africa's crisis in the 1980s would recognize that all small, low-income economies were being buffeted by factors beyond their control, including shifts in terms of trade, in capital flows, and in world interest rates. Calling on small, low-income economies to adjust their own economies was like exhorting passengers in a lifeboat to paddle faster when their raft is in the middle of the Atlantic Ocean in a hurricane. No matter how impressive the efforts of the passengers, it is unlikely that their paddling will bring them to safety. Without a coherent approach to international conditions, it was clear to some economists that the "adjustment" programs being foisted on one country at a time would not work. The fallacy in the Fund and Bank's approach was, as Tony Kil-lick expressed in 1990, that adjustment "has come to be viewed primarily as something to be undertaken by deficit countries, with no equivalent pressure for action on surplus countries" (Killick 1989, 1990).

The problem for Fund or Bank staff, even if sympathetic to this approach, was twofold. A different approach required resources that did not seem to be avail-able; and it countered the new ideological predilections of their most powerful shareholders. The support and influence of major shareholders in the Fund and Bank was a critical feature of the institutions' work in Africa in the early 1980s. Having extended loans to African countries throughout the 1960s and 1970s for a variety of geostrategic, postcolonial, economic, and domestic political reasons, the industrialized countries found themselves in relationships with aid-dependent states that could not repay even the most concessional loans. They turned to the IMF and World Bank for help and the institutions duly became more active in Africa.

Loans from the IMF and World Bank in the 1980s reflected new stringent con-straints: a squeeze on resources as their industrialized country members re-sponded to general economic downturn; and a new ideological imprimatur imposed very rapidly and forcefully in each institution when the Reagan admin-istration took office (Boughton 2001, Kapur et al. 1997, interview with former U.S. IMF Executive Director Charles Dallara 1995). These constraints meant that it was easier for the IMF and World Bank to call on borrowers to tighten their belts than it was to extract more resources from industrialized country members, or indeed even their cooperation in macroeconomic coordination. Further re-inforcing this approach was the fact that as the institutions became more involved in lending to Africa, their priority became to ensure that short-term repayment schedules were met and hence their own resources assured.

Implementing the Mission in the 1980s

By the end of the 1980s both the IMF and the World Bank had each staked sig-nificant material and intellectual resources in their work in Africa. They coor-dinated the region's relations with creditors, setting down the conditions debtors needed to meet in order to continue borrowing not just from the institutions themselves but from all donors. This position gave the international financial in-stitutions significant bargaining power since sub-Saharan African countries be-came massively indebted throughout the decade. As illustrated below, the total debt of countries on the continent doubled between 1979 and 1985 and dou-bled again by the early 1990s. The value of their external debt as a share of gross national product (GNP) rose from around 25 percent in 1980 to more than 80 percent in 1994. As the IMF and World Bank became more involved in Africa, indebted countries began to use bilateral loans from individual donor agencies to repay the IMF and the World Bank who were necessarily their "preferred creditors." The result was both to create reverse flows of funds to the IMF (see

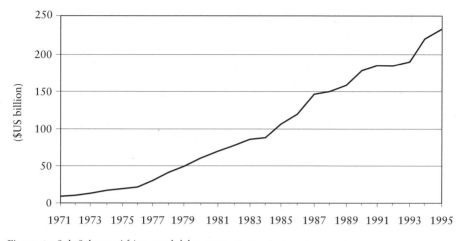

Figure 6.1 Sub-Saharan Africa, total debt, 1971–1995

figure 6.3 below) and to create strong political pressure for a change in the debt strategy.

The IMF was at the heart of the rescheduling of African debt. Any country needing to reschedule its debts to governments had first to conclude a deal with the IMF and then present itself to the "Paris Club" to negotiate a new repayment schedule. The Paris Club was (and still is) a forum in which creditor governments could gang up on individual debtor countries, demanding concessions defined by the IMF. The process has been described by participants as "a deliberately complex obstacle course, full of chicanery" (James 1996, 523) and as a necessarily "unpleasant affair" (Rieffel 1985, 15).

The reschedulings of the 1980s led to a vast increase in the debt burden of African countries. As debt-service payments were postponed outstanding debt was increased as debt-servicing obligations were added to the capital sum. While

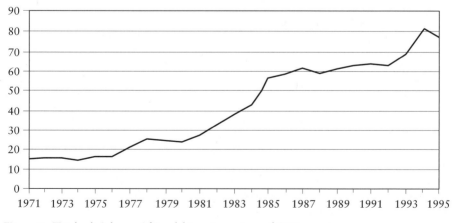

Figure 6.2 Total sub-Saharan Africa debts as percentage of GNP, 1971–1995

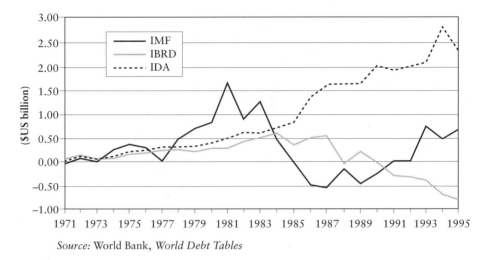

Source: World Bank, *World Debt Tables*

Figure 6.3 Sub-Saharan Africa, net flows of lending from international agencies, 1991 –1995

the IMF lay at the heart of the rescheduling process, the World Bank attempted to coordinate donors more generally through consultative group meetings for donors on a country-by-country basis, and on specific sectors. This would later be described as a particularly thankless task (Kapur et al. 1997, 739) but it included the creation in 1988 of the Special Program of Assistance for Africa, which was supposed to act as a focal point for coordinating the balance of payments portion of external assistance to sub-Saharan Africa with all major official donors.

A second role the IMF and World Bank played in respect of Africa was as lenders to debt-ridden African countries. But IMF creditor nations seriously limited the resources the institutions were willing to lend to Africa. In March 1986 the Structural Adjustment Facility (SAF) was created in the IMF with $3.2 billion to provide loans to the poorest countries (defined as those eligible for assistance from the Bank's International Development Association) with balance of payments difficulties. However, after strong U.S. opposition to new or easy money, the facility was meagerly funded from repayments on previous loans to the IMF's Trust Fund, and accompanied by particularly stringent conditionality (Boughton 2001, 646).

A second attempt to increase IMF lending was made in late 1987 when the Enhanced Structural Adjustment Facility (ESAF) was created, which had larger funding and offered a longer support framework (IMF 1988, 120). Again however, the United States was very reluctant to contribute to a new facility. The U.S. administration argued that it needed to concentrate on securing appropriations for the International Development Association (IDA) from Congress and refused to countenance selling some of the IMF's gold stock in order to finance the new facility (and U.S. approval was a sine qua non since such as sale required 85 percent of total voting power on the Board of the Fund). Eventually the United States made a very modest contribution of about 4 percent of the total grant commitments of the ESAF, leaving it to the IMF to establish a trust fund negotiated with ad hoc contributions from other countries, among whom Japan became by far the largest contributor.

The Enhanced Structural Adjustment Facility magnified the bargaining power of the IMF vis-à-vis Africa. It combined much-needed loans with particularly far ranging and high-level conditionality covering medium-term policy changes and short-term monetary and fiscal management. It was a prerequisite for loans from all other bilateral donors and other international funding programs. Fund conditions were thus "at the top of the hierarchy of donor conditionality" not because of the amount of resources that the Fund transferred but because the Fund was the lead coordinator (IMF External Evaluation 1998, 26).

The World Bank's role in the adjustment process was a complementary one to that of the IMF. The Bank's agenda was to reshape the role of the state and increase the role of markets and the private sector in African economies. In practice, however, the Bank soon found that its most feasible goals were to liberalize trade policies and to devalue overvalued exchange rates. These goals were much easier to achieve than deeper institutional reform within borrowing countries; furthermore liberalization and currency reform were prerequisites for ESAF lending. Within this framework, the World Bank increased its lending to Africa through its concessional arm in the 1980s (see figure 6.3 above) and increased its overall stake in the continent. During the early 1980s the Bank came to deploy the largest share of staff and budgetary resources to sub-Saharan Africa: a third of its regional staff resources, an increasing percentage of research time producing numerous special regional reports, and a plethora of special initiatives and programs launched (Kapur et al. 1997, 731–72). The Bank's concessional lending to Africa increased from less than a quarter of IDA from 1977 to 1979 to nearly half of IDA from 1988 to 1990 and was further increased by a Special Facility for Africa created in January 1985 based principally on contributions from France, Italy, the Netherlands, Germany, Japan, the United Kingdom, and a transfer from the Bank's net income (Kapur et al. 1997, 733). Much of the Bank's new lending was aimed at bringing about policy reforms within African borrowing members. Obviously, to be effective in this role more than monetary incentives were needed.

A third role, played by the IMF and World Bank in Africa in the 1980s, and by far the most contentious, was their attempt jointly to induce particular economic reforms. Their roles in coordinating assistance and lending to African countries gave them some bargaining power. However, as we saw in Mexico and Russia analyzed in earlier chapters of this book, the IMF and World Bank depend on sympathetic national policymakers to bring about policy change. Their interlocutors need to be interested in pursuing policies prescribed by the IMF and World Bank. Furthermore, they must be situated within institutional arrangements, which permit them to implement such measures. In Africa, the Fund and Bank attempted to shape economic policy in what they saw as a hostile political context—they were somewhat weak and lost in an alien terrain. By contrast, critics saw them as tremendously powerful and arrogant—blind to the political needs and constraints of even the most well-intentioned policymakers. So how powerful were they?

The case of Senegal, a leading recipient of aid per capita in Africa from 1980 to 1987, illustrates the way politics, economics, and conditionality were intertwined. In the late 1970s economic crisis and a collapse in revenue from peanut exports on which Senegal depended brought reformer Abdou Diouf to power, first as prime minister and then as president (Mbodji 1991). In a first flurry of reform, Prime Minister Diouf launched an adjustment program with the World Bank supported by a $60 million structural adjustment loan approved on 18 December 1980 (World Bank 2004a) and a loan from the IMF's Extended Fund Facility. The IMF loan carried tough conditions requiring the government to cut its current account deficit by more than half, almost double net public savings by 1985, increase overall investment from 16 percent in 1981 to 18 percent in 1985, and achieve a 4 percent annual growth rate of GDP (World Bank 1989e; Ka and Van de Walle 1994, 309).

Both multilateral loans soon ran into difficulties. Bad weather affected exports and necessitated greater food imports, public debt was higher than originally admitted, and fiscal revenues actually declined from 1981 to 1984 (Ka and Van de Walle 1994, 311). The IMF loan was discontinued in January 1981 and replaced by a one-year standby arrangement. The World Bank canceled the second tranche of its structural adjustment loan in June 1983 because of noncompliance. For a government facing a sharp drop in the export price of peanuts and in the run-up to an election, it was increasingly difficult to sustain unpopular, contractionary reforms (Landell-Mills and Ngo 1991, 48; Mbodji 1991, 124–25). For some analysts this demonstrated that Diouf's political base was too narrow and technocratic with insufficient grounding in political parties, the political process, and electoral politics of Senegal—a constraint that soon began to change (Ka and Van de Walle 1994).

Immediately after the 1983 elections in Senegal, Diouf began to consolidate his political power. He eliminated the post of prime minister and limited the power of the National Assembly, strongly reinforcing his position as president. He also began to usher a new breed of technocrats into positions of authority across all ministries, enhancing and streamlining the capacity of the government to negotiate with external aid and lending agencies and to undertake new economic policies. Principal among the new breed of officials was Mamoudou Toure, a former IMF official who was to lead Senegal's structural adjustment effort from 1985.

By mid 1984 Senegal enjoyed three newly approved World Bank loans and a new IMF loan (IMF-Senegal 2004, World Bank 2004a). The government embarked on a program of economic reform that was approved by a World Bank–organized consultative group meeting in December 1984 (Landell-Mills and Ngo 1991). Subsequently, government expenditure was slashed, credit was controlled, and fiscal and current account deficits were both cut. As Senegal struggled with an exchange rate fixed within the CFA franc zone and fluctuating against the dollar, it relied heavily in the period 1980–87 on foreign aid flows, which grew by about 18 percent per year, totaling about one fifth of Senegal's GDP. Much of this aid was coordinated with IMF and World Bank lending, further enhancing the potential leverage of the organizations.

By 1987 the president's reform agenda faced powerful opposition. Although Senegal's public finance situation had improved by this point, as World Bank economists have written, "The bulk of the program was achieved through containment of expenditures and reliance on extraordinary revenues generated from petroleum and rice imports" (Landell-Mills and Ngo 1991, 50). Austerity and cuts in government spending soon led to student boycotts, school closures, strikes, and union opposition to the government. In the aftermath of the 1988 election a state of emergency was called by the government as opponents of the government went on a rampage, and even once order had been restored, public demonstrations against reform continued. In the spring of 1989 riots took on an ethnic dimension as tensions with neighboring Mauritania spilled over in the streets of Dakar, forcing Mauritanian shopkeepers out.

The IMF and World Bank had succeeded in supporting the government to undertake stabilization, but longer-term reforms seemed to be slipping rapidly out of reach. The key technocrats in charge of structural adjustment—Mamoudou Toure and Cheikh Hamidou Kane—both left government in March 1988. Meanwhile, key structural adjustment policies were reversed in the face of the need to shore up political support and the government's lack of revenue. For example, the government had removed trade protective tariffs as a core part of a relatively successful new industrial policy (Boone 1991). By 1988, the policy was reversed because the government needed the revenues that tariffs produced and a small number of large, powerful businesses lobbied against it (Ka and Van de Walle 1994). While outside commentators accuse the IMF, World Bank, and donors of having imposed conditions that were too detailed and copious to be implemented and too seldom enforced (Ka and Van de Walle 1994, 329), Senegalese critics of structural adjustment in that country argue that it imposed unsustainable and unacceptable costs in health, sanitation, education, and literacy (Ndiaye 2003).

The IMF and World Bank had enjoyed some key preconditions for their success. They had incentives to offer Senegal and sympathetic interlocutors within the government with whom to work. They had shown themselves able to suspend, cancel, and defer loans when conditionality was not met. Yet after the first phase of stabilization and structural adjustment, further reform seemed virtually impossible. In retrospect, a survey of the assumptions underpinning reform and the evidence of impact makes this finding unsurprising.

During the 1980s, the IMF and World Bank justification for their programs in Senegal was that once the government undertook stabilization and a first phase of adjustment, it would achieve an annual growth rate of around 3.8 percent. This prediction was based on some extraordinary premises. For example, it was assumed that liberalization in agriculture and industry would produce an immediate "supply response." In other words, farmers could and would rapidly increase production in response to greater market freedom. Similarly, industry would expand as privatization and liberalization attracted new credit and permitted new export sectors to flourish. Unsurprisingly (given all other cases of stabilization and structural adjustment) new policies would take much longer to produce change, and in Senegal there were technical and environmental factors along with wide fluctuations in world market prices of exports and low international peanut prices that prevented an expansion of food production and exports (Landell-Mills and Ngo 1991, 52). In respect of industry, the establishment of new private sector activity and increased investment would require at the very least a more developed banking system. More generally, in the words of one scholar examining the evidence in the textile industry, "Senegal's Structural Adjustment programs offered no economically viable or politically acceptable means of restructuring the existing textile industry" (Boone 1991, 146). What does the failure of IMF and World Bank predictions tell us?

Hemmed in by their own resource constraints, yet desiring to play a role in a large number of countries across the world, the Fund and Bank had their own reasons for adopting policy prescriptions that cast an onus on developing country borrowers to adjust and to keep adjusting even in the absence of any evidence of economic growth. Conditionality had to be premised on a prediction of growth or the institutions would be explicitly trying to persuade patients to take medicine that was bad for them. At the same time neither the Fund nor the Bank could lend or catalyze lending that would directly fund growth-inducing investment. Furthermore, both the Fund and the Bank had to ensure that borrowers repaid them for previous loans and this put a stringent priority on stabilization.

In Senegal the harsh effects of adjustment were magnified by the country's inability to devalue its currency. As a member of the West African Monetary Union, Senegal was locked into the CFA franc zone arrangements. In essence this left the government with only two real instruments of adjustment: cutting government expenditure, and controlling exports and imports. The overvalued CFA franc made the latter extremely difficult.

Why did the IMF (and World Bank) accept and support Senegal's currency arrangement? In economic terms a permanently fixed and externally guaranteed exchange rate coupled with a supranational central bank should promote low inflation and encourage savings, investment, and growth. These benefits have been reviewed by several IMF and World Bank economists (Bhatia 1985, Devarajan and de Melo 1987, Elbadawi and Majd 1992). Certainly low inflation was achieved within the franc zone and some scholars go further and positively correlate the currency arrangement with growth (Devarajan and de Melo 1987, Guillaumont et al. 1988). However, these studies also show that members did not benefit equally. Indeed, smaller countries such as Senegal did much worse than the larger members (Medhora 2000). Furthermore, the most obvious benefit of the currency arrangement—exchange rate stability—may well have been illusory for Senegal since the real effective exchange rate was more unstable than the nominal effective exchange rate (de Macedo 1986). In economic terms there was (and still is) genuine debate and disagreement as to the merits and demerits of Senegal's currency arrangement through the 1980s.

For the IMF and World Bank there was a further political reason underpinning support for Senegal's currency arrangement. This highlights an already-mentioned structural constraint at work facing the institutions. As one of France's former colonies and largest aid recipients, decisions about Senegal are led by France's preferences, with other powerful shareholders in the international institutions loath to intervene in respect of what they recognize as a special sphere of influence. Senegal's currency arrangements in the 1980s were part of France's CFA-franc zone encompassing the West African Monetary Union and a currency union among the central African states across which France guaranteed the convertibility of the common currency—the CFA franc (Medhora 1992). France vigorously opposed CFA franc devaluation and fought the Bank's and Fund's recommendations in this respect.

At a more general level the structural constraint of special spheres of influence has at times permitted major shareholders to pursue geostrategic goals in the context of the Cold War, to reinforce former colonial ties, or to bolster narrow economic interests, sometimes with catastrophic consequences for development. The extreme cases of this were the support provided to Nicaragua under Somoza, to the Philippines under Marcos, and to Zaire under Mobutu. In these cases the IMF and World Bank were not lending on technical economic or developmental grounds. Rather they were following the directions of their major shareholders, who permitted dictators to amass vast personal fortunes leaving behind a crippling debt burden which these impoverished countries have been forced subsequently to service (Kremer and Jayachandran 2003). That said, even in cases where the structural constraint was not a determining factor, the results of the IMF and World Bank's loans to Africa in the 1980s were extremely disappointing.

Conditionality and structural adjustment simply did not work in the 1980s. The large number of evaluations undertaken by the IMF and the World Bank themselves provides ample proof. Combing through their studies, which use a variety of methodologies, it is difficult to find any evidence that countries that entered into programs of structural adjustment with the IMF and World Bank did any better than countries that did not.[1] Their critics argue that this was at least in part because their prescription was both wrong and in itself damaging.

Was the Prescription Wrong?

Independent analysts have argued that the Bank and Fund misdiagnosed the problem in African economies in the 1980s, making inappropriate forecasts for recovery and applying the wrong policy conditions. Far from facilitating nec-

---

[1] See the excellent summary of the IMF work from Khan 1988 onward in Boughton 2001 and the ESAF review (IMF External Evaluation 1998). The World Bank reviews include World Bank 1989a (*Adjustment Lending*); World Bank 1989e (*Africa's Adjustment*), and World Bank 1989f (*Sub-Saharan Africa*).

essary adjustments and reform, the conditionality pushed by the international financial institutions drove countries into a vicious circle of stagnation and poverty.

What was needed for effective structural adjustment was a boost in low domestic savings so that countries could fund the investments necessary for structural change and growth. It required increased imports of raw materials and spare parts, which necessitated additional foreign exchange. And for structural adjustment to work, there needed to be political support and a sense of confidence and sustainability in policies undertaken. The converse, the "import compression" or "import strangulation" phenomenon, resulted in serious underutilization of existing capacity (due to the shortage of critical inputs), not just a limited ability to invest in order to expand it.

Instead, a narrow set of structural adjustment targets were imposed by the Fund and Bank in the context of increasingly onerous debt repayments schedules. A vicious cycle was created. Governments forced to meet enormous debt repayments obligations did not have foreign exchange resources to finance imports and without necessary imports, exports could not be increased, thus further reducing the capacity to purchase imports. Debt servicing also claimed domestic savings needed for investment and the maintenance of capital stock (Killick 1989 calculates some 20–25 percent of domestic savings being absorbed in debt repayments). The lack of investment was exacerbated by the uncertainties introduced by "debt overhang," which further discouraged investment and diverted governments away from longer-term problems of structural reform (Killick 1989, 1990). The result was to grind economies to a halt rather than to permit restructuring that would bring about growth.

The impact of IMF conditionality (on which World Bank lending hinged) was rigorously analyzed by an expert group commissioned by the board of the IMF in 1996. Their brief was to analyze the most far-ranging and high-level conditionality applied by the Fund—the ESAF, or Enhanced Structural Adjustment Facility. Designed to deliver concessional financing to low-income countries, ESAF required medium-term policy changes across the economy as well as shorter-term monetary and fiscal management targets. Although the amounts lent from ESAF were small, the associated conditionality was highly leveraged because compliance with the IMF's ESAF conditionality was a prerequisite for most aid and lending (in technical jargon, there is "nonreciprocal cross-conditionality"), particularly program assistance.

The goal of ESAF was to enhance investment and growth in low-income countries by channeling funds not to governments (who complied with conditionality) but mostly to a country's central bank to bolster reserves and thereby to promote confidence and greater investment in a country's economy. The key to the success of ESAF was enhancing investment.[2]

---

[2] The goal of ESAF is set out in an IMF Board decision of 15 December 1987: "To promote in a balanced manner, both balance of payments viability and growth, through mobilization of domestic and external resources." There were only three situations in which ESAF loans actually provided budget support to governments (its best effect according to the External Evaluation): (1) where the extra reserves produce

The External Evaluation of ESAF substantiated several powerful criticisms of IMF conditionality, some of which had previously also been leveled at the World Bank's structural adjustment lending.

A first problem with ESAF conditionality was that it simply did not seem to work. In many countries ESAF targets were not met. The review found that three-quarters of ESAF programs collapsed or were interrupted (IMF External Evaluation 1998, 32). Perhaps more seriously, the evaluation cited the evidence that where ESAF programs were being followed, they seemed to have no impact on investment flows (IMF External Evaluation 1998, Rodrik 1995). Finally, the review found that conditionality can be counterproductive in the sense that "one of the IMF's most valuable functions is the signal of credibility that it provides to private investors by approving a program. This signal becomes noisy as its recipients become aware that the design of approved programs may be faulty and that program interruptions are indeed common" (IMF External Evaluation 1998, 32).

A second set of problems detailed in the report might be summarized (although the experts did not summarize in this way) as the IMF's overly doctrinaire and short-term focus on reducing budget deficits in ESAF countries. This had several very negative effects. Three effects mentioned in the evaluation are particularly worth elaborating.

By putting such priority on balancing the budget, the Fund supported policies that had adverse long-term effects. For example, the Fund resisted lowering import tariffs, without analyzing the longer-term consequences on growth. In respect of privatization, the Fund was so keen to use the sale of assets to improve the budget deficit that it paid little heed to the way privatization was undertaken and the consequent longer run efficiency implications (or social implications). Among other cases, the evaluators cite the privatization of the public telephone company in Cote d'Ivoire, which resulted in a highly profitable monopoly charging much higher prices and setting back the development of access to infrastructure necessary for development. According to the ESAF report, the IMF simply did not adequately trade off the short-run fiscal benefits and the long-run social costs in such cases. It left this work to the World Bank to pursue in an entirely separate way, which did not work.

A further effect of the Fund's single-minded focus on balancing the budget was that the institution was too quick to assume an end to external aid to countries and this hindered the prospects for growth in the poststabilization phase. The Fund's emphasis has been to plan radically to reduce "aid dependency." Yet, as the ESAF report argues, poststabilization low-income countries need more money not less—so as to begin to invest. Instead the IMF's approach (exemplified by Uganda) was to force a reliance on trade and petroleum taxes that were very costly in terms of growth.

---

income which could be transferred to the governments; (2) where the exchange rate appreciated, facilitating imports but penalizing exports; (3) in the CFA franc zone where ESAF loans were used entirely for budget support because France's support of the common currency made reserves unnecessary.

Compounding the damage of obsession with budgetary balance was the Fund's exaggeration of countries' fiscal deficits. The independent evaluation details the way the Fund included only pure grants in its calculations of fiscal balance, excluding the grant element in all other loans and treating them instead as commercial loans. In respect of IDA loans, the external evaluation team argued that some 70 percent should be treated as grant aid. By not treating IDA loans in this way, the IMF probably discouraged investment and pushed for too stringent a budget contraction (IMF External Evaluation 1998, 33).

A third set of problems with IMF conditionality lay in their design. Several countries were encouraged to undertake financial and exchange rate liberalization before they had stabilized their economies. The results were disastrous, not only making stabilization unnecessarily difficult but leading to broader economic collapse. As the ESAF report details, in Zimbabwe and Zambia the policy sequence led to economic crisis as the government lost fiscal control and interest rates rose, deterring any investment. In Zambia the share of public expenditure in GDP halved in a two-year period. In Zimbabwe deep cuts in health and education spending could have been avoided.

A related problem in conditionality—which affected both the IMF and World Bank—was a reliance on unleashing market effects to bring about structural reforms. In reality, specific structural reforms needed to complement liberalizing measures. For example, in Zambia privatization in agriculture needed to be complemented with early reforms to improve rural transport, extension, and storage. Without these, farmers simply "got stuck" (IMF External Evaluation 1998).

The ESAF report criticisms of the IMF were not new and some had already been applied to the World Bank. In the 1980s and early 1990s both the IMF and the World Bank had been criticized for basing their structural adjustment programs on overly optimistic projections (Helleiner 1987, Van der Hoeven and Van der Kraaij 1994). Key assumptions regarding the demand in industrial countries for primary commodities, terms of trade, private flows, and costs of servicing commercial debt all went in the opposite direction to that assumed in the Fund's programs. The Fund itself acknowledged this at a very early point (IMF 1982, 96) and similarly the World Bank would later conclude that the external economic environment "turned out to be substantially worse than was assumed at the start of the 1980s" making "adjustment slower and more difficult than initially expected" (World Bank 1989e). In 2002 a report of the IMF's Independent Evaluation Office detailed that the IMF had projected a mean export growth rate of 10.5 percent in countries making prolonged use of Fund resources. In reality the mean export growth rate in these countries was 7.4 percent. Similarly, real GDP growth in prolonged-use countries had been projected at 4.1 percent (again as a mean) whereas the actual growth rate was 3.5 percent (Independent Evaluation Office 2002).

Over-optimism in the IMF has frequently reflected a desire on the part of staff and the country to ensure that the board would accept a loan program. But this does not obviate the subsequent problem that over-optimistic projections have knock-on effects for program design, funding needs, and expectations about meeting conditions.

IMF missions in countries making prolonged use of IMF resources have typically been staffed by more junior personnel, those less willing and less able to challenge head office orthodoxy. In sub-Saharan Africa IMF missions were often more rigid, interacting with local officials on the details of programs that had already been broadly constructed in Washington (IMF External Evaluation 1998, Independent Evaluation Office 2002).

The content of World Bank conditionality had been criticized from a number of sources. As mentioned above, the Bank relied heavily on reforms in prices and market signals yet as one analysis of reform in rural Africa puts it, "reliance on markets may not necessarily ensure competitive processing or marketing of crops, where monopolies exist, or where historical factors explain oligopolistic tendencies" (Lele 1988, 204). The Bank had been overly optimistic about the prospects for traditional exports, particularly where several countries were being simultaneously advised to expand their exports of a particular commodity (Cassen 1994, Koester et al. 1987). The push for rapid privatization—as per the Washington consensus—was misguided (Adam 1994) and displayed too little regard for the ways it could be instrumentalized by politicians to consolidate power and direct profits toward favored groups and sectors as has been documented in the case of Cameroon (Van de Walle 1989, Konings 1989).

Too often, Bank conditionality was based on simplified but incorrect presumptions about both the situation on the ground and the likely impact of adjustment policies. For example, Bank staff in the 1980s worked on the premise that all over Africa government employees were overpaid and overemployed. This assumption reflected an idea popular at the Bank that the rapid and excessive expansion of government service in the immediate aftermath of independence had produced too many public sector employees (Goldsmith 1999). Critics argue that the Bank's perception was based on out-of-date and faulty evidence. The assumption of too many overpaid civil servants was contradicted by the Bank's own subsequent data and analysis (Lindauer, Meesook, and Suebsaen 1986; Dipak Muzumdar cited in Kapur et al. 1997, 737). In Anglophone African countries over the 1970s and 1980s civil service salaries had in fact collapsed by more than 80 percent of their real value (Robinson 1990). In many countries, an increase in the number of civil servants was accompanied by a dramatic decline in quality and remuneration (Van de Walle 2002). A better analysis of the problem, as the World Bank would later admit following consultations with African leaders, institutions, and donors, was not that Africa needed "less government" but that it needed "better government best pursued through technical assistance, institution-building, public expenditure reviews and the like" (Agarwala et al. 1994).

In fashioning reforms, Bank and Fund officials discounted the realities of formal and informal financial markets and structures (Johnson 1994). In Nigeria for example, financial sector liberalization hugely increased corruption within the banking sector (Lewis and Stein 1997). Similarly, trade liberalization often resulted in an exploitation of new opportunities for fraud and rent-seeking behavior (Van de Walle 2002, Hibou 1996). Finally, the World Bank was heavily criticized for paying insufficient attention to areas where greater public investment was needed and most especially for inadequate efforts being made to protect the poor and public programs beneficial to them (Stewart 1994).

The critiques of the Fund and Bank prescriptions for African economic reform suggest that conditionality was too often aimed at narrow, measurable, short-term targets. There also seem to have been too few incentives for the organization and staff to achieve the longer-term aims of each institution. By contrast the incentives facing officials of each organization weighed heavily in favor of setting and achieving short-term targets. The result was too little attention paid to analyzing or taking into account the clear trade-offs arising between short-term and long-term goals.

Political pressures also pushed and shaped the conditionality of the IMF and World Bank. Most obviously, politically powerful members imposed a resource constraint. Each institution has to cut a robe to fit its available cloth and to some degree this explains the incentive on both the IMF and the World Bank to stay blind to the (obvious) fact that the debt position of most African borrowing members in the 1980s was unsustainable and that stabilization and adjustment was not producing the effects necessary to reverse that position .

This seeming blindness of the Fund and Bank to the failure of their approach to sub-Saharan Africa persisted even as the studies of the IMF and the World Bank themselves demonstrated that stabilization and adjustment failed to elicit positive investment effects (World Bank 1989a, 1989e, 1989f; Khan 1990; Killick 1990; Corbo and Rojas 1992; Elbadawi and Majd 1992; Bird 1995; Killick 1995). It permitted structural adjustment to be offered as the most convenient diagnosis and prescription for agencies needing to ensure that repayments were made in a timely fashion without catalyzing accelerating needs for further financial assistance.

The most politically mobilizing criticism of structural adjustment as pursued by both the IMF and the World Bank was that it had an unacceptably harsh impact on the poor and vulnerable in economies across Africa. In 1986, UNICEF launched a report on The State of the World's Children, calling for "adjustment with a human face" (Cornia et al. 1987). Study after study of the impact of adjustment in Africa and elsewhere pronounced adverse effects on the poor or at the very least highlighted how little attention had been paid to protecting the poor (Havnevik 1987, Bassett 1988, Hodges 1988, Helleiner 1987, Van der Hoeven and Van der Kraaij 1994). Public sector job retrenchments, job losses in other areas, cutbacks in food subsidies and other welfare provisions, as well as a loss in the quality of welfare provision, the effects of the general economic slowdown, and the lack of any political voice in the process of adjustment all exacted a high price on the poor in sub-Saharan Africa. An internal Bank memorandum reflecting on the impact of adjustment noted that "adjustment through further economic contraction is not a feasible alternative in a continent where per capita income levels are no higher than they were twenty years ago" (internal memorandum written in 1986, cited in Kapur et al. 1997, 732).

If the Bank and Fund had wanted to prioritize protecting the poor in the 1980s, they needed to build into stabilization and structural adjustment programs protections of five core aspects of the lives and opportunities of the poor: access to productive assets such as land; the quality and availability of extension services which increased the returns of the poor from the assets they did have; employment opportunities; access to education and health services; and supplementary resources, such as food subsidies (see UNICEF 1986 and the World Bank staff paper published in 1987: Demery and Addison 1987).

To plan economic adjustment with a human face would require the IMF and World Bank to work differently. To protect the poor, they would need to use local information about who was poor in any country and how they might be protected. Such information is unlikely to be held by Fund and Bank interlocutors in the Ministry of Finance or Central Bank. As the External Evaluation of ESAF noted: "It is not possible to devise, a priori, safety net interventions that will work across ESAF programs" in different countries. There is no substitute for detailed country-level work using socioeconomic survey data. However, to the extent that information was available, the Bank and Fund failed to use it to build safety nets into the design of ESAF programs (IMF External Evaluation 1998, 18). The IMF could make better use of the household poverty expertise of the World Bank in integrating projections of social impact into program design and monitoring the outcomes. At the very least the IMF and World Bank could work together to share information and their respective expertise. This had not happened in the 1980s.

The Bank and Fund Modify Their Approach

By the late 1980s a growing wave of criticism of structural adjustment and of the Bank and Fund washed over donor countries. Indeed some donor countries broke the link of bilateral aid to the region with IMF programs (James 1996, 525). Nongovernmental organizations (NGOs) in Canada, Scandinavia, and in the United States took up a vociferous role urging their governments to address the hardship being suffered by people in heavily indebted countries. In September 1987 American NGOs held a press conference delivering a letter calling for greater World Bank efforts on poverty and signed by 153 members of the U.S. Congress and 40 senators (Kapur et al. 1997, 368).

External pressures on the World Bank were leveraged by two big funding struggles. First the Bank had begun negotiations to replenish its concessional lending fund—called in Bank jargon IDA 8. This occurred in the context of the disastrous previous negotiations on IDA 7, in which the United States had cut funding. Second, the Bank was also negotiating a general capital increase, and in that context the whole adjustment with a human face issue was raised, with the U.S. Treasury committing to report to Congress on the Bank's involvement with NGOs, poverty programs, women's programs, micro-enterprises, and other issues (Kapur et al. 1997, 368).

The Bank and Fund considered some measures to alleviate the impact of adjustment on the poor. For example, the World Bank called for more external financing to reduce the social costs of adjustment and gradually began to accept that compensatory services and public works projects might usefully ensure some protection for the poor. At the same time, staff began to focus on how government social services might be channeled more directly to the poor through targeted, needs-based benefits, funded by charges and user-fees paid by the better-off (Nelson 1995, 23). Similarly the IMF began an internal debate about how to monitor poverty impacts and protect programs from external shocks. This led to the creation of a new Compensatory and Contingency Financing Facility (CCFF) in 1988, which integrated the preexisting Compensatory Financing Facility with a new external contingency mechanism.

In practice, there was little modification to the overall approach of the Fund and Bank. Both institutions held to their existing paradigm, which assumed that stabilization and adjustment were prerequisites to alleviating poverty. Official Bank and Fund documents all robustly promulgated the view that adjustment was a necessary step toward poverty alleviation. For example, in the World Bank's 1992 review of structural adjustment we find several assertions that adjustment reduced the incidence of poverty, that the "distributional effects of well-designed policies often favour the poor," and that "adjustment is much better for the poor than non-adjustment" (World Bank 1992, 19–20). But the evidence does not back up these claims. One central assumption was that adjustment would improve the rural/urban terms of trade and therefore, because poverty in rural areas was far greater than in urban areas, reduce poverty overall. However, critics combing the actual available figures on poverty have found no hard evidence to back this claim. For example, one study found that poverty was high and increasing in most of sub-Saharan Africa in the 1980s in both adjusting and nonadjusting countries, belying the claim that adjustment was better for the poor (Stewart 1995, 138–70).

Why was it so difficult to modify Bank and Fund conditionality? Adjustment programs in sub-Saharan Africa in the 1980s demonstrated a high degree of uniformity and consistency on the part of each of the IMF and the World Bank in diagnosing the problems of these economies and in prescribing solutions (Killick et al. 1984).[3] In outlining structural adjustment measures staff from both the Fund and Bank drew heavily on in-house theoretical propositions and predilections, which were not always supported by substantiating evidence. As discussed in chapter 2, there were strong incentives for staff members and their immediate interlocutors to use such a template. Originality in design would only increase the likelihood of a proposed loan being rejected. By contrast, using a template reduced the responsibility of the individuals writing the agreement for its content. Simply put, if the program turned out to be wrong but followed the institutional template, responsibility would fall more heavily on the institution than the authors of the program.

---

[3] Cf. an unpublished study by William Kingsmill which argues that there was some variation in the content of World Bank programs even though the broad thrust of the programs was the same (cited in Killick 1990, 16).

More recent evidence about the institutions' modus operandi in Africa points to another reason for a template approach to have dominated their programs on the continent. A recent IMF evaluation provides figures about how much staff time has been put into designing and monitoring programs in countries that have the longest ongoing programs with the IMF (into which category most of Africa falls). The evaluation published in 2002 highlights that far fewer staff resources are invested in the programs of these countries than in the more successful "temporary" users of IMF resources. It also shows the very high degree of turnover of staff and mission chiefs working with countries, with less than half of any mission team having been involved in the same country in the previous two years (Independent Evaluation Office 2002, Annex VI).

Similarly in the World Bank a recent report on low-income countries under stress (LICUS) notes that most of these countries "have typically not received much Senior Management attention . . . and little investment in economic and sector work, so that World Bank Group knowledge of these countries is often seriously deficient" (World Bank 2002c, vii). Under these time and staffing constraints, it is difficult to see how either the Fund or Bank might acquire expertise about the subtle and complex economic, political, and social implications of reform in any one country. Yet a final criticism emphasizes how vital such knowledge is.

The most difficult, irrefutable, and profoundly challenging critique for both the IMF and the World Bank is that their work in fostering economic reform has ignored or wished away political realities—in Africa just as much if not more as in other countries. To some degree the institutions have recognized this. To quote a working paper produced in the World Bank's evaluation department in 2000 "development constraints are structural and social, and cannot be overcome through economic stabilization and policy adjustment alone—they require a long-term and holistic vision of needs and solutions" (Branson and Hanna 2000).

A deeper critique of the institutions' policies is that political realities have turned rational policies into instruments of deeply damaging change, incurring perverse effects and hindering the prospects of positive development outcomes. The argument is not necessarily that the theory of structural adjustment is wrong. Indeed, many have questioned the extent to which stabilization and adjustment measures were ever actually implemented in Africa (Van de Walle 2001). One worldwide survey of 305 IMF programs from 1979 to 1993 found implementation failure in 53 percent of cases where failure was defined as a country not implementing 20 percent or more of the program's conditions (Killick 1996). In a different study of World Bank adjustment loans, the same author found that 75 percent of adjustment loans faced problems of noncompliance (Killick 1998).

The core political economy argument about reform in Africa is that IMF, World Bank, and other donors' conditionality made an unintended difference to politics rather than to economics. For example, Nicolas Van de Walle makes a powerful argument that conditional loans produced an entrenchment and reinforcement of patrimonial politics in Africa. He argues that two decades of economic reform have produced three key trends. First, there has been a centralization of power as staffing, control of economic reform, and control of the rent-seeking opportunities have all converged on the office of the president. Second, at the behest of the head of state, "reforms" have been used to direct benefits to specific groups in the economy, whether they are tribal, regional, or political. Third, the state has withdrawn from development, leaving nongovernmental organizations often run by the elite (who profit from them) to enter into the business of providing health, education, and so forth in an even less accountable, potentially more clientelistic way than governments (Van de Walle 2002).

Although both the IMF and the World Bank have recognized the need to take political circumstances into account, this recognition is very difficult to act on. How could the institutions acquire the kinds of knowledge required to take political, social, and institutional factors into account? At a fairly theoretical level, the IMF has probed a number of political science approaches to understanding reform feasibility and sustainability, the most recent of which is a review commissioned by the Independent Evaluation Office (Wimmer 2002). In the World Bank more practical attempts have been made to advance "reform readiness analysis" (World Bank 1999b). However, to cite World Bank researchers in the evaluation department: "This tool demands detailed knowledge of a proposed reform and of the political situation surrounding it, knowledge often unavailable to outsiders" (Branson and Hanna 2000, 6). As a result any change in either institution has been very slow and partial even though the institutions have long expounded the need for more sensitivity to political constraints. That said, other exigencies forced a change in strategy by the end of the 1980s.

A Growing Problem within the Institutions

By the early 1990s the strategy vis-à-vis the poorest, most indebted countries was not working. Debt levels and debt service payments were continuing to increase. In spite of debt rescheduling and reduction efforts, the debt stock of most ESAF-supported countries had doubled between 1985 and 1995, current account deficits had seen little reduction, and savings performance had been disappointing (IMF External Evaluation 1998, 23). Overall, to adapt the words of historian Harold James, the experience of the IMF and the World Bank with Africa had been "profoundly dispiriting, disappointing, and disillusioning" (James 1996, 543). So-called "structural adjustment with growth" was neither being consistently pursued, nor was it leading to the promised growth and recovery.

In 1996 the Fund and Bank responded to the failure of the debt strategy in Africa with the launch of the Heavily Indebted Poor Countries (HIPC) Initiative to provide exceptional assistance to heavily indebted poor countries. To quote the IMF: "For these countries, even full use of traditional mechanisms of rescheduling and debt reduction—together with continued provision of concessional financing and pursuit of sound economic policies—may not be sufficient to attain sustainable external debt levels within a reasonable period of time and without additional external support" (IMF 2001d). Eligible countries were defined as those facing an unsustainable debt burden beyond available debt-relief mechanisms, and an established track record of reform and sound policies through IMF- and World Bank-supported programs.

What brought about a new debt initiative? To some degree it was the NGOs and critics of structural adjustment who shamed and pressured the most powerful G-7 governments into action in the early and mid 1990s, however, they had an even stronger influence on the subsequent shift in policy. In the mid 1990s their calls coincided with pressing practical exigencies, which began to force a shift in the strategy toward the poorest countries.

Throughout the 1980s and early 1990s the G-7 blindly refused to accept that many of their loans (both bilateral and multilateral) to the poorest and most heavily indebted countries would never be repaid. Even in the face of figures showing an obviously unsustainable debt burden and mounting poverty and devastation, the G-7 continued to reaffirm a debt strategy that eschewed debt reduction and instead looked to indebted developing countries to reschedule their debt obligations while pursuing stringent adjustment measures (G-7/G-8 Research Archive at www.toronto.edu/g-7).

The only glimmer of a prospect for debt reduction was made in the Paris Club forum for government creditors. In 1988 these official creditors agreed to "Toronto terms" (followed up by successor "London terms," "Naples terms," "Lyon terms," and "Cologne terms") laying out a menu of options through which creditors could modestly reduce the debt service obligations of their poorest borrowers subject to stringent conditionality. The lack of greater action in respect of the world's poorest, most indebted countries stood in marked contrast to the more decisive actions taken in respect of the middle-income, transition, and emerging countries whose situations more directly impacted on the economies of powerful industrialized countries (Evans 1999, Serieux 2001, and see chapter two).

Even the very modest reduction in debt service achieved by the Paris Club through a lowering of the interest rate on rescheduled debt was vociferously opposed by several creditor governments, among whom a consensus had to be reached in the Paris Club. Three arguments dominated negotiations. These would recur throughout all debates on debt in the 1980s and 1990s.

A first argument against debt relief was that it was wrong to let countries off paying. The sanctity of contracts had to be upheld, and not to do so would invite other (e.g., middle-income debtors) not to repay. This was a principle particularly emphasized by Germany in negotiations.

A second argument against debt relief was that it would undermine IMF conditionality by heralding incentives for failure.

A third argument against a new approach to debt was that creditors could not afford the cost of debt reduction, particularly in the straightened circumstances of the fiscally contractionary 1980s.

Against the arguments for not changing the status quo were the simple facts that many debtors were not repaying their debts, nor meeting their IMF conditions. Furthermore, most creditors were being forced to extend new credit to them anyway. Two British participants in negotiations among the G-7 recall having laid out these arguments to other participants (Evans 1999, Lawson 1992.)

In practice even once the new Paris Club rescheduling framework was in place, it did little to address the seriousness of the debt crisis in the poorest, most heavily indebted countries. Under the Toronto terms creditors could reduce debt service by about a third (this proportion increased under subsequent terms) by choosing from a menu consisting of partial reduction, rescheduling, or rescheduling in a way that would reduce debt. The debt figures from eligible countries reveal that creditor actions under this agreement did little to moderate these countries' increasing debt burdens (see figures 6.1 and 6.2 above).

As countries faced mounting difficulties in meeting their obligations to the IMF and World Bank (which if they failed to meet, would cut off funding), bilateral creditors deferred repayments to themselves and essentially provided loans to countries so that they could repay the IMF and the World Bank. Development assistance budgets thus rapidly turned into funds being directed to the IMF and World Bank. Zambia offers a good example of what was happening. Between 1991 and 1993 Zambia made a net transfer to the IMF of $335 million in an effort to pay past debts—a sum which Oxfam points out was equivalent to total government spending on health and education (Oxfam 1996). Zambia was making its repayments mainly from foreign aid. With a 14 percent current account deficit, Zambia had zero debt servicing capacity. The $335 million earmarked for debt repayments in 1993 was more than half of the $550 million or so pledged to that country in development assistance over the same period.

The position of the IMF and World Bank was becoming less and less tenable in the 1990s. Loans conditional on stabilization and structural adjustment had not catalyzed new flows of finance nor growth nor better debt sustainability in heavily indebted countries. Throughout the 1980s new loans and conditionality had ensured that most poor debtor countries did not fall into arrears (as the IMF terms it) or nonaccrual status (as the World Bank describes a country more than 180 days in arrears on its payments). However, as the debts of the poorest countries mounted and were gradually becoming dominated by their debt to the Fund and Bank, the unsustainability of this debt ultimately risked eroding the institutions' own financial credibility.

As "preferred creditors," the IMF and World Bank enjoyed being first in line for repayment throughout the 1980s. Debtors had to repay them in full or face being cut off from all other debt financing, including trade credits. Until 1984 the IMF had only ever taken action on three cases of nonrepayment (Cuba, Egypt, and Cambodia), all of which were due to powerful political circumstances (Boughton 2001, chap. 16). The World Bank had never declared a member country in "nonaccrual status" until 1984.

In April 1984 the IMF faced three borrowers overdue by more than six months in their repayments and a further eight overdue by at least six weeks (Boughton 2001, 757–846). In that same year, the World Bank placed Nicaragua in "nonaccrual status," and by 1989, nine countries with loans comprising 4 percent of the Bank's portfolio were in nonaccrual status (Kapur et al. 1997, 1058–73; McKenzie 2002). Simply put, the institutions were beginning to face a debt crisis of their own.

In the IMF by 1990, eleven countries were in protracted arrears (payments in arrears for six months or more) to the tune of nearly 14 percent of outstanding Fund credits (Boughton 2001, 764). In total, at the end of December 1998, some forty heavily indebted poor countries had outstanding and disbursed debts of US$39.247 billion to the World Bank group (mainly IDA), of which $746 million were in arrears, and US$8.192 billion to the IMF of which US$1.660 billion were in arrears (IDA/IMF 1999). Clearly both institutions now urgently needed to reduce their nonperforming loans and thereby any risk to their own financial credibility.

The arrears crisis initially brought out different responses in the Fund and Bank. At first the IMF's response to arrears—at the behest of its powerful share-holders led by the United States—was to try to penalize countries in arrears through both financial and nonfinancial means in order to deter countries from not repaying. In 1985 the board raised the interest rate charged on outstanding obligations (the "rate of charge"), thus passing the full cost of arrears onto all borrowing countries making repayments. This was soon altered so as to pass the extra cost directly onto those countries in arrears through "special charges." However, in 1986 a new burden-sharing arrangement was agreed in response to the argument that the membership as a whole had approved arrangements that had subsequently gone wrong and therefore the whole membership should bear the cost. This paved the way for the Fund to work toward a more cooperative strategy to help the arrears countries to return to a more sustainable course (Boughton 2001, 812).

The World Bank at first muddled through in negotiations with countries in arrears. It was able to use its concessional lending arm—the IDA—to disburse new credits to severely indebted, low-income countries so as to ensure that they kept up with their IBRD loan repayments. In several cases economic decline made non-repaying borrowers eligible for such credits. In the short-term IDA became "a means to bail out the Bank" (Kapur et al. 1997, 1067). In 1991 the Bank announced a new "carrot and stick" arrears policy. Countries would be encouraged to keep repaying through a waiver of a part of interest charges on a year-by-year basis. However, the payment deadlines would be tighter as would the penalties attached to these deadlines (Kapur et al. 1997, 1064).

Throughout the 1990s the IMF and the World Bank fought to maintain their preferred creditor status vis-à-vis private and official creditors. They also fought a little with one another. The Bank worried that countries would use their loans to repay the Fund, and the Fund worried that the reverse would happen. These concerns led to detailed negotiations and agreements between the two institutions regarding their respective roles in supporting and receiving payments from borrowers in arrears (Kapur et al. 1997, 1071).

In summary, by the mid 1990s it was clear that the financial credibility of the IMF and the World Bank could be threatened by members' failure to repay. At the same time, a small number of powerful member countries, urged on by an active NGO campaign, were beginning to press for action to extend debt reduction into the realm of multilateral debt. The United Kingdom, the Netherlands, and the Nordic states in particular began arguing for a reduction in the debt owed by the poorest, most heavily indebted countries to the IMF and World Bank. Opposing their stance (predictably given previous rounds of discussion) were the United States and Germany.

The official positions of the Fund and Bank were extraordinarily conservative at this point. The IMF remained resolutely opposed to relief in respect of debts owed to it. In the World Bank, although some staff set up a taskforce that gave a realistic appraisal of the urgent need for a radical new approach—and indeed outlined one—they were blocked by senior management who opposed any change in the status quo (World Bank 1995).

Inching toward a New Strategy

When the Heavily Indebted Poor Countries (HIPC) Initiative was launched in 1996, for the first time major creditor countries agreed that debt owed to the multilateral institutions by the poorest countries would need to be reduced. Nonetheless, the initiative was a poor and unworkable compromise reached among creditor countries. To be eligible for relief, a highly indebted poor country had first to undertake three years of structural adjustment (the technical conditions of which were drafted by the Fund and Bank staff) and exhaust all traditional debt relief, at which point the country could be considered for relief, which would become available only after three more years of adjustment.

Like all its predecessor debt strategies, HIPC required heavily indebted countries successfully to undertake deep economic restructuring and long-term improvements in performance even as they continued to be hobbled by a crippling burden of debt. To quote the IMF, countries had to tackle "the whole range of factors currently limiting their growth performance, including poor infrastructure, the lack of effective policy making institutions, and governance problems" (IMF 1998b). As in the case of Senegal discussed above, to ask governments to do this with no resources and in the context of hostile politics catalyzed by stabilization, economic contraction, and increasing poverty was to ask the impossible.

Although unworkable, the HIPC initiative highlighted the three elements that were required for a change in the debt strategy. First, there had to be new ideas about how to reduce debt. Second, there had to be resources available to do it. Third, there had to be a revision of conditionality to fit the new strategy.

New ideas were provided by technical work done by economists within the Fund and Bank and other development agencies. In the words of a senior British official engaged in the negotiations at the time: "Many of the individuals in the institutions had come to the conclusion that debt reduction was needed. This was not the policy of some key shareholders and therefore not of the IMF and World Bank management, but the staff played important roles behind the scenes in giving support to the UK and other initiatives" (Evans 1999, 274). The new technical work opened up the possibility of a policy change. Once the technical basis for debt reduction was established, the Fund and Bank needed to resolve two further issues.

The new debt strategy needed to be financed. One proposal was to use a revaluation of a portion of the IMF's gold stocks. However, this was opposed by the United States and also by Germany whose opposition led protesters to lay mock gold bars outside the German embassy in London. The United States was reticent in spite of the U.S. Treasury secretary's repeated declarations of support for HIPC (U.S. Treasury 1998a, 1998b). It would not be until 2000 that the U.S. administration finally made its first ever request to the Congress to agree to a contribution toward multilateral debt relief.

A final necessary element for a new debt strategy was to rewrite conditionality. The existing approach was not working. However, its failure provoked two different responses among economists within the Bank and Fund (as well as among critics outside the organizations). Innovators argued that the institutions should reconceive conditionality to ensure greater "ownership" by borrowing countries. Traditionalists argued that the institutions simply had to be tougher in applying existing conditionality.

When UK chancellor Gordon Brown proposed a review of HIPC in September 1998, the traditionalists feared that this would lead to wrong criticism or dilution of the institutions' prescriptions. On this view, the continuing lack of growth in Africa was not due to any problem with the content of conditionality. Rather it was due to the failure of governments to restructure and provide incentives to the private sector. In the words of the World Bank in 1994, "Even among the strongest adjusters, no country has gone the full distance in restructuring its economy" (World Bank 1994, 1). The crisis in Africa was "predominantly a consequence of the failure of domestic policy and of the institutions the state helped to develop and sustain" (Sahn 1994, 366). The solution lay in tough love and the more stringent application of conditionality—as enshrined in the 1996 HIPC.

The weakness in the traditionalist approach was that it neatly split sound economic prescription (the work of the Fund and Bank) from practical implementation and sustainability (the duty of the borrowing state). It sidestepped the fact that regardless of who was to blame, Fund and Bank conditionality was simply not working in Africa. By contrast, innovators, particularly within the Bank, began to open up and consider what this failure suggested about both the content and the process of defining conditionality (World Bank 1996).

The New Strategy—A Revolutionized Washington Consensus?

In 1999 a new, enhanced HIPC was launched that would potentially affect some thirty-four African debtors.[4] It was heralded as "deeper, broader and faster" than

---

[4] It included the following highly indebted poorest countries in Africa: Angola, Benin, Burkina Faso, Burundi, Cameroon, Central African Republic, Chad, Comoros, Congo, Côte d'Ivoire, Democratic Re-

the existing HIPC. It was faster in the sense that most countries would get relief at an earlier point in the process. It was deeper because the amount of assistance would be determined by their actual debt position at that time (the so-called "decision point") whereas previously, debt relief was based on a debtor's projected position at a later time (the "completion point"). It was broader because conditionality would now be defined by a country's poverty reduction strategy anchored by a "broad-based participatory process." And where countries needed more time to develop such a strategy, the initial relief could be based on an interim strategy setting out their commitment to and plans for developing such a strategy (IMF 1999c, International Development Association 1999 and 2002).

Change had to take place. By 1999 it had become clear that the 1996 HIPC was failing. By 1999, the debt of HIPC-eligible countries had quadrupled (from about $59 billion in 1980 to about $205 billion in 1999). On average, countries now faced debt burdens more than four times larger than their export earnings, and equivalent to more than their entire GDP (Birdsall and Williamson 2002). These facts mobilized debt-relief politics in industrialized countries.

Throughout the 1990s many NGOs had been monitoring the work of the IMF and World Bank and calling for more action on debt. However, in the late 1990s they became better organized and visible, and began to mobilize serious levels of public support on the issue. At the G-8 Summit in Birmingham in May 1998 an astonishing seventy thousand Jubilee 2000 supporters formed a Human Chain around Birmingham City Center urging the meeting of world leaders to forgive the debts of the world's poorest countries. As national and international media covered the event, even its organizers were amazed by the number of people, churches, charities, and civic organizations who had come out to demonstrate on the issues of debt and poverty.

Capitalizing on their success, by the end of 1998 a high-profile NGO campaign under the umbrella organization of Jubilee 2000 dominated the international media debate about debt. Although they addressed themselves to the IMF and World Bank, the real impact of their campaign was on voters within powerful creditor countries. "When a plea for debt relief becomes the common cause of a coalition that embraces both the Pope and the pop world, creditors should take notice," wrote the *Financial Times* in their leader of 17 February 1999. "The case for appropriate and radical action," the newspaper continued, "is compelling. Debt servicing imposes an impossible burden, particularly in Africa. Mozambique spends more on repaying debt than it spends on health: this is a country where one in five children die before the age of five. In Tanzania, payments consume more than the entire primary school budget" (*Financial Times* 17 February 1999, 21).

Creditor governments had rejected multilateral debt relief for both ideological and financial reasons. Ideologically, opposition focused on the adverse con-

---

public of the Congo, Ethiopia, Gambia, Ghana, Guinea, Guinea-Bissau, Kenya, Liberia, Madagascar, Malawi, Mali, Mauritania, Mozambique, Niger, Rwanda, São Tomé and Principe, Senegal, Sierra Leone, Somalia, Sudan, Tanzania, Togo, Uganda, and Zambia.

sequences of weakening contractual obligations undertaken by borrowers and on the impossibility of ensuring that relief would be well used. This was memorably expressed by Senator Phil Gramm:

> It is a pretty hard sell to talk about forgiving billions of dollars of debt to countries that borrowed money from us and, in too many cases, simply squandered or stole it, and now they do not want to repay it. They riot, they protest, they demand, but those things do not work in College Station, Texas. In College Station, Texas, when you borrow money from the bank or finance company or from your brother-in-law, you are expected to pay it back (Gramm to U.S. Senate 18 October 2000).

In the upper echelons of the IMF and World Bank, this argument had its attractions but it was being rapidly superseded by the simple fact that large amounts of debt on their books were now recognized as unrepayable—putting at risk the financial solidity of the institutions. And among the wider public within industrialized countries the argument for "no relief" was rapidly losing sway.

In industrialized countries, opponents to debt relief soon found that they were losing the argument to a groundswell of public opinion. In late 1998 the new center-left government in Germany turned around that country's traditional opposition to debt reduction, and let it be known that debt relief would be showcased at the G-8 Summit to be held in Cologne in 1999 (Elliott 1998). Tellingly, no fewer than five of the eight countries attending the Summit produced debt relief proposals (Chote 1999).

In the United States, as Senator Biden would later declare to the Senate, the campaign to reduce debt drew together right-wing Christians such as Reverend Pat Robertson and left-wing legislators such as Maxine Waters (Address in the U.S. Senate, 12 Oct 2000). In a more complaining tone in his closing remarks to the 106th Senate, Senator Phil Gramm declared, "I had a group of holy people come to my office the other day to lobby for this debt forgiveness. I do not think since Constantine the Great called his ecumenical council in Nicaea has there been a larger gathering of holy people in one place than the people who came to see me about supporting debt forgiveness" (U.S. Senate, 18 October 2000). The impact of public pressure such as those faced by Senator Gramm helped to unblock a new approach.

Public pressure on the debt strategy focused on two features that would shape a new approach. The first was poverty reduction. The original HIPC had mainly left poverty alleviation to other agencies and processes, requiring only that the international financial institutions monitor progress toward the OECD 1996 Development Assistance Committee goals of poverty reduction and social development. The old approach reflected the view that poverty alleviation was best "supported by the international community through various instruments, including lending, policy dialogue, and social expenditure reviews" rather than through explicit IMF and World Bank programs (IMF 1998b). The enhanced debt relief initiative changed this.

In 1999, the IMF joined the World Bank in voicing a new focus on poverty, recognizing "increasing evidence that entrenched poverty and severe inequality in economic opportunities and asset endowments can themselves be impediments to growth" (IMF 1999c). In large part the new focus on poverty was a direct response to the concerns of people and governments within industrialized countries. Two decades of indebtedness in Africa had exacerbated poverty within the poorest countries. Any new debt relief initiative would have to demonstrate that it was attempting to remedy this.

The second new element of the enhanced strategy was its explicit commitment to let countries and their peoples "take the lead." Bank and Fund conditionality was to be based on strategies developed locally with the active participation of civil society and NGOs as well as donors and international institutions. The key concepts driving the new process would be "participation" and "ownership." "Participation" captured a new "on-the-ground" approach to working with local communities and nongovernmental organization. This mirrored what was happening in Washington, D.C., as more NGOs became involved in input, advocacy, and the monitoring of results of HIPC.

"Ownership" captured a rethinking being undertaken within the Bank and Fund as to how each might improve the commitment of governments to reform and thereby the effectiveness of conditionality. It dovetailed with a public anxiety about the institutions imposing harsh terms on governments. The new emphasis on ownership permitted the institutions to respond both to critics of their harshness and critics of their ineffectiveness.

The role of NGOs in influencing the debt strategy was significant. From 1998 onward large well-organized NGOs (mostly from industrialized countries) successfully carved out a place for themselves in the official review of HIPC. Their campaign for debt reduction targeted both the IMF and the World Bank, accusing the institutions of failing to listen or heed the views of people within the most indebted countries. Many NGOs presented themselves as proxies for otherwise marginalized people, at least in negotiations at the international level. In this role, they played a very active part in the review of HIPC. To cite a joint report of the Fund and Bank:

> From the very beginning the HIPC process has benefited from consultation with civil society in all parts of the world. . . . Recently, a number of organizations have produced detailed and insightful analyses on the HIPC Initiative and debt relief more broadly. We want to build on this existing consultative process as we carry out this year's comprehensive review. (IMF 1999c)

The Fund and Bank proceeded to formalize the input of NGOs in the 1999 review, creating a broad-based consultative exercise managed at the headquarters in Washington. This shaped the rhetoric of the enhanced debt strategy. It also further established a pattern of engagement with NGOs—whether at headquarters in Washington or in the field—in formulating poverty reduction strategies.

For the Bank and Fund as institutions (i.e., for their management and staff), the new participatory approach had direct political benefits. Increasing openness to NGOs both softened critiques of the organizations and enhanced the leverage of management over the creditor governments in which most of the powerful, well organized, and mobilized NGOs were based. Robert Wade proposes to us that the new alliance "may be understood, in part, as an attempt to build a broad constituency of support precisely so that the Bank is not completely beholden to the U.S. government and a narrow range of US 'gotcha' NGOs" (Wade 2001). However, as Wade goes on to note, much of the new alliance and broadened Bank agenda was "largely rhetorical and aimed at satisfying external Part I [i.e. creditor] entities rather than intended to have any effect on the goods and services delivered to the borrowers in return for loans" (Wade 2001).

A second effect of the new alliance with NGOs is that it boosted the resources available for the institutions to use in implementing the new debt strategy, as the World Bank heralds on its website:

> In 1999, the Jubilee 2000 global coalition and hundreds of other interested NGOs participated with the Bank in a six-month review of the HIPC Initiative. The contributions to the HIPC review from civil society directly resulted in the doubling of debt relief pledged by international creditors, accelerated implementation, and the linking of relief to poverty reduction strategies. (www.worldbank.org)

At the global level the new participation of NGOs opened up the debate about debt relief and mobilized political support in industrialized countries, forcing governments and the international financial institutions to engage with a wider audience and a wider range of interlocutors.

At the national level in borrowing countries, the participation by NGOs provoked a new debate about who participates and why in IMF and World Bank consultations and public outreach exercises. Critics argue that a very selective process of engagement has emerged that privileges some groups over others and too often bypasses the broader "civil society" (Scholte 2001). A second criticism is that too often the new participation excludes or marginalizes existing political institutions such as political parties and parliaments (Eggers, Florini, and Woods 2004). The growing antagonism between Southern and Northern NGOs, and indeed the intense suspicion on the part of Southern governments of Northern NGOs, exacerbated these problems.

The other key element of the enhanced HIPC was "ownership," a concept that emerged from several in-house studies and external evaluations undertaken in both the IMF and the World Bank that detail the degree to which traditional conditionality was not working. "Improving ownership" was seen as a way to ensure greater national commitment for policies and increasing public accountability through policy debate and better monitoring of expenditure and outcomes.

The clearest expression of the new ownership approach lies in the 1997–98 World Bank's Comprehensive Development Framework (CDF), although there had previously been significant informal discussion about ownership, both within the Bank and even more so within the DAC and donor community. For example, the "radical" initiative on aid relationships in Tanzania, which centered on ownership, and in which the Bank was directly involved, preceded the CDF. Within the IMF, rather a latecomer, the ownership issue received a significant impetus from the external ESAF review. Drawing on earlier research into the Bank's relations with its borrowers (World Bank 1989f, World Bank 1996b), the CDF aimed to "put the country in the driver's seat, both 'owning' and directing the policy agenda, with the Bank and the country's other partners each defining their support in their respective business plans." The key was to find "mechanisms to bring people together and build consensus." The Bank's role would be to support the process, which would forge stronger partnerships allowing for strategic selectivity, a reduction of wasteful competition, and an emphasis on the achievement of concrete results (World Bank 2001b).

The rhetoric of ownership is powerful. Much more difficult has been practical clarification of how to operationalize and muster strong staff support for the new approach. In its early renditions, increased ownership was frequently understood by staff to mean that they should better explain conditionality and its rationale to local groups (Piciotto and Weaving 1994). In respect of its poorest borrowers, the Bank's own findings highlight serious difficulties in attempting to alter its policies and its modus operandi (World Bank 2002c). In spite of these problems, the most recent study of the Bank's evaluation department provides empirical evidence of why greater ownership will lead to more effective development assistance (Operations Evaluation Department 2003).

For the IMF the new participatory approach to negotiating conditions for debt relief posed a yet more substantial challenge. The institution voiced its desire "to be ready to assess new approaches and to recognize and support a healthy process of experimentation and innovation. Fund staff will be open to considering alternative adjustment paths, taking into account their impact on the poor" (IMF 1999c). However, this would always be difficult for an organization used to monitoring concrete specific actions through intensive internal review processes. The new framework called for a more fluid approach and one that required the institution to balance several competing "key features." The Fund would have to narrow its approach to ensure more selective structural conditionality and more emphasis on measures to improve public resource management and accountability. At the same time, however, the framework calls on the Fund to broaden its approach so as to embed poverty reduction in overall strategies, ensure budgets are pro-poor, and undertake social impact analysis. The IMF, with its emphasis on fast crisis response, is bound to have a great deal more trouble with participatory processes (Boughton and Mourmouras 2002).

At a more general level, ownership poses a larger challenge to both the IMF and the Bank, requiring them to undertake a degree of self-denial—to facilitate specific outcomes but at the same time to abjure from imposing conditionality. To sharpen up their expertise but to hold it back in preference for the new broader, country-based, participatory approach to designing policies. Fund staff speaking to assessors of the new initiative voiced fears that in the end this trade-off is one of "ownership" versus "quality" (Adam and Bevan 2001, 4). In practice, however, the result has been to change little.

The Impact of the New Strategy

In 2003 the Jubilee Research group described the progress of HIPC as "glacial," referring to the fact that only eight countries (rather than a projected twenty-one) had reached completion point and therefore benefited from stock-of-debt reduction (Jubilee 2003). According to the IMF and the World Bank, two obstacles have rendered progress very slow. First, there has been a lack of adequate funding for the initiative. Creditor governments have failed to convert support for the initiative into "firm commitments" and to provide adequate "topping up" funding to increase debt relief, especially since so many HIPC countries are suffering from the global economic downturn and a fall in commodity prices (International Development Association 2002). Furthermore, many countries need further grants, particularly the most vulnerable countries, some of whom are too far in arrears and too conflict-affected even to qualify for interim assistance.

Critics argue that the Fund and Bank could themselves put more of their resources into debt relief—net income from the Bank and gold sales from the Fund (Jubilee 2003). The Bank and Fund respond that this would weaken their capacity to provide financial support to low-income countries, including the HIPCs (International Development Association 2002). It would also cast some of the costs of debt relief onto their borrowers.

The lack of committed funding to debt relief means—to cite a report by the Bank's operations evaluations department—that the Fund and Bank cannot hope to improve both debt sustainability and poverty alleviation in the most heavily indebted countries. Debt sustainability requires redesigning the ways resources are delivered to countries—something the institutions can do. Poverty reduction requires increasing the resources delivered to poor countries—for which the Fund and Bank must rely on other aid flows (Operations Evaluation Department 2003, 57). On this logic, the enhanced debt strategy is a less radical revision than it seems. Constrained by resources, the Bank and Fund must still rely heavily on indebted countries "adjusting" so as better to be able to service their debts and invest in poverty alleviation.

A second reason for the slow progress on debt relief lies in the conditionality attached to HIPC. The new conditionality requires countries to produce a poverty reduction strategy in a consultative and participatory way. Where this is difficult, countries can use an interim procedure to access relief. However, the old conditionalities must also still be met. In the absence of much greater funding, adjustment is still the mainstay of the debt strategy. And this continues to be difficult and contentious.

To qualify for debt relief, countries are required to meet macroeconomic targets in respect of inflation, fiscal balance, and their external position, as well as to implement structural and sectoral reforms (IMF 2001e). Critics accuse the IMF of applying these targets to crisis-ridden countries with far too great a vigor. They argue that the Fund is forcing countries off-track for debt relief by applying overly conservative fiscal targets and focusing too much on privatization in the conditionality attached to HIPC. Some fourteen of the nineteen program countries in the HIPC process have fallen "off track" at least once (Jubilee 2003, 3).

To some degree the institutions' own review tells a similar rather pessimistic story. Summarizing the experience of HIPC-eligible countries, the staff of the IMF and World Bank detail slippages in fiscal policy and delays in structural reforms and privatization measures to explain why several countries, such as Ghana, Malawi, the Central African Republic, Senegal, Rwanda, and Tanzania, have been slow in qualifying (IMF/World Bank 2002).

A fundamental question here is whether the conditionality—for these countries at this time—is right. Or, more pointedly, what explains the priorities reflected in the ongoing conditionality? Does it reflect the needs and economic conditions of each country? Or is it being overly shaped by the resource constraints of the institutions?

The enhanced HIPC promised a new process for fashioning conditionality—one that focused on participation and ownership. Yet, the evidence suggests that in practice little has changed. Take two countries discussed earlier in this chapter—Senegal and Zambia. Each has run into difficulties in its path toward eligibility for debt relief. In Senegal the IMF and World Bank write that external debt stock indicators have worsened significantly as a result of lower export projections than anticipated and that progress in economic reforms has been slow (International Development Association 2002, 65). Particular sticking points in Senegal's performance have been in respect of privatizing the peanut industry and privatizing and deregulating electricity.

About Zambia the institutions are more sanguine: "All structural performance criteria and benchmarks were met" they announced in 2002 (International Development Association 2002, 69), heralding the government's commitment to a speedy privatization of the Zambia National Commercial Bank (ZNCB) in a later press release (IMF 2002). However, low world prices for copper and the closure of mines in Zambia have meant lower export earnings in Zambia and therefore an ongoing unsustainable burden of debt.

Instantly recognizable in the cases of Senegal and Zambia are two factors that have marked Africa's last two decades: the devastating impact of external factors and in particular lower world prices and markets in commodities; and the unabated continuation of structural conditionalities whose urgency, sequencing, and efficacy in countries facing extreme economic (and often political) crisis are at the very least a matter of debate. The argument is not that in the abstract structural adjustment is wrong. It is that countries suffering extreme political and social stress do not enjoy the conditions necessary for all such reforms to be beneficial. These pre-conditions include the core infrastructure, political capital, and transparent, effective institutions, which are necessary in order to proceed with wholesale programs of privatization and liberalization.

In conversations with country experts in both the IMF and the World Bank, it is clear that many staff in both institutions know this. There has doubtless been a great deal more rhetoric about ownership than actual change in practices. However, there have been some significant changes by donors at the country level where an increased proportion of aid from some countries is taking the form of budget support or sectoral programs. For example, the UK Department for International Development reports that some 15 percent of its bilateral aid program is being disbursed in budget support and other forms of program aid (DFID 2004a, 117–18 and 162–63). Furthermore, at least in respect to some countries, there is an improvement in donor coordination (Renzio 2004, OECD/DAC 2004). However, there are larger institutional imperatives, which prevent the core approach from changing.

What Is Driving the IMF and World Bank?

Three obvious tensions arise out of the way the Bank and Fund might adapt to better achieve their mission in Africa. Each takes us back to the institutions' sources of power and autonomy explored in the first two chapters of this book. In the first place, each institution has long relied on its specialist "expertise" as a rationale for conditionality and as a source of influence in persuading governments to undertake reform. In giving advice, experts in each institution face very powerful incentives not to deviate from standardized prescriptions. The more standard the template of conditionality they negotiate, the less any individual staff member will have to justify his or her actions. It is a risk-averse strategy for staff whose time is short and whose expertise is more theoretical than empirical.

Equally, for each institution a template makes life easier. It makes it easier to claim that all borrowers are being treated equally. Furthermore, the closer the institution's advice reflects a consensus among professional economists, the easier it will be for the institution to justify its prescriptions in terms of specialist expertise. All of this will be threatened if ownership and participation were genuinely to take hold in the modus operandi of each institution.

A genuine local ownership of policies, resulting from broad local participation in Africa, would likely produce more complex and diverse policy packages. The Bank has recently noted the tension "between the Bank's country focus and its implementation of more comprehensive and rigorous operational standards" (World Bank 2002b, vi). Taking steps away from their professionalized economic expertise takes each institution into uncharted territory—not just as economists but also as institutions with norms, practices, and structures, which have developed because they are useful to the institutions.

A second tension in the new mission in Africa takes us back to the financial structure of the Fund and Bank and the nature of lending they undertake. Institutional reform and poverty alleviation take considerably longer to achieve than the kinds of macroeconomic and microeconomic structural adjustment measures that have been promulgated in conditionality to date. The ESAF review discussed above demonstrated that the institutions tend to focus their energy and hard conditionality on short-term monitorable targets rather than broader long-term goals.

A new broader mission in Africa, which strengthens the processes of decision-making rather than just focusing on targets, will be much more difficult to implement, measure, and monitor. Institutional change, degrees of participation and ownership, and poverty alleviation are all multifaceted and complex goals. A recent study of the "new approach" to IMF conditionality found that the new poverty reduction strategy papers "have tended to be rather general, weakly prioritised and of variable quality" (Killick 2002).

The essential question is whether short- and medium-term conditional financing instruments can achieve the longer-term goals of the IMF and the World Bank. If they cannot, the institutions need to retool or to delegate to other institutions better placed to undertake the longer-term mission.

A third and final tension in the IMF and World Bank's mission in Africa is that between "borrower ownership" and "donor control." The aid community is now discussing longer-term and more concessional lending or grants that will not necessarily be channeled through the Fund or Bank—such as the Global Fund for AIDS/HIV Tuberculosis and Malaria and the new Millennium Challenge Account. The contradiction arising from these new funds is that they offer yet another donor-controlled modality of development assistance. Just as some economists are drawing the lesson from debt relief that aid works best where it is fungible (Birdsall and Williamson 2002), the new "global fund" model of governance proposes assistance that is less fungible and more highly directed and controlled by international donors. Indeed, policymakers within Africa have argued that this new approach further hollows out any possibility of genuine participation or ownership in the budgetary process within countries (Tumusiime-Mutebile 2002).

The Bank and Fund risk being caught somewhere between their new mission and a new model of financing development. Their new mission attempts to inject enhanced participation and ownership into their work and necessarily devolves (or will in the future devolve) responsibility and control to borrowers. Yet the new model of development funding injects greater donor control or at the very least greater donor scrutiny of "concrete, provable results."

The problem for the Fund and Bank is this. They are under increasing pressure to demonstrate results. This is captured in the ferocious critiques of the institutions mounted both by the U.S. Congress through a commission it appointed in 2000 (Meltzer Commission 2000) and by the remarks of the then-incoming U.S. secretary of treasury Paul O'Neill (Blustein 2001b). Yet their mission is being rewritten to set goals that are, by definition, more difficult to evaluate and to prove successful.

A final comment needs to be made about the relationship between the IMF and the World Bank. The new debt relief initiative has brought the Fund and Bank into greater areas of potential conflict with one another. As had occurred before, the respective roles of the IMF and the World Bank had to be very carefully negotiated and elaborated (a proposal for them to work together on joint programs had failed to gain support). The documentation about HIPC subtly reveals the tension between the institutions. To quote the Fund's definition of their relationship:

The staffs of the Fund and Bank will need to cooperate closely and seek to present the authorities with a coherent overall view, focusing on their traditional areas of expertise in line with past agreements between the two institutions. . . . In order to fulfil their role in assisting in preparation of the macroeconomic strategy, the Fund staff will need to be able to interpret the work of the Bank and other institutions. However, consistent with the views of the Board, the Fund staff will not attempt to supplement or substitute for Bank work in poverty analysis or the development of social policies. (IMF 1999c)

In substance the World Bank has been assigned to take the lead in advising countries on the design, cost assessment, and monitoring of poverty reduction strategies; the design of sectoral strategies and structural reforms such as privatization and regulatory reform; the strengthening of institutions including public expenditure reviews; and the provision of social safety nets.

The IMF's role is to lead in its traditional areas of responsibility such as in promoting prudent macroeconomic policies, structural reforms in areas such as exchange rate and tax policy, and issues related to fiscal management, budget execution, fiscal transparency, and tax and customs administration. The division of labor leaves many areas of overlap, mostly notably in governance issues such as "establishing an environment conducive to private sector growth," trade liberalization, and financial sector development.

Beneath the polite language of collaboration, liaison between the IMF and the World Bank was found to be "seriously deficient" in the external evaluation of ESAF (IMF External Evaluation 1998, 34). The expert reviewers found that as the Fund broadened its agenda into areas of the World Bank's expertise, it was still not working closely with the Bank on the ground. While "expressions of goodwill" abound, no attempt had been made to undertake the "major institutional change" necessary if technical advice were to be improved. Indeed, they found no evidence of even the minimal requisite formalization of procedures for cross-institutional teamwork and decision rules (IMF External Evaluation 1998, 34).

The IMF and World Bank have found it extremely difficult to facilitate successful economic growth, development, and policy reform in line with their conditionality in Africa. This is puzzling from the outside because the institutions look very powerful vis-à-vis Africa. They have leverage due to their resources and knowledge. Their borrowers in Africa are among the least likely to have access to alternative sources of finance. Powerful shareholders are less likely than elsewhere to override the authority of the institutions to meet their own geopolitical goals. In sum, Africa is the one region in which we might expect the staff of the institutions to act relatively independently of the ideologies and preferences of the most powerful member states. Under these conditions, the technical expertise and research of the IMF and the World Bank might well be expected to come to the fore.

The experience of sub-Saharan Africa highlights weaknesses within the international financial institutions. Those weaknesses cannot all be attributed to political pressures from outside. In Africa countries seem to have been poorly served by the research and lending practices of the Fund and Bank. The most recent evaluations undertaken by the World Bank staff and the IMF's independent evaluation office highlight the shortcomings of their respective missions to date (Independent Evaluation Office 2002, World Bank 2002c). Too often specific policy advice has been fashioned according to easy blueprints rather than hard research—ideological presumptions rather than tested theories. Certainly the institutions have had limited resources with which to fashion policies for poor, indebted countries. But even within those constraints, it would seem that they economized on staff time in designing programs for their most needy borrowers, they were very slow to seize and shape the issue of debt relief in respect to sums owed to themselves, and most poignantly of all even after two decades of engagement their main borrowers in sub-Saharan Africa seem no closer to the promise of economic growth, and are still highly indebted to the IMF and World Bank. This experience, set alongside that of emerging market economies such as Mexico, and transition countries such as Russia, discussed in earlier chapters, necessitates consideration of how each institution could be reformed.

Chapter 7

REFORMING THE IMF AND WORLD BANK

The IMF and the World Bank are extraordinary international institutions. Their money, remit, and expertise endow them with a power about which other international organizations can only dream. The fact that they are automatically funded and earn income from their lending and investments gives them a degree of independence unrivaled by other institutions. They exist to foster global monetary cooperation and financial stability, facilitate international trade, promote high employment and sustainable economic growth, reduce poverty, and improve the living standards of people in the developing world. They can pursue these aims through lending and conditionality as well as through research. They employ the largest number of applied economists of any institution in the world, aggregating an awe-inspiring bank of economic data and applied research.

Critics assail the IMF and World Bank from all sides. They accuse the institutions of being U.S. dominated. They charge them with peddling poor quality economic advice. Each institution is indicted for supporting or even promoting corrupt and oppressive regimes. This chapter reviews and builds on the evidence assembled in this book. It argues that the work of the Fund and Bank is affected by the preferences of their most powerful members, by their own bureaucratic motives, and by politics within countries with whom they work. They are not purely technical institutions. Economists are naïve to assume that the Fund and Bank would work better if they were insulated from the hurly burly of politics. The agencies cannot escape the political decisions and debates they sit within. What would make them more effective is a governance structure that better mediated the competing interests they face. This chapter seeks to lay out that structure.

What Drives the Institutions?

Three forces drive and shape what the IMF and World Bank try to do. First, there are the interests of their most powerful member countries—very much led by the

United States. Powerful countries define the outer perimeter within which each organization works. Often, this means particular agencies within a powerful country—such as the U.S. Treasury. This sets down a general direction for the institution, but seldom defines the detail of what each of the IMF and World Bank do.

The second set of forces is economic ideas, fashions, and orthodoxies, as shaped by the needs of each institution. The well-known Washington consensus is one example. Fiscal and monetary prudence were bastions of a consensus emerging in economics as well as in politics by the end of the inflation-prone 1970s. For the IMF, this offered a clear starting-point for dealing with the chaos of the debt crisis. For the World Bank, the consensus on adjustment through privatization, deregulation, and sectoral reform did the same. It offered a conditionality-heavy but relatively resource-light way to deal with a large number of member countries in crisis at the same time. The alternatives would have required more staff effort and time, more resources, and greater political largesse on the part of major shareholders.

The third set of forces is bureaucratic. They take us into the offices of the staff and management to discover pressures and incentives within which they work. In the World Bank a disbursement culture has long prevailed for the obvious reason that it is IBRD lending which sustains each institution. Staff are rewarded for lending more not less. In the IMF staff face pressures to come up with programs that are approved not just by their senior managers but by the borrowing government. The way to achieve this is to maximize the amount that can be lent by massaging growth projections and the link to make a larger loan possible.

Other pressures shape the detail of the work. Consider the individual staff member sent to a faraway country to negotiate loan conditions. He or she could attempt an altogether innovative approach that drew on local customs and circumstances. But that would be both time-consuming and risky. It would attract considerable scrutiny and questioning by senior managers and the Board back in D.C. If things went wrong, the individual designer would be held to account. By contrast, if the staff member simply replicates what the organization has done in all other countries, the program becomes collectively the organization's responsibility.

Traced through time, the three forces shaping the IMF and World Bank explain how and why each organization has developed a particular mission. Chapter 1 began this journey depicting agencies born in the cauldron of the Second World War, delivered by statesmen who dramatically rewrote the rules of economic cooperation among states. The result was not simply a projection of U.S. interests. A powerful set of ideas and circumstances informed a bold new model which accorded the institutions important degrees of independence. Over time that independence has eroded. The IMF and World Bank have come under increasing U.S. influence. Yet political differences within the United States and uncertainty about how best to achieve the goals of each institution have opened up scope for other factors to shape the work of the IMF and World Bank. Prime among these is the study of economics, as explored in chapter 2.

Economics does not give perfect answers to how governments should run economies. The growth of any economy depends heavily on its vulnerability to shocks, many of which lie beyond its control—exchange rate movements, commodity price shifts, private capital movements, the weather and natural disasters, and volatile aid flows. Equally, the effects of economic policy depend on the nature of a country's infrastructure and industrial capacity, and the state of its political institutions. Yet since at least the 1980s the IMF and World Bank have promulgated a relatively simple answer to what government should do, and that is to stabilize, liberalize, privatize, and deregulate.

The advice and policy prescriptions of the IMF and World Bank have not emerged as a result of pure economic research and debate. Rather, the institutions have adapted economic ideas to fit their available resources and instruments. Facing new challenges, each institution has dashed in using tools already at hand. Necessarily, each has left behind economic theories or policy prescriptions which would require greater resources or a different expertise. This greatly narrows the consensus forged within the institutions and used to prescribe conditionality for countries. In turn, the narrow consensus can become a trap for the institutions, creating fertile conditions for groupthink and a fixation on a particular interpretation of events, screening out alternative scenarios and thereby failing to foresee crises.

On the other side of the work of the IMF and World Bank lie member governments with whom they must work. Developing, transition, and emerging economies all borrow from the institutions. Chapter 3 explored the ways the Fund and Bank coerce or persuade able and willing interlocutors in these countries. In respect of needy governments, they have considerable bargaining power. Each institution can lend or withhold resources, disburse or suspend payments, and impose various forms of conditions. Yet influence depends heavily on whether they can find and work with the right (as seen from the perspective of the Bank and Fund) government officials.

Sometimes Fund and Bank officials find themselves working with sympathetic policy-makers in borrowing countries who are willing and able to embrace at least the main priorities preferred by the institutions. The willingness of interlocutors is influenced by their circumstances as well as their training and mindset. For example, in many countries the 1980s debt crisis helped to discredit existing ideas about economic policy and demolished the resources necessary to implement them. In that context, debtor governments sought new policies. The so-called Washington consensus offered a solution that fit both within the immediate resource constraint faced by governments and within international political pressures to which they were subjected. The consequence was an emphasis on squeezing expenditure rather than more effective investment.

But not all governments implemented Washington consensus policies. Where finance officials enjoyed power in a centralized government relatively insulated from other political pressures, they had more scope to undertake reforms under the tutelage of the IMF and World Bank. The prospects of change were yet greater where the bureaucracy could be swiftly reconfigured to reflect new priorities. It is under these conditions that the international institutions have more influence. But is this ideal?

All economic policy redistributes benefits, risks, and opportunities. Those who win from a policy are always likely to argue that it is the optimal policy, best reflecting national interests. Losers will argue the opposite. The key question is who should decide which measure is adopted? Some argue that expert economists should decide. Indeed, in the same vein they argue that economic reform should be pursued as rapidly as possible so as to forestall political mobilization against change (Krueger 2004). Politics, in other words, should be kept out because it mainly opens up opportunities for rent-seekers. In this view, the legitimacy of economic policy should rest on its outcomes—such as economic growth.

The problem with the technocratic view is that it assumes that we know what measures will bring about economic growth or indeed balanced growth—not in a general way but in a specific way. Experts, in other words, have hard facts to use in adjudicating among competing alternatives. Yet once economists step outside of pure theory they find it difficult to forecast the growth effects of competing policies (Helleiner 1982). In the Bank and Fund such forecasts are shaped not just by poverty or distributional effects but by the institutional and political preferences of powerful member governments. A clear example is IMF and World Bank work in support of HIPC debt relief where staff take the amount of relief as a given (i.e. what donors are prepared to put on the table) and then make overly optimistic projections in respect to an indebted country's macroeconomic growth, tax collection, and fiscal balances to ensure that HIPC sustainability and MDG criteria are met.

This pries open the question of legitimacy. It means that economic policy as prescribed by the Fund and Bank cannot be justified in purely technical terms. Not least because their work is at least partly driven by a political process within each institution. Furthermore, the implementation of policies preferred by the Fund and Bank relies on political processes within borrowing countries. These cannot be wished away. Interest groups within countries often succeed in capturing and distorting the way economic policy is implemented. In some cases this occurs in precisely the political conditions favored by the Fund and Bank for other reasons. The very same conditions that facilitate Fund- and Bank-favored "rational economic policy"—centralization and insulation from politics—can equally facilitate unbalanced policy capture by interest groups. In Mexico from 1982 to 1988, for example, private sector groups lobbied very actively to shape trade liberalization (Kraemer 1995), and in some sectors they were joined by foreign investors to promote protectionist tariffs (Grether and Marcelo 1999). In Russia, two notorious privatization programs were captured by powerful private sector interests (Hellman 1998, Hellman et al. 2000, and see chapter 5).

Participation and political competition in economic policy does not prevent corruption and inefficiency but it can make it more difficult to hide the "policy capture" that so often takes place by powerful interest groups (Hellman 2000). In more open and contested political systems finance officials can be subjected to the scrutiny and constraints of party politics, electoral cycles, and widespread social debate and protest. This often thwarts the "rational" reform conditions supported by the IMF and World Bank and marginalizes their influence. However, the messy and complex processes of democratic decision-making at least provide an imperfect and rudimentary form of political accountability.

At the core of a democratic political process is not simply the fact that governments are elected. Rather, the ideal democratic decision-making process is one bounded by agreed rules, usually including open consultation and deliberation and fairness in procedure. The rules are enforced by institutions that hold policymakers to account, including public and legal bodies such as judges, courts, ombudsmen, government auditors and evaluators, as well as private groups. People within the system may disagree with a particular decision and indeed bear losses from it. However, a general belief in the legitimacy and fairness of the system itself sustains it.

For the IMF and the World Bank open, participatory, and consultative decision-making processes open up a number of dilemmas. In their rhetoric both institutions have begun to shift their ultimate goals away from specific economic measures and toward a broader vision of persuading governments to build better and more accountable institutions of governance. Such a shift, however, has some perverse implications for the institutions, as illustrated by the cases of Mexico, Russia, and by the work of the IMF and World Bank in sub-Saharan Africa.

In Mexico up until 1994 the transformation of the economy was heralded by many as an exemplar of how the Washington consensus might be applied. As documented in chapter 4, a small group of Mexican policymakers worked very closely with officials from the IMF and World Bank—including in secret meetings and negotiations—to forge an agenda of reform that affected the whole economy. The influence of the Bank and Fund was at a high point when interlocutors sympathetic to their agenda had consolidated a grip across the bureaucracy that ran Mexico. Subsequently, however, the realm of the economic technocrats has been limited by democratization, which has brought to power a mixture of opposition forces and breathed life into Mexico's (previously rubberstamping) Congress. This has narrowed the power of the technocrats and with it the influence of the IMF and World Bank.

Hidden yet further within the Mexico story is a recognition by both the IMF and the World Bank that sometimes their analysis is not "first rate." In interviews, IMF officials in the early 1990s argued that the IMF had to field its best economists and advice in Mexico since that country's officials were so highly qualified. More recently, the World Bank has noted that in Mexico it has needed to do "exceptionally good work, combining world-class international experiences and analytical skills with deep knowledge of the country and its institutions" (World Bank 2004d, 23). Later the same report speaks of the Bank having more influence where it provides "first-class policy analysis" (World Bank 2004d, 24). Both the IMF and the Bank recognize that in some instances and in respect to some countries their advice is not the best. This is borne out by evaluations into their advice to Russia, and in their advice to some of the poorest African countries where some of their least impressive technical work was proffered to governments. This further erodes the claim that technical knowledge should supervene over the democratic process.

In Russia the institutions had a tough job. As instruments of a wider Western agenda to stabilize Russia and support governments that were not hostile to the West, both the IMF and the World Bank soon found their usual bargaining power constrained by the political priorities of their most powerful members. Major Western powers did not delegate tasks to the Fund or Bank in a clear-cut way. At times the international financial institutions were expected to "do their job," at other times they were expected to tailor their work to secure political rather than economic results. Little surprise then that many Fund and Bank staff believe they would have been more successful had their conditions not been constantly diluted by special terms and exceptions made by the United States and others. Yet, this is not obvious.

In Russia, as elsewhere, the Bank and Fund needed interlocutors who were both ideologically willing and institutionally able to implement prescribed solutions. But politically Russia was difficult. Although decision-making in Russia was relatively centralized, as chapter 5 detailed, Yeltsin's presidential style involved constant trade-offs between Congress and executive. This gave little by way of a constant platform to interlocutors most sympathetic to the IMF and World Bank. On the roundabout of Russian "court politics" there was little the international institutions could do to strengthen their position or that of the agencies they were placed within. In that context, both the IMF and World Bank had little leverage in Russia. Their loans at most tipped a couple of tactical battles among the ruling policymakers.

But even had the Fund and Bank faced more propitious political circumstances in Russia, were their prescribed reforms the right ones? Was each institution in command of the best solutions, and were these solutions reflected in the conditions applied in loans? Economists continue to debate which of the various alternative policies might have had the best effects in Russia—there is evidence for and against particular measures. What we can say is that Fund and Bank priorities were not shaped purely by economic research and analysis. Policies were prioritized by the IMF and World Bank according to political pressures, judgments, and opportunities, as well as by institutional exigencies and resource constraints. This severely dents the view that Fund and Bank conditionality is legitimized by the fact that it represents the best economic solution and that which is most likely to foster economic growth.

Unlike Russia, across countries in sub-Saharan Africa the IMF and World Bank have had a freer hand to set conditionality and to use their bargaining power with governments. For these reasons, the continent should be a showcase for the technical expertise of the IMF and World Bank. Unlike Mexico and Russia, the country-level work of each international institution is not overridden by threats to international financial stability or the need to stabilize a nuclear arsenal. Nowhere has good quality economic advice been more needed. Many African governments have limited capacity to analyze global economic trends and shocks, yet their economies are hugely influenced by such forces. The IMF and World Bank also have a very strong bargaining position in sub-Saharan Africa. Many borrowing governments face a disastrous external position and few have other sources of finance. Bilateral aid flows have long tended to follow behind IMF and World Bank accreditation, loans, and programs. In brief, the Fund and Bank have been powerful gatekeepers to all aid flows.

The experience of sub-Saharan Africa underscores deep challenges for the international financial institutions. The Fund and Bank rely for influence on interlocutors who are both willing and able. Borrowers must be represented by officials who are willing to take up and act on the priorities highlighted by the institutions. And the relevant officials must have the political authority and jurisdiction to implement such measures. In Africa, as revealed in chapter 6, this was often not the case. That said, a second powerful question arises: were the prescribed reforms the right ones?

The countries of sub-Saharan Africa seem to have been poorly served by the research and lending practices of the Fund and Bank. The most recent evaluations undertaken by the World Bank staff and the IMF's independent evaluation office highlight the shortcomings of their respective missions to date (Independent Evaluation Office 2002, World Bank 2002c). Too often specific policy advice has been fashioned according to easy blueprints rather than hard research—ideological presumptions have triumphed over tested theories.

It is true that the Fund and Bank have limited resources with which to research and fashion policies for poor indebted countries. The available data are often poor, they have limited time, and a large canvass to cover. But even within those constraints, it would seem that they economized on staff time in designing programs for their most needy borrowers. They were very slow to seize and shape the issue of debt relief in respect of sums owed to themselves. Most poignantly of all, even after two decades of engagement their main borrowers in sub-Saharan Africa seem no closer to the promise of economic growth, and are still highly indebted to the IMF and World Bank.

The experience in sub-Saharan Africa, set alongside that of emerging market economies such as Mexico, and transition countries such as Russia, demands that changes be considered. But what kinds of changes? The analysis of this book highlights that hiring different economists to work in each organization would change little unless the incentives within which they work are also altered. The Fund and Bank adopt particular economic models and priorities as a function of what is politically feasible, what is institutionally rational, and what is credible based on the available resources from creditor governments. Like it or not the process is influenced by politics within and outside of each institution. For these reasons, we need to scrutinize politics within each organization and ask whether it adequately balances competing demands and pressures from their various stakeholders. The result of that political process determines in the end what each institution does.

What Role for the IMF and World Bank?

Underpinning this study is a belief that the IMF and the World Bank can play a useful and constructive role vis-à-vis the people represented by governments who borrow from them. Yet much of the evidence assembled in this book demonstrates ways in which the Fund and Bank have failed their borrowers. Their initial degree of independence has seeped away. Their lending has become overpriced and is often pro-cyclical, which means that instead of counterbalancing the inflow and outflow of volatile markets, the IMF and World Bank loans are often part of the herd. Their conditionality has been driven by political and bureaucratic pressures more than by evidence and technical expertise. Their political impact is often adverse. IMF loans are seen as protecting those responsible for a crisis by postponing their day of reckoning. World Bank loans seem to provide ample space for vested interests in both rich and poor countries to pursue private profit at the expense of public good.

Yet the IMF and World Bank have important tasks to complete. To date they have successfully magnified and accelerated the expansion of global commerce. Yet they were created to help manage and balance globalization, not simply to accelerate it.

The Bretton Woods twins are public institutions. Their founding documents direct them to ensure balanced growth, high levels of employment and income, and the development of productive resources in all their member countries. Their mission is to go where markets fail to reach, to intercede when markets fail, and to mitigate the harsh effects of volatility in the global economy. Put in economic terms, their role is to manage global externalities, and global and domestic market failures. To this end, there are distinctive roles each can play.

The IMF in the Global Economy

The international monetary system is driven and energized by global capital markets. But those markets create externalities and sometimes fail in ways that produce systemic risks, irrational behavior, contagion, spillovers from other countries' bad policies, and currency crises. All of these give governments strong reasons to cooperate in order to mitigate their vulnerability. This implies several roles for the IMF.

When a financial crisis explodes, the IMF has traditionally lent money and imposed conditionality on crisis-affected governments as a way to contain the crisis. But it has been difficult for the Fund to find an even-handed way to intervene. In the 1980s it only assisted countries that first paid their commercial creditors in full. This cast the institution into the role of debt-collector. Subsequently the institution is still searching for the right position even though it has now reversed its policy not to lend to countries in arrears on their payments to private creditors. A yet more fundamental constraint is that the resources the IMF can lend to a crisis-stricken country are now dwarfed by massive and growing capital market flows.

The solution favored by the management of the IMF is to increase the jurisdiction of the institution—to give it a central role in managing financial crises based on legal powers rather than financial resources. Hence in 2001 the senior management of the institution proposed a "Sovereign Debt Rescheduling Mechanism" which would permit a crisis-afflicted country to call for a standstill of all payments with support from the IMF (Krueger 2001). However, this approach was firmly rejected by the United States (Taylor 2002).

A different role for the IMF in financial crises is advisory—offering member governments advice about how to mitigate the effects of a crisis, including the use of precautionary measures or capital controls. In the past this role has been compromised by the institution's failure to provide balanced advice. The Fund has long been associated with pushing hard for members to open up to foreign investment—or "capital account liberalization" as it is called. That policy in some cases increased the vulnerability of member countries (Prasad et al. 2003). It also made it taboo for economists within the institution to evaluate the potential use of limited capital controls or precautionary measures. The challenge for the IMF now is for its members to formulate a clear policy in this area (Independent Evaluation Office 2005). This is difficult in part because the institution cannot afford to be associated with any automatic imposition of capital controls (this would make it impossible to approach the Fund in a crisis). It is also difficult because there is a tradition of opposing capital controls among the staff.

A further advisory role for the IMF in financial crises relates to the institution's duty to ensure that governments are not forced to take measures destructive of national prosperity (to quote the Articles of Agreement of the IMF). It is striking that although the Fund has been involved in financial crises for over twenty years, it has not analyzed how different macroeconomic responses to a crisis impact social distribution and recovery. Meanwhile, outsiders claim that countries taking IMF advice and assistance do worse than countries who do not (Bordo and Schwartz 1998 and 2000). The IMF could usefully deploy its impressive research capacity and experience at least to begin collecting data that would help determine which crisis-management strategies might most mitigate the harshest social effects of a financial crisis.

In theory the Fund is well-placed to offer its members a more effective system of mutual insurance. For many emerging markets the current global monetary system poses a sharp triple risk of exchange rate crash, a sovereign debt default, and a domestic banking crisis. Some countries are attempting to protect themselves by building up massive foreign exchange reserves. In East Asia, for example, by the end of May 2002, monetary authorities had doubled their reserves to a level of some 38 percent of the world total and well beyond what standard monetary theory suggests they needed (Aizenman and Marion 2003). Since then, reserves in Asia have doubled once again. The IMF foresees them reaching US$1430.4 billion by 2005, up from a level of US$496.9 billion in 2002 (IMF 2005, 269).

The cost of self-insurance to Asian countries is very high. Less costly would be for countries to offer one another mutual insurance (as occurs in monetary unions or in bilateral swaps arrangements). However the most efficient way to mutually insure would be across regions and countries, pooling different and less correlated risks. The IMF offers a multilateral framework for such pooling. However, as the organization is currently structured it does not deliver.

In the IMF all members can draw automatically on the first tranche (25 percent) of the quota they lodge in the IMF. These sums however are too small to make a difference to a country in a liquidity crisis. One way to increase available resources would be dramatically to increase the IMF's quotas so that countries could draw automatically on a greater sum. Alternatively, the rules for drawing on existing credit could be changed. Undergirding either idea, however, is an assumption that members of the IMF share a confidence in the institution as a mutual insurance scheme. In the absence of some radical changes in governance, conditionality, and voting, such confidence is unlikely to emerge, especially from East Asian countries who since 1997 seem to have opted to ignore the institution rather than attempt to reform it.

Exchange rates are another neglected area of influence for the IMF. Exchange rates were a primary reason for creating the IMF back in 1944. The Great Depression had provided ample evidence of the downside to countries competitively devaluing with no restrictions. Yet the IMF has virtually no role in managing exchange rates today. It conducts surveillance, monitoring, and assistance in data dissemination in economies around the world. However, it plays no role as an independent arbiter of what constitutes a fair exchange rate. This leaves individual countries threatening trade sanctions and the like on the basis of their own unilateral judgments about the exchange rates of others. More broadly, the lack of multilateral coordination on exchange rates further exacerbates the pressures on developing countries currently trying to negotiate the perils of a fixed or floating rate.

Finally, in low-income countries as well as across all its membership the IMF has a role as a standard-setter and adviser. In theory, it could deploy its research, data, and expertise to assist members in identifying vulnerabilities and opportunities they face regionally and internationally, and offer practical ranges of solutions to those problems. Nowhere could this role be more valuable than in the poorest, least resourced countries of the world. Yet these countries do not perceive of the institution as experts to whom they can turn for practical, impartial advice. They experience the IMF as an institution which sets down terms and demands responses from them. As detailed in chapter 6, too often those terms have been blanket market-opening targets rather than a sharing of experience and advice aimed at helping a government manage integration into the world economy in a way which ensures a balanced and equitable pattern of growth within its borders.

Fairly radical reform is required for the IMF to redirect its research and policy so as to play an advisory and standard-setting role in a way that would better advantage its borrowers, and particularly its poorest and least developed borrowers. For this reason, again we are returned to the need for changes in the governance structure of the institution.

The World Bank and the Global Economy

The potential role for the World Bank is different from that of the IMF. The IBRD pools the credit ratings of its members, backed by their guarantees, to raise funds from capital markets to lend to members needing to borrow for development or for post-war reconstruction. Raising capital in this way can work even among much smaller groups of small and poor countries as evidenced to a limited degree by the Andean Development Cooperation. However, the larger the number of countries participating in such a pool, the more cheaply and effectively an institution can raise capital. In theory, the World Bank is ideally placed to raise development finance on behalf of all its membership.

Three things have altered the availability and costs of World Bank resources. First, wealthy non-borrowing members have reduced their contributions to the institution (as will be discussed in detail below). Second, an increasingly onerous bureaucratic process has grown up within the World Bank—principally as a way for the large bureaucracy to mitigate risks within its own walls. Finally, the conditions attached to loans have grown in breadth and depth. The result of the three forces described is that developing countries are displaying a diminishing appetite for borrowing from the World Bank. The financial consequences are elaborated later in this chapter.

Alongside lending, the World Bank is at the heart of global research and the production of technical advice on development. By "pooling" research resources, all countries stand to gain. However, the internal incentives and governance structure of the Bank have channeled research and policy prescriptions toward a very general level of overly prescriptive advice. The Bank's research has focused heavily on trade liberalization and the benefits of market-opening. Less attention has been paid to producing country-specific—and regionally sensitive—advice about the different kinds of infrastructure and social capital which could enable members to better exploit global markets.

A further "pooling" function the Bank could play is coordination in international development assistance which is notoriously fragmented, duplicative, and cluttered with a large number of donors tripping over each others' bilateral rather than multilateral efforts. Here, for example, the World Bank's International Development Association (IDA) offers concessional finance to poorer countries, serving not just as a source of finance but as a coordinated aid mechanism. This reduces transaction costs and improves information in a way that could be much more greatly leveraged by donors. However, at present donor countries typically contribute to IDA but at the same time set up multiple mechanisms for disbursing aid bilaterally. A recent such initiative was the Millennium Challenge Corporation (MCC) created by the United States. The set-up costs of the MCC alone were $5 million dollars in its first nine months. It took a further two years for the new institution to make its first loan (Millennium Challenge Corporation 2004). Multilateralism has the potential to cut out these costs as well as the yet more damaging ones inflicted on aid recipients by a fragmented and duplicative aid system.

Both the IMF and the World Bank have policy advice to offer. Yet their conditionality has attracted widespread criticism from outside the institutions as well as critical appraisal from within. A widely accepted conclusion has been that greater "ownership" by borrowing countries is required to make policy advice effective. To this end the Fund and Bank are now doing more consultation and better public relations in borrowing countries and building a stronger presence on the ground (as many other donors are also doing). The result, however, is not the kind of "ownership" their experience suggests is necessary. Lacking is the shift in responsibility, priority-setting, and choice which has been indicated by previous failures of conditionality. Furthermore, at a more political level, the greater presence on the ground by the Bank and Fund and more intensive and widespread relations may well be further smothering local officials, reducing "ownership" rather than fostering nationally owned initiatives.

Steps which might genuinely confer ownership of policy on borrowing countries are much more difficult. They require the IMF and World Bank to put away their preconceived priorities and targets and to roll back their templates of economic policy goals and ideals. Their relationship with their borrowing members would have to become a genuine conversation—initiated by borrowers—rather than a school-masterly tirade however politely delivered. Conditionality might have to be consigned to the scrap-heap or at least completely rethought. Imagine conditioning lending on a simple judgment as to whether a government adequately accounts to its own people for its revenue and expenditure. And where governments are too weak or too corrupt to qualify, making no pretense of attempting to positively impact on governance. We will return to this below.

New approaches to conditionality within the Bank and Fund push each institution toward inherently more political decisions about to whom they should lend. To this end, reforming their governance is imperative to give assurance that such decisions will not simply reflect the interests and political preferences of a handful of powerful states. In sum, the IMF and World Bank have important roles to play in the world economy as public institutions. Each institution now needs a governance structure which would permit it to fulfill its role.

The Flawed Political Process at the Heart of the IMF and World Bank

In theory the IMF and World Bank each represent 184 countries who collectively fund and run each organization. Yet most of these countries have little say over either organization. More than three-quarters of the members of each of the IMF and World Bank are not directly represented on the Board of Executive Directors. Nor are they represented in the senior management of either institution. Many have virtually no nationals even working on the staff. These are the countries who are most deeply affected by each of the institutions.

A small number of economically powerful countries run the institutions. They dominate the board where they have a majority of the weighted votes. They choose the leadership and senior management in each organization. Little surprise that their interests and views are closely watched and heeded by the management and staff of each organization. Behind these governments line up powerful companies who stand to gain or lose from decisions. In the World Bank, the vast business of bidding to deliver World Bank projects—be it building dams, or writing new codes for governments—creates huge incentives for the private sector to lobby and to influence decisions being made in Washington. Equally the effects of IMF interventions and policies—particularly in emerging markets—push Wall Street, bond-holders, and other financial institutions to organize and lobby their own governments and the Fund itself. Adding to the political fray are non-governmental organizations pressing a variety of Northern and Southern concerns and interests, most (but not all) of whom are based in wealthy countries.

In respect of the IMF, the dominance of industrialized countries is yet clearer due to the role of the Group of Seven. A subgrouping of G-7 Finance Ministry deputies regularly convenes to discuss the issues confronting the organization and the world economy, updated and advised by the U.S.-appointed first deputy managing director of the IMF. It is this group rather than the formal oversight body— the International Monetary and Financial Committee (IMFC)—which guides the institution, or as a report in 2004 puts it, assumes the strategic guiding role in respect of the IMF (Kenen et al. 2004).

Other countries in the IMF have little say. To a large degree the same is true in the World Bank. This is in part a result of the way the board of each organization is structured. A handful of members have every incentive to do their job thoroughly, the rest have virtually no incentive. The five largest members of each organization appoint their own Executive Director (the United States, Japan, Germany, France, and UK) whose work is backed up by staff working in the director's office in Washington, D.C., as well as teams in home ministries working on Fund and Bank related issues. All other countries gravitate into groupings or "constituencies" of countries, which elect a director to represent them. That director wields the collective vote of all of his or her members. The power and influence of each director is affected by the voting power they represent as well as the quantity and quality of staff and resources they can mobilize both in the director's office as well as in their member countries.

There is little if any power in numbers in the Bank or Fund. For example, the twenty-four-country African group in the IMF collectively wields 1.42 percent of total voting power. This means that if a country such as Rwanda wished to push a concern about debt relief, it would need first to persuade other countries in its twenty-four-member constituency (some nineteen of which are already HIPC countries). That would be a first small step. Rwanda's constituency would then need to persuade other groups of countries likely to share the same concerns. The obvious group is the other African constituency whose nineteen members (of whom ten are already HIPC countries) wield 3 percent of the vote. But having gathered consent from some forty-three members of the organization, the coalition would still only wield 4.41 percent of votes. A third constituency to approach might be that of fellow HIPC countries Laos and Myanmar, a constituency that includes some emerging markets such as Malaysia and Singapore and commands 3.18 percent of the vote. Some fifty-five members of the organization might now be mobilized behind the concern. Yet their collective share of votes in the organization—7.61 percent—would be insufficient even to veto a proposal, let alone positively to push one.

Compare the situation of borrowing countries to that of the G-7, which wields 47.13 percent of the vote (with Italy and Canada wielding the votes of constituencies in which each has over three-quarters of the voting power). In practice this means that the G-7 finance deputies have a strong incentive regularly to consult and to formulate shared views on issues. After all, these views will become the agenda of the IMF Board, commanding pretty close to a majority of voting power. Similarly development agencies in the same group of countries can consult and press issues in the board and committees of the World Bank. By contrast, there is no incentive for developing countries to do the same.

A direct knock-on effect of the power of the agenda-setters is that they command the attention of the staff and management in each organization. Small surprise that the Fund's senior management are happy to advise and provide the G-7 finance deputies with the necessary briefings to guide their decision-making. Similarly, the senior management in the World Bank respond with alacrity to requests for information, support, research, or particular kinds of evaluation when these requests are made from their most powerful shareholders. Conversely, other countries have little incentive even to formulate such requests, let alone to make them.

Further unbalancing the workings of the boards of the IMF and World Bank is the fact that two very different systems of accountability are at work. There is little by way of an overarching set of standards for executive directors. The job of holding directors to account is largely left to national authorities, but this produces an unbalanced result.

Executive directors from the United States, Japan, Germany, France, and the United Kingdom are held directly to account by the government that appoints each. If a director fails to perform, fails to follow instructions of his or her government, or manages the office badly, he or she can be summarily removed and replaced. By contrast no country in a constituency can require their executive director to resign. Once elected a director stays in office until his or her two-year term has expired. No member can require their resignation (Gold 1974, 65).

Yet more surprisingly, executive directors representing multiple countries have only a diluted responsibility to represent the views of their members. The Articles of Agreement of the IMF and of the World Bank require directors to wear two hats, one as official of the institution (which pays his or her salary) and a second as representative of member countries. The IMF's legal counsel has argued that a director is not obliged to defer to the views of his or her member states, nor to cast votes in accordance with their instructions. The votes of the director will be "valid even if they are inconsistent with any instructions he may have received from his constituents" (Gianviti 1999, 48). So on what basis are the director's actions legitimate? And how can they be held to account?

The coup de grâce for the accountability of the boards of the IMF and World Bank is that their proceedings are not published. Elected directors are not bound to follow the instructions of their members, they cannot be removed, they are not subject to formal reviews or evaluation, and their actions are not made public.

The transcripts of board meetings cannot be accessed in any timely way. The IMF produces summaries of board discussions but the full record of meetings cannot be accessed except after at least ten years under the IMF's archives policy. The World Bank has recently begun to publish the formal minutes of its board meetings, but these give little indication of the positions taken by directors—who act in part as representatives—on the board. In neither institution can members outside of the boardroom know what positions are being taken on issues by those ostensibly representing them.

The governance structure of the IMF and the World Bank gives strong incentives to the directors of a small number of wealthy board members closely to represent their country's interests and to perform at the highest level. Conversely, directors representing all other countries face no such incentives. They may—and often do—perform well. But without any formal incentives, the matter is left purely to chance.

The unbalanced incentives facing directors are complemented by an equally unbalanced workload. The most work-intensive countries in the Bank and Fund are in large groups represented by just one director. The least work-intensive countries have their own director and a large staff at his or her disposal both in the institution and in their home agencies. Take the twenty-four-member African constituency in the IMF, of which nineteen are currently in Poverty Reduction and Growth Facility (PRGF) debt relief programs. The director's office needs to undertake almost forty on-site missions and present semiannual reviews to the board, as well as preparing some twenty-four countries' article IV Consultations (typically on an annual basis), Poverty Reduction Strategy Papers (PRSP) Joint Staff Assessments, or informal board meetings on country matters to update on country developments, and prepare for board discussions on the progress of each member under the HIPC Initiative. There are also field missions for members undertaking a voluntary assessment of international standards, missions related to Financial Sector Assessment Programs, as well as possible technical assistance missions. Little surprise that only executive directors from the wealthiest countries seem to have the time or the will to engage in longer-term strategic discussions about the role and structure of each institution.

Much of the good governance and global governance rhetoric of the 1990s was about inclusion, participation, and ownership. Developing countries were urged to take charge of their own destinies and to be more forthcoming in producing their own economic agendas. Yet there is no incentive for them to do so in the governance of the IMF or the World Bank. Indeed, there are many obstacles. The governance structures of the institutions produce a dramatic asymmetry of accountability whereby paradoxically those countries least affected by the decisions and actions of the World Bank and IMF have the most influence and the most capacity to hold either institution to account. Many justify this state of affairs by pointing out that "he who pays the piper should get to call the tune," but that risks misrepresenting how the IMF and World Bank are respectively financed.

Who Pays the Piper?

Do the wealthiest and most powerful members of the IMF and World Bank fund the organizations? In fact, the running costs of both organizations are paid mostly by borrowing members.[1] The charges they have to pay on loans join the proceeds of investment made by each institution to cover the salaries of board members and senior management and staff; the buildings; research, monitoring, and evaluation activities; safeguard policies in the World Bank; and perhaps most astonishingly of all, huge payments by the IMF to its wealthy creditor countries who are remunerated for the quotas they lodge with the organization.

The core capital of each organization relies on the participation of their wealthiest nonborrowing members. The IMF's core capital comprises quotas lodged by every member, with the largest quotas being lodged by the wealthiest countries. In the World Bank a very small amount of core capital is paid in by all members, but the Bank's credit rating reflects the "callable capital" or guarantees given by all members—the largest being from the wealthiest members—to back the bonds sold by the institution. In the past both the IMF and the World Bank relied on wealthy nonborrowing countries for both their capital and their running costs, but that equation has changed dramatically over time.

Financing the IMF

Originally the IMF's members all lodged parts of their quota with the organization, thereby creating a pool of resources that could be lent to any member in need at low and stable interest rates. This would encourage countries to turn for help to the IMF before getting into serious difficulty and thereby bolster global financial and monetary stability. If the IMF needed more resources, it could borrow from members (which it has done several times: IMF 2001g, 75) or from the markets (which it has never done). The Fund later began to supplement its resources from investments and from members' contributions to special trust funds.

Radical change in the IMF came when wealthy nonborrowing countries began to demand that they be paid by the organization. This began with a relatively modest demand in 1968 that creditors be paid interest on a portion of the quota they lodged with the IMF. Later, the Reagan administration in the United States aggressively pushed for creditors to be paid at market interest rates.[2] The United States also insisted that creditors should not have to shoulder the burden of bad loans—a view promulgated robustly even though some such loans had been made for geostrategic reasons under strong pressure from the United States and

---

[1] On one calculation, in 1982 the Fund's debtors were contributing 27.7 percent of the Fund's administrative expenses, by 2002 this figure had risen to 75 percent. By contrast, the contribution of wealthy creditor countries had dropped from 72.3 percent to 25 percent (Mohammed 2003).

[2] U.S. law mandated the U.S. executive director to work toward raising the remuneration rate to the SDR interest rate (Boughton 2001, 908). The SDR interest rate is determined weekly by reference to short-term market interest rates on the currencies used for SDR valuation.

other creditors, such as to Zaire, and other arrears resulted directly from sanctions imposed by creditor countries, such as in Vietnam and Panama. Finally, the Reagan administration pushed for borrowing charges to be increased so that the institution could generate a net income. By the mid 1980s the United States had gotten its way. By 2003 the remuneration of creditors was costing the IMF double the organization's total administrative expenses (IMF 2004b, 154).

As the IMF increased what it paid to wealthy creditor members, it also increased what it charged borrowers—and it continues to increase that rate. Until 1977 rates of charge were low and concessional. In a first series of steps they rose to close to market rates on short-term loans (Boughton 2001, 909). Subsequently they have continued to rise. In 1999 the rate of charge was set at 113.7 percent of the SDR rate. By 2004 it had risen to 154 percent of the SDR rate. The SDR rate reflects the short-term market interest rate of the four currencies used to value the SDR (which is the international reserve asset of the IMF). Put simply, loans at concessionary rates had given way to loans at market rates in all but the special loans the organization makes from Trust Funds (such as HIPC).

Further fueling increases in borrowing charges has been a policy set in 1981 that borrowing charges should generate a target net income for the organization. An initial target of 3 percent of beginning-of-period reserves was set for net income in 1981. That target rose to 5 percent in 1985 and subsequently to 7.5 percent in 1987–88 before being pegged back at 5 percent. Put simply, since 1981 borrowers have also been asked to fund an increase in the precautionary balances of the institution.

The costs of running the IMF have increased in the last decade as it has expanded its activities better to fulfill its role of ensuring international financial stability. For example, in the wake of the East Asian financial crises in the late 1990s the IMF's oversight activities have been expanded to include the development of benchmarks of good practices on data dissemination, fiscal transparency, monetary and financial policy transparency, and in banking supervision (in cooperation with other agencies). By 2003 the institution had produced 343 Reports on the Observance of Standards and Codes (ROSCs) for some eighty-nine economies—reports that aim to pinpoint areas of institutional weakness, advise policy actions, and focus technical assistance (IMF 2003b). Similarly, in 1999 a Financial Sector Assessment Program (FSAP) was developed with the World Bank to detect potential vulnerabilities in the financial system of member countries and reduce the likelihood and magnitude of financial crisis. By 2003 some ninety-five countries had participated in the scheme (IMF 2003c).

Who is paying for the IMF's expanded activities? A quota increase which came into effect in 1999 means that most members (including borrowers) have contributed to an increase in the institution's resources from SDR 145.6 billion (about US$204 billion) to SDR212 billion (about US$297 billion), increasing the institution's useable resources by about SDR45 billion (about US$63 billion). However, the overall costs of new actions urged on the IMF and World Bank in the wake of the East Asian crisis are virtually all being borne by borrowers. The additional work required to complete reports on the observance of standards and codes (ROSCs) on fiscal and data transparency is performed by Fund staff and paid for out of the administrative and operational expenses of the organization. In respect of FSAPs and ROSCs relating to the financial sectors, national agencies provide about 20 percent of professionals working on such assessments but the rest of the cost is borne by the IMF (and by the World Bank, which participates in FSAPs in non-OECD countries). Paradoxically, while the lending activities of the institution are supposed to pay for most of its activities, it is the non-borrowing creditors who have set and pushed the expanded agenda of the IMF.

Borrowers now pay a high premium for using IMF resources. Indeed, a new Supplementary Reserve Facility created for emerging markets in crisis proposed yet higher interest rates. Creditors, by contrast, are remunerated for their contributions. The result is that borrowers are paying a larger share of a larger budget as the Fund's administrative expenses have increased from 189.4 million SDRs in 1991 to 530.8 million SDRs in 2002 (Mohammed 2003, 20). This means that the IMF—in fulfilling its global public goods functions—has come to rely ever more heavily on its borrowers since without their borrowings and payments, the IMF would run higher and higher deficits (as it did in the 1970s Boughton 2001, 899). A similar reasoning applies to the rather differently structured finances of the World Bank.

Financing the World Bank

The World Bank's main lending arm, the IBRD, does not use periodic donations from rich countries to lend to the poor. It is only the concessional lending arm of the Bank that does this. Mostly, the IBRD raises money in capital markets and lends that money to developing, emerging, and transition economies. In essence it uses guarantees provided by its wealthy members to enable it to sell triple-A rated bonds in capital markets.[3] These "debt securities," which are issued in a variety of currencies, are sold to both institutional and retail investors. The money so raised is then lent to borrowers. Borrowers pay the cost of funding the loan plus a lending spread that helps fund the Bank's reserves, investments, and administrative expenses.

Backing the Bank's issues of debt securities are three things. First but no longer foremost, there is the capital stock of the institution contributed (or at least promised) by every member. Countries do not actually pay these amounts to the Bank, nor is there an expectation that they would need to. Instead they pay in a tiny fraction. The rest is "callable capital"—a kind of guarantee pooled together by the promises of all members. Of the U.S. contribution of $31,965 billion, some $29,966 billion remains uncalled.

A second but increasingly important source of financial strength of the IBRD

---

[3] All members pay in a small fraction of their capital subscription, the rest is pledged as "callable capital" on which no call has been or would ever be made unless the Bank were to go bankrupt and need to pay off its bondholders.

is its principal asset—its loans to member countries and their record in meeting their debt-service obligations to the Bank. This record sustains the high credit-rating of the IBRD. The third financial foundation of the Bank is what it earns through investments of its own income from lending. To give a sense of the proportion of this contribution, in June 2004 the IBRD had loans and guarantees outstanding to the value of $119.275 billion. Its reported loan income (from fees and charges) was $4.403 billion (down from $8.143 billion in 2001), and its investment income was $304 million (down from $1.540 billion in 2001) (World Bank 2004d, vol. 2, 3–4).

Over time what has changed in the Bank is the relative burden of paying for the World Bank. As with the IMF, in the 1980s the Reagan administration began to push for an increase in the Bank's loan charges so as to increase the reserves of the organization and to cover the costs of failing loans falling into nonaccrual status. In 1979 the "spread" or amount the IBRD charged to its borrowers over and above what it was paying to raise the money it was lending them, was 0.5 percent plus a commitment fee of 0.75 percent. But during the early 1980s this increased dramatically as a result of three decisions.

As monetary problems afflicted its European nonborrowing members, they urged the IBRD to stay away from their capital markets. The IBRD had then to turn to the much more costly U.S. bond market which favored shorter maturity, variable-yield instruments (Kapur et al. 1997, 1025). The result was more costly finance, the cost of which was passed on to borrowers. Additionally, as of early 1982 the Bank imposed a 1.5 percent front-end fee on all new IBRD loans "to forestall any potential decline in the IBRD's income over the medium term" (World Bank 1982, 52). This effectively doubled the spread on the Bank's loans. In that same year, the IBRD also began lending at variable rates. The result of these changes was to drop the nominal grant element of loans from about 14 percent in 1974–78 to minus 2 percent in the period 1980–84 (Kapur et al. 1997, 1028). The resulting build up of reserves meant that by 1985 the front-end fee was reduced to 0.5 percent. And in 1988 the Bank's finances were boosted by the third ever general capital increase in the Bank—an increase to the tune of $74.86 billion, which took effect on 28 April 1988, just as Bank disbursements were slowing (World Bank 1989b, 61).

As charges on loans have increased, the Bank has increased its reserves-loans ratio and built up an additional "surplus account" to add to its financial strength (and reduce the risks covered by its members' guarantees). The Bank also increased its "net income."

A further shift was made in 1998 when the G-7 led a coalition to vote to further augment the Bank's net income and reserves—a highly contentious decision that increased borrowing costs to the developing, transition, and emerging-market members of the Bank (Kapur 2002).

Borrowers now pay the IBRD the cost to the institution of raising money plus a spread comprising an interest charge (calculated as a percentage of balance disbursed to the borrower and paid semiannually), a commitment charge (calculated as a percentage of balances committed and yet to be disbursed and paid semiannually), and a front-end fee calculated as a percentage of total amount committed and paid up-front.

Borrowers are being expected to pay more to the World Bank not just to build up the institution's reserves but also to cover the costs of an expansion in the Bank's activities. Between the mid 1970s and the mid 1990s the Bank's administrative expenses per project doubled (Kapur 2002, 346).[4] At the behest of its wealthy shareholders, the Bank spent money on special initiatives. In the 1990s, some US$30 million of the Bank's net income was paid for the G-7–requested study of the economy of the former Soviet Union (mentioned in chapter 5). Further resources were put into a trust fund for Bosnia, and a trust fund for the Gaza Strip and the West Bank. Debt relief for the poorest countries placed a further demand on the Bank's net income. Meanwhile staff time and resources were also increasingly required to implement stricter Bank operational standards (fiduciary and safeguards policies, discussed in greater detail below).

The Bank's expanded activities have doubtless all been worthy. However, should borrowing members bear the cost? The special initiatives in the Soviet Union, Bosnia, and Palestine have all been projects closely associated with political initiatives of the G-7. Yet rather than funding these worthy projects from their own aid budgets, the G-7 effectively turned the costs over to the borrowing members of the IBRD.

The World Bank's concessional lending arm is financed in a different way and here wealthy countries do provide most of the funds and enjoy overall control. The International Development Association (IDA) is a fund replenished every three years, mostly from a core group of donors who conduct lengthy negotiations about who will contribute what. IDA13 refers to this pot of money in the period 2002–05. About half its money (US$13 billion of approximately US$23 billion) came from contributions from donor countries. A further chunk of resources comes from borrowers' repayments (about US$4 billion in IDA13), investment income, money left over from previous replenishments, and contributions from the IBRD's net income (approximately US$900 million in IDA13).

The original 1960 voting structure of the IDA reflected the initial subscriptions to the Fund. But it was decided early on that replenishment contributions would not automatically change voting rights (International Development Association 2001). Indeed, as U.S. contributions slipped from its initial clear leadership position, it has retained the largest share of votes. Up until 2005 the largest cumulative contributor to IDA was Japan which gave 22.07 percent of the Fund's resources (International Development Association 2005). Yet Japan's voting share up to 2005 was 9.14 percent and has now dropped to 8.92 percent—below that of the United States whose cumulative contribution up to IDA13 was

---

[4] Since the late 1990s and a compact not to increase further the Bank's administrative expenses, they seem not to have increased dramatically. The Bank's 1996 *Annual Report* shows a total administrative budget for 1994 of US$1.3884 billion and a similar figure for 1995 and 1996 (Appendix 6, 235), as does the 1998 *Annual Report* for 1997 and 1998 (Appendix 5, 153). The 2001 *Annual Report* suggests a slight reduction to US$1.094 billion in 1999 and then to US$1.006 billion in 2001 with these figures continuing into 2002 and 2003, rising to US$1.113 billion in 2004 (*Annual Report* 30 June 2004, 33).

21.74 percent but which enjoyed 12.07 percent of votes. In IDA14 the United Kingdom is contributing the same amount as the United States (each are contributing 13.18 percent of the Fund), yet the United Kingdom has 4.72 percent of the vote while the United States has 11.61 percent of the vote.

Since at least the early 1990s the donors have exercised a very heavy hand in the lending of the IDA, using replenishment negotiations not just to set goals for the Fund, but to detail recommendations and even to specify the share of lending that should go to specific sectors and countries. The donor-set goals, as reviewed by the World Bank's Operations Evaluation Department in 2002, have been unrealistic with respect both to what can be achieved and the requisite budget resources—indeed this led to efforts in IDA13 and IDA14 negotiations to include some borrower representatives in replenishment negotiations (OED 2002). However, the IDA governance structure does not permit borrowing countries to contribute or buy subscriptions in the Fund so as to gain a voice.

The Implications of Who Funds the Institutions

The IMF and the various agencies of the World Bank are multilateral institutions created to ensure growth, stability, and equity in the world economy for the benefit of all countries. The wealthy members of each organization have mostly defined precisely how these goals should be met, in several instances expanding the activities of each organization and thereby increasing their running costs. Yet wealthier nonborrowing countries have reduced their own contributions and liability at the same time as they have leaned more heavily on the institutions to fulfill global public goods functions. This has left an increasing burden on borrowing members.

The paradox of contemporary arrangements is highlighted by the role of the heads of each organization. The wealthy countries have long arrogated to themselves the right to choose the head and senior management of the Bank and Fund. For this reason the Bank president is always American and the managing director of the Fund is always a West European who is closely shadowed by an American first deputy managing director. Yet borrowing countries now shoulder the costs not just of the salaries of these officials but also of the new initiatives or corporate restructuring that each new incumbent tends to bring with him.

There are deep flaws in the reasoning that wealthy countries pay for the IMF and World Bank and should therefore run the organizations. The argument is neither wholly true nor conducive to effective institutions. A substantial burden of costs is being borne by borrowing members of each institution. But a deeper problem was recognized by the founders some sixty years ago. In a debate on the issue of who should govern the institutions, Harry Dexter White (representing the United States), argued that to accord voting power strictly proportionate to the value of the subscription would give the one or two powers control over the Fund. This, he argued, would destroy the truly international character of the Fund, and seriously jeopardize its success (cited in Gold 1972, 19). There are several reasons to believe that White was right.

The United States has used its dominant position in each of the Bretton Woods twins to radically reshape their finances since the 1980s, as well as to reinforce and elaborate the conditionality associated with their loans. Other wealthy industrialized countries have either supported or permitted this to happen. This has made borrowing from each of the institutions more costly. The first casualty of this is the willingness of countries to use the organizations. Recall for a moment that the rationale for low loan charges in each organization was to attract members to use them. This has been dumped at a cost.

High borrowing charges and onerous conditionality make the IMF at best the very last port of call for developing, emerging market, or transition economies. Rather than approaching the Fund for assistance in a timely way when a crisis still might be forestalled, countries do all they can to avoid the institution. This has been demonstrated in individual cases such as Korea (as discussed in chapter 2) but more dramatically when the IMF set up a new special facility for emerging markets at risk of contagion—a facility bearing a yet higher rate of charge and conditionality than the IMF's own competing product, the normal "standby" arrangement. Unsurprisingly not a single member availed itself of the new facility. Increasing charges have steadily eroded the incentive on members to approach the Fund. In turn, this erodes the extent to which the Fund can work with members to prevent or manage crises. In the World Bank the main lending arm (the IBRD) is suffering equally from its increased charges and conditions and the "hassle factor" associated with Bank loans. As creditors have forced up the rates at which the Bank lends, so too it has begun to push away some of the Bank's most successful borrowers.

Neither the Fund nor the Bank can fulfill their main objectives without cooperation from developing, emerging, and transition economies. Core among these objectives is to ensure a degree of balance in the world economy—to ensure that untrammeled global markets did not simply result in a "rich take all" system. Yet the institutions themselves are today distributing money from poor to rich countries as borrowers increasingly shoulder the burden not just of bad loans but also of building up the reserves of each organization and of remunerating creditor members in the IMF.

Who Sings the Loudest—Is It Really NGOs?

NGOs have had a roller-coast relationship with the Fund and Bank. Hailed as the champions of transparency and democracy in the 1990s, in 2005 they are attacked by some for usurping their position and pursuing an agenda that hurts the poor and those they purport to represent. Indeed, at least one organization has been set up for the purpose of exposing the unaccountable nature of some NGOs (www.ngowatch.org). Amid the loud debate about NGOs, however, there is a lack of clarity about their actual role.

There are three roles NGOs have played in the last decade in respect of the IMF and World Bank. These include an operational role delivering aid; a policy-advisory role in respect of governments and officials including within the international institutions; and an accountability role in respect of Bank and Fund projects, policies, and governance. These roles are worth clarifying.

The operational role assumed by NGOs emerged in the 1980s when governments led by Ronald Reagan, Margaret Thatcher, and Helmut Kohl were pressing to reduce the role of governments. NGOs were seen as an alternative way to deliver aid. Large Northern NGOs could be contracted by government. This would create more of a market in aid with greater flexibility and adaptation. For some Northern NGOs this meant becoming rather heavily dependent on their contracts with Northern governments. On the other side of the equation, NGOs in developing countries rose up to receive aid. In the ideal case this permits innovation and grassroots projects to flourish, strengthening civil society on the ground and offering a solution to lack of government capacity. But critics argue that channeling aid around and away from governments erodes democracy and creates incentives for individuals to reinvent themselves as NGOs and to replicate the kinds of corruption, diversion, and clientelism that formed the basis of the critique against aid to governments in the first place. All that said, NGOs from both North and South have been and still are a crucial link in delivering aid across much of the developing world.

Flowing out of that role, NGOs have also taken up a policy-advisory role in respect of aid and development assistance. Many operational NGOs from both North and South are included in IMF and World Bank consultations—in country as well as at headquarters in Washington. As detailed in chapter 6, in the process of putting together Poverty Reduction Strategy Papers, governments are encouraged explicitly to work with NGOs. This is challenging for both borrowing governments, and the staff of the Bank and Fund who strive to meet deadlines and disburse loans in a timely way within a set of aspirations which are much more long term.

A third role NGOs have come to play concerns transnational advocacy of particular issues—especially concerning the environment. Coming to prominence in the 1970s and 1980s, environmental and other NGOs have highlighted adverse impacts of World Bank projects and IMF structural adjustment across the developing world. In the 1980s, a group of environmental NGOs joined forces with members of the U.S. Congress to press the World Bank to answer to their claims (Wade 1997). The Bank began more closely to scrutinize its own performance. In 1992 two investigative reports were produced. The first was the Morse Commission—an independent review of India's Sardar Sarovar loan projects that uncovered that the Bank had failed properly to implement its own policies such as on resettlement and energy. The second was an internal review of the Bank's lending portfolio (the Wapenhans Report), which was leaked to the press and contained damning evidence of the "culture of approval" wherein Bank staff face a much stronger incentive to disburse loans than to ensure that their own rules are met.

Not just NGOs but a combination of pressures from the U.S. government, from within the Bank, and from among NGOs caused a minor revolution in the

World Bank in 1993–94. The Bank tightened its safeguards policies, which direct Bank staff properly to assess the impact of Bank-supported projects on the environment, cultural property, and indigenous peoples, and mandated a new standard of transparency. Topping this off, the Bank board created an Inspection Panel, which would enforce the institution's safeguards policies—in a sense countervailing the "disbursement culture" that had been identified by the Wapenhans Report. Any community of people affected by a Bank project could now push for an investigation into whether the Bank staff had complied with the institution's own rules and policies. Alongside the panel, the Bank announced a new disclosure policy in 1994 opening the institution to greater scrutiny from the outside.

For NGOs the changes in the World Bank were empowering. The public was granted greater access to information about what the Bank was doing. Nongovernmental actors were given access to a mechanism of accountability in respect of the Bank's own rules and procedures.

The revolution in the Bank's accountability also significantly altered—and complicated—the incentives within which Bank staff worked. Unsurprisingly, it soon became the bête noir of some staff within the Bank and various supporters outside the organization. Critics averred that the new standards and mechanisms added significantly to the cost of preparing Bank loans, forcing the staff to work with one eye constantly on the Inspection Panel (Wade 2000). More recently, it has been argued that environmental protection and the like have added dramatically to the Bank's costs of doing business, leading major borrowers to simply walk away from the Bank (Mallaby 2004a). To some degree if the safeguards and Inspection Panel have been at all effective, they will have altered staff behavior, and likewise had implications on costs. However, these claims have been somewhat overstated.

The Bank reported in 2001 that project supervision had risen in cost from US$130 million in 2001 to US$149 million in 2002, due to "higher fiduciary and safeguard standards," while the unit costs of "supervision" in lending rose from US$67,000 in FY1997 to US$74,000 in 2001 (World Bank 2001d, 33). These increases reflect a number of factors. As of the late 1990s, the World Bank tightened up three areas of its operational policies. One area was new higher standards of transparency, monitoring, and evaluation of the economic effectiveness of its projects. A second area is fiduciary policies, which cover rules governing financial management, procurement, and disbursement. A third area is safeguard policies that include Environmental Assessments and specific policies designed to prevent unintended adverse effects on things such as natural habitats, pest management, cultural property, involuntary resettlement, indigenous peoples, safety of dams, projects on international waterways, and projects in disputed areas. The third category is that on which most rage about safeguards has been focused, yet it accounts for about a third of the costs of the operational policies overall (World Bank 2001c).

Undergirding the arguments about how much World Bank safeguards policies cost is a deeper debate that pits the values of environmentalism and opposition to the forcible resettlement of peoples against the goals of modernization, growth, and poverty reduction. This reverberates in the globalization versus anti-globalization debate. It has long affected both the IMF and the World Bank. It has been most clearly expressed in furors surrounding World Bank support for large infrastructural projects such as hydroelectric dams which require resettlements of peoples and directly affect the environment to the end of modernization. Such decisions and the conditionality attached to them are deeply contentious, affecting the lives and opportunities of many.

Infrastructure projects such as dams are deeply contentious because they affect the lives and opportunities of many. The way a dam is built affects those who may benefit from the irrigation water or electricity produced, as well as those who are displaced to build a dam. When the World Bank is involved it ought, in theory, to offer impartial and technically accurate advice. However, both the Bank's role and a borrowing government's decision are further complicated by the role international companies play in competing for the contracts to build and manage such dams. Transparency International finds that firms often try to influence decision-making in their favor by bribing officials, or by colluding with their competitors, or both, and that corrupt governmental officials become involved (Wiehen 1999, and see www.worldbank.org/html/extdr/pb/dams). When the World Bank is involved, very often major shareholders in the institution champion the interests of their own construction and electricity companies before, during, and after a loan is made. All of this makes the job of providing impartial and technically accurate advice to potentially dam-building borrowers extremely fraught.

Unlike NGOs, the private sector lobbies the Bretton Woods institutions much more quietly. Typically private sector advocacy is well-organized, highly funded, well-supported by the government, and highly effective. For example, in the wake of the debt crisis in the early 1980s, the financial sector created the Institute of International Finance to represent banks and investors affected by the crisis. This is now just one of several organizations representing private sector investors. In 2003 the organization spent over US$16 million advancing the interests of its members through research and advocacy (Institute of International Finance 2003).

In the World Bank, private sector influence is also powerful, although mostly exercised through governments. For example, the U.S. government invests heavily in ensuring that U.S. companies benefit from the World Bank's procurement contracts. The U.S. Department of Commerce maintains a liaison office at the World Bank (and at four other multilateral development banks) to inform and advise U.S. companies on bidding for contracts arising out of World Bank loans. It also operates as a resource for U.S. companies engaged in disputes over World Bank projects. This agency's work is supported by at least eight other government agencies, each of which has a brief to assist U.S. business in making the most of opportunities afforded by World Bank loans. These include the U.S. Trade and Development Agency; the U.S. Trade Representative; the Departments of State, Homeland Security and Transportation; the Export-Import Bank of the United States; the Overseas Private Investment Corporation; and the Foreign Agricultural Service.[5]

The Bank—and the IMF—each need a political process at their helm that can fairly weight and counterbalance private interests with public goals. Governments and their representatives on the board do not work within incentives which clearly prioritize the public goals of the governments they are supposed to support—not least because private interests permeate the governments on all sides of the equation. This is as true in Washington as it is in the capitals of borrowing countries.

Over the past two decades large transnational advocacy NGOs have tried to hold each of the Bretton Woods institutions to account for their decisions. They have shone an uncomfortable and often inconsistent spotlight into the workings of the organizations. They have enraged borrowing countries, staff within the Fund and Bank, private sector investors, and critics who ask with what legitimacy NGOs presume to intercede. The obvious riposte to this is to ask what kind of governance structure cedes so easily to the demands of nongovernments— whether they are NGOs or private sector interests? The Fund and Bank are susceptible to a range of pressures, interest groups, special pleadings, political preferences, and ideological fashions. This chapter has argued that the political process for mediating these pressures could be vastly improved.

Changing the Tune

Independent boards have been advocated for each of the Fund and Bank by commentators keen to reform the institutions. To quote an eminent set of proposals to reform the IMF: "The obvious solution is to strengthen the independence of the Executive Board. If Directors are too inclined to take advice from their governments, then the Articles of Agreement should be amended to discourage them from so doing. The analogy with central bank independence is direct. The Statute of the European System of Central Banks, for example, prohibits members of the Board of the European Central Bank from taking advice from their governments. There is no reason why the IMF's Articles of Agreement could not follow suit" (De Gregorio et al. 1999, 91). This proposal self-consciously drew from an earlier report advocating a more independent central bank for the UK (CEPR 1993). A similar demand for greater independence of the board in the World Bank is also often made.

But the IMF and World Bank are not like Central Banks. They cannot be held to account purely with reference to a specified output such as inflation. The goals of the Fund and Bank are more wide-ranging. The IMF was told by its member

---

[5] The World Bank's Contracts Award Search database details to whom contracts are awarded—which companies and from which countries: see http://web.worldbank.org/WBSITE/EXTERNAL/PROJECTS/ 0,,menuPK:51565~pagePK:95864~piPK:95915~theSitePK:40941,00.html.

governments to take on a wide range of tasks in 2004. These included assistance to members affected by volatile oil prices, poverty reduction, effective and even-handed surveillance, and trade liberalization (IMFC 2004). The World Bank in the same year was directed to intensify its analytical work on the potential sources of growth from remittances and ways to mobilize them, to focus on infrastructure needs of member countries, to help the Doha Round of trade negotiations to succeed, to assist in the meeting of the Millennium Development Goals, and so on (World Bank 2004b). These goals are not like an inflation target. They could not be used to hold an independent executive board to account.

There are other more practical reasons for rejecting the idea of independent boards for the IMF and World Bank. Some independence is already entrenched in the Articles of Agreement of both the Bank and the Fund. The role of executive directors is not to represent their country. Rather, directors are responsible for the conduct of the general operations of the organization (IBRD Article V.4.a; IMF Art XII.3.a). They are deliberately not employees of their national agencies, rather they are employees of the Fund or Bank. They sit full-time in Washington, D.C., precisely as an insulation against undue political interference from capitals. The independence of each organization is further entrenched by provisions requiring the president or managing director and all staff to discharge their offices owing their duty entirely to the organization and to no other authority (article V.5.c in IBRD, article XII.4.c in IMF). The same articles call on every member to respect the international character of this duty and to refrain from all attempts to influence the management or staff in the discharge of their duties.

Despite their charters, politics has seeped into the board of each organization—and beyond. This is hardly surprising. As discussed above, the decisions of the Bank and Fund create winners and losers—and not just in borrowing countries. Within wealthy countries, corporations who bid for World Bank contracts or investment funds hoping for an IMF intervention will gain or lose from the institutions' decisions. Each lobbies vigorously their own governments and the institutions themselves. A theoretically independent executive board would not cause these interests to go away, nor their advocates. It would yet further distance most countries from the institutions. It would most likely leave a powerful system of informal influence to the private sector, nongovernmental organizations, and government officials based in Washington D.C.

What each institution needs is a board that can mediate competing interests in a way that is representative, transparent, and accountable. Adequate representation does not necessarily mean a UN-style system of one-country one-vote that would render the boards unwieldy. The present board structure offers a potentially useful framework for representing all members yet being small enough to be workable. Lacking is an incentive for the most powerful vote holders to consult and build coalitions across a wide range of members when they can command an easy majority of voting power among themselves. Equally lacking are incentives on developing, emerging, and transition economies to use their seats on the board and to use coalitions among themselves to affect the strategic direction and priorities of each institution.

Changing voting power is not the best solution to this problem. A series of complex formulae are used to ascertain the share of votes of each member of the Fund and Bank. Reforms have been proposed from several quarters (IMF 2001f; Van Houtven 2002; Buira 2005, 14–15). But changing voting distribution requires taking votes away from some members and giving them to others—a process that in the 1980s led to tortuous negotiations to increase Japan's share (Ogata 1989, Lister 1984, Rapkin and Strand 1996). Furthermore the calculations in proposals already mentioned would not result in a change that would give incentives to involve small, poorer countries in decision-making.

Basic votes offer a similarly flawed solution to the inclusion problem. In previous periods an allocation of basic votes to every member of the Bank and Fund ensured a slightly more equal distribution of votes among member states.[6] At the founding of the institutions, basic votes represented just over 10 percent of votes whereas they now represent just 2.8 percent of total votes in the World Bank and a similar proportion of votes in the IMF. The result has been subtly to bolster—over time—the erosion of equality among members in the institution. If basic votes were to be brought back to their original level, in the twenty-three-member African constituency of the World Bank voting power would rise from 3.41 to 4.06 percent. In the twenty-five-country African constituency, voting power would rise from 1.99 to 2.81 percent.[7] These changes are significant but would not achieve the goal of ensuring wider participation and coalition-building across the institution.

There is a simple way to change governance in each organization. Leaving voting power and shares to one side, decisions could be made by a double majority. Big powerful countries would then have to build coalitions among the more numerous small countries. An incentive would be created for greater inclusion in decision-making (more on this below).

Once there is an incentive to include smaller poorer countries in discussions and decisions within the IMF and World Bank, those countries' representatives need more clearly and effectively to be held to account. As we saw above, only directors from a small number of wealthy countries can directly hold their representatives to account. In the case of the United States the U.S. Congress is involved in approving the appointment of the U.S. executive director and subsequently demanding reports from him or her. The U.S. Congress also uses the investigative and oversight capacity of the U.S. General Accounting Office better to understand the policies and effects of the international financial organizations. More recently parliaments, including those in the United Kingdom, Ireland, France, and Italy, have begun to call for greater transparency and reporting to them about their governments' policies in the multilaterals.

Meanwhile directors from all other countries in the Fund and Bank have lit-

---

[6] Basic votes are attributed to the membership in a fixed amount regardless of the size of a member's quota. Each member is in total allocated 250 basic votes plus 1 vote for each part of its quota—in the IMF equivalent to 100,000 SDR (IMF: Art. XII, Sec. 5). See Lister (1984), Woods (1998) and Boughton (2003).

[7] These calculations are based on figures produced by the Development Committee (World Bank 2004b).

tle incentive to be anything but virtually independent of their members. There are no formal mechanisms through which their members can hold them to account. Yet more egregiously, there is no transparency about board decisions, which would permit greater oversight of the actions of either rich or poor board members. These gaps need addressing through greater accountability, effectiveness, and transparency of all board members.

Better accountability is also necessary in respect of the head of each organization. Serving and chairing the board, each leader is in theory elected by all executive directors. In practice, as already mentioned, each head is appointed and held to account by the U.S. and European shareholders respectively. The World Bank president is selected by the U.S. administration in a process controlled by the U.S. Treasury and characterized by great secrecy. In a similar vein, the largest EU members in the IMF control the nomination of a West European candidate. In 2000, in breach of established convention, developing countries nominated their own candidate in a particularly shambolic selection, and this spurred a review of current procedures. The process is significant because it skews the accountability of each organization, making the leader accountable to those who appoint him. In turn the accountability of the staff is skewed because they all report to the leader. Headship selection is a core part of the overall accountability of each organization and at present that process is deeply flawed.

The work of the staff in the Fund and Bank is influenced by the way each agency is organized. Ideally any Fund or Bank staffer would face incentives to ensure that his or her institution best met its goals. Yet often more bureaucratic priorities get in the way. The narrow goals of ensuring that the institution runs smoothly, presenting a coherent face to the world, reducing costs where necessary, or spending its budget take precedence over the wider goals of reducing poverty, enhancing global financial stability, and so on.

Typical trade-offs are highlighted in issues such as how staff are deployed. Rotating the staff around different countries, or using temporary contracts can give the institution greater flexibility, give staff cross-country expertise, and in the old diplomatic parlance, prevent staff from going native and overly sympathizing with locals. However, as argued earlier in this book, the Fund and Bank are ill-served by staff who have not had the opportunity to acquire deep knowledge of particular circumstances within a country or of the culture of recipients and beneficiaries. A further casualty of short-term assignments is that they give no incentive to the staff to prioritize longer-term effects of their projects or policies (Ostrom et al. 2001). More broadly, there are few if any concrete incentives for staff missions from the Bank or Fund to ensure that projects or policies are sustained beyond the short-term lending period. Neither the evaluation of lending activities, nor procedures for staff promotion include such incentives. Finally, the "disbursement culture" in the World Bank, mentioned earlier in the book, is typical of most aid agencies keen to prove that they can use their budget within its annual allocation period and are deserving of more. That culture is at odds with the Bank's current emphasis on lending in ways that better serve governance, ownership, and participation in decision-making in borrowing countries.

The contradiction between bureaucratic incentives and institutional goals is highlighted in attempts by the Fund and Bank to foster greater ownership by borrowers of policies and projects. Each institution has tried to incorporate a commitment to greater ownership into their work. The difficulty is that greater ownership by borrowers necessarily means less control by the staff and nonborrowers of the organizations. This shift of control is very clearly expressed in one seminal study of aid and incentives. Four conditions are outlined as vital for some degree of ownership in aid or lending in the pursuit of a sustainable policy or project (Ostrom et al. 2001, xx). First, beneficiaries need to have enunciated a demand for the aid or policy. Second, they need to exercise some control over the resources made available. Third, they need to allocate at least some of their own assets to the project or program so they have a real stake in it. Finally, clear responsibility needs to have been assigned to them, and they must participate in decisions regarding the continuance or noncontinuance of a project (Ostrom et al. 2001, xx). These are challenging findings for the IMF and World Bank.

Politically the problem for the Bank and Fund is that they are trying to incorporate "ownership" into the way they do business at a time when nonborrowers are also demanding that the institutions be yet more accountable and responsive to them. Like Dr. Doolittle's Pushmepullyou animal, the Fund and Bank are being pushed by their largest shareholders to give more control to borrowers and—at the same time—being pulled back to permit more control by the large shareholders. The contradiction is clearly expressed in the report of the commission created by the U.S. Congress in 1998 to frame U.S. demands for reforming the IMF and World Bank. The report calls on the IMF and World Bank to be more responsive to the U.S. Congress, and at the same time calls on the institutions to rely "more on incentives and local decision-making and much less on programs and conditions imposed by multilateral agencies" (Meltzer Commission 2000). Missing entirely from the analysis is a recognition that the U.S. Congress itself has demanded and shaped those very programs and conditions it accuses the multilateral agencies of imposing.

Six Important Reforms

The Bank and Fund need to be governed in a way that is more representative, transparent, and accountable. A number of key potential reforms stand out to address the flaws highlighted above.

A Rebalancing of Who Pays

In the first place, the burden of who pays for the institutions needs to be redistributed. Wealthy countries stepped away from funding the IMF and World Bank in the 1980s, forcing each institution to depend more on the charges it set on its borrowers. Yet those same wealthy countries today are demanding that the IMF and World Bank provide a wider-than-ever range of global public goods, including disseminating financial and banking standards; clamping down on terrorist

TABLE 7.1
Loan disbursements (gross)

Year	Disbursement amount (in billions of dollars)
1996	13.321
1997	14.009
1998	19.283
1999	18.100
2000	13.332
2001	11.784
2002	11.256
2003	11.921
2004	10.109

Sources: Information for 1996, 1997, and 1999 from AR 1998, 212; 2004 numbers from AR 2004, vol. 2, 4.

financing; helping reach the Millennium Development Goals; fighting the wider war on poverty and disease, especially the HIV/AIDS pandemic; and assisting in providing a more stable global security climate. Simply put, those setting this agenda need to be prepared more amply to contribute to achieving it.

Borrowers may already be showing that they are not prepared to shoulder the burden thrust on them. They may not have many voting rights on the board but the income-generating borrowers of each institution can vote with their feet. In development financing, the World Bank's loans to its middle-income and IBRD borrowers have been dropping in recent years, as evidenced in the institution's annual reports, which show that loan disbursements have dropped from a high of US$19.283 billion in 1998 to US$10.109 billion in 2004 (see table 7.1). One direct result for the Bank is a steadily dropping loan income from around US$8 billion earned each year from 1999 to 2001 to US$4.4 billion earned in 2004 (World Bank 2004d, vol. 2, 4).

The IMF is equally shrinking. Its disbursements have dropped from 25 billion SDR in 2002 to 4 billion in 2004 (www.imf.org). Emerging economies are choosing not to use Fund resources, which have become so much more expensive and more conditional than they were prior to the 1980s and in relation to other sources of finance. As already discussed, some emerging economies are seeking to ensure that prospectively they will never need to use the IMF—by stockpiling their own foreign exchange reserve.

As borrowers walk away from the costly and highly conditional loans now on offer, the result is to leave each institution with a shrinking capacity to fulfill a growing mission. A first element of a solution is therefore to require more systematically that those who define the institutions' missions should be prepared to pay more to fulfill it—and that they must concede a stronger voice to those who share in those costs with them. This would bolster the cooperative and multilateral mission and capacity of each institution, just as Harry Dexter White proposed some sixty years ago.

Greater Inclusion through Double-Majority Voting

A wider range of members needs to be included in the decision-making of each institution. One way to achieve this is to alter the decision-making rule (Strand and Rapkin 2005, Jakobeit 2005). In both the Fund and the Bank some decisions already require both a special majority of voting power and a special majority of governors.[8] If a majority of voting power and a majority of countries in each organization were required to pass measures, the G-7 would need to find not just one further executive director's vote but also the support of half the membership. This reform would immediately create an incentive for the powerful members of the board to forge alliances with a larger number of borrowing countries—large and small. Equally, it would give borrowing members an incentive to participate more actively, more constructively, and with greater input into the strategic decisions made in each organization.

Publication of Board Transcripts

The discussions and decisions made by the board of each institution should be available for immediate public scrutiny. They are already carefully prepared and filed in each organization. They should be published in a timely way. The Fund publishes a summary of board discussions and the Bank has recently begun to publish the formal minutes of board meetings. But the full transcripts, including positions taken by directors, should be published. This would permit board members to be held more openly to account for positions they take in decisions of the board. It would permit people in member countries at least to know why a decision was taken and at whose behest in either of these public institutions. For these reasons, this measure has been recommended by many (e.g. Meltzer Commission 2000, Department for International Development 2000, De Gregorio et al. 1999).

Reporting to Parliaments

A fourth important reform adds a further element of accountability to the members of each institution's board. Parliaments in some industrialized countries already require reporting direct from the executive director representing them in one or other institution. More recently, demands have been made by international groups such as the Parliamentary Network on the World Bank, which was set up in 2000 (www.pnowb.org), and national groups such as the Frente Parlamentar in Brazil, which has called for legislation to ensure that information on loan agreements is made public, and for creating mechanisms to facilitate greater participation of officials and civil society in the design of programs

---

[8] In both the IMF and the IBRD an amendment of the Articles requires three-fifths of the members, having 85 percent of the total voting power (IBRD Art VIII; IMF Article XXVIII). In the IBRD the suspension of a member requires the support of a majority of the governors, exercising a majority of the total voting power (IBRD Art VI).

(www.rbrasil.org.br/frenteparlamentar). These demands are for greater accountability about what each institution decides and how it implements its decisions. Two caveats are in order about the effectiveness of broader accountability.

Broadening accountability differs from the outreach of staff in each organization to parliaments and others. Having seen their reforms rebuffed by parliaments in Russia, Turkey, and Indonesia, the IMF now encourages its staff to reach out (where governments permit) to a broader range of stakeholders including parliamentarians to build support for economic reforms. The Bank has been engaged in this for a longer time. However, actual progress toward engaging parliaments in their work has been slow. In preparing Poverty Reduction Strategy Papers (PRSP), both the Fund and the Bank have required low-income governments to undertake more participatory processes. The official review of the first stage of the process noted that the "role of parliaments . . . has generally been limited, although individual parliamentarians have been involved in some countries" (International Development Association 2002, 22). More staff outreach has the potential to complement greater accountability of board members but it is no substitute.

On its own, broadening the oversight of borrowing country directors would have little significance. Borrowing members need first to be empowered so that their stances matter (such as through double-majority voting) and the very large size of several current constituencies needs to be reduced—obviously a director attempting to report to twenty-four different countries' legislatures would have time for little else.

Representative Leadership Selection Process

A fifth necessary reform is leadership selection in each organization. As mentioned, the present process skews accountability across each organization toward the large shareholding members who still arrogate to themselves the right to appoint. The board of the IMF has already discussed changing these arrangements to ensure "a plurality of candidates representing a diversity of members across regions regardless of nationality" (IMF 2001h). A working group drawn from both the Fund and Bank Boards formally proposed in 2001 that there should at least be clear criteria for identifying, nominating, and selecting qualified candidates and that there should be transparency in the subsequent process (IMF 2001h). So far these proposals have gone nowhere. In 2005 the selection of a new World Bank president took place as secretly and as controlled by the United States as every previous selection. Blueprints for change have been ignored, yet an open and meritocratic leadership selection in the IMF and World Bank would confer greater legitimacy and result in better-balanced accountability in both organizations.

Staff Incentives

Finally, the incentives for staff need rewriting. Both the Fund and Bank have underscored the need to enhance ownership of policy and projects by borrowers. This is unlikely to be achieved without governance reforms at the levels not just of the board but also of the staff. Previous sections highlighted that such measures could include ensuring that staff spend longer working in particular countries not just to acquire greater knowledge but also to create a clearer incentive to consider long-term goals within borrower countries. Equally important could be devolution of a genuine degree of control to borrowers over the resources lent and processes for evaluating their use, and finally, counterveiling more strongly the incentives within each agency to disburse (which will only strengthen as their lending drops).

The six reforms proposed are not a magic solution to global economic inequality and discord but they would help the Fund and Bank better focus on their core purposes and serve their borrowing members. They would do this by changing the way decisions are made in the IMF and World Bank. Deliberately, the focus is on *how* decisions are made rather than *what* decisions are made. This is because the important decisions taken by institutions are not (and cannot be) based on absolute or objective economic truths. Each member government, and the IMF and World Bank, must balance private initatives with public purpose, weighing competing priorities and making decisions which create winners and losers. For this reason they need to be structured so as to balance competing interests appropriately—not just through formal representation but through influence, voice, and accountability. From a procedural point of view, the public affected by their decisions needs to perceive the process as fair, even if as individuals they object to a particular decision because it adversely affects them.

The modest suggestions for change would rebalance power and accountability so as to give borrowing members more direct voice within each institution. At the same time, the proposed changes would also ensure that these governments are in turn held more to account within their own countries. More power would come with more responsibility and accountability.

At least some borrowing governments would not support a reinvigoration of the public purposes highlighted at the outset of this chapter—a new approach to financial crises, attention to the social consequences of financial crisis management, better aid coordination, and a rethinking of conditionality. Some governments may fear impeding the short-term availability of private finance, or losing leverage (gained from conditionality and loans) over particular parts of their own political system, or focusing yet more attention on social distribution within their own borders. More generally, they may see their broader interests as being met by tagging along behind the most powerfully country in the international system—the United States.

But many other countries in the IMF and World Bank participate in a multilateral system of economic coordination and cooperation because it is the best way to resolve specific collective action problems, to ensure the provision of particular public goods, and to manage globalization. For them, reform of the governance structures of the international financial institutions is a necessary first step toward reinvigorating these reasons for their very existence.

Globalization increases the potential workload of each multilateral institution. More capital flows, more trade, and more investment spell more opportunities for entrepreneurs across the global economy. The flipside is more risk, more financial crises, and more dislocation within and across countries.

Enter public institutions. Just as governments within industrialized countries provide social insurance for their citizens, so too the IMF and World Bank exist to mitigate the harshest effects of markets on countries and peoples across the world. But to do this effectively they need to be responsive to all countries that make up their membership and especially to those most harshly affected by global markets and failures.

The IMF and World Bank were born with an ability to do just this. Their finances made them relatively independent. Their political structures carefully balanced stakes across those making contributions and those whose representation and cooperation is vital for the organizations to fulfill their mandates. But they evolved—particularly in the 1980s—into institutions increasingly financed by poor and directed by the rich.

The place to begin a renaissance of the IMF and World Bank is at home—in their headquarters in Washington D.C.—where some simple reforms to the governance of each institution could empower the people who work in them and governments who work with them much more powerfully to fulfill their core mission—not as the handmaidens of globalization, but as the stabilizers and insulators of an increasingly volatile and risk-prone international economy.

REFERENCES

Cited Interviews (description of position at time of interview or communication)

Aspe, Pedro. 1995. Former minister of finance, Mexico. Mexico City.
Beza, Ted. 1995. Director, Western Hemisphere Department, IMF. Washington, DC.
Binswagen, Hans. 1995. World Bank division chief for agriculture in Mexico and Central America. Washington, DC.
Brady, Nicholas. 1994. Former U.S. secretary of the treasury. Washington, DC.
Bravo Aguilera, Luis. 1994. Former under-secretary of foreign trade. Mexico City.
Camdessus, Michel. 1996. Managing director IMF. Interview by Ngaire Woods on BBC Radio 4, Analysis Program.
Clavijo, Fernando. 1994. Economic adviser to President Salinas. Mexico City.
Dallara, Charles. 1995. Managing director of the Institute of International Finance. Washington, DC.
Federov, Boris. Former minister of finance, Russia. Ottawa.
Husein, Shahid. 1995. Senior vice president of World Bank. Washington, DC.
Illiaronov, Andrei. 1996. Economic adviser to the president. Moscow.
Knox, David. 1995. Former vice president of World Bank for Latin America. Oxford, UK.
Loser, Claudio, and Eliot Kalter. 1994. Deputy director and staff member, Western Hemisphere Department, IMF. Washington, DC.
Marino, Roberto. 1994. Alternate director (from Mexico), IMF. Washington, DC.
Molina, Humberto. 1994. Deputy director, Bancomext. Mexico City.
Naim, Moises. 1995. Former minister of finance, Venezuela. Washington, DC.
Ortiz, Guillermo. 1994. Undersecretary of Finance Ministry. Mexico City.
Petricioli, Gustavo. March 1995. Former secretary of the treasury (of Mexico). Washington, DC.
Rozental, Andrés. 1994. Undersecretary, Ministry of Foreign Affairs. Mexico City.
Silva Herzog, Jesús. 1994. Minister of tourism, former minister of finance. Mexico City.
Steckhan, Rainer. 1995. Director for special operations in the Latin American and Caribbean region, World Bank. Washington, DC.
Van Wijnbergen, Sweder. 1994. World Bank economist. London.

Books, Periodicals, Documents

Abugre, Charles, and Nancy Alexander. 1998. Nongovernmental organizations and the international monetary and financial system. *International monetary and financial issues for the 1990s.* Vol. 9, 107–25. Geneva: UNCTAD.
Adam, Christopher. 1994. Privatization and structural adjustment in Africa. In *Negotiating structural adjustment in Africa,* ed. Willem Van der Geest, 137–60. New York: UNDP and Heinemann.
Adam, Christopher, and David Bevan. 2001. *PRGF stocktaking exercise on behalf of DFID.* Oxford: Oxford University. Mimeo.

Adler, Emanuel. 1987. Seizing the middle ground: Constructivism in world politics. *European Journal of International Relations* 3 (3): 319–63.

Adler, Emanuel, and Peter Haas. 1992. Conclusion: Epistemic communities, world order, and the creation of a reflective research program. *International Organization* (Winter).

Agarwala, Ramgopal, Pushpa Schwartz, and Jean Ponchamni. 1994. *Sub-Saharan Africa: A long-term perspective study.* Washington, DC: World Bank.

Aggarwal, Vinod. 1996. *Debt games: Strategic interaction in international debt rescheduling.* Cambridge: Cambridge University Press.

Aizenman, Joshua, and Nancy Marion. 2003. Foreign exchange reserves in East Asia: Why the high demand? *Pacific Basin Notes* 11.

Alesina, A., and Allan Drazen. 1991. Why are stabilizations delayed? *American Economic Review* 81 (5): 1170–88.

Alesina, Alberto, and Roberto Perotti. 1996. Income distribution, political instability, and investment. *European Economic Review* 40: 1203–28.

Annett, Anthony. 2000. Social fractionalization, political instability and the size of government. *IMF Working Papers* 00/82. Washington DC, IMF.

Aravena, J. 1991. *Debt reduction schemes, theoretical issues and empirical results for Chile.* Louvain la Neuve: CIACO.

Arbatov, Georgii. 1992. Neo-Bolsheviks of the IMF. *New York Times,* 7 May.

Arthur, W. Brian. 1989. Competing technologies, increasing returns, and lock-in by historical events. *Economic Journal* 99: 116–31.

———. 1990. Positive feedbacks in the economy. *Scientific American* (February): 92–99.

Ascher, H. 1983. New development approaches and the adaptability of international agencies—the case of the World Bank. *International Organization* 37 (3): 415–39.

Ascher, William. 1992. The World Bank and U.S. control. In *The United States and multilateral institutions: Patterns of changing instrumentality and influence,* ed. K. Mingst and M. Karns. London: Routledge.

Aslund, Anders. 1995. *How Russia became a market economy.* Washington, DC: The Brookings Institution.

———. 1996. Reform vs. "rent-seeking" in Russia's economic transformation. *Transition* 2 (2) (OMRI Transitions Online): 12–16.

———. 1997. *Russia's economic transformation in the 1990s.* London: Pinter.

———. 1999. Why has Russia's economic transformation been so arduous? World Bank Annual Bank Conference on Development Economics: 28–30.

———. 2000. Russia and the international financial institutions. Paper presented to the International Financial Institution Advisory Commission. 18 January.

Aspe, Pedro. 1993. *Economic transformation: The Mexican way.* Cambridge: MIT Press.

Axelrod, Robert. 1986. An evolutionary approach to norms. *American Political Science Review* 80: 1095–1111.

Babb, Sarah. 2001. Managing Mexico: Economists from nationalism to neoliberalism. Princeton, NJ: Princeton University Press.

Baker, James. 1985. Testimony to U.S. House of Representatives Committee on Banking, Finance, and Urban Affairs. Hearing on U.S. proposals on international debt crisis. 99th Congress, first session. 22 October. Serial Number 99–39.

Baldwin, David. 1965. The international bank in political perspective. *World Politics* 18 (1): 68–81.

Balino, Tomas J. T., David S. Hoelscher, and Jakob Horder. 1997. Evolution of Monetary Policy Instruments in Russia. IMF Working Paper No. 97/180. 1 December, 1997.

Banco Nacional de Comercio Exterior. 1984. *Comercio Exterior.* Mexico.

Bartley, Robert L. 1997. The Peso folklórico: Dancing away from monetary stability. In *México 1994: Anatomy of an emerging-market crash,* ed. S. Edwards and M. Naím. Carnegie Endowment for International Peace: Washington, D.C.

Bassett, Thomas. 1988. Development theory and reality: The World Bank in northern Ivory Coast. *Review of African Political Economy* 41: 45–59.

Barnett, Michael, and Martha Finnemore. 2004. *Rules for the world: International organizations in global politics.* Ithaca: Cornell University Press.

Bates, Robert. 1981. *States and markets in tropical Africa: The political basis of agricultural policy.* Series on Social Choice and Political Economy. Berkeley: University of California Press.

Bates, R., and A. Kreuger. 1993. *Political and economic interactions in economic policy reform: Evidence from eight countries.* Oxford: Basil Blackwell.

Bauer, Peter. 1984. *Reality and rhetoric: Studies in the economics of development.* London: Weidenfeld and Nicolson.

Baum, Warren C., and Stokes M. Tolbert. 1985. *Investing in development: Lessons of World Bank experience.* New York: Oxford University Press.

Bazdresch, C., N. Bucay, S. Loaeza, and N. Lustig. 1993. *México auge, crisi y ajuste.* Mexico City: Fondo de Cultura Economica.

Bekkr Aleksander. 1996. Credit is "on vacation." *Current Digest of Post-Soviet Press* 48 (23), Columbus, Ohio.

Bhatia, Rattan. 1985. The West African Monetary Union: An analytical review. IMF Occasional Paper No. 35. Washington, DC: IMF.

Biersteker, T. J. 1993. *Dealing with debt: International financial negotiations and adjustment bargaining.* Boulder, CO: Westview Press.

Bini Smaghi, L. 2004. A single EU seat in the IMF? *Journal of Common Market Studies* 42 (2): 229–48.

Bird, Graham. 1995. *IMF lending to developing countries: Issues and policies.* London: Routledge.

——. 1996. Borrowing from the IMF: The policy implications of recent empirical research. *World Development* 24: 1753–60.

——. 1999. Crisis averter, crisis lender, crisis manager: The IMF in search of a systemic role. *World Economy* 22 (7).

Bird, Graham, and Dane Rowlands. 2000. IMF lending: How is it affected by economic, political, and institutional factors. mimeo.

Birdsall, Nancy, and John Williamson. 2002. *Delivering on debt relief: From IMF gold to a new aid architecture.* Washington, DC: Center for Global Development, Institute for International Economics.

Blackwell, Michael, and Simon Nocera. 1989. Debt-equity swaps. In *Analytical issues in debt,* ed. J. A. Frenkel, M. P. Dooley, and P. Wickham. Washington, DC: IMF.

Blanco, H. 1994. *Las negociaciones comerciales de México con el mundo.* Mexico City: Fondo de Cultura Economica.

Blaug, Mark. 1987. *Economic history and the history of economics.* New York: NYU Press.

Block, Fred. 1977. *The origins of international economic disorder: A study of United States international monetary policy from World War II to the present.* Berkeley: University of California Press.

Blustein, Paul. 1998. IMF battens down for more ill wind. *Washington Post,* 29 July 1998, A16.

——. 2001a. *The chastening: Inside the crisis that rocked the global financial system and humbled the IMF.* New York: PublicAffairs.

——. 2001b. O'Neill again criticizes World Bank. *Washington Post,* 28 June 2001, E01.

Blyth, Mark. 1997. Any more bright ideas? The ideational turn of comparative political economy. *Comparative Politics* 29 (2): 229–50.

Bogdanowicz-Bindert, Christine. 1985. Testimony before U.S. House of Representatives Committee on Banking, Finance, and Urban Affairs. Hearing before the Subcommittee on International Development Institutions and Finance. External debt in the developing world. 27 June. 99th Congress, first session. Serial Number 99–25.

Bohlen, Celestine. 1998. In hour of crisis, Kremlin brings Gorbachev economic team back. *New York Times,* 15 September, A1.

Boiko, Boris. 1996. Duma "raid' on central bank is Yeltsin's gain. *Current Digest of Post-Soviet Press* 48 (23), Columbus, Ohio.

Boone, Catherine. 1991. Politics under the specter of deindustrialization: Structural adjustment in practice. In *The political economy of Senegal under structural adjustment,* ed. Christopher Delgado and Sidi Jammeh. 127–49. New York: Praeger.

Bordo, Michael, and Anna Schwartz. 1998. Under what circumstances, past and present, have international rescues of countries in financial distress been successful? Working Paper 6824. Cambridge, MA: National Bureau of Economic Research.

——. 2000. Measuring real economic effects of bailouts: Historical perspectives on how countries in financial distress have fared with and without bailouts. NBER Working Paper No. 7701. Cambridge, MA: National Bureau of Economic Research.

Boughton, James M. 2001. *Silent revolution: The International Monetary Fund, 1979–1989.* Washington, DC: International Monetary Fund.

——. 2002. *Why White, not Keynes? Inventing the post-war international monetary system.* Washington DC., IMF mimeo.

——. 2003. *Governing the IMF: Issues for Asia.* Washington, DC: IMF. Mimeo.

Boughton, James M., and Alexandros T. Mourmouras. 2002. Is policy ownership an operational concept? Working Paper No. 02/72. 1 April. Washington, DC: IMF:

Bouzas, R., and S. Keifman. 1985. Argentina: El Plan asutral y las negociaciones financiers externas. *America Latina Internacional* 1 (6): 113–19.

Boycko, Maxim, Andrei Shleifer, and Robert Vishny. 1995. *Privatizing Russia.* Cambridge, MA: MIT Press.

Brandt, Willy (Brandt Commission). 1980. *North-south: A program for survival:* The report of the independent commission on international development issues under the chairmanship of Willy Brandt. Cambridge, MA: The MIT Press.

Branson, William, and Nagy Hanna. 2000. *Ownership and conditionality.* World Bank OED Working Paper No. 8. Available at www.worldbank.org/html/oed.

Bretton Woods Project. 2004. Mott foundation grant reporting form. London: Bretton Woods Project.

Brint, Steven. 1994. *In an age of experts: The changing role of professionals in politics and public life.* Princeton, NJ: Princeton University Press.

Broms, Bengt B. 1959. *The doctrine of equality of states as applied in international organizations.* Helsinki: University of Helsinki.

Bruhn, K. 1997. *Taking on Goliath: The emergence of a new left party and the struggle for democracy in Mexico.* University Park: Pennsylvania State University Press.

Bruno, M., and Hollis Chenery. 1962. Development alternatives in an open economy. *Economic Journal* 72 (285): 79–103.

Buira, Ariel, ed. 2005. *Reforming the governance of the IMF and World Bank.* London: Anthem Press.

Burki, Shahid Javed, and Guillermo E. Perry. 1998. *Beyond the Washington consensus: Institutions matter.* Washington, DC: World Bank.

Bush, Keith. 1992. *RFE/RL Research Report.* 10 April.

———. 1993. IMF pessimistic about new loans. Radio Free Europe Archive, 62.

Bush, Keith, and Robert Lyle. 1993. Criticism from World Bank. Radio Free Europe Archive, 63.

Callaghy, Thomas. 1990. Lost between state and market: The politics of economic adjustment in Ghana, Zambia, and Nigeria. In *Economic crisis and policy change,* ed. Joan Nelson. 257–319. Princeton, NJ: Princeton University Press.

Calvo, Guillermo, Carlos Diaz-Alejandro, and World Institute for Development Economics Research. 1989. *Debt, stabilization, and development: Essays in memory of Carlos Diaz-Alejandro.* Oxford: WIDER.

Calvo, Guillermo, and Enrique Mendoza. 1994. Trade reforms of uncertain duration and real uncertainty—a first approximation. IMF Working Papers 94/45. Washington, DC: International Monetary Fund.

Castro, Claudio de Moura, and Toukel Alfthan. 1996. *Supporting reform in the delivery of social services: a strategy.* Washington, DC: Inter-American Development Bank.

Camdessus, Michel. 1993. *IMF Survey,* 22 February 1993. Washington, DC: IMF.

———. 1994. Supporting transition in Central and Eastern Europe: An assessment and lessons from the IMF's five years' experience. Second Annual Francisco Fernandez Ordez Address. 21 December. Madrid.

———. 1995. Russia's transformation efforts at a turning point. Address to the US-Russia Business Council. 29 March. IMF Press Release 95/5.

Carey, J. M., and M. S. Shugart. 1995. Incentives to cultivate a personal vote: A rank ordering of electoral formulas. *Electoral Studies* 14 (4): 417–39.

Cassen, Robert. 1994. Structural adjustment in Sub-Saharan Africa. In *Negotiating structural adjustment in Africa,* ed. Willem Van der Geest, 7–13. New York: UNDP and Heinemann.

Centeno, M. A. 1994. *Democracy within reason: Technocratic revolution in Mexico.* University Park: Pennsylvania State University Press.

Centeno, M. A., and S. Maxfield. 1992. The marriage of finance and order—changes in the Mexican political elite. *Journal of Latin American Studies* 24 (part 1): 57–85.

Centre for Economic Policy Research (CEPR). 1993. *Independent and accountable: a new mandate for the Bank of England.* CEPR Reports. London: Centre for Economic Policy Research.

CEPAL. 1984. América Latina: crisis y opciones de desarrollo. *Cepal Review* 22 (April).

Chakravarthi, Raghavan. 1989. South's share in world manufactured exports grows, but . . . SUNS— South-North Development Monitor: From GATT-Uruguay Round to the WTO (Geneva). www.sunsonline.org/trade/areas/environm/ (accessed 10 December 2004).

Chayes, Abram, and Antonia Chayes. 1993. On compliance. *International Organization* 47: 175–205.

Chote, Robert. 1999. Change of heart on debt relief for the poorest countries. *Financial Times,* 20 April, 6.

Claessens, Stijn., 1990. *Market-based debt reduction for developing countries.* Policy and Research Department. Washington, DC: World Bank.

Claessens, S., and S. Wijnbergen. 1990. Secondary market prices under alternative debt reduction strategies: An option pricing approach with an application to Mexico. CEPR Discussion Paper Series 415.

Clark, I. 1996. Inside the IMF: Comparisons with policy-making organisations in Canadian governments. *Canadian Public Administration* 39 (2): 157–91.

Clarke, Stephen. 1967. *Central bank cooperation: 1924—31*. New York: Federal Reserve Bank of New York.

Cline, William. 1984. *Systemic risk and policy response*. Washington, DC: Institute for International Economics.

———. 1995. *International debt reexamined*. Washington, DC: Institute for International Economics.

Commander, Simon, Irina Dolinskaya, and Christian Mumssen. 2000. Determinants of barter in Russia—An empirical analysis. IMF Working Paper WP/00/155. Washington, DC: IMF.

Conway, Patrick. 1994. IMF lending programs: Participation and impact. *Journal of Development Economics* 45: 365–91.

Corbo, Vittorio, Morris Goldstein, and Mohsin Khan, eds. 1987. *Growth-oriented adjustment programs.* Washington, DC: IMF.

Corbo, Vittorio, and Patricio Rojas. 1992. "World Bank-supported adjustment programs: Country performance and effectiveness." In *Adjustment lending revisited: Policies to restore growth*, ed. Vittorio Corbo, Stanley Fischer, and Steven B. Webb. 23–36. Washington, DC: World Bank.

Cordoba, J. 1994. Mexico. In *The political economy of policy reform*, ed. J. Williamson. Washington, DC: Institute for International Economics.

Cornia, Giovanni Andrea, Richard Jolly, and Frances Stewart, eds. 1987. *Adjustment with a human face: Protecting the vulnerable and promoting growth.* Oxford: Clarendon Press.

Corwin, Julie A. 1998. Tax Service seizes oil companies' assets. Radio Free Europe/Radio Liberty Newsline. 6 August 1998.

Cottarelli, Carlo, and Curzio Giannini. 2002. Bedfellows, hostages, or perfect strangers? Global capital markets and the catalytic effect of IMF crisis lending. IMF Working Papers No. 02/193.

Cox, Gary. 1990. Centripetal and centrifugal incentives in electoral systems. *American Journal of Political Science* 34 (4): 903–35.

Cox, Robert. 1979. Ideologies and the NIEO. *International Organization* 33 (2): 257–80.

Cox, Robert, W., and Harold Karan Jacobson. 1973. *The anatomy of influence: Decision making in international organization.* New Haven, CT: Yale University Press.

Cukierman, Richard Webb, and B. Neyapti. 1992. Measuring the independence of central banks and its effect on policy outcomes. *World Bank Economic Review* 6 (3): 353–98.

Current Digest of the Post-Soviet Press (CDPP). 1991. Vol. 43 (43).

———. 1992. Vol. 44 (14).

Darity, William, and Bobbie Horn. 1988. *The Loan pushers: The role of commercial banks in the international debt crisis.* Cambridge: Ballinger.

Deane, Phyllis. 1978. *The evolution of economic ideas.* Cambridge: Cambridge University Press.

De Gregorio, Jose, Barry Eichengreen, Takatoshi Ito, and Charles Wyplosz. 1999. *An independent and accountable IMF.* Geneva: International Center for Monetary and Banking Studies.

De La Madrid Hurtado, M. 1982. *Plan basico 1982–1988 y plataforma electoral.* Mexico City: Partido Revolucionario Institucional.

Dell, Sidney. 1981. *On being grandmotherly: The evolution of IMF conditionality.* Vol. 144 of *Princeton essays in international finance.* Princeton, NJ: Princeton University Press.

———. 1982. Stabilisation: The political economy of overkill. *World Development* 10 (8).

Dell, Sidney, and Roger Lawrence. 1980. *The balance of payments adjustment process in developing countries.* New York: Pergamon.

De Macedo, J. B. 1986. Collective pegging to a single currency: The West African monetary union. In *Economic adjustment and exchange rates in developing countries*, ed. S. Edwards and L. Ahamed. Chicago: University of Chicago Press.

Demery, Lionel, and Tony Addison. 1987. *Alleviation of poverty under structural adjustment.* Washington, DC: World Bank.

De Moura Castro, C., and T. Alfthan. 1994. *Budget cuts in education: Policy or politics.* Washington, DC: Inter-American Development Bank.

Department for International Development (DFID). 2000. *Eliminating world poverty: Making globalisation work for the poor.* London: Department for International Development.

———. 2004a. *Departmental Report.* April. London: Department for International Development.

———. 2004b. *Statistics on international development 2004.* October. London: Department for International Development.

Devarajan, S., and J. de Melo. 1987. Evaluating participation in African monetary unions: A statistical analysis of the CFA zones. *World Development* 15 (4): 483–96.

De Vries, Margaret Garritsen. 1976. *The International Monetary Fund 1966–1971: The system under stress.* Vols. 1, 2. Washington, DC: IMF.

———. 1985. *The International Monetary Fund, 1972–1978: Cooperation on trial.* Washington, DC: IMF.

——. 1987. *Balance of payments adjustment, 1945–1986: The IMF experience.* Washington, DC: IMF.

DiMaggio, Paul, and Walter Powell. 1991. *The new institutionalism in organizational analysis.* Chicago: University of Chicago Press.

Dixit, A. K. 1996. *The making of economic policy: A transaction-cost politics perspective.* Cambridge: MIT Press.

Dolowitz, D. P., and D. Marsh. 2000. Learning from abroad: The role of policy transfer in contemporary policy-making. *Governance—An International Journal of Policy and Administration* 13 (1): 5–24.

Domínguez, Jorge I., ed. 1997. *Technopols: Freeing politics and markets in Latin America in the 1990s.* University Park: Pennsylvania State University Press.

Domínguez, Jorge, and James McCann. 1996. *Democratizing Mexico: Public opinion and electoral choices.* Baltimore, MD: Johns Hopkins University Press.

Dooley, Michael. 1986. An analysis of the debt crisis. IMF Working Paper 86/14. Washington, DC: IMF.

——. 1988. Buy-backs and market valuation of external debt. IMF Staff Papers. Washington, DC: IMF: 215–29.

Dornbusch, Rudiger, and Alejandro Werner. 1994. Mexico: Stabilization, reform, and no growth. Brookings Papers on Economic Activity. Issue 1: 253–315.

Drazen, Allan. 2001. Conditionality and ownership in IMF lending: A political economy approach. Mimeo.

Drazen, Allan, and V. Grilli. 1993. The benefit of crises for economic reforms. *American Economic Review* 83 (3): 598–607.

Dreher, Axel. 2003. The influence of elections on IMF program interruptions. *The Journal of Development Studies* 39 (6): 101–20.

Dubinia, Sergei. 2004. Pathways through financial crises workshop. Participant contribution at workshop held at University College, Oxford, UK.

Eberstadt, Nicholas, and Clifford Lewis. 1995. Privatizing the World Bank. *The National Interest* 40 (Summer).

Economic Commission for Africa. 1980. The Lagos plan of action. At http://www.uneca.org/itca/ariportal/docs/lagos_plan.PDF.

——. 1982. *Declaration of Tripoli.* 30 April. Tripoli: Conference of Ministers, Economic Commission for Africa.

——. 1989. *African alternative framework.* Addis Ababa: Economic Commission for Africa.

Economist. 1993. Mexico: Survey—into the spotlight—a latin big bang. *Economist* 13.

Edwards, Martin. 2003. Domestic institutions and economic performance under IMF programs, 1979–1995. Mimeo. Texas Tech University.

Edwards, Sebastian. 1995. *Crisis and reform in Latin America: From despair to hope.* New York: Oxford University Press for the World Bank.

——. 1996. A tale of two crises: Chile and Mexico. Manuscript (available at www.anderson.ucla.edu/faculty/sebastian.edwards/papers.htm).

Edwards, S., and M. Naim, eds. 1997. *Mexico 1994: Anatomy of an emerging-market crash.* Washington, DC: Carnegie Endowment for International Peace.

Edwards, Sebastian, and J. A. Santella. 1993. Devaluation controversies in the developing countries: Lessons from the Bretton Woods era. In *A retrospective on the Bretton Woods system,* ed. Michael Bordo and Barry Eichengreen, 405–55. Chicago: University of Chicago Press.

Edwards, Sebastian, and G. Tabellini. 1991. Explaining fiscal policies and inflation in developing countries. *Journal of International Money and Finance* 10 (suppl. S): S16–S48.

Eggers, Ann Florini, and Ngaire Woods. 2005. Democratizing the IMF. In *Accountability of the International Monetary Fund,* ed. Barry Carin and Angela Wood. 38–61. Aldershot: Ashgate and IDRC.

Eichengreen, Barry. 1989. Hegemonic stability theories of the international monetary system. In *Can nations agree: Issues in international economic cooperation,* 255–98. Washington, DC: Brookings Institution.

——. 1996. *Golden fetters: gold standard and the great depression 1919–39.* New York: Oxford University Press.

Eijffinger, S. C. W., and J. de Haan. 1996. Central bank independence—Only part of the inflation story: A comment. *Economist* 144 (4): 658–66.

Elbadawi, Ibrahim, and Nader Majd. 1992. Fixed parity of the exchange rate and economic performance in the CFA zone. PRE Working Papers WPS 830. Washington, DC: World Bank.

Electricity Regulatory Authority (Uganda). 2003. Uganda seeks new investor. Gulu: Electricity Regulatory Authority. 16 August. At www.era.or.ug/article.asp?id=102.

Elliott, Larry. 1998. Germany raises hope of deal on debt relief. *The Guardian* 7 December 1998: 3.

Erlanger, Steven. 1992. Yeltsin to seek more time to repay old Soviet debts. *New York Times* 5 July, A6.

Escobar, A. 1995. *Encountering development: The making and unmaking of the third world*. Princeton, NJ: Princeton University Press.

European Bank for Reconstruction and Development (EBRD). 1997. *1997 Transition Report*. London: EBRD.

Evans, Huw. 1999. Debt relief for the poorest countries: Why did it take so long? *Development Policy Review* 17 (3).

Evans, Peter. 1995. *Embedded autonomy: States and industrial transformation*. Princeton, NJ: Princeton University Press.

Evans, Peter, and Martha Finnemore. December 2001. Organizational reform and the expansion of the South's voice at the Fund. G-24. At http://www.g24.org/evans-fi.pdf.

Evans, P., S. Haggard, and R. Kaufman, eds. 1992. *The politics of economic adjustment: International constraints, distributive conflicts, and the state*. Princeton, NJ: Princeton University Press.

Evans, Peter, H. Jacobson, and R. Putnam. 1993. *Double-edged diplomacy: International bargaining and domestic politics*. Berkeley: University of California Press.

Evans, Peter, Dietrich Rueschemeyer, and Theda Skocpol. 1985. *Bringing the state back in*. Cambridge: Cambridge University Press.

Feldstein, Marty. 1998. Refocusing the IMF. *Foreign Affairs 77*.

Ferguson, J. 1990. *The antipolitics machine: "Development," depoliticization, and bureaucratic domination in Lesotho*. New York: Cambridge University Press.

Fernandez, R., and D. Rodrik. 1991. Resistance to reform—status-quo bias in the presence of individual-specific uncertainty. *American Economic Review* 81 (5): 1146–55.

Ffrench-Davies, Ricardo. 1987. Latin America: Debtor-creditor relations. *Third World Quarterly* 9 (4).

Financial Times. 1999, Editorial of 17 February, 21.

———. 1988. Editorial of 26 September 1988.

Fine, Ben, and Degol Hailu. 2000. Convergence and consensus: the political economy of stabilization and growth. Centre for Development Policy and Research. Discussion Paper 1400. London: School of Oriental and African Studies.

Finnemore, Martha. 1996. Norms, culture, and world politics: Insights into sociology's institutionalism. *International Organization* 50: 325–47.

Finnemore, Martha, and Kathryn Sikkink. 1999. International norm dynamics and political change. In *Exploration and contestation in the study of world politics*, ed. Peter Katzenstein, Robert Keohane, and Stephen Krasner, 247–77. Cambridge: MIT Press.

Fish, M. Steven. 1998. The determinants of economic reform in the post-communist world. *East European Politics and Societies* 12 (Winter): 31–78.

Fischer, Stanley. 1998a. Reforming the international monetary system. David Finch Lecture, Melbourne.

———. 1998b. *The Russian economy at the start of 1998*. 9 January. Washington, DC: IMF.

———. 2001. The Russian economy: Prospects and retrospect. Speech to Higher School of Economics. Moscow. 19 June.

Folkerts-Landau, David, and Carl-Johan Lindgren. 1998. Toward a framework for financial stability. World Economic and Financial Surveys. Washington, DC: IMF.

Fomin, Roman. 2001. End of Vladimir Gusinsky's empire, media-most holding liquidated. *Pravda* 10.

Franck, Thomas. 1992. The emerging right to democratic governance. *American Journal of International Law* 86: 46–91.

Frankel, Francine. 1978. *India's political economy, 1947–1977*. Princeton, NJ: Princeton University Press.

Freeland, Chrystia. 1998. IMF ready to throw Russian lifeline. *Financial Times,* 25 June, 2.

Frenkel, Jacob, Michael Dooley, and Peter Wickham, eds. 1989. *Analytical issues in debt*. Washington, DC: IMF.

Frenkel, J. A., and Morris Goldstein. 1991. Monetary policy in an emerging European economic and monetary union—Key issues. *International Monetary Fund Staff Papers* 38 (2): 356–73.

Fried, Edward, and Philip Trezise. 1989. *Third world debt: The next phase*. Washington, DC: Brookings Institution.

Frieden, Jeffry. 1991a. Invested interests: The politics of national economic policies in a world of global finance. *International Organization* 45 (4): 425–51.

———. 1991b. *Debt, development, and democracy: Modern political economy and Latin America*. Princeton, NJ: Princeton University Press.

Frischtak, Leila, and Izak Atiyas. 1996. *Governance, leadership and communication: Building constituencies for economic reform*. Washington, DC: The World Bank.

Furtado, Celso. 1959. *The economic growth of Brazil: A survey from colonial to modern times*. English translation published in 1965. Berkeley: University of California Press.

G-24. 1986. G-24 Communiqué. Thirty-Fourth Meeting Of Ministers.

——. 1991. Communiqué of Intergovernmental Group of Twenty-four on international monetary affairs. Forty-fifth Meeting of Ministers. 12 October. Bangkok, Thailand. At www.g24.org.

——. 1992. Communiqué of Intergovernmental Group of Twenty-four on international monetary affairs. Forty-sixth Meeting of Ministers. 26 April. Washington, DC. At www.g24.org.

Gaddy, Clifford G., and Barry W. Ickes. 1998. Russia's virtual economy. *Foreign Affairs* 77 (5): 53–67.

Gaidar, Yegor. 1997. The IMF and Russia. AEA Papers and Proceedings 87 (2) (May): 13–17.

——. 1999. Lessons of the Russian crisis for transition economies. February. Moscow: Institute for the Economy of the Transition Period. At www.iet.ru.

Gardner, Richard N. 1964. *In pursuit of world order: U.S. foreign policy and international organizations.* New York: Praeger.

——. 1969. *Sterling-dollar diplomacy: The origins and prospects of our international economic order.* New York: Oxford University Press.

——. 1980. *Sterling-dollar diplomacy in current perspective: The origins and the prospects of our international economic order.* New York: Columbia University Press.

——. 1985. Sterling-dollar diplomacy in current perspective. *International Affairs* (Winter): 21.

Geddes, Barbara. 1994. How politicians decide who bears the cost of liberalization. In *Transition to market economy at the end of the 20th century,* ed. I. T. Berend. Munich: Sudosteuropa-Gesselschaft.

——. 1995. The politics of economic liberalization. *Latin American Research Review* 30 (2): 195–214.

Geertz, Clifford. 1964. Ideology as a cultural system. In *Ideology and Discontent,* ed. David Apter. 47–76. London: Macmillan.

Geithner, Timothy. 1998. Under-Secretary of Treasury for International Finance. Statement to U.S. House of Representatives. 21 April. At www.house.gov/htbin/fe_srchget/comms/ba00/42198tre.htm).

——. 1999. Under-Secretary of Treasury for International Finance. Statement to the Senate Banking, Housing and Urban Affairs Committee. 9 March.

General Accounting Office (GAO). 1999. International Monetary Fund: Approach used to establish and monitor conditions for financial assistance. 22 June 1999. GGD/NSAID-99-198.

——. 2000. Foreign Assistance: International efforts to aid Russia's transition have had mixed results. November 2000. GAO-0108.

General Agreement on Tariffs and Trade (GATT). 1993. *Mexico: trade policy review.* Geneva: GATT.

Gianviti, Francois. 1999. Decision-making in the International Monetary Fund. In *Current developments in monetary and financial law,* edited by the International Monetary Fund, 31–67. Washington, DC: International Monetary Fund.

Gil-Diaz, F., and A. Carstens. 1996. *Pride and prejudice: The economics profession and Mexico's financial crisis, 1994–95.* Mexico City: Banco de Mexico.

Gisselquist, David. 1981. *The political economics of international bank lending.* New York: Praeger.

Gold, Joseph. 1972. *Voting and decisions in the International Monetary Fund.* Washington, DC: IMF.

——. 1974. *Membership and nonmembership in the International Monetary Fund: A study in international law and organization.* Washington D.C.: International Monetary Fund.

——. 1977. *Voting majorities in the Fund: Effects of second amendment of the articles.* Washington, DC: IMF.

——. 1989. *The Fund agreement in the courts.* Vols. I–IV. Washington, DC: IMF.

Goldman, Marshall. 1994. *Lost opportunity: Why economic reforms in Russia have not worked.* New York: Norton.

Goldsmith, Arthur A. 1999. Africa's overgrown state revisited: Bureaucracy and economic growth. *World Politics* 51 (4): 520–46.

Goldstein, Judith, and Robert Keohane. 1993. Ideas and foreign policy: An analytical framework. In *Ideas and Foreign Policy,* ed. Judith Goldstein and Robert Keohane. Ithaca: Cornell University Press.

Goldstein, Morris, and Peter J. Montiel. 1986. Evaluating fund stabilisation programs with multicountry data: Some methodological pitfalls. IMF Staff Papers 33, 304–44.

Gomulka, Stanislav. 1995. The IMF-supported programs of Poland and Russia, 1990–1994: Principles, errors and results. *Journal of Comparative Economics* 20 (3).

Goodman, J., and L. Pauly. 1993. The obsolescence of capital controls: Economic management in an age of global markets. *World Politics* 46 (1): 50–82.

Gould, Erica. 2003. Money talks: Supplementary financiers and International Monetary Fund conditionality. *International Organization* 57 (3): 551–86.

Gould-Davies, Nigel, and Ngaire Woods. 1999. Russia and the IMF. *International Affairs* 75 (January).

Gourevitch, Peter. 1978. The second image reversed: The international sources of domestic politics. *International Organization* 32: 881–911.

Graham, George. 1994. IMF-World Bank warning on Russia. *Financial Times,* 7 January, 2.

Graham, L. 1990. *The state and policy outcomes in Latin America.* New York: Praeger.

Gramm, Phil. 2000. Speech in the Senate ending the 106th Congress. US Senate. 18 October 2000 (S10650-1).

Gran, G. 1986. Beyond African famines: Whose knowledge matters? *Alternatives* 11: 275–96.

Grant, Robert M. 2002. AES Corporation: Rewriting the rules of management. At www.blackwell publishing.com/newgrant/docs/17AES.pdf.

Granville, Brigitte. 1999. *A messy business: The exchange rate strategy.* London: Royal Institute for International Affairs.

Green, Marshall. 1990. *Indonesia: Crisis and transformation, 1965–1968.* Washington, DC: Compass Press.

Greenhouse, Steven. 1993a. IMF may loosen conditions for aid to Russia economy. *New York Times,* 22 December, A1.

——. 1993b. IMF delays $1.5 billion loan to Russia because reform is stalled. *New York Times,* 20 September, A3.

Grether, Jean-Marie de Melo, and Jaime Olarreaga Marcelo. 1999. Who determines Mexican trade policy? World Bank Policy Research Working Paper 2187. September. Washington, DC: World Bank.

Griffith-Jones, S. 1988. *Managing world debt.* Hemel Hempstead, UK: Harvester Wheatsheaf.

Gruber, Lloyd. 2000. *Ruling the world: Power politics and the rise of supranational institutions.* Princeton, NJ: Princeton University Press.

Guillaumont, P., S. Guillaumont, and P. Plane. 1988. Participating in African monetary unions—An alternative evaluation. *World Development* 16 (5): 569–76.

Gurria, J. A. 1988. Debt restructuring: Mexico as a case study. In *Managing World Debt,* ed. S. Griffith-Jones. Hemel Hempstead, UK: Harvester Wheatsheaf.

——. 1993. *La politica de la deuda externa.* Mexico City: Fondo de Cultura Economica.

Gwin, Catherine. 1997. *U.S. relations with the World Bank, 1945–1992.* Vol. 2 of *The World Bank: Its first half century.* Ed. Devesh Kapur, John Lewis, and Richard Webb, 195–274. Washington, DC: Brookings Institution.

Gwin, C., and R. Feinberg. 1989. *The International Monetary Fund in a multipolar world: Pulling together.* Washington, DC: Overseas Development Council.

Haas, Ernst. 1990. *When knowledge is power: Three models of change in international organizations.* Berkeley: University of California Press.

Haas, P. 1989. Do regimes matter? Epistemic communities and Mediterranean pollution control. *International Organization* 43: 377–405.

——. 1992. Knowledge, power, and international policy coordination. Special Issue. *International Organization* 46.

Haggard, Stephan. 1986. The politics of adjustment: Lessons from the IMF's extended fund facility. In *The politics of international debt,* ed. Miles Kahler, 157–86. Ithaca: Cornell University Press.

——. 2000. *The political economy of the Asian crisis.* Washington, DC: Institute of International Economics.

Haggard, Stephan, and Robert Kaufman. 1989. The politics of stabilization and structural adjustment. In *Developing country debt and economic performance: The international financial system,* ed. Jeffrey Sachs, 210–20. Chicago: University of Chicago Press.

——. 1995. *The political economy of democratic transitions.* Princeton, NJ: Princeton University Press.

Haggard, Stephan, and Beth A. Simmons. 1987. Theories of international regimes. *International Organization* 41 (3): 491–517.

Haggard, Stephan, and Steven B. Webb. 1994. *Voting for reform: Democracy, political liberalization, and economic adjustment.* New York: Oxford University Press for the World Bank.

Hale, David. 1996. Lessons from the Mexican crisis of 1995 for the post–Cold War international order. Draft chapter for The World Bank Report on Mexico. February.

——. 1998. How Russia caused a global financial crisis. 31 August. At www.davidhaleonline.com/reports/pdf/russia_crisis.pdf accessed on 21/07/03).

Hall, Peter. 1986. *Governing the economy: The politics of state intervention in Britain and France.* Oxford: Oxford University Press.

——, ed. 1989. *The political power of economic ideas: Keynesianism across nations.* Princeton, NJ: Princeton University Press.

Hall, H. Keith, and Douglas Nelson. 1992. Institutional structure in the political economy of protection: Legislated versus administered protection. *Economics & Politics* 4 (1): 61–77.

Hanson, Stephen. November 2000. Can Putin rebuild the Russian state. Program on New Approaches to Russian Security Policy Memo Series, Number 148.

Hansson, Ardo. 2003. The trouble with the rouble: Monetary reform in the former Soviet Union. In *Changing the economic system in Russia,* ed. Anders Aslund and Richard Layard. New York: St. Martin's Press.

Havnevik, Kjell, ed. 1987. *The IMF and the World Bank in Africa.* Uppsala: Scandinavian Institute for Africa Studies.

Helleiner, Eric. 1994. *States and the reemergence of global finance: From Bretton Woods to the 1990s.* Ithaca: Cornell University Press.

Helleiner, Gerald. 1981. The Refsnes seminar—economic-theory and North-South negotiations. *World Development* 9 (6): 539–55.

——. 1982. *For good or evil: Economic theory and North-South negotiations.* Toronto: University of Toronto Press.

——. 1986a. Balance-of-payments experience and growth prospects of developing-countries—a synthesis. *World Development* 14 (8): 877–908.

——, ed. 1986b. Africa and the International Monetary Fund. Papers Presented at a Symposium Held in Nairobi, Kenya. 13–15 May. Washington, DC: IMF.

——, ed. 1987. *Africa and the International Monetary Fund.* Washington, DC: IMF.

Helliwell, John. 1994. Empirical linkages between democracy and economic growth. *British Journal of Political Science* 24: 225–48.

Hellman, Joel. 1997. Constitutions and economic reform in the postcommunist transitions. In *The rule of law and economic reform in Russia,* ed. Jeffrey Sachs and Katharina Pistar. Boulder, CO: Westview Press.

——. 1998. Winners take all: The politics of partial reform in postcommunist-transitions. *World Politics* 50 (2): 203–34.

Hellman, Joel, Geraint Jones, and Daniel Kaufman. 2000. Seize the state, seize the day: An empirical analysis of state capture, corruption, and influence in transition. World Bank Policy Research Working Paper No. 2444. Washington, DC: World Bank.

Heredia, Blanca. 1987. Profits and politics. In *Government and private sector in contemporary Mexico,* ed. S. Maxfield and R. Anzaldua. San Diego, CA: Center for US-Mexican Studies.

Hibou, Beatrice. 1996. L'Afrique est-elle protectionniste? Les chemins buissonniers de la libéralisation extérieure, collection "Les Afriques." Paris: Karthala.

Hirsch, Fred. 1969. *Money international.* Harmondsworth, UK: Penguin.

Hiscox, Michael. 1999. The magic bullet? The RTAA, institutional reform, and trade liberalization. *International Organization* 53 (4): 669–98.

——. 2002. *International trade and political conflict: Commerce, coalitions, and mobility.* Princeton, NJ: Princeton University Press.

Hodges, Tony. 1988. Ghana's strategy for adjustment with growth. *Africa Recovery* 2 (3): 16–21.

Hoffman, Lily. 1989. *The politics of knowledge: Activist movements in medicine and planning.* Albany: State University of New York Press.

Horsefield, J. K., ed. 1969. *The International Monetary Fund 1945–1965: Twenty years of international monetary cooperation.* Vol. 3. *Documents.* Washington, DC: IMF.

Hough, Jerry, Evelyn Davidheiser, and Susan Goodrich Lehman. 1996. *The 1996 Russian presidential election.* Washington, DC: Brookings Institution.

Husain, Ishrat, and Ishac Diwan. 1989. *Dealing with the debt crisis.* Washington, DC: World Bank.

Ikenberry, J. 1990. The international spread of privatization policies: Inducements, learning and "policy bandwagonning." In *The political economy of public sector reform and privatization,* ed. E. N. Suleiman and J. Waterbury. Boulder, CO: Westview Press.

——. 1992. A world economy restored: Expert consensus and the Anglo-American postwar settlement. *International Organization* 46: 289–321.

Ilchman, Warren, and Norman Uphoff. 1969. *The political economy of change.* Berkeley: University of California Press.

Independent Evaluation Office of the IMF. 2002. *Evaluation of prolonged use of IMF resources.* Washington, DC: IMF.

——. 2003a. *The IMF and recent capital account crises: Indonesia, Korea, Brazil.* Washington, DC: IMF.

——. 2003b. *Fiscal adjustment in IMF-supported programs.* Washington DC: IMF.

——. 2004. *The IMF's approach to capital account liberalization.* Washington, DC: IMF.

Institute of International Finance (IIF). 2003. Annual report. Washington, DC: Institute of International Finance.

International Development Association (IDA). 1998. *Additions to IDA resources: Twelfth replenishment.* Washington, DC: IDA.

——. 2001. *The IDA deputies: An historical perspective.* November. Washington, DC: International Development Association 13. At http://siteresources.worldbank.org/IDA/Resources/Seminar%20PDFs/deputS.pdf (accessed 20 May 2005).

——. 2005. *Additions to IDA resources: Fourteenth replenishment.* Report from the executive directors of the International Development Association to the Board of Governors. 10 March. Washington, DC: International Development Association.

International Development Association (IDA)/IMF. 1999. *Heavily Indebted Poor Countries (HIPC) Initiative—Update on costing the enhanced HIPC initiative.* 7 December. Washington, DC: IMF.
——. 2002. Review of the Poverty Reduction Strategy Paper (PRSP) approach: Early experience with interim PRSPs and full PRSPs. 26 March. International Development Association and International Monetary Fund. At www.worldbank.org/poverty/strategies/review/earlyexp.pdf
International Financial Institutions Advisory Commission (IFIAC). 2000. *Report of the International Financial Institutions Advisory Commission.* At http://phantom-x.gsia.cmu.edu/IFIAC/.
International Monetary Fund. 1976. Annual report. Washington, DC: IMF.
——. 1982. World economic outlook: A survey by the staff of the IMF. Occasional Paper 9. Washington, DC: IMF.
——. 1985. *Mexico: Recent economic developments.* IMF Staff Mission. 20 May. Washington, DC: IMF.
——. 1987. Theoretical aspects of the design of fund-supported adjustment programs. Occasional Paper 55. Washington, DC: IMF.
——. 1988. Annual report. Washington, DC: IMF.
——. 1993. Annual report. Washington, DC: IMF.
——. 1994a. *Economic review: financial relations among countries of the former Soviet Union.* Washington, DC: IMF.
——. 1994b. *Country report on Mexico following Article IV consultations.* January 1994. Washington, DC: IMF.
——. 1995a. *Country report on Mexico.* Washington, DC: IMF.
——. 1995b. *International capital markets: Developments, prospects, and policy issues.* Washington, DC: IMF.
——. 1995c. Report to the Executive Board on the IMF and Mexico (Confidential Report of a review conducted for the managing director by former head of IMF European Department, Sir Alan Whittome: "the Whittome Report"). I am very grateful to officials who I cannot name who shared the contents of this report with me in 1996.
——. 1996. IMF approves three-year EFF credit for the Russian Federation. Press release 96/13. Washington, DC: IMF.
——. 1997a. *Good governance: The IMF's role.* Washington, DC: IMF.
——. 1997b. Russian Federation—recent economic developments. IMF Staff Country Report 97/63. Washington, DC: IMF.
——. 1997c. IMF adopts a decision on new arrangements to borrow. IMF Press release 97/5. January 27, 1997. Washington, DC: IMF.
——. 1997d. *Legal and institutional obstacles to growth and business in Russia.* Washington, DC: IMF (European II Department).
——. 1998a. *World economic outlook. Financial crises: Causes and indicators.* May. Washington, DC: IMF.
——. 1998b. *HIPC initiative: The IMF's response to critics.* September. Washington, DC: IMF.
——. 1998c. *World economic outlook: Financial turbulence and the world economy.* October. Washington, DC: IMF.
——. 1998d. Press release 98/5.
——. 1998e. IMF announces appointment of Donal Donovan as director of IMF-Singapore regional training institute. Press release 98/17. 5 May 1998.
——. 1998f. Press briefing transcript. 13 July.
——. 1998g. Press release 98/31.
——. 1998h. Transcript of IMF press conference. 28 August.
——. 1998i. World economic outlook and international capital markets: Interim assessment. Washington, DC: IMF.
——. 1999a. Direction of trade statistics. March. Washington, DC: IMF.
——. 1999b. Liberalizing capital movements: Some analytical issues. *Economic Issues* 17. Washington, DC: IMF.
——. 1999c. *The poverty reduction and growth facility (PRGF)—operational issues.* 13 December. Prepared by the Policy Development and Review Department, IMF, in consultation with the Area Departments, Fiscal Affairs Department, and the staff of the World Bank. Washington, DC: IMF.
——. 2000a. IMF managing director's letter to GAO. 26/10/2000.
——. 2000b. *Russia country report.* Washington, DC: International Monetary Fund.
——. 2001a. *Streamlining structural conditionality: Review of initial experience.* July. Policy Development and Review Department. Washington, DC: IMF.
——. 2001b. Russian Federation: Postprogram monitoring discussion, staff report, and public information notice on the executive board discussion. July. IMF Country Report Number 01/102. Washington, DC: IMF.

——. 2001c. Diversity annual report. Washington, DC: IMF.

——. 2001d. HIPC. Washington, DC: IMF.

——. 2001e. Guidelines on joint staff assessments of PRSPs. Washington, DC: IMF. At www.imf.org/external/np/prsp/2001/042001.htm#annex2.

——. 2001f. (Cooper Report) Report to the IMF executive board of the quota formula review group. 12 April. Washington, DC: IMF. At www.imf.org/external/np/tre/quota/2000/eng/qfrg/report/index.htm.

——. 2001g. Financial organization and operations of the IMF. Pamphlet Series. Washington, DC: IMF (Treasurer's Department).

——. 2001h. Draft joint report of the working group to review the process for selection of the president of the World Bank and managing director of the IMF. Washington, DC: IMF (28 April). At www.imf.org/external/spring/2001/imfc/select.htm).

——. 2002a. Staff report for the 2002 Article IV consultation, Mexico. 13 August. IMF country report 02/237. Washington, DC: IMF.

——. 2002b. Biennial review of the implementation of the fund's surveillance and of the 1977 surveillance decision: Surveillance in a program environment. 15 March. Policy Development and Review Department. Washington, DC: IMF.

——. 2002c. Human Resources Department. Washington, DC: IMF.

——. 2002d. The design of the sovereign debt restructuring mechanism—further considerations. 27 November. Washington, DC: IMF.

——. 2002f. Update on the financing of PRGF and HIPC operations and the subsidization of postconflict emergency assistance. Washington, DC: IMF.

——. 2002g. Annual Report. Washington, DC: IMF.

——. 2002h. IMF completes review under Zambia's PRGF arrangement and approves US$55 million. News Brief No. 02/117. November 27. Washington, DC. IMF.

——. 2003a. Staff report for the 2003 Article IV consultation: Mexico. 17 September. Washington, DC: IMF.

——. 2003b. International standards: Strengthening surveillance, domestic institutions, and international markets. Washington, DC: IMF.

——. 2003c. Financial sector assessment program—review, lessons, and issues going forward. Washington, DC: IMF.

——. 2004. Annual Report. Washington, DC: IMF.

——. 2005. World economic outlook: Globalization and external imbalances. April. Washington, DC: IMF. At http://www.imf.org/external/pubs/ft/weo/2005/01/index.htm.

International Monetary and Financial Committee (IMFC). 2004. Communiqué of the International Monetary and Financial Committee of the Board of Governors of the International Monetary Fund. 2 October. Washington, DC: IMF. At www.imf.org/external/np/cm/2004/100204.htm.

IMF, External Evaluation. 1998. External evaluation into ESAF: A report by a group of independent experts. Washington, DC: IMF.

——. 1999a. External evaluation of IMF surveillance: A report by a group of independent experts. Washington, DC: IMF.

——. 1999b. External evaluation of IMF research activities: A report by a group of independent experts. Washington, DC: IMF.

IMF-Senegal. 2004. Transactions with the IMF—Senegal. Washington, DC: IMF. At www.imf.org/external/np/tre/tad/ (accessed 10 December 2004).

IMF and World Bank. 1999. Heavily indebted poor country (HIPC) debt initiative. Review and consultation prepared by the staffs of the International Monetary Fund and World Bank. 9 February. Washington, DC: IMF and World Bank.

IMF, World Bank, European Bank for Reconstruction and Development, and Organization for Economic Cooperation and Development. 1991. A Study of the Soviet Economy. Vols. 1, 2. Washington, DC: IMF.

Intriligator, Michael. 1997. Round table on Russia: A new economic policy for Russia. Economics of Transition 5 (1): 225–27.

Ize, A. I. 1990. Trade liberalization, stabilization, and growth: Some notes on the Mexican experience. Washington, DC: IMF.

Jacobsen, John. 1995. Much ado about ideas: The cognitive factor in economic policy. World Politics 47 (2): 283–310.

Jakobeit, Cord. 2005. Enhancing the voice of developing countries in the World Bank: Selective double majority voting and a pilot phase. In Reforming the governance of the IMF and World Bank, ed. Ariel Buira, 213–34. London: Anthem Press.

James, Harold. 1996. *International monetary cooperation since Bretton Woods.* Washington, DC: International Monetary Fund and Oxford University Press.

Johnson, Melanie. 1994. Financial sector reforms in structural adjustment programmes. In *Negotiating structural adjustment in Africa,* ed. Willem Van der Geest, 175–85. New York: UNDP and Heinemann.

Johnson, J., and S. Wasty. 1993. Borrower ownership of adjustment programs and the political economy of reform. World Bank Discussion Paper 1999. Washington, DC: World Bank.

Johnson, Simon, and Marzena Kowalska. 1994. Poland: The political economy of shock therapy. In *Voting for reform: Democracy, political liberalization, and economic adjustment,* ed. Stephan Haggard and Steven B. Webb. New York: Oxford University Press.

Johnstone, R, S. Darbar, and C. Echeverria. 1997. Sequencing capital account liberalisation: Lessons from experience in Chile, Indonesia, Korea, and Thailand. IMF Working Paper. Washington, DC. IMF.

Joshi, Vijay, and Ian Little. 1994. *India: Macroeconomics and political economy, 1964–1991.* Washington, DC: World Bank.

Joyce, Joseph P. 2004. The Adoption, implementation and impact of IMF programs: A review of the evidence. *Comparative Economic Studies.* 46 (3).

Jubilee. 2003. *Real* Progress Report on HIPC (prepared by Romilly Greenhill and Elena Sisti, September 2003). London: Jubilee.

Ka, Samba, and Nicolas Van de Walle. 1994. Senegal: Stalled reform in a dominant party system. In *Voting for reform: Democracy, political liberalization, and economic adjustment,* ed. Stephan Haggard and Steven B. Webb. New York: Oxford University Press.

Kagarlitsky, Boris. 1998. Testimony to the General Oversight and Investigations Subcommittee. House of Representatives Committee on Banking and Financial Services. 10 September. At http://www.house.gov/banking/91098kag.htm.

Kahler, Miles. 1992a. Multilateralism with small and large numbers. *International Organization* 46 (3): 681–708.

——. 1992b. External influence, conditionality, and the politics of adjustment. In *The politics of economic adjustment,* ed. Stephan Haggard and Robert Kaufman. Princeton, NJ: Princeton University Press.

——. 1992c. The United States and the International Monetary Fund: Declining influence or declining interest? In *The United States and multilateral institutions: Patterns of changing instrumentality and influence,* ed. K. Mingst and M. Karns, 91–114. London: Routledge.

——. 2001. *Leadership selection in the major multilaterals.* Washington, DC: Institute for International Economics.

Kaletsky, Anatole. 1983. *The costs of default.* New York: Twentieth Century Fund.

Kapstein, Ethan B. 1992. *The political economy of national security.* New York: McGraw Hill.

Kapur, Devesh. 1994. Background Paper on Mexico based on interviews with Bank officials. Prepared for Brookings Institution and World Bank History Project.

——. 2000. Who gets to run the world. *Foreign Policy* 121 (November/December).

——. 2002. The common pool dilemma of global public goods: Lessons from the World Bank's new income and reserves. *World Development* 30 (3): 337–54.

Kapur, Devesh, John Lewis, and Richard Webb. 1997. *The World Bank: Its first half century.* Vol. 1. Washington, DC: Brookings Institution.

Kapur, Ishan, and Emmanuel Van der Mensbrugghe. 1997. External borrowing by the Baltics, Russia, and other countries of the former Soviet Union: Development and policy issues. IMF Working Paper Number WP/97/72. Washington, DC: IMF.

Katzenstein, Peter, Robert Keohane, and Stephen Krasner. 1998. International organization and the study of world politics. *International Organization* 52 (4): 645–85.

——, eds. 1999. *Exploration and contestation in the study of world politics.* Cambridge: MIT Press.

Kaufman, Robert R. 1990. Stabilization and adjustment in Argentina, Brazil, and Mexico. In *Economic crisis and policy choice: The politics of adjustment in the third world,* edited by Joan Nelson. Princeton, NJ: Princeton University Press.

Keck, Margaret E., and Kathryn Sikkink. 1998. *Activists beyond borders: Advocacy networks in international politics.* Ithaca: Cornell University Press.

Kenen, Peter, B. Schafer, Nigel Wicks, and Charles Wyplosz. 2004. *International economic and financial cooperation: New issues, new actors, new responses.* Geneva: International Center for Monetary and Banking Studies and Centre for Economic Policy Research.

Keohane, Robert. 1984. *After hegemony: Cooperation and discord in the world political economy.* Princeton, NJ: Princeton University Press.

Keohane, R., and H. Milner. 1996. *Internationalization and domestic politics.* Cambridge: Cambridge University Press.

Keynes, John Maynard. 1920. *The Economic consequences of the peace.* New York: Harcourt, Brace, Howe.

———. 1971–1989. *The collected writings of John Maynard Keynes.* Ed. Donald Edward Moggridge, Elizabeth S. Johnson, and Royal Economic Society. London: Macmillan.

Khan, Mohsin. 1990. Macroeconomic effects of Fund-supported adjustment programmes. IMF Staff Papers. Vol. 37, No. 2, June.

Killick, Tony. 1989. *A reaction too far: Economic theory and the role of the state in developing countries.* ODI Development Policy Studies. London: Overseas Development Institute.

———. 1990. Markets and governments in agricultural and industrial adjustment. Working Paper No. 39. London: Overseas Development Institute.

———. 1995. *IMF programmes in developing countries: Design and impact.* London and New York: Routledge and Overseas Development Institute.

———. 1998. *Aid and the political economy of change.* London: Routledge.

———. 2002. *The "streamlining" of IMF conditionality: Aspirations, reality & repercussions.* London: UK Department for International Development.

Kimenyi, M., and J. Mbaka. 1993. Rent-seeking and institutional stability in developing countries. *Public Choice* 77. 385–405.

Kindleberger, Charles. 1977. *America in the World Economy.* New York: Foreign Policy Association.

Kirk, Donald. 2000. Korean crisis: Unraveling of the miracle in the IMF era. New York: St Martin's Press.

Kissinger Commission. 1984. *National Bipartisan Commission on Central America.* January. Washington, DC: Government Printing Office.

Knight, Malcom, and J. A. Santaella. 1997. Economic determinants of Fund financial arrangements. *Journal of Development Economics* 54: 405–36.

Knorr, Klaus. 1948. The Bretton Woods institutions in transition. *International Organization* 2: 19–38.

Koester, Ulrich, and Ernst-August Nuppenau. 1987. The income efficiency of government expenditure on agricultural policy. *Intereconomics* (March/April): 74–75.

Konings, Piet. 1989. La liquidation des plantations Unilever et les conflits intra-élite dans le Cameroun anglophone. *Politique Africaine* No. 35 (October): 132–35.

Kopper, Hilmar. 1997. The World Bank's European funding. Vol. 2 of *World Bank: Its first half century,* ed. Devesh Kapur, John P. Lewis, and Richard Webb, 435–72. Washington, DC: Brookings Institution.

Koremenos, B., C. Lipson, and D. Snidal. 2001a. Rational design: Looking back to move forward. *International Organization* 55 (4).

———. 2001b. The rational design of international institutions. *International Organization* 55 (4).

Kraatz, Matthew S. 1998. Learning by association? Inter-organizational networks and adaptation to environmental change. *Academy of Management Journal.* 41 (6): 621–43.

Kraemer, Moritz. 1995. The political economy of trade reform in Mexico 1982–1988. Ibero-America Institute for Economic Research Discussion Paper 66. Gottingen: Ibero-America Institute for Economic Research.

Krasner, Stephen. 1991. Global communications and national power: Life on the Pareto frontier. *World Politics* 43 (3): 336–66.

———. 1999. *Sovereignty: Organized hypocrisy.* Princeton, NJ: Princeton University Press.

Kremer, Michael, and Seema Jayachandran. 2003. *Odious debt.* Washington, DC: IMF.

Krueger, Anne. 2001a. International financial architecture for 2002: A new approach to sovereign debt restructuring. Speech to the National Economists' Club Annual Members' Dinner at the American Enterprise Institute. 26 November. Washington, DC.

———. 2001b. A new approach to sovereign debt restructuring. Indian Council for Research on International Economic Relations. At http://www.imf.org/external/np/speeches/2001/122001.htm.

———. 2003. Maintaining the momentum: Emerging market policy reform in 2004. Keynote Address at the Asia Society Conference: Investing Across Emerging Markets 2004New York, November 20.

Krugman, Paul. 1999. Analytical afterthoughts on the Asian crisis. 12 September. At http://web.mit.edu.krugman/www/MINICRIS.htm.

Kugler, Jacek. 1987. The politics of foreign debt in Latin America: A study of the debtors' cartel. *International Interactions* 13 (2): 115–44.

Kupchinsky, Roman. 2002. Tracking down IMF billions. Radio Free Europe/Radio Liberty Reports. Vol. 2, no. 25. 27 June.

Kuzcynski, Pedro Pablo Godard. 1988. *Latin American debt.* Baltimore, MD: Johns Hopkins University Press.

LaFraniere, Sharon. 1998. Russian bailout fails to ease market fears. *Washington Post,* 28 July 1998: A1.

Lakatos, I., and A. Musgrave, eds. 1970. *Criticism and the growth of knowledge.* Cambridge: Cambridge University Press.

Lake, Anthony. 1989. *Somoza falling.* New York: Houghton Mifflin.

Landell-Mills, Pierre, and Brian Ngo. 1991. Creating the basis for long-term growth. In *The political economy of Senegal under structural adjustment,* ed. Christopher L. Delgado and Sidi Jammeh. Westport, CT: Greenwood Publishing Group.

Lawson, Nigel. 1992. *The view from no. 11: Memoirs of a Tory radical.* London: Bantam Press.

Legro, Jeffrey. 1997. Which norms matter? Revisiting the failure of internationalism. *International Organization* 51: 31–63.

Lehman, H., and J. McCoy. 1992. The dynamics of the 2-level bargaining game: The 1988 Brazilian debt negotiations. *World Politics* 44: 600–644.

Lele, Uma. 1988. *Agricultural growth, domestic policies, the external environment, and assistance to Africa: Lessons of a quarter century.* Washington, DC. World Bank.

Levy, Daniel, and Kathleen Bruhn. 2001. *Mexico: The struggle for democratic development.* Berkeley: University of California Press.

Lewis, John. 1997. *India's political economy: Governance and reform.* Oxford: Oxford University Press.

Lewis, P., and H. Stein. 1997. Shifting fortunes: The political economy of financial liberalization in Nigeria. *World Development* 25 (1): 5–22.

Lewis, W. A. 1954. Economic development with unlimited supplies of labour. *Manchester School of Economic and Social Studies* 22 (May): 139–91.

Lindauer, David, Oey Astra Meesook, and Parita Suebsaen. 1986. Government wage policy in Africa: Summary of findings and policy issues. CPD Discussion Paper 24. Washington, DC: World Bank.

Lissakers, Karin. 1991. *Banks, borrowers, and the establishment: A revisionist account of the international debt crisis.* New York: Basic Books.

Lister, Frederick. 1984. *Decision-making strategies for international organizations: The IMF Model.* Vol. 20, nook 4. Denver: Graduate School of International Studies, University of Denver.

Lloyd, John. 1993. Moscow reformer criticises US stance. *Financial Times,* 24 December, 2.

Locke, Mary. 2000. Funding the IMF: the debate in the US Congress. *Finance and Development* 37 (3): 56–59.

Lofchie, Michael. 1994. The new political economy of Africa. In *Political development and the new realism in sub-Saharan Africa,* ed. David E. Apter and Carl G. Rosberg, 145–83. Charlottesville: University Press of Virginia.

Lohmann, Susanne, and Sharyn O'Halloran. 1994. Divided government and U.S. trade policy: Theory and evidence. *International Organization* 48 (4): 595–632.

Lopez Gallo, M. 1989. *El elegido.* Mexico: Ediciones el Caballito.

Lopez Portillo, J. 1988. *Mis Tiempos.* Mexico City: Fernandez Editores.

———. 1995. Economic thought and economic policy-making in contemporary Mexico: International and domestic components. Submitted for D.Phil, Oxford University.

Loser, Claudio, and Eliot Kalter. 1992. *Mexico: The strategy to achieve sustained economic growth.* Washington, DC: IMF.

Loxley, John. 1986. Alternative approaches to stabilization in Africa. Papers presented at a symposium held in Nairobi, Kenya. 13–15 May. In *Africa and the International Monetary Fund,* ed. Gerald Helleiner, 117–47. Washington, DC: IMF.

———. 1990. Structural adjustment in Africa: Reflections on Ghana and Zambia. *Review of African Political Economy* 17 (47): 8–28.

Lustig, N. 1992. *Mexico: The remaking of an economy.* Washington, DC: Brookings Institution.

———. 1995. *The Mexican peso crisis: The foreseeable and the surprise.* Washington, DC: Brookings Institution.

Lyle, Robert. 1998. Transition nations active in IMF loans. 6 August 1998: Radio Free Europe/Radio Liberty Newsline.

Machinea, Jose Luis. 1990. *Stabilization under Alfonsin's Government: a frustrated attempt.* Documento CEDES/42 Buenos Aires: Centro de Estudious de Estado y Sociedad.

MacIntyre, Andrew. 1989. Corporatism, control, and political change in the "new order" Indonesia. In *Observing political change in Asia,* ed. R. J. May and W. J. O'Malley. Bathurst, UK: Crawford House Press.

———. 1993. The politics of finance in Indonesia. In *The politics of finance in developing countries,* ed. Stephan Haggard, Chung Lee, and Sylvia Maxfield, 123–64. Ithaca: Cornell University Press.

Mahieu, Géraldine, Dirk Ooms, and Stéphane Rottier. 2003. *EU representation and the governance of the International Monetary Fund.* Brussels: European Commission.

Mahoney, James. 2000. Path dependence in historical sociology. *Theory and Society* 29: 507–48.

Mallaby, Sebastian. 2004a. NGOs: Fighting poverty, hurting the poor. *Foreign Policy* 144 (September/October): 50ff.

———. 2005. *The World's Banker: A story of failed states, financial crises, and the wealth and poverty of nations.* New Haven: Yale University Press.

March, James G., and Johan P. Olsen. 1989. *Rediscovering institutions: The organizational basis of politics.* New York: Free Press.

Mares, David. 1985. Explaining choice of development strategies: Suggestions from Mexico, 1970–1982. *International Organization* 39 (4): 667–97.

Margolin, Ruslan. 2000. The Russian financial crisis: From craze to crash. *The Stern Journal* (Spring): 9–17.

Martin, Lisa. 1999. The political economy of international cooperation. In *Global public goods: International cooperation in the 21st century,* ed. Inge Kaul, Isabelle Grunberg, and Marc A. Stern, 51–64. New York: UNDP.

———. 2000. Agency and delegation in IMF conditionality. Manuscript prepared for workshop on Political Economy of International Finance, Harvard University. October.

Martin, Lisa, and Beth Simmons. 1998. Theories and empirical studies of international institutions. *International Organization* 52 (4): 729–57.

Martinez, G., and G. Farber. 1994. *Desregulacion economica (1989–1993).* Mexico City: Fondo de Cultura Economica.

Mason, Edward, and Robert Asher. 1973. *The World Bank since Bretton Woods.* Washington, DC: Brookings Institution.

Matecki, B. E. 1956. Establishment of the international finance corporation: A case study. *International Organization* 10: 261–75.

Maxfield, Sylvia. 1990. *Governing capital: International finance and Mexican politics.* Ithaca: Cornell University Press.

Mbaka, J., and C. Paul. 1989. Political instability in Africa: A rent-seeking approach. *Public Choice* 63: 63–72.

Mbodji, Mohamed. 1991. The politics of independence: 1960–86. In *The political economy of Senegal under structural adjustment,* ed. Christopher Delgado and Sidi Jammeh. New York: Praeger.

McDonald, David A., and Eunice Njeri Sahle, eds. 2002. *The legacies of Julius Nyerere: Influences on development, discourse, and practice in Africa.* Trenton, NJ: Africa World Press.

McDonald, Keith. 1995. *The sociology of the professions.* London: Sage.

McFaul, Michael. 1995. *Privatization, conversion and enterprise reform in Russia.* Boulder, Colorado: Westview Press.

———. 1999. Lessons from Russia's protracted transition from communist rule. *Political Science Quarterly* 114 (1): 103–30.

———. 2001. *Russia's unfinished revolution: Political change from Gorbachev to Putin.* Ithaca: Cornell University Press.

McKenzie, David. 2002. An econometric analysis of IBRD creditworthiness. Policy Research Working Paper WPS2822. Washington, DC. World Bank.

Mearsheimer, John J. 1995. The false promise of international institutions. *International Security* 19: 5–49.

Medhora, Rohinton. 1992. The West African monetary union: Institutional arrangements and the link with France. *Canadian Journal of Development Studies* 13 (2): 151–80.

———. 2000. *Dollarization in the Americas: Lessons from the Franc zone?* Ottawa: International Development Research Center.

Meltzer Commission. 2000. *International Financial Institution Advisory Commission Final Report.* March. Washington, DC. At http://www.eldis.org/static/DOC7563.htm.

Mendelson, Sarah. 2001. Democracy assistance and political transition in Russia. *International Security* 25 (4): 68–106.

Meyer, John, and John Boli. 1997. World society and the nation-state. *American Journal of Sociology* 103 (1): 144–81.

Meyer, John, and B. Rowan. 1977. Institutional organizations: Formal structure as myth and ceremony. *The American Journal of Sociology* 83, 340–63.

Migdal, Joel. 1988. *Strong societies and weak states: State-society relations and state capabilities in the third world.* Princeton, NJ: Princeton University Press.

Mikesell, Raymond. 1994. *The Bretton Woods debates: A memoir.* Princeton, NJ: International Finance Section, Department of Economics, Princeton University.

Miller-Adams, Michelle. 1997. *The World Bank in the 1990s: Understanding institutional change.* New York: Columbia University Press.

Millennium Challenge Corporation. 2004. Financial Statements. Washington, DC: Millennium Challenge Corporation.

Milner, Helen, and Robert Keohane. 1996. *Internationalization and domestic politics.* Cambridge: Cambridge University Press.

Milward, Alan. 1984. *The reconstruction of Western Europe 1945–51.* London: Methuen.

Ministry of Finance, Mexico. 1999. *Mexico: Challenges and opportunities at the turn of the century.* Mexico City: Ministry of Finance. At www.shcp.gob.mx/english/docs/991007.html.

Mistry, Percy. 1994. Exchange-rate adjustment: A review of developing countries' experience. In *Negotiating structural adjustment in Africa,* ed. Willem Van der Geest, 115–36. New York: UNDP and Heinemann.

Mody, Ashoka, and Diego Saravia. 2003. Catalyzing capital flows: Do IMF-supported programs work as commitment devices? IMF Working Papers Working Paper No. 03/100. Washington, DC: IMF.

Mohammed, Aziz Ali. 2003. Burden-sharing at the IMF. G-24 Working Papers. Washington, DC: G24.

Morales, E., and C. Ruiz. 1989. *Crecimiento, equidad y financiamiento externo.* Mexico City: Fondo de Cultura Economica.

Moravcsik, Andrew. 1998. *The choice for Europe: Social purpose and state power from Messina to Maastricht.* Ithaca: Cornell University Press.

Morris, Stephen. 1995a. *Political reformism in Mexico: An overview of contemporary Mexican politics.* Boulder, CO: Lynne Rienner.

——. 1995b. The struggle of the PRD in Mexico. SECOLAS Annals 26: 26–41.

Morrow, James. 1994. Modeling the forms of international cooperation: Distribution versus information. *International Organization* 48 (3): 387–424.

Morvant, Penny. 1996. Yeltsin pledges to fight poverty. Radio Free Europe/Radio Liberty Newsline. 2 January 1996.

Mosley, Layna. 2000. Room to move: International financial markets and national welfare states. *International Organization* 54 (4).

Munter, Pyivi. 2003. Russia pays off more Paris Club debt. *Financial Times,* August 21.

Mussa, Michael. 2002. *Argentina and the Fund: From triumph to tragedy.* Washington, DC: Institute for International Economics.

Myerson, Roger. 1994. Analysis of democratic institutions: Structure, conduct, and performance. Evanston, IL.: Center for Mathematical Studies in Economics and Management Science, Northwestern University.

Naim, Moises. 1993. *Paper tigers and minotaurs: The politics of Venezuela's economic reforms.* Washington, DC: Carnegie Endowment for International Peace.

——. 1995. *Latin America's journey to the market: From macroeconomic shocks to institutional therapy.* San Francisco: International Center for Economic Growth.

Ndiaye, Abdourahmane. 2003. Foreign debt, structural adjustment programs, and poverty in Senegal. ATTAC. At http://attac.org/fra/list/doc/ndiayeen.htm.

Nelson, Joan, Jacek Kochanowicz, Kalman Mizsei, and Oscar Munoz. 1994. *Intricate links: Democratization and market reforms in Latin America and Eastern Europe.* Washington, DC: Overseas Development Council.

Nelson, Paul. 1995. *The World Bank and nongovernmental organizations: The limits of apolitical development.* London: Macmillan.

Nesirky, Martin. Russia wants IMF cash, faces Oct 7 protests. Reuters. 5 October 1998.

New York Times. 1992. News summary: Russia to seek debt extension. 5 July, A1.

Nezavisimaya Gazeta. 1997. *Current Digest of the Post-Soviet Press* 51 (8).

Nicita, Alessandro. 2004. Who benefited from trade liberalization in Mexico? Measuring the effects on household welfare. World Bank Policy Research Working Paper 3265. April. Washington, DC: World Bank.

Oxford Analytica. 2001. Russia: New industrial groups keep competitors at bay. *Oxford Analytica Brief* 4 September 2001. Oxford: Oxford Analytica.

Odling-Smee, John, and Gonzalo Pastor. 2002. The IMF and the ruble area, 1991–93. *Comparative Economic Studies* 44 (4): 3–30.

O'Donnell, Guillermo. 1985. External debt: Why don't our governments do the obvious? *CEPAL Review* 27: 27–34.

——. 1987. Brazil: What future for debtors' cartels. *Third World Quarterly* 9 (4): 1157–66.

Ogata, Sadako. 1989. Shifting power relations in multilateral development banks. *Journal of International Studies* 22.

Olson, Mancur. 1982. The rise and decline of nations: Economic growth, stagflation, and social rigidities. New Haven: Yale University Press.

Operations Evaluation Department, World Bank (OED). 1999. Indonesia: Country assistance note. 29 March. Washington, DC: World Bank.

———. 2001. *Mexico country assistance evaluation*. 28 June. Washington, DC: World Bank.

———. 2002. *Assisting Russia's transition: An unprecedented challenge*. Washington, DC: World Bank.

———. 2003. *Towards country-led partnership*. Washington, DC: World Bank.

Organization for Economic Cooperation and Development (OECD), World Bank, IMF, and EBRD. 1991. *A study of the Soviet economy*. Paris: OECD.

OECD/DAC. 2004. *Results of the OECD-DAC survey on harmonisation and alignment*. 16 December. Paris: OECD Development Cooperation Directorate. At www.oecd.org/department/0,2688,en_2649_15577209_1_1_1_1,00.html.

———. 2005. Paris declaration on aid effectiveness: ownership, harmonisation, alignment, results and mutual accountability. High Level Forum. 2 March. Paris: OECD/DAC.

OECD and Catherine Gwin. 2002. *IDA's partnership for poverty reduction: An independent evaluation of fiscal years 1994–2000*. Washington, DC: OED, World Bank.

Ortiz, Guillermo. 1994. *La reforma financiera y la desincorporacion bancaria*. Mexico City: Fondo de Cultura Economica.

Ostrom, Elinor, Clark Gibson, Sujai Shivakumar, and Krister Andersson. 2001. *Aid, incentives, and sustainability: An institutional analysis of development cooperation*. 11 December. SIDA Studies in Evaluation. Gothenburg, Sweden: SIDA.

OXFAM. 1996. Multilateral debt: The human costs. Oxfam Position Paper. February. Oxford: Oxfam.

Paarlberg, Robert. 1985. *Food trade and foreign policy: India, the Soviet Union, and the United States*. Ithaca: Cornell University Press.

Park, Daekeun and Changyong Rhee. 1998. Currency crisis in Korea: Could it have been avoided? Working Paper. Seoul: Seoul National University.

Parrish, Scott. 1996. Yeltsin pledges to stay the course. Radio Free Europe/Radio Liberty Newsline. 2 January 1996.

Parsons, Craig. 2002. Showing ideas as causes: The origins of the European Union. *International Organization* 56 (1): 47–84.

Pastor, Manuel, and Carol Wise. 1994. The origins and sustainability of Mexico free-trade policy. *International Organization* 48 (3): 459–89.

———. 2001. From poster child to basket case. *Foreign Affairs* (November/December).

Patel, I. G. 1968. *Foreign Aid*. Bombay: Institute of Public Enterprise.

Pauly, Louis. 1997. *Who elected the bankers: Surveillance and control in the world economy*. Ithaca: Cornell University Press.

Penrose, Ernest Francis. 1953. *Economic planning for the peace*. Princeton, NJ: Princeton University Press.

Peters, Gretche. 2002. In Mexico, war between Fox and congress escalates. *Christian Science Monitor,* 16 April, 7.

Philip, George. 2002. The presidency, the parties, and democratization in Mexico. *Democratization* 9 (3): 131–48.

———. 2003. Ideas and policy transfer: The Mexican civil service reform change of bureaucracy. *Future Governance* 13.

Piciotto, Robert, and Rachel Weaving. 1994. A new project cycle for the World Bank? *Finance and Development* 31 (42): 42–44.

Polak, J. J. 1957. Monetary analysis of income formation and payments problems. *IMF Staff Papers*. November. Vol. 6, 1–50.

———. 1997. The IMF monetary model: A hardy perennial. *Finance and Development* 34 (4): 16–19.

Polak, J. J., and Research Department. 1997. The IMF monetary model at forty. 1 April. Washington, DC: IMF.

Polak, J. J., and W. H. White. 1955. The effect of income expansion on the quantity of money. *IMF Staff Papers*. Vol. 4 (August). Washington, DC: IMF.

Pollard, Robert A. 1985. *Economic security and the origins of the cold war, 1945–1950*. New York: Columbia University Press.

Portfolio Management Task Force (Wapenhans Report). 1992. *Effective implementation: Key to development impact*. October. Washington, DC: World Bank.

Prasad, Eswar, Kenneth Rogoff, Shang-Jin Wei, and M. Ayhan Kose. 2003. *Effects of financial globalization on developing countries: some empirical evidence*. Washington, DC: IMF.

Pravda. 2003. Russian bank disappears without settling with creditors. 21 January.

Presupuesto, Secretaria de Programacion y. 1987. *Antologia de la Planeacion en Mexico 1917–1985*. Vol. 9. Mexico City: CFE.

PriceWaterhouseCoopers. 1999. Auditors' report by the independent audit firm PricewaterhouseCoopers on the accuracy of financial reports of the central bank of the Russian federation for the year ended December 31, 1999. Moscow: PricewaterhouseCoopers Audit (ZAO PwK Audit).

Prowse, Michael. 1991. IMF creates section to deal with the former USSR. *Financial Times,* 14 December, 2.

Przeworski, A., and F. Limongi. 1993. Political regimes and economic growth. *Journal of Economic Perspectives* 7 (3): 51–69.

Przeworski, A., and J. R. Vreeland. 2000. The effect of IMF programs on economic growth. *Journal of Development Economics* 62 (2): 385–421.

Putnam, Robert. 1988. Diplomacy and domestic politics: The logic of two-level games. *International Organization* 42 (3): 427–60.

Radelet, Steve, and Jeffrey Sachs. 1998. The East Asian financial crisis: Diagnosis, remedies, prospects. *Brookings Papers on Economic Activity* 1: 1–90.

RFE/RL. 1997a. Luzhkov says dependence on IMF is "national disgrace." Radio Free Europe/Radio Liberty Newsline. 30 December 1997.

——. 1997b. Russia not to borrow from IMF after 1999. Radio Free Europe/Radio Liberty Newsline. 18 September 1997.

——. 1997c. Newsline. Radio Free Europe/Radio Liberty Newsline.

——. 1998a. Yeltsin uses phone diplomacy to secure loan. Radio Free Europe/Radio Liberty Newsline, 13 July 1998.

——. 1998b. Mixed reaction to bailout agreement. Radio Free Europe/Radio Liberty Newsline, 15 July 1998.

——. 1998c. Newspapers concerned about IMF's influence. Radio Free Europe/Radio Liberty Newsline. 30 April 1998.

——. 2002. Radio Free Europe/Radio Liberty Newsline 2 (4).

Ramcharan, Rodney. 2002. How does conditional aid (not) work. IMF Working Paper WP/02/183. Washington, DC: IMF.

Ramirez, Carlos. 1982. Tllo Macias, Avance desde la Nacionalizacion; Silva Herzog, Marcha Atras. *Proceso* 306 (8).

Ramirez, Miguel D. 1989. *Mexico's economic crisis: Its origins and consequences.* New York: Praeger.

Ramos, Alejandro, José Martínez, and Carlos Ramírez 1987. *Salinas de Gortari: candidato de la crisis.* Mexico: Plaza y Valdes.

Rapkin, David, and Jonathan Strand. 1996. U.S.-Japan leadership sharing in the IMF and the World Bank. Paper presented at ISA Conference, San Diego. 16–20 April.

Reddaway, Peter. 1994. Prepared statement to the hearing before the Committee on Banking, Housing and Urban Affairs, United States Senate. Impact of IMF/World Bank policies toward Russia and the Russian economy. 8 February. S.HRG.103–508, 76–78.

Remmer, Karen L. 1984. *Party competition in Argentina and Chile.* Lincoln: University of Nebraska Press.

——. 1986. The politics of economic stabilisation: IMF standby programs in Latin America, 1954–1984. *Comparative Politics* 19 (1): 1–24.

——. 1990. Democracy and economic crisis: The Latin American experience. *World Politics* 42: 315–35.

Renzio, Paolo de. 2004. *Incentives for harmonisation in aid agencies: A report to the DAC task team on harmonisation and alignment.* London: Overseas Development Institute.

Rieffel, Alexis. 1985. *The role of the Paris Club in managing debt problems.* Essays in International Finance 161. Princeton, NJ: Princeton University Press.

Riegle, Donald. 1994. Introductory remarks by chairman to the hearing before the Committee on Banking, Housing and Urban Affairs, United States Senate. Impact of IMF/World Bank policies toward Russia and the Russian economy. 8 February 1994. S.HRG.103–508.

Righter, Rosemary. 1995. *Utopia lost: The United Nations and the world order.* London: The Century Foundation.

Rivlin, Benjamin. 1996. UN reform from the standpoint of the United States. UN University Lectures 11. Tokyo: The United Nations University.

Robinson, Derek. 1990. *Civil service pay in Africa.* Geneva: International Labour Office.

Rodrik, Dani. 1995. Why is there multilateral lending? NBER Working Papers 5160. Washington, DC: National Bureau of Economic Research.

——. 1996. Understanding economic policy reform. *Journal of Economic Literature,* 34 (March): 9–41.

Rogoff, Kenneth. 2002. Rethinking capital controls: When should we keep an open mind? *Finance and Development* 39.

Rogozinski, J. 1993. *La privatizacion de empresas paraestatales.* Mexico City: Fondo de Cultura Economica.

Roubini, Nouriel. 1991. Economic and political determinants of budget deficits in developing countries. *Journal of International Money and Finance* 10 (1): 49–72.

Rowlands, Dane. 2001. The response of other lenders to the IMF. *Review of International Economics* 9 (3): 531–46.

Rudland, Peter. 1996. Replacement for Chubais named. Radio Free Europe/Radio Liberty Newsline. 26 January 1996.

Ruggie, John Gerard. 1982. International regimes, transactions, and change: Embedded liberalism in the postwar economic order. *International Organization* 36 (2).

——. 1998. What makes the world hang together? Neo-utilitarianism and the social constructivist challenge. *International Organization* 52 (4): 855–85.

Russian Economic Trends. 1992. 1 (1).

Rustomjee, Cyrus. 2005. Improving southern voice on the IMF board: Quo vadis shareholders? In *Accountability of the International Monetary Fund,* ed. Barry Carin and Angela Wood. Aldershot: Ashgate and IDRC, 2005.

Rutland, Peter. 1996. The IMF: Savior or Sinner? OMRI Analytical Brief 10.

Ruttan, Vernon. 1996. *United States development assistance policy: The domestic politics of foreign economic aid.* Baltimore: Johns Hopkins University Press.

Sachs, Jeffrey. 1986. Managing the LDC debt crisis. Brookings Papers on Economic Activity 2. Washington, DC: Brookings Institution, 397–431.

——. 1989. The debt overhang of developing countries. In *Debt, stabilization, and development: Essays in memory of Carlos Diaz-Alejandro,* ed. Ronald Findlay, Guillermo Calvo, Pentti Kouri, and Jorge Brage de Macedo. Oxford. Blackwell Publishers.

——. 1991. Goodwill is not enough. *Economist.* 21 December.

——. 1992. The grand bargain. In *The post-Soviet economy: Soviet and western perspectives,* ed. Anders Aslund. London: Pinter Publishers.

——. 1994. Prepared statement to the hearing before the Committee on Banking, Housing and Urban Affairs, United States Senate. Impact of IMF/World Bank policies toward Russia and the Russian economy. 8 February. S.HRG.103–508, 74–75.

——. 1995. Why Russia has failed to stabilize. In *Russian economic reform at risk,* ed. Anders Aslund. London: Pinter Publishers.

——. 1998. Creditor panics: Causes and remedies. Prepared for Cato Institute. 22 October. At www.cato.org/events/monconf16/sachs.pdf.

Sachs, Jeffrey, and Harry Huizinga. 1987. U.S. commercial banks and the developing country debt crisis. Brookings Papers on Economic Activity 2. Washington, DC: Brookings Institution.

Sachs, Jeffrey, and David Lipton. 1993. Remaining steps to a market-based monetary system. In *Changing the economic system in Russia,* ed. Anders Aslund and Richard Layard. New York: St Martin's Press.

Sachs, Jeffrey, Aaron Tornell, and Andres Velasco. 1995. The real story. *International Economy* (March/April).

Sachs, J., A. Tornell, and A. Velasco. 1995. The collapse of the Mexican peso: What have we learned? NBER Working Paper 5142.

Sahn, David, ed. 1994. *Adjusting to policy failure in African economies.* Ithaca: Cornell University Press.

Salinas de Gortari, C. 1989. *The Mexico we want by 1994.* Mexico City: Presidency of Mexico.

Sanford, Jonathan. 1988. U.S. policy toward the multilateral development banks: The role of congress. *George Washington Journal of International Law and Economics* 22: 1–115.

——. 1999. IMF and World Bank: US contributions and agency budgets. CRS Research Reports for Congress. 9 December. Washington, DC: Congressional Research Service.

Sanger, David E. 1998. Finance ministers agree to explore Clinton IMF plan. *New York Times,* 4 October, A1.

Santaella, J. A. 1996. Stylized facts before IMF-supported adjustment. *IMF Staff Papers* 43, 502–44.

Schloss, Henri H. 1958. *The bank for international settlements.* Amsterdam: North-Holland Publishing Co.

Scholte, Jan Aart. 2001. Civil society voices and the international monetary fund. Mimeo. Warwick: Centre for the Study of Globalization and Regionalization.

Secretaría de Programación y Presupuesto (SPP). 1987. *National plan for industrial development.* Mexico City: SPP.

Serieux, John. 2001. Debt of the poorest countries: Anatomy of a crisis kept on hold. *Canadian Journal of Development Studies* 22 (2): 305–42.

Shadlen, Kenneth. 1999. Continuity amid change: Democratisation, party strategies, and economic policy making in Mexico. *Government and Opposition* 34 (3): 397–419.

Sherk, Donald. 1994. Emerging markets and the multilateral development banks. *Columbia Journal of World Business* 29 (2): 44–52.

Sikkink, Kathryn. 1991. *Ideas and institutions: Developmentalism in Brazil and Argentina.* Ithaca: Cornell University Press.

Silva, E. 1993. Capitalist coalitions, the state, and neoliberal economic restructuring in Chile, 1973–1988. *World Politics* 45: 526–29.

———. 1996. From dictatorship to democracy: The business-state nexus in Chile's economic transformation, 1975–1994. *Comparative Politics* 28 (April): 229–320.

Silva Herzog, Jesús. 1993. México hoy, en el Nuevo entorno internacional. *Revista Mexicana de Política Exterior* 38 (Spring 1993).

Sirowy, L., and A. Inkles. 1990. The effects of democracy on economic growth and inequality—a review. *Studies in Comparative International Development* 25 (1): 126–57.

Skidelsky, Robert, and Pavel Erochkine. 2003. *Russia's choices: The Duma elections and after.* London: Centre for Global Studies.

Soesastro, M. Hadi. 1989. The political economy of deregulation in Indonesia. *Asian Survey* 29 (9): 853–69.

Solís, L. 1970. *La realidad economica Mexicana: Retrovision y panorama.* Mexico: Editorial Siglo XXI.

Solomon, Robert. 1977. *The international monetary system, 1945–1976: An insider's view.* New York: Harper & Row.

———. 1982. *The International monetary system, 1945–1981.* New York: Harper and Row.

Southard, Frank. 1979. The evolution of the International Monetary Fund. Essays in International Finance 135. Princeton, NJ: International Finance Section, Dept of Economics, Princeton University.

Spaventa, Luigi. 1983. Two letters of intent: External crises and stabilisation policy, Italy 1973–77. In *IMF conditionality,* ed. John Williamson, 441–73. Washington, DC: Institute for International Economics.

Stallings, B. 1992. International influence on economic policy: Debt, stabilization, and structural reform. In *The politics of economic adjustment,* ed. S. Kaufman and R. Haggard. Princeton, NJ: Princeton University Press.

———, ed. 1995. *Global change, regional response: The new international context of development.* Cambridge: Cambridge University Press.

Steinmo, Sven. 1989. Political institutions and tax policy in the United States, Sweden, and Britain. *World Politics* 41 (4): 500–535.

Stern, Nicholas, with Francisco Ferreira. 1997. The World Bank as "intellectual actor." Vol. 1 of *The World Bank: Its first half century,* ed. Devesh Kapur, John Lewis, and Richard Webb. Washington, DC: Brookings Institution.

Stewart, Frances. 1994. Are adjustment policies in Africa consistent with long-run development needs? In *Negotiating structural adjustment in Africa,* ed. Willem Van der Geest, 99–114. New York: UNDP and Heinemann.

———. 1995. *Adjustment and poverty: Options and choices.* London: Routledge.

Stiglitz, Joseph. 1999. Whither reform: Ten years of the transition. Keynote address of the World Bank Annual Conference on Development Economics. Washington, DC: World Bank.

———. 2000. The insider: What I learned at the world economic crisis. *New Republic* (April): 56.

———. 2002. *Globalization and its discontents.* New York: W. W. Norton.

Stinchcombe, Arthur. 1998. *Constructing social theories.* New York: Harcourt Brace and World.

Stone, Diane. 2002. *Banking on knowledge: The genesis of the global development network.* London: Routledge.

Stone, Randall. 2002. *Lending credibility: The International Monetary Fund and the postcommunist transition.* Princeton, NJ: Princeton University Press.

Story, Dale. 1982. Trade politics in the third world: A case study of the Mexican GATT decision. *International Organization* 36 (4): 767–94.

Strand, Jonathan and David Rapkin. 2005. Voting power implications of a double majority voting procedure in the IMF's Executive Board. In *Reforming the governance of the IMF and World Bank,* ed. Ariel Buira, 235–50. London: Anthem Press.

Strange, Susan. 1974. The IMF. In *The anatomy of influence: decision making in international organization,* ed. Robert W. Cox and Harold K. Jacobson. New Haven: Yale University Press.

Summers, Lawrence. 1999. The right kind of IMF for a stable global financial system. 14 December. London: London Business School.

Sutton, Mary. 1982. Indonesia 1966–70: economic management and the role of the IMF. Working Paper 8. London: Overseas Development Institute.

Szymczak, P. 1992. International trade and investment liberalization: Mexico's experience and prospects. In *Mexico: The strategy to achieve sustained economic growth,* ed. C. Loser and E. Kalter. Washington, DC: IMF.

Tavernier, Yves. 2001. Les activités et le contrôle du Fonds monétaire international et de la Banque Mondiale. *Assemblée Nationale Rapport d'Information No. 3478.* 19 December. Paris: Assemblée Nationale, Onzième Législature.

Taylor, John. 2002. Sovereign debt restructuring: A US perspective. Sovereign debt workouts: Hopes and hazards? Institute for International Economics, Office of Public Affairs, Department of the Treasury. Washington, DC. At http://www.ustreas.gov/press/releases/po2056.htm.

Tew, Brian. 1970. *International monetary cooperation, 1945–70.* London: Hutchinson.

t'Haart, Paul. 1990. *Groupthink in government: A study of small groups and policy failure.* Baltimore: John Hopkins University Press.

Thacker, Strom. 1999. The high politics of IMF lending. *World Politics* 52 (1): 38–75.

Thapar, Raj. 1991. *All those years.* New Delhi: Seminar Publications.

Treisman, Daniel. 1999. *After the deluge: Regional crises and political consolidation in Russia.* Ann Arbor, MI: University of Michigan Press.

Tsebelis, George. 1995. Decision making in political systems: Veto players in presidentialism, parliamentarianism, multicameralism, and multipartyism. *British Journal of Political Science* 25: 289–325.

Tucker, Robert. 1977. *The inequality of nations.* New York: Basic Books.

Tumusiime-Mutebile, Emmanuel. 2002. New scenarios for future debt-relief and financing for low income countries. Briefing document prepared for Working Group on Global Financial Governance. Available at http://users.ox.ac.uk/~ntwoods/wg3%202002%20mtg3%20Report.pdf.

Tussie, Diana. 1995. *The Inter-American Development Bank.* London: Lynne Rienner.

Tussie, D., and M. Botzman. 1990. Sweet entanglement: Argentina and the World Bank 1985–89. *Development Policy Review* 8: 393–409.

Uchitelle, Louis. 1992. IMF and Russia reach accord on loan aid and spending limits. *New York Times,* 6 July, A1.

Uganda Economic Study Team. 1987. Advisers appointed June–July 1986, to advise on short and medium term economic policy in Uganda. Ottawa: International Development Research Center.

Ugwumba, Chidozie. 2002. Freeloading bankers: How the global economy's rule makers thrive on subsidies from an impoverished and disenfranchised city. Washington, DC. 50 Years is Enough—US Network for Global Economic Justice at http://www.50years.org/action/s28/report.html.

UNICEF. 1986. *State of the world's children.* United Nations Children's Fund. New York: Oxford University Press.

United Nations Conference on Trade and Development (UNCTAD). 1988. Eleventh general report on the implementation of the generalized system of preferences. February. Geneva: UNCTAD.

U.S. House of Representatives. Committee on Banking, Finance and Urban Affairs. 1985a. Hearing before the Subcommittee on International Development Institutions and Finance. External debt in the developing world. 27 June. 99th Congress, first session, Serial Number 99–25.

——. Committee on Banking, Finance and Urban Affairs. 1985b. Hearing before the Subcommittee on International Development Institutions and Finance. Role of multilateral development institutions in global economy. 27 June. 99th Congress, first session, Serial Number 99–29.

——. Committee on Banking, Finance and Urban Affairs. 1985c. Hearing on U.S. proposals on international debt crisis. 22 October. 99th Congress, first session, Serial Number 99–39.

——. Committee on Banking, Finance and Urban Affairs. 1989. Hearing before the Subcommittee on International Development Finance, Trade and Monetary Policy. Impact of accounting and regulatory procedures on the third world debt problem. 27 June. 101st Congress, Serial Number 101–39.

——. 2000. Russia's road to corruption: How the Clinton administration exported government instead of free enterprise and failed the Russian people. September. 106th Congress. Washington, DC: U.S. House of Representatives. At http://www.fas.org/news/russia/2000/russia/partoo–cover.htm.

U.S. State Department. 1994. *1993 country reports on economic practices and trade: Russia economic policy and trade practices.* February. Washington, DC: U.S. State Department.

U.S. Statutes at Large. No. 373, tit. 5, sec. 511(b).

U.S. Treasury. 1998a. Rubin welcomes debt relief for Bolivia. RR-2699. 23 September. Washington, DC: US Treasury.

——. 1998b. Rubin welcomes debt relief for Uganda. RR-2358. 8 April. Washington, DC: US Treasury.

——. 2002. Thoughts on the global economy. Speech by Kenneth Dam (deputy U.S. treasury secretary) to the World Affairs Council of Washington, DC. 25 January. Washington, DC: US Treasury Press Release PO-948.

Valente, Marcela. 2002. Argentina: Economy minister abandons a sinking ship. Inter-Press Service.

Van der Hoeven, Rolph, and Fred Van der Kraaij. 1994. Structural adjustment and beyond in sub-Saharan Africa. The Hague: Ministry of Foreign Affairs (DGIS).

Van de Walle, Nicolas. 1989. Privatization in developing countries: A review of the issues. *World Development* 17 (5): 601–16.

——. 2001. *African economies and the politics of permanent crisis, 1979–1999.* Cambridge: Cambridge University Press.

Van Dormael, Armand. 1978. *Bretton Woods: Birth of a monetary system.* New York: Holmes and Meier.

Van Houtven L. 2002. Governance of the IMF: Decisionmaking, institutional oversight, transparency, and accountability. *IMF Pamphlet Series No. 53,* International Monetary Fund.

Varshney, A. 1989. Ideas, interest, and institutions in policy change—transformation of India's agricultural strategy in the mid-1960s. *Policy Sciences* 22 (3–4): 289–323.

Vassiliev, Dmitri Glinski. 2000. The essence of Putinism: The strengthening of the privatized state. November. Program on New Approaches to Russian Security Policy Memo Series 147.

Vaubel, Roland. 1986. A public choice approach to international organisation. *Public Choice* 51: 39–57.

Veit, Lawrence. 1976. *India's second revolution: The dimensions of development.* New York: McGraw-Hill for the Council on Foreign Relations.

Viera da Cunha, Paulo, and Maria Valeria Junho Pena. 1998. The limits and merits of participation. World Bank Working Paper Series. At http:/econ.worldbank.org/docs/594.pdf.

Vreeland, James Raymond. 1999. *The IMF: Lender of last resort or scapegoat?* New Haven, CT: Yale University Press.

——. 2000. The institutional determinants of IMF Programs. Delivered at the Leitner Work-In-Progress Seminar, Yale University.

Wade, Robert Hunter. 1996. Japan, the World Bank, and the art of paradigm maintenance: The East Asian miracle in political perspective. *New Left Review* 217 (May–June): 3–36.

——. 1997. Greening the Bank: The struggle over the environment, 1970–1995. Vol. 2 of *The World Bank: Its first half century,* ed. Devesh Kapur, John Lewis, and Richard Webb. 611–734. Washington, DC: Brookings Institution.

——. 2000. A defeat for development and multilateralism: the World Bank has been unfairly criticised over the Qinghai Resettlement Project. *Financial Times,* 4 July.

——. 2001. The U.S. role in the malaise at the World Bank: Get up Gulliver! G-24 paper. At http://ksghome.harvard.edu/~.drodrik.academic.ksg/WadeG24.pdf.

Wallis, Darren. 2001. The Mexican presidential election and congressional elections of 2000 and democratic transition. *Bulletin of Latin American Research* 20 (3): 304–23.

Wall Street Journal. 26 September 1988.

Walter, Andrew. 1993. *World power, world money: The role of hegemony and international monetary order.* London: Harvester Wheatsheaf.

Waterbury, John. 1999. The long gestation and brief triumph of import-substituting industrialization. *World Development* 27 (2): 323–41.

Watson, Maxwell, Russell Kincaid, Caroline Atkinson, Eliot Kalter, and David Folkerts-Landau. 1986. *International capital markets: Developments and prospects.* Washington, DC: IMF.

Wedel, Janine. 1998. *Collision and collusion: The strange case of western aid to Eastern Europe, 1989–1998.* New York: St. Martin's Press.

Wegner, Daniel M., and Robin R. Vallacher. 1980. *The self in social psychology.* New York: Oxford University Press.

Weir, Margaret. 1989. Ideas and politics: the acceptance of Keynesianism in Britain and the United States. In *The political power of economic ideas: Keynesianism across nations,* ed. Peter Hall. Princeton, NJ: Princeton University Press.

Weisbrot, Mark. 1998. Testimony to the General Oversight and Investigations Subcommittee, House of Representatives Committee on Banking and Financial Services. 10 September. At http://www.house.gov/banking/91098ppp.htm.

Whitehead, Laurence. 1989. Latin American debt: An international bargaining perspective. *Review of International Studies* 15: 231–49.

Whitlock, Eric. 1993. US urges IMF to provide Russia more aid. Radio Free Europe/Radio Liberty. No. 60. 29 March 1993.

Wiehen, Michael. 1999. Transparency and corruption of building large dams. Paper prepared for World Commission on Dams. Berlin: Transparency International.

Williams, John. 1947. *Postwar monetary plans, and other essays.* New York: Knopf.

Williamson, John. 1988. *Voluntary approaches to debt relief.* Washington, DC: IIE.

———. 1990. *Latin American adjustment: How much has happened.* Washington, DC: Institute for International Economics.

———. 1994. *The political economy of policy reform.* Washington, DC: Institute for International Economics.

———. 2002. Is Brazil next? International Policy Briefs PB02-7 (August). Washington, D.C.: Institute for International Economics.

Wilson, J. Q. 1989. *Bureaucracy: What government agencies do and why they do it.* New York: Basic Books.

Wimmer, Andreas, with Indra de Soysa and Christian Wagner. 2002. Political science tools for assessing feasibility and sustainability of reforms. 25 September. Washington, DC: Independent Evaluation Office of the IMF.

Woods, Ngaire. 1995. The role of economic ideas in international relations: Beyond rational neglect. *International Studies Quarterly* 39: 161–80.

———. 1998. Governance in international organizations: The case for reform in the Bretton Woods institutions. Vol. 9 of *International monetary and financial issues for the 1990s.* Geneva: UNCTAD/Group of Twenty-Four.

World Bank. 1979. Internal memorandum. Washington, DC: World Bank.

———. 1981. Berg report: Accelerated development in Sub-Saharan Africa. Washington, DC: World Bank.

———. 1982. Annual report. Washington, DC: World Bank.

———. 1989a. *Adjustment lending: An evaluation of ten years of experience.* Washington, DC: World Bank.

———. 1989b. Annual report. Washington, DC: World Bank

———. 1989c. OED report 8041. Washington, DC: World Bank.

———. 1989d. *World debt tables 1988–1989.* 1. Washington, DC: World Bank Publications.

———. 1989e. *Africa's adjustment and growth in the 1980s.* Washington, DC: World Bank.

———. 1989f. *Sub-Saharan Africa: From crisis to sustainable growth.* Washington, DC: World Bank.

———. 1990. *World development report 1990.* Washington, DC: World Bank.

———. 1992. *Structural and sectoral adjustment lending: World Bank experience (1980–1992).* Washington, DC: World Bank (Operations Evaluation Department).

———. 1994. *Adjustment in Africa: Reforms, results and the road ahead.* Washington, DC: World Bank.

———. 1995. The multilateral debt facility for heavily indebted poor countries. Taskforce from Development Economics, Financial Policy, and Resources Mobilisation. Controller, Africa Region. Confinancing and Advisory Services, Legal, and External Affairs. 25 July. Washington, DC: World Bank.

———. 1996a. Report on Mexico for the Executive Board, World Bank. 15 October. SecM96–1053. Washington, DC: World Bank

———. 1996b. Participation sourcebook. Washington, DC: World Bank.

———. 1997a. Annual report. Appendix 13. Washington, DC: World Bank

———. 1997b. Russian Federation—Second Structural Adjustment Loan Project. PID5759. 23 December, 1997. Washington, DC: World Bank

———. 1998a. Global development finance, country tables. Washington, DC: World Bank.

———. 1998b. World development report. Washington, DC: World Bank).

———. 1998c. Annual report. Appendix 13. Washington, DC: World Bank

———. 1998d. World Bank press release. 99/1919/ECA. Washington, DC: World Bank

———. 1999a. Russia: country assistance strategy. Washington, DC: World Bank.

———. 1999b. World Bank prem notes. Washington, DC: World Bank

———. 2000. Annual report. Washington, DC: World Bank.

———. 2001a. Russia coal sector reform. Washington, DC: World Bank. At www.worldbank.org/participation/ghanidoc.htm.

———. 2001b. The comprehensive development framework: overview. Washington, DC: World Bank. At http://www.worldbank.org/cdf/overview.htm.

———. 2001c. *Cost of doing business: Fiduciary and safeguard policies and compliance.* Washington, DC: World Bank.

———. 2001d. *Annual report.* Washington, DC: World Bank.

———. 2002a. *Private sector development strategy: Directions for the World Bank Group.* Washington, DC: World Bank.

———. 2002b. World development report 2002. Washington, DC: World Bank.

———. 2002c. World Bank group work in low-income countries under stress: A task force report. September. Washington, DC: World Bank. At http://www1.worldbank.org/operations/licus/Documents.html.

——. 2002d. Annual report on operations evaluation. Washington, DC: World Bank.

——. 2002e. Russian Federation: Country assistance evaluation. Washington, DC: World Bank. At http://www.worldbank.org/oed/russia_cae/.

——. 2003. African development indicators. Washington, DC: World Bank.

——. 2004a. Country information—Senegal. Washington, DC: World Bank. At http://web.worldbank.org/WBSITE/EXTERNAL/COUNTRIES/AFRICAEXT/SENEGALEXTN/0,,menuPK:296308~pagePK:141159~piPK:141110~theSitePK:296303,00.html).

——. 2004b. Development Committee communiqué. Washington, DC: World Bank. 2 October. At www.imf.org/external/np/cm/2004/100204a.htm).

——. 2004c. Projects—Mexico. Washington, DC: World Bank. At http://web.worldbank.org/external/default/main?menuPK=338429&pagePK=141155&piPK=141124&theSitePK=338397#active. Accessed 10 December 2004.

——. 2004d. *Annual report.* Washington, DC: World Bank.

——. 2004e. *The World Bank operational manual.* At wbln0018.worldbank.org/institutional/manuals/opmanual.nsf. Washington, D.C.: World Bank.

Yergin, Daniel. 1978. *Shattered peace: The origins of the cold war and the national security state.* London: Deutsch.

Yevstigneyev, Vladimir. 1996. Russia and the credit policy of the IMF and IBRD. *Mirovaya ekonomika i mezhdunarodnye otnosheniya* no. 6.

Yoon, Hwan Shin. 1991. The role of elites in creating capitalist hegemony in post-oil boom Indonesia. Special Issue. *Indonesia* (Journal of the Mario Einaudi Center for International Studies): 127–43.

INDEX

Numbers in italics refer to tables and figures.

accountability. *See* transparency
Adam, Christopher, 157, 172
Adler, Emmanuel, 67, 76
Africa
  debt burdens, 146–47, *147, 148,* 154, 168
  economic crisis, sources of, 141
  economic decline (1990–2001), *143*
  interest groups, 80–81, *81–82*
  See also specific countries
Africa mission, 44, 141–78
  arrears crisis, 164–66
  Cameroon, 157
  conditionality and, 143–44, 148, 149, 150,
    154–56, 161–62
  conditionality template, 160–61, 175
  Côte d'Ivoire, 155
  debt rescheduling, 146–48
  economic prescriptions, 149–50, 154–59
  Ghana, 174
  IMF bargaining power, 141–42, 146–47,
    149, 184–85
  Malawi, 174
  Mauritania, 151
  misdiagnoses, 144, 153–54, 156
  mission debate, 142–46
  Mozambique, 168
  Nigeria, 157
  prediction errors, 151–52
  Rhodesia, 143
  Rwanda, 174
  Senegal, 150–53, 174
  short-term focus, 146, 175–76
  structural constraints, 153, 158, 161
  sympathetic interlocutors, 185
  Tanzania, 145
  World Bank bargaining power, 141–42,
    146–47, 184–85
  Zaire, 153, 195
  Zambia, 49, 143–44, 156, 164, 174
  Zimbabwe, 156
  See also HIPC Initiatives
African Alternative Framework, 144–45
Agarwala, Ramgopal, 157
Aggarwal, Vinod, 47, 51
Aid India Consortium, 73
Aizenman, Joshua, 187–88
Aleksashenko, Sergei, 126
Alesina, Alberto, 76, 80
Alfthan, T., 71
Andean Development Cooperation, 189
Anglo-American Loan Agreement (1946), 33
Annett, Anthony, 79
Aravena, J., 52
Arbatov, Georgii, 105
Arbenz, Jacobo, 33
Argentina, 51, 66, 68, 78
arrears crisis, 164–66
Ascher, H., 77
Asher, Robert, 13, 19, 25, 36, 43, 44, 45–46,
  70, 74
Aslund, Anders, 104, 113, 114, 121, 135,
  137, 138
Aspe, Pedro, 59, 66, 85, 97, 99, 100
"Assisting Russia's Transition" (OED), 109
Atiyas, Izak, 78

Babb, Sarah, 66
Baker, James, III, 49–50, 52
Baker Plan, 49–50
Baldwin, David, 25

Balino, Tomas J. T., 115, 117
Banco Nacional de Comercio Exterior, 49
Bank Advisory Group, 89
Bank for International Settlements (BIS), 20
bargaining power
    economic reform and, 70–72
    IMF (*See* IMF, bargaining power)
    Mexico, 86–87, 90–91, 94
    Russia, 113
    World Bank (*See* World Bank, bargaining
        power)
Bartlett, Manuel, 96
Bartley, Robert L., 100
Bassett, Thomas, 158
Bates, Robert, 80–81
Bauer, Peter, 143
Baum, Warren C., 25
Bayne, N., 67
Bay of Pigs invasion (1961), 33
Bekkr, Aleksander, 123
Bell Mission, 73
Berezovsky, Boris, 123, 132
Berg, Elliot, 144
Berg report, 144
Bevan, David, 172
Beza, Ted, 89
Bezerovsky, Boris, 126
Bhatia, Rattan, 152
Biden, Joseph R., Jr., 169
Bini Smaghi, L., 33
Binswagen, Hans, 72, 92, 96, 98
Bird, Graham, 70n1, 79, 158
Birdsall, Nancy, 168, 176
BIS (Bank for International Settlements), 20
Black Tuesday (Russia), 118
Blackwell, Michael, 52
Blanco, H., 85
Blaug, Mark, 69
Block, Fred, 16, 18, 21
Blustein, Paul, 40, 70, 130, 176
Bogdanowicz-Bindert, Christine, 49
Bogomolov, Oleg, 105
Bohlen, Celestine, 105
Boiko, Boris, 123
Bolivia, 52
Boone, Catherine, 151, 152
Bordo, Michael, 20, 187
Boughton, James, 5, 8, 9, 13, 32, 50, 52, 61,
    172, 196
    on Africa mission, 143, 144, 146, 148, 164,
        165
    on Bretton Woods conference, 17, 20, 21
    on IMF-World Bank collaboration, 50–51
    on remuneration for IMF creditors, 24,
        194n2, 195
Bouzas, R., 68
Boycko, Maxim, 111
Brady, Nicholas, 52
Brady Plan, 52, 95, 97
Brandt Commission, 47

Branson, William, 45–46, 161, 162
Bravo Aguilera, Luis, 86, 93
Brazil, 49, 78, 81, 210
Bretton Woods conference, 16–21
Brint, Steven, 54
Broms, Bengt B., 23
Brown, Gordon, 167
Bruhn, K., 101
Bruno, M., 43
Buira, Ariel, 206
bureaucracy, economic reform and, 76–77
Bush, George H. W., 110
Bush, Keith, 112, 115

callable capital, 196, 196n3
Callaghy, Thomas, 143
Calvo, Guillermo, 51, 57, 60
Camacho, Manuel, 100
Cambodia, 164
Camdessus, Michel, 51, 108n2, 109, 113,
    118, 121, 124–25, 131
Cameroon, 157
Canadian International Development Research
    Centre, 145
capital account liberalization
    East Asian financial crisis and, 136–37
    IMF advocacy of, 1, 43, 126–28, 136–37
    Russia and, 126–28, 136–37
capture economies, 136
Cárdenas, Cuauhtémoc, 101
Carey, J. M., 79
Carstens, A., 57
Cartagena Consensus, 49
Cassen, Robert, 157
Cavallo, Domingo, 66, 68
CCFF (Compensatory and Contingency Fi-
    nancing Facility), 129, 160
CDF (Comprehensive Development Frame-
    work), 171–72
Centeno, M. A., 90, 91, 96
Central African Republic, 174
CEPAL, 49
CEPR, 204
Ceylon, 36
CFA-franc zone, 153
Chakravarthi, Raghavan, 145
Chechnya, 118
Chenery, Hollis, 43
Chernomyrdin, Viktor, 112, 114, 128, 131
Chiapas uprising (Mexico), 57, 100
Chile, 36, 44, 52, 81
China, 22
Chubais, Anatoly, 118, 122, 125
Citibank, 51
Claessens, Stijn, 52
Clark, I., 53
Clarke, Stephen, 20
Clavijo, Fernando, 93
Cline, William, 47, 51, 52
Clinton, Bill, 115

Cold War, 33–36
Colombia, 36
Colosio, Luis Donaldo, 96, 100
Commander, Simon, 133
Compensatory and Contingency Financing Facility (CCFF), 129, 160
completion point, 168
Comprehensive Development Framework (CDF), 171–72
Conable, Barber, 141
Consultative Group on Indonesia, 75
Corbo, Vittorio, 52, 158
Cornia, Giovanni Andrea, 5, 158
Corrales, Javier, 66
Corwin, Julie A., 130
Costa Rica, 52
Côte d'Ivoire, 155
Cottarelli, Carlo, 71
Country Assistance Strategy paper, 102
Cox, Gary, 79
Cox, Robert, 47
Cuba, 33, 164
Cukierman, Richard Webb, 76
Current Digest of the Post-Soviet Press, 109, 112
Czechoslovakia, 35–36

Dallara, Charles, 146
Darity, William, 47
Davidheiser, Evelyn, 112
Deane, Phyllis, 69
debt reduction debate
    creditor governments, 163–64, 166, 168–69
    NGOs, 163, 165–66, 168, 170–71
    popular opinion, 168, 169
    See also HIPC Initiatives
decision point, 168
De Gregorio, Jose, 204
de Haan, J., 76
de la Madrid, Miguel, 85, 88, 89, 91
Dell, Sidney, 17, 25, 42, 48
de Macedo, J. B., 152
de Melo, J., 152
democracy, economic policy and, 5, 182–83
De Moura Castro, C., 71
Devarajan, S., 152
developing countries
    IMF/World Bank influence, 27, 191
    obstacles to progress, 145
    Russia bailout and, 108
    statist approach to development, 142
De Vries, Margaret Garritsen, 13, 25, 31, 34, 36, 40, 41
DFID, 175
DiMaggio, Paul, 66
Diouf, Abdou, 150
Diwan, Ishac, 50, 52
Dolinskaya, Irina, 133
Dolowitz, D. P., 66

Domínguez, Jorge, 66, 101
Dooley, Michael, 52
Dornbusch, Rudiger, 59, 60, 99
double-majority voting, 206, 210
Dow Jones, 129, 130
Drazen, Allan, 68, 80
Dreher, Axel, 79
Dubinin, Sergei, 131

East Asia, foreign reserves, 187
East Asian financial crisis
    capital account liberalization and, 136–37
    Russia and, 127–28
Eastern Oil, 130
EBRD (European Bank for Reconstruction and Development), 104, 107, 127
Economic Commission for Africa, 142, 143, 144–45
The Economic Future of Europe (Funk), 16n1
economic reform, 65–82
    bargaining power and, 70–72
    bureaucracy and, 76–77
    epistemic communities and, 67–68
    interest groups and, 80–82
    political processes and, 5, 68–69, 182–83
    political structures and, 76–80
    sympathetic interlocutors and, 72–76, 76–77
    technocrats and, 65–66, 68–69
Economic Transformation: The Mexican Way (Aspe), 59
Economist, 34, 51, 95
Ecuador, 81
Edwards, Martin, 36, 76, 79
Edwards, Sebastian, 58, 60, 79, 99
Eggers, Ann Florini, 130, 171
Egypt, 36, 81, 164
Eichengreen, Barry, 17, 20
Eijffinger, S. C. W., 76
Elbadawi, Ibrahim, 152, 158
Enhanced Structural Adjustment Facility (ESAF), 148–49, 154–55n2, 154–56, 159
epistemic communities, 67–68
Erlanger, Steven, 113
ESAF (Enhanced Structural Adjustment Facility), 148–49, 154–55n2, 154–56, 159
Escobar, A., 55
European Bank for Reconstruction and Development (EBRD), 104, 107, 127
European Economic Community, 144
Evans, Huw, 163, 164, 166
Evans, Peter, 54, 67, 76
EXIMBANK, 102, 204

Farber, G., 85
Fedorov, Boris, 115, 116–17
Feldstein, Marty, 40
Ferguson, J., 55
Fernandez, R., 80

Ferreira, Francisco, 53
Ffrench-Davies, Ricardo, 49
Financial Sector Assessment Program (FSAP), 195–96
Financial Strengthening Program, 101
Financial Times, 51, 95, 168
Fine, Ben, 41
Finnemore, Martha, 12, 54, 67, 77
Fischer, Stanley, 126, 127, 128, 129, 137
Fish, Steven, 77
Fleming, J. Marcus, 41
Florini, Ann, 130, 171
Folkerts-Landau, David, 57
Fomin, Roman, 132
foreign direct investment, protectionism and, 81
Fox, Vicente, 101
France, 52, 130, 149, 206
    IDA contributions, 28
    IMF/WB influence, 27, 32
    Senegal and, 153
Frank, Oliver, 73
Frankel, Francine, 73
Freeland, Chrystia, 129
Frenkel, J. A., 40, 52
Fried, Edward, 52
Frieden, Jeffry, 80, 86
Frischtak, Leila, 78
FSAP (Financial Sector Assessment Program), 195–96
Funk, Walther, 16n1
Furtado, Celso, 15

G-7, 112
    debt strategy, 163
    IMF influence, 191, 192
    World Bank influence, 197, 198
G-24, 50, 108
GAB (General Agreements to Borrow), 31
Gaddy, Clifford G., 133
Gaidar, Yegor, 110, 111, 112, 114, 115, 117, 124
Gandhi, Indira, 37, 74
GAO. *See* General Accounting Office
García Paniagua, Javier, 91
Gardner, Richard N., 17, 18, 19, 20, 21
GATT, 81
Gazprom (natural gas company), 114, 121, 124, 128, 131
Geddes, Barbara, 76
Geertz, Clifford, 69
Geither, Timothy, 30
General Accounting Office (GAO), 120, 121, 123, 206
    World Bank lending to Russia, 111n5, 116, 129, 138
General Agreements to Borrow (GAB), 31
Generalov, Sergei, 130
Gerashchenko, Viktor, 112, 131

Germany, 47, 149
    debt reduction debate and, 163, 166, 167, 169
    IDA contributions, 28
    IMF/World Bank influence, 27, 32
Ghana, 81, 174
Giannini, Curzio, 71
Gianviti, François, 192
Gil-Diaz, F., 57
Gisselquist, David, 20, 31
GKO/OFZ market, 127–28
GKOs (short-term couponless bonds), 126
Global Fund for Aids/HIV Tuberculosis and Malaria, 176
Gold, Joseph, 23, 27, 48, 192
Goldman, Marshall, 135
Goldsmith, Arthur A., 157
Goldstein, Morris, 40, 52
Gomulka, Stanislav, 105
González Casanova, Pablo, 95
Gore, Al, 118
Gould, Erica, 12
Gould-Davies, Nigel, 13–14
Graham, George, 118
Graham, L., 103
Gramm, Phil, 169
Gran, G., 55
Granville, Brigitte, 127
Green, Marshall, 33
Greenhouse, Steven, 117, 118
Grether, Jean Marie de Melo, 81, 182
Grilli, V., 80
Gruber, Lloyd, 17
Guillamont, P., 152
Gurria, J. A., 85, 89
Gusinksy, Vladimir, 132
Gwin, C., 29

Haas, Ernst, 67, 77
Haggard, Stephen, 5, 18, 68, 76, 79, 81
Hailu, Degol, 41
Hale, David, 59, 61, 62
Hall, H. Keith, 76
Hall, Peter, 22, 76
Hanna, Nagy, 45–46, 161, 162
Hanson, Stephen, 132
Hansson, Ardo, 135
hard conditionality, 70
Haussman, Ricardo, 52
Havnevik, Kjell, 158
Heavily Indebted Poor Countries Initiatives. *See* HIPC Initiatives
Helleiner, Eric, 31, 42, 47, 53, 156, 158, 182
Hellman, Joel, 76, 82, 122, 136, 182
Heredia, Blanca, 68, 85
Hibou, Beatrice, 157
HIPC Initiative (1996), 162–63
    eligibility, 163, 166

events leading to, 163–66
failure of, 168
opposition to, 166–67
poverty alleviation approach, 169
See also debt reduction debate
HIPC Initiative (1999), 167–68n4, 167–74
   criticism of, 173–74
   eligibility, 173
   NGOs and, 168, 170–71
   participatory policy approach, 168, 170, 171–72, 173
   poverty alleviation approach, 169–70
   See also debt reduction debate
HIPC Trust Fund, 29
Hirsch, Fred, 17
Hodges, Tony, 158
Hoffman, Lily, 66
Horn, Bobbie, 47
Horsefield, J. K., 13, 17, 18, 25, 45
Hough, Jerry, 112
Huizinga, Harry, 48, 53
Hull, Cordell, 21
Hungary, 35
Husain, Ishrat, 50, 52
Husein, Shahid, 72, 78, 82, 92, 94, 96

IBRD (International Bank for Reconstruction and Development), 108, 200
   amendment process, 210
   borrower rates, 197–98
   funding of, 196–98
   mandate, 20
   member suspension process, 210n8
Ickes, Barry W., 133
IDA (International Development Association), 28–29, 165, 168, 173, 174, 189, 211
   funding of, 28–29, 198–99
   governance structure, 198–99
   U.S. Congress and, 28–29
Ikenberry, John, 18, 20, 21, 22, 68–69
Ilchman, Warren, 80
Illiaronov, Andrei, 111
IMFC (International Monetary and Financial Committee), 191, 205
IMF External Evaluation, 46, 143, 149, 155–56, 157, 159, 162, 176–77
IMF (International Monetary Fund), 5, 8
   access to information, 72
   arrears crisis, 164–66
   capital account liberalization, advocacy of, 1, 43, 126–28, 136–37
   Cold War, subservience to, 34–36
   Compensatory and Contingency Financing Facility, 129, 160
   financial programming models, 40–43
   Latin American debt crisis and, 47–48, 50–51, 52
   loan disbursements, shrinking of, 209

   Mexican financial crisis and, 56–57, 58–59, 60, 61, 100
   precedents for, 20
   responsibilities, 9, 44
   South Korean financial crisis and, 56, 57–58, 59, 61–62
   staff appointments and deployments, 26, 53–54, 54n1, 207
   technical expertise, 71, 110n4, 179
   trade liberalization, advocacy of, 99
   World Bank, comparison to, 6–9
   World Bank collaboration, 50–51, 176–77
   See also Africa mission; Independent Evaluation Office; Mexico mission; Russia mission
IMF, bargaining power, 4–5, 70–72, 179
   Africa mission, 141–42, 146–47, 149, 184–85
   Mexico mission, 87, 89, 183
   Russia mission, 106, 107, 110, 113, 114, 116–17, 122, 126, 133, 134–35, 184
IMF, criticisms of, 1, 2, 5, 9, 179
   Africa mission, 3, 155–56, 156–57
   analyses, depth of, 46, 55, 183
   economic reform prescriptions, 2, 104, 137, 153, 155–56, 157
   Mexico mission, 3
   political realities, dismissal of, 161–62
   poverty alleviation, neglect of, 158–59
   projections, over-optimistic, 156–57
   Russia mission, 3, 131, 137
IMF, financial structure, 23–24, 194–96
   creditor countries, 31–32, 108, 194–95, 194n1, 196, 199–200
   debtor countries, 195–96, 199–200
IMF, governance structure, 7, 8, 190–93
   amendment process, 210
   executive directors, 192–93, 205
   transparency, 9, 192–93
   voting, 22–23, 27, 191–92
IMF, governance structure reform
   double majority voting, 206, 210
   funding distribution, 208–9
   independent boards, 204–5
   representative leadership process, 211
   staff incentives, 211–12
   transparency, 206–7, 210–11
IMF, institutional features
   bureaucracy, 2, 4, 180
   cohesiveness/rigidity, 9, 56, 63
   hierarchical structure, 7, 55
   independence, 27–28, 179
   orthodoxy, 157
   professionalism, 54–55
   self-censorship, 62
IMF, lending structure
   arrears policy, 71
   borrower rates, 195, 200
   conditionality, 7, 25–26, 70–71

IMF, mandate, 2, 3, 9, 179, 186
  balance of payments adjustment, 20, 44,
    109
  capital account liberalization, 1
  exchange rate management, 20, 44, 108
  expansion of, 204–5
  financial stability, oversight of, 195
  transition, 108–9
IMF, mandate reform, 186–88
  advisor, 187
  crisis management, 186–87
  exchange rate management, 188
  mutual insurance provision, 187–88
  participatory engagement of borrower coun-
    tries, 3, 189–90, 207–8
  standard-setter, 188
IMF, political constraints, 2, 4–5, 65, 69
  debtor country parliaments, 78
  developing countries, 191
  G-7, 191, 192
  political institutions, 78–79
  private sector, 190–91
  U.S., 4, 15, 27, 29–31, 34–36, 108, 180,
    200
  U.S. Congress, 29–31, 32, 206
import strangulation, 154
Independent Evaluation Office, 41–42, 157,
    187
  on Africa mission, 142, 156, 161, 178, 185
  on South Korean financial crisis, 57, 58, 59,
    61
India, 37, 38, 44, 73–74
Indonesia, 33, 36, 75, 78, 99, 129
Inspection Panel (World Bank), 8, 202
Institute of International Finance, 203
Inter-American Development Bank, 33, 49–
    50, 52, 67, 98, 102
interest groups, 80–82, 182
  See also NGOs; private sector
Inter-Governmental Group on Indonesia, 75
International Bank for Reconstruction and
    Development. See IBRD
International Development Association. See
    IDA
International Monetary and Financial Com-
    mittee (IMFC), 191, 205
International Monetary Fund. See IMF
Iran, 33, 75
Iraq, 33
Ireland, 130, 206
Italy, 149, 206
Ize, A. I., 93

Jakobeit, Cord, 210
James, Harold, 13, 44, 47, 109, 147, 159, 162
  on Bretton Woods conference, 16n1, 17, 18,
    20, 24, 25
  on IMF stabilization programs, 34, 41
Japan, 28, 29, 32, 52, 129, 149, 198
Jayachandran, Seema, 153

Johnson, J., 78
Johnson, Lyndon B., 37, 74
Johnson, Melanie, 157
Johnson, Simon, 106
Johnstone, R., 61
Joshi, Vijay, 73, 74
Jubilee 2000, 168
Jubilee 2003, 173

Ka, Samba, 150, 151
Kadannikov, Vladimir, 122
Kahler, Miles, 26, 66
Kaletsky, Anatole, 47
Kalter, Eliot, 87, 95, 97, 99
Kane, Cheikh Hamidou, 151
Kapstein, Ethan B., 68
Kapur, Devesh, 13, 33, 54, 73, 75, 92, 146,
    159, 197
  on Africa mission, 141, 144, 148, 149, 157
  on arrears crisis, 164, 165
  on World Bank expansion, 28, 198
  on World Bank financial structure, 24
  on World Bank focus on projects, 25, 44
  on World Bank technical expertise, 25, 26,
    45
Kapur, Ishan, 137
Kaufman, Robert R., 68, 76
Keck, Margaret E., 21
Keifman, S., 68
Kenen, Peter, 191
Kennan, George, 33
Keohane, Robert, 18
Keynes, John Maynard, 16, 20
  on Bretton Woods conference, 17–18, 19,
    20
  IMF balance of payments deficit proposal,
    42
  IMF mandate proposal, 25
  on IMF quota allocations, 22
Khan, Mohsin, 5, 52, 158
Khasbulatov, Ruslan, 112, 115
Killick, Tony, 5, 42, 46, 142, 146, 154, 158,
    160, 176
  on failure of conditionality, 4, 71, 161
Kimenyi, M., 82
Kindleberger, Charles, 18
Kingsmill, William, 160n3
Kiriyenko, Sergei, 124, 128, 130, 131
Kirk, Donald, 40
Kissinger Commission Report (1984), 47, 91
Kizha, Georgii, 112
Knox, David, 72, 94, 95
Koester, Ulrich, 46, 157
Kohl, Helmut, 47, 142–43, 201
Konings, Piet, 157
Kopper, Hilmar, 28
Koremenos, B., 18
Kowalska, Marzena, 106
Kraatz, Matthew S., 66
Kraemer, Moritz, 81, 182

Krasner, Stephen, 39
Kremer, Michael, 153
Krueger, Anne, 48, 73, 76, 81, 82, 93, 182, 187
Krugman, Paul, 42
Kugler, Jack, 49
Kuhn, Thomas, 69

LaFraniere, Sharon, 130
Lagos Plan of Action (1980), 142, 143
Lakatos, I., 69
Lake, Anthony, 33
Landell-Mills, Pierre, 150, 151, 152
Latin America
    Washington consensus, embrace of, 65–66
    See also specific countries
Latin American debt crisis, 31, 47–52
    Baker Plan, 49–50
    Brady Plan, 52
    IMF and, 47–48, 50–51, 52
    Miyazawa Plan, 52
    Polak model determination of, 48
    U.S. and, 51, 52
    U.S. Congress and, 48–49, 51
    World Bank and, 50–51, 52
Latin American debtors' group, 94
Lawrence, Roger, 42
Lawson, Nigel, 164
League of Nations, 20
Lehman, H., 112
Lele, Uma, 157
Levy, Daniel, 101
Lewis, John, 13, 37, 43, 44, 73, 74, 75, 157
Lindauer, David, 157
Lingren, Carl-Johan, 57
Lipson, C., 18
Lipton, David, 135
Lipton, Michael, 80
Lissakers, Karin, 51, 52, 53, 95
Lister, Frederick, 23, 27, 206
Little, Ian, 73, 74
Livshits, Alexander, 125
Lloyd, John, 118
Locke, Mary, 130
Lofchie, Michael, 142
Logo Vaz-Sibneft, 132
Lopez Portillo, J., 86, 88, 91
Loser, Claudio, 87, 93, 95, 97, 99
Loxley, John, 145
Lustig, N., 56, 93
Luzhkov, Yuri, 126
Lyle, Robert, 115, 130

Machinea, Jose Luis, 51
MacIntyre, Andrew, 75
Mahieu, Géraldine, 27
Majd, Nader, 152, 158
Malawi, 174
Mallaby, Sebastian, 202
Marcelo, Jaime Olarreaga, 81, 182

March, James G., 77
Marcos, Ferdinand, 153
Mares, David, 85, 88
Margolin, Ruslan, 128
Marino, Roberto, 86
Marion, Nancy, 187–88
Marsh, D., 66
Marshall Plan (1947), 33
Martin, Lisa, 12
Martinez, G., 85
Maslyukov, Yuri, 131
Mason, Edward, 13, 19, 25, 36, 43, 44, 45–46, 70, 74
Mau, Vladimir, 118
Mauritania, 151
Maxfield, Sylvia, 90, 96
Mbaka, J., 82
Mbodji, Mohamed, 150
McCann, James, 66, 101
MCC (Millennium Challenge Corporation), 176, 189
McDonald, David A., 145
McDonald, Keith, 54
McFaul, Michael, 110, 111, 115, 136
McKenzie, David, 164–65
McNamara, Robert, 28, 44–45, 88, 145
Medhora, Rohinton, 152, 153
Media-Most group, 132
Meesook, Oey Astra, 157
Meltzer Commission, 30, 176, 208
Menatep, 132
Mendelson, Sarah, 111
Mendoza, Enrique, 57
Mexican financial crisis (1994), 56–57, 58–59, 60–61, 62, 100
Mexico
    Bancomext, 92, 93
    Budget and Planning Ministry, 90, 93, 98
    Central Bank, 89, 90, 93–94, 98
    Chiapas uprising, 57, 100
    debt crises, 88–89
    Finance Ministry, 90, 92, 98, 101, 102
    financial crisis (1994), 56–57, 58–59, 60–61, 62, 100
    Foreign Affairs Ministry, 92
    Gobernación, 90
    interest groups, 81, 182
    Ministry of National Patrimony and Industrial Development (SEPAFIN), 88
    National Industrial Development Bank, 92
    National University (UNAM), 99
    Pact for Welfare, Stability, and Growth, 58
    political structure, 77, 78, 87
    PRI, 101
    state bargaining power, 86–87, 90–91, 94
    Trade Ministry, 93–94
    U.S. relations, 86–87, 89, 91, 94, 95
Mexico mission, 75, 88–102
    first phase (1976–1982), 84, 87, 88–90
    second phase (1982–1988), 84, 87, 90–94

Mexico mission (*continued*)
    third phase (1988–1994), 84, 87, 95–100
    fourth phase (1994 onward), 84, 87–88,
       101–2
    access to information, 72, 92
    agricultural reform, 97–98
    IMF bargaining power, 87, 89, 183
    IMF lending, 102
    political reform, 100–101, 183
    radicals, 86, 90, 91, 94
    secrecy, 97
    state bargaining power, 86–87, 90–91, 94
    structuralists/economic nationalists, 88–89
    sympathetic interlocutors, 91–94, 96, 98–
       100
    technocrats, 65–66, 78, 88, 89, 90, 91–92,
       96, 102
    trade liberalization debate, 85–86, 88–89,
       92–94
    U.S. lending, 95
    World Bank bargaining power, 87, 93, 183
    World Bank lending, 95, 102
Meyer, John, 66
Migdal, Joel, 82
Mikesell, Raymond, 22
Millennium Challenge Corporation (MCC),
    176, 189
Miller-Adams, Michelle, 77
Milward, Alan, 33
Miyazawa Plan, 52
Mobutu Sese Seko, 153
Mody, Ashoka, 71
Mohammed, Aziz Ali, 194n1, 196
Moldova, 78
Molina, Umberto, 92
Morales, E., 99
Moravcsik, Andrew, 19
Morgan Guaranty Bank, 52
Morris, Stephen, 101
Morrow, James, 33
Morse Committee, 201
Morvant, Penny, 122
Mosley, Layna, 71
Most Bank, 132
Mourmouras, Alexandros T., 172
Mozambique, 168
Mulford, David, 52
Mumssen, Christian, 133
Muñoz Ledo, Porfirio, 95
Munter, Pyivi, 133
Musgrave, A., 69
mutual insurance, 187–88
Mutual Security Act (U.S., 1951), 34
Muzumdar, Dipak, 157
Myerson, Roger, 79

NAB (New Arrangements to Borrow), 31
Naim, Moises, 66, 77
Ndiaye, Abdourahmane, 151
Nehru, Jawaharlal, 37

Nelson, Douglas, 76
Nelson, Joan, 66, 68, 77
Nelson, Paul, 160
Nemtsov, Boris, 125
neoclassical economics, 54–55
Netherlands, 29, 149, 166
New Arrangements to Borrow (NAB), 31
New York Times, 113, 117
Neyapti, B., 76
Nezavisimaya Gazeta, 126
Ngo, Brian, 150, 151, 152
NGOs (nongovernmental organizations), 159,
    191, 201
    criticism of, 171, 200
    debt reduction debate and, 163, 165–66,
       168, 170–71
    IMF/World Bank transparency watchdog,
       201–2
    See also interest groups
Nicaragua, 33, 164
Nigeria, 157
NK Rosneft (oil company), 128
Nocera, Michael, 52
nongovernmental organizations. *See* NGOs
Nordic countries, 166

Odling-Smee, John, 118
O'Donnell, Guillermo, 49
OECD (Organization for Economic Coopera-
    tion and Development), 109, 127
OECD Development Assistance Committee,
    144, 175
OED (Operations Evaluation Department),
    75, 172, 173, 199
    on Mexico mission, 99, 102
    on Russia mission, 104, 105, 109, 110,
       113–14, 116
OFZs (ruble-denominated coupon bonds), 127
Ogata, Sadako, 32, 206
Olsen, Johan P., 77
Olson, Mancur, 80
ONAKO (oil company), 130
O'Neill, Paul, 176
Oneximbank, 123, 132
Ooms, Dirk, 27
OPEC countries, 144
Operations Evaluation Department. *See* OED
Organization for African Unity, 142
Organization for Economic Cooperation and
    Development. *See* OECD
Ortiz, Guillermo, 85, 93
ORT television channel, 132
Ostrom, Elinor, 207, 208
Overseas Private Investment Corporation, 204
ownership. *See* participatory policy approach
Oxfam, 164

Paarlberg, Robert, 38
Pakistan, 37
Panama, 195

Paris Club, 147, 163–64
Park, Daekeun, 58
Parliamentary Network on the World Bank, 210
Parrish, Scott, 122
participatory policy approach, 3
    HIPC Initiative and, 168, 170, 171–72, 173
    IMF/World Bank reform and, 3, 189–90, 207–8
    prerequisite conditions, 208
Pastor, Manuel, 51, 118
Paul, C., 82
Pauly, Louis, 20
Penrose, Ernest Francis, 21
Perotti, Roberto, 76
Peru, 36, 49
Peters, Gretche, 101
Petricioli, Gustavo, 89, 92
Philip, George, 101
Philippines, 36, 75, 153
Piciotto, Robert, 172
Polak, Jacques, 40–41, 108n3
Polak model, 40–41, 43
    Latin American debt crisis determination, 48
Poland, 35
policy capture, 182
political movement hypothesis, 34, 35
political proximity hypothesis, 34, 35
Pollard, Robert A., 21
Popov, Vladimir, 130
Portanin, Vladimir, 132
Portfolio Management Task Force, 39
Potanin, Vladimir, 123–24
Powell, Walter, 66
Prasad, Eswar, 136, 187
Pravda, 132
Preston, Lewis, 115
PriceWaterhouseCoopers, 117, 121
Primakov, Yevgeny, 131
private sector, 80–82, 190–91, 203–4
Prowse, Michael, 110n4
Przeworski, A., 79
Putin, Vladimir, 132–33
Putnam, Robert, 67

"Questions and Answers on the International Monetary Fund" (U.S. Treasury), 25

Radelet, Steve, 42, 135–36
Radio Free Europe/Radio Liberty Newsline (RFE/RL), 126, 128, 129, 130
Ramcharan, Rodney, 68
Ramirez, Carlos, 88
Rapkin, David, 32, 206, 210
rational economic policy, 182
Reagan, Ronald, 47, 142–43, 146, 194–95, 197, 201
Remmer, Karen L., 68, 76
Renzio, Paolo de, 175

"Replenishment and Scarce Currencies" (IMF), 42
Reports on the Observance of Standards and Codes (ROSCs), 195–96
RFE/RL (Radio Free Europe/Radio Liberty Newsline), 126, 128, 129, 130
Rhee, Changyong, 58
Rhodesia, 143
Rieffel, Alexis, 147
Righter, Rosemary, 23
Rivlin, Benjamin, 23
Robinson, Derek, 157
Rodrik, Dani, 80, 155
Rogoff, Kenneth, 59
Rogozinski, J., 85
Rojas, Patricio, 158
Romania, 35–36
ROSCs (Reports on the Observance of Standards and Codes), 195–96
Rottier, Stéphane, 27
Roubini, Nouriel, 79
Rowan, B., 66
Rowlands, Dane, 79
Rozenthal, Andrés, 86, 92
ruble zone, 135–36
Ruggie, John Gerard, 22
Ruiz, C., 99
Russia, 79
    Central Bank of Russia, 112, 117, 122
    Communist Party, 120
    deficit reduction, 117
    Duma, 78, 117, 128, 130
    East Asian financial crisis and, 127–28
    economic collapse, 104–5, 105, 114–15
    financial crisis (1998), 128–32
    geostrategic importance, 107, 135
    interest groups, 182
    loans-to-shares scandal, 119–22, 123–24
    ORT television channel, 132
    privatization, 119–22, 123–24, 128, 136
    ruble zone, 135–36
    state bargaining power, 113
    tax collection, 124, 124–25, 130, 133
    Temporary Extraordinary Commission on Strengthening Tax and Budget Discipline, 125
Russia mission, 106–40, 184
    bailout, 108, 129–30
    capital account liberalization, 126–28, 136–37
    conditionality, compromise of, 114–17, 118–19, 122, 123, 134–35, 137
    economic reform prescriptions, 109–12, 125
    financial crisis (1998), 128–32
    IMF bargaining power, 106, 107, 110, 113, 114, 116–17, 122, 126, 133, 134–35, 184
    IMF lending, 108, 113, 116, 118, 120, 123, 126, 129, 133

Russia mission (*continued*)
  IMF mistakes, 135–38, 139
  mandate, 107–9
  oligarchs, 112–13, 114, 121–22, 123–24,
    125–26, 131, 132–33
  state bargaining power, 113
  U.S. and, 107–8, 115
  World Bank bargaining power, 106, 107,
    110, 113–14, 122, 134–35, 184
  World Bank lending, 108, 111n5, 113–14,
    116, 118, 120, 123, 129, 130, 133–34,
    138
  World Bank mistakes, 138–39
Russian Economic Trends, 111
Russian financial crisis (1998), 128–32
Russian Reform Monitor, 138
Rutland, Peter, 105
Ruttan, Vernon, 34, 37
Rwanda, 174

Sachs, Jeffrey, 42, 56
  on Latin American debt crisis, 48, 51, 52,
    53
  on Russia's economic transition, 105, 108,
    112, 119, 135
SAF (Structural Adjustment Facility), 148
Sahle, Eunice Njeri, 145
Sahn, David, 167
Salinas de Gortari, Carlos, 85, 88, 91, 95, 96,
  99
SAL (Structural Adjustment Lending) pro-
  grams, 50
Sanger, David E., 131
Saravia, Diego, 71
Saudi Arabia, 31, 32
Schloss, Henri H., 20
Scholte, Jan Aart, 171
Schwartz, Anna, 20, 187
SDR (special drawing right), 31n3
  interest rate, 194n2, 195
Seleznev, Gennadii, 130
Senegal, 150–53, 174
Seo, Jungkun, 81
Serieux, John, 163
Serra Puche, Jaime, 87, 96
Sevodnya (newspaper), 123
Shadlen, Kenneth, 101
Sherk, Donald, 62
Shleifer, Andrei, 111
Shugart, M. S., 79
SIDANCO (oil company), 130
Sikkink, Kathryn, 21, 67
Silva Herzog, Jesús, 85, 86, 89, 90, 92
Simmons, Beth A., 18
Smith, Ian, 143
Smolensky, Alexander, 132
Snidal, D., 18
Soesastro, M. Hadi, 75
soft conditionality, 70–71
Solís, L., 90

Solomon, Robert, 31
Somoza Garcia, Anastasio, 33
South Africa, 36
South Korea, 5, 70, 81
  financial crisis (1997), 40, 56, 57–58, 59,
    61–62, 129
"Sovereign Debt Rescheduling Mechanism"
  proposal, 186–87
Soviet Union, 22, 37
Special Facility for Africa, 149
Special Program of Assistance for Africa,
  148
SPP, 88, 91
Statute of the European System of Central
  Banks, 204
Steckhan, Rainer, 87, 90, 91, 92, 94, 95, 96,
  98
Stein, H., 157
Steinmo, Sven, 76
Stern, Nicholas, 53
Stewart, Frances, 158, 160
STF (Systemic Transformation Facility), 116,
  118
Stiglitz, Joseph, 2, 46, 104
Stone, Randall, 66
  on Russia mission, 112, 113, 115, 117, 118,
    122, 126, 131
  on U.S. influence, 12, 36
Story, Dale, 85, 88
Strand, Jonathan, 32, 206, 210
Strange, Susan, 53
Structural Adjustment Facility (SAF), 148
Structural Adjustment Lending (SAL) pro-
  grams, 50
Subramaniam, C., 73–74
Suebsaen, Parita, 157
Suharto, 33, 75
Supplementary Reserve Facility, 196
Sutton, Mary, 75
sympathetic interlocutors, 5, 72–76, 181
  Africa, 185
  economic reform and, 76–77
  India, 73–74
  Indonesia, 75
  Mexico, 91–94, 96, 98–100
  Russia, 184
Systemic Transformation Facility (STF), 116,
  118
Szymczak, P., 85

Tabellini, G., 79
Talbott, Strobe, 118
Tanzania, 145, 168, 172, 174
Tavernier, Yves, 130
technical expertise
  IMF, 71, 110n4, 179
  World Bank, 45, 71, 179
Tellez, Luis, 97
Tello, Carlos, 88
Temporary Extraordinary Commission on

Strengthening Tax and Budget Discipline
(Russia), 125
t'Haart, Brian, 60
Thacker, Strom, 12, 34–35
Thapar, Raj, 73
Thatcher, Margaret, 47, 142–43, 201
Thioune, R., 151
Tolbert, Stokes M., 25
Tornell, Aaron, 56
Toure, Mamoudou, 150, 151
trade liberalization, 157
   Africa mission, 149
   IMF and, 99, 157
   Mexican debate over, 85–86, 88–89, 92–
      94
   World Bank and, 1, 67–68, 92–94, 99, 157
transparency
   IMF, 9, 192–93, 206–7, 210–11
   World Bank, 8, 192–93, 202, 207, 210–11
Transparency International, 203
Treisman, Daniel, 124, 125
Tresize, Philip, 52
Tsebelis, George, 79
Tucker, Robert, 143
Tumusiime-Mutebile, Emmanuel, 176
Turkey, 36, 75, 78, 79, 81
Tussie, Diana, 67

Uchitelle, Louis, 113
Uganda Economic Study Team, 145
United Kingdom, 47, 130, 206
   Bretton Woods conference, 21, 25
   civil service bureaucracy, 77
   debt reduction debate and, 166
   IDA and, 28, 149, 199
   IMF/World Bank influence, 22, 27, 32
UNICEF (United Nations Children's Fund),
   144, 158
UNCTAD (United Nations Conference on
   Trade and Development), 145
UNDP (United Nations Development Pro-
   gram), 144
UN Economic Commission for Latin America,
   67
U.S., 48
   aid community, 37
   Bretton Woods conference, 17–18, 21, 24,
      25
   competing foreign policy cliques, 37–38
   debt reduction debate and, 166, 167, 169
   Department of Commerce, 203
   Federal Reserve, 47
   Foreign Agricultural Service, 204
   Homeland Security, 204
   IDA contributions and voting share, 198–
      99
   IMF, influence over, 4, 15, 27, 29–31, 34–
      36, 108, 180, 200
   IMF expansion of mandate, rejection of,
      187

IMF voting power, 22, 23, 27
India relations, 36–38, 73–74
Latin American debt crisis and, 51, 52
Mexico relations, 86–87, 89, 91, 94, 95
Mutual Security Act, 34
political structure, 77
remuneration of IMF creditors, advocacy of,
   194–95, 194n2
Russia mission and, 107–8, 115
SAF and ESAF, opposition to, 148–49
State Department, 117, 204
Trade and Development Agency, 203
Trade Representative, 203
Treasury, 4, 25, 30, 167
World Bank, influence over, 4, 15, 27, 28–
   29, 108, 180, 200
   See also General Accounting Office; U.S.
   Congress
U.S. Agency for International Aid (USAID),
   37, 107, 111
U.S. Congress, 21
   Bretton Woods conference, 19
   criticism of IMF/World Bank, 159, 176, 201
   IDA and, 28–29
   IMF, influence over, 29–31, 32, 206
   India and, 37
   Latin American debt crisis and, 48–49, 51
   Russia bailout and, 129–30
   UN, influence over, 23
   World Bank, influence over, 28–29, 32, 206
   See also Meltzer Commission
Uphoff, Norman, 80
USAID, 37, 107, 111

Valente, Marcela, 78
Vallacher, Robin R., 60
Van der Hoeven, Rolph, 156, 158
Van der Kraaij, Fred, 156, 158
Van der Mensbrugghe, Emmanuel, 137
Van de Walle, Nicholas, 82, 142, 150, 151,
   157, 161
Van Dormael, Armand, 16, 18, 20
Van Houtven, L., 206
Van Wijnbergen, Sweder, 92, 93, 95, 97, 98
Varshney, Ashutosh, 38, 73, 74, 81
Vassiliev, Dmitri Glinski, 133
Vaubel, Roland, 12
Velasco, Andres, 56
Venezuela, 51, 82
veto power, 27
Vietnam, 28, 195
Vietnam war, 37, 38
Vinson, Fred M., 17–18
Vishny, Robert, 111
Volcker, Paul, 52
Vreeland, James Raymond, 68, 79

Wade, Robert, 8, 29, 32, 171, 201, 202
Wallis, Darren, 100
Wall Street Journal, 51

Wapenhans Report, 6, 201
Washington consensus, 48, 53, 180, 181
    Argentina and, 66, 68
    good governance and, 106
    Latin America and, 65–66
Wasty, S., 78
Waterbury, John, 142
Watson, Maxwell, 50
Weaving, Rachel, 172
Webb, Richard, 13, 75, 76
Wedel, Janine, 108
Wegner, Daniel M., 60
Weir, Margaret, 77
Weisbrot, Mark, 105
Werner, Alejandro, 59, 60, 99
White, Harry Dexter, 16, 20–21, 22, 23, 25,
    199
White, W. H., 40
Whitehead, Laurence, 49
Whitlock, Eric, 115
Wiehen, Michael, 203
Wijnbergen, S., 52
Williams, John, 33
Williamson, John, 42, 52, 53, 168, 176
Wilson, James Q., 77
Wimmer, Andreas, 64, 162
Wise, Carol, 51
Woods, Ngaire, 69, 130, 171
World Bank, 5–6, 9
    access to information, 72, 92
    administrative expenses, 198n4
    arrears crisis, 164–66
    Cold War, subservience to, 33–34
    Comprehensive Development Framework,
        171–72
    disbursement culture, 39, 180, 201, 207
    expansion, 28–29
    IMF, comparison to, 6–9
    IMF collaboration, 50–51, 176–77
    India and, 37, 73–74
    Inspection Panel, 8, 202
    Latin American debt crisis and, 50–51, 52
    loan disbursements, shrinking of, 209, 209
    Mexican financial crisis and, 56, 57, 58–59,
        60–61, 62, 100
    objectivity policy, 26, 34, 45
    poverty alleviation approach, 160
    precedents for, 20
    safeguard policies, 202
    staff appointments and deployments, 26,
        53, 54n1, 207
    Structural Adjustment Lending programs,
        50
    technical expertise, 45, 71, 179
    trade liberalization, advocacy of, 1, 67–68,
        92–94, 99
    transmission of ideas, 67
    See also Africa mission; IBRD; IDA; Mexico
        mission; OED; Russia mission
World Bank, bargaining power, 4–5, 70–72,
    93, 179
    Africa mission, 141–42, 146–47, 184–85
    Mexico mission, 87, 93, 183
    Russia mission, 106, 107, 110, 113–14,
        122, 134–35, 184
World Bank, criticisms of, 1, 3, 9, 179
    analyses, depth of, 45–46, 55, 183
    economic reform prescriptions, 104, 153,
        157
    political realities, dismissal of, 161–62
    poverty alleviation, neglect of, 158–60
    public investment, neglect of, 157–58
World Bank, financial structure, 24, 196–99
    callable capital, 196, 196n3
    debtor vs. creditor countries, 199–200
    investment income, 197
    member country lending, 196–97
    trust fund dependence, 29
    U.S. contributions, 108
    See also IDA
World Bank, governance structure, 7, 8, 190–
    93
    board selection, 207
    executive directors, 192–93, 205
    voting, 22–23, 27, 191–92
World Bank, governance structure reform,
    206–7, 208–12
    double majority voting, 206, 210
    funding distribution, 208–9
    independent boards, 204–5
    representative leadership selection process,
        211
    staff incentives, 211–12
    transparency, 207, 210–11
World Bank, institutional features
    bureaucracy, 2, 4, 180, 189
    groupthink, 63
    hierarchical structure, 55
    independence, 27–28, 179
    professionalism, 54–55
    self-censorship, 62, 99
    transparency, 8, 192–93, 202, 207
World Bank, lending structure, 189
    borrower rates, 200
    conditionality, 8, 25–26, 70, 167
    nonaccrual policy, 71
World Bank, mandate, 1–2, 3, 8, 9, 44, 179,
    186
    development, 43–45
    expansion of, 198, 205
    original debate over, 24–25
World Bank, mandate reform, 188–90
    development capital, raising of, 188–89
    international development assistance coordi-
        nation, 189
    participatory engagement of debtor coun-
        tries, 3, 189–90, 207–8
    research resources, pooling of, 189

World Bank, political constraints, 2, 45, 65, 69
  creditor countries, 4, 179–80
  debtor countries, 4–5
  G-7, 197, 198
  political institutions, 78–79
  private sector, 190–91, 203–4
  U.S., 15, 27, 28–29, 108, 180, 200
  U.S. Congress, 28–29, 32, 206
World Bank, reform measures, 3–4
  decentralization, 56
  safeguard policies, 202–3
  transparency, 202
World Bank, tensions
  debtor participation *vs.* donor control, 207–8
  modernization *vs.* environmentalism, 202–3

Yeltsin, Boris, 109–10, 184
  economic reforms, 111

election campaign, 122, 123–24
privatization scheme, 119
reformers, political appointment of, 115, 117, 118, 125, 128
Russian financial crisis (1998) and, 129, 131
Russian oligarchs and, 114, 132–33
Yergin, Daniel, 33
Yevstigneyev, Vladimir, 105
Yoon, Hwan Shin, 75
Yugoslavia, 33, 36

Zaire, 153, 195
Zambia, 49, 81, 143–44, 156, 164, 174
Zambia National Commercial Bank (ZCNB), 174
Zedillo, Ernesto, 96, 100–101
Zimbabwe, 156
Zyuganov, Gennady, 120, 122